THE PRINTED PAGE IS EVERYMAN'S UNIVERSITY

THE CIVILIZATION OF THE AMERICAN INDIAN

C. JAS. E. THOMPSON COMPANY, KNOXVILLE, TENN.

View of the beautiful country in East Tennessee which the Cherokee Indians were obliged to leave

INDIAN REMOVAL

The Emigration of the Five Civilized
Tribes of Indians

GRANT FOREMAN

Norman
UNIVERSITY OF OKLAHOMA PRESS

4-14-88

Books by GRANT FOREMAN
PUBLISHED BY THE UNIVERSITY OF OKLAHOMA PRESS, NORMAN
Indian Removal (1932, 1953)
Fort Gibson (1936, 1943)
Muskogee: The Biography of an Oklahoma Town (1943)
A History of Oklahoma (1942, 1945)
Editor of A Pathfinder in the Southwest (1941)
Marcy and the Gold Seekers (1939)
Sequoyah (1938)
Editor of Adventure on Red River (1937)
Indians and Pioneers (1936)
Down the Texas Road (1936)
The Five Civilized Tribes (1934, 1938)
Advancing the Frontier (1933)

BY OTHER PUBLISHERS

The Last Trek of the Indians (Chicago, 1946)
The Adventures of James Collier (Chicago, 1937)
Editor of Indian Justice: A Cherokee Murder Trial as Reported
by John Howard Payne (Oklahoma City, 1933)
Indians and Pioneers (New Haven, 1930)
Editor of A Traveler in Indian Territory: The Journal of
Ethan Allen Hitchcock (Cedar Rapids, 1930)
Pioneer Days in the Early Southwest (Cleveland, 1926)

BROCHURES

Beginnings of Protestant Christian Work in Indian Territory
(Muskogee, 1951)
The Five Civilized Tribes: A Brief History and a Century of
Progress (Muskogee, 1948)
Muskogee and Eastern Oklahoma (Muskogee, 1946)

To the memory of
ROBERT L. WILLIAMS
who did much
to make and to preserve
Oklahoma history

AFTER TWENTY YEARS

Indian Removal at the time of its publication twenty years ago represented the most complete account that had been written concerning the removal of the Five Civilized Tribes from the Southeast to the Indian Territory. It is gratifying that this new edition is to be issued by the original publishers, the University of Oklahoma Press.

The book has been out of print for many years but there has been a constant and insistent demand for it which, happily, the reissuance at this time will now satisfy.

Although I have been engaged in historical research concerning these Indians ever since *Indian Removal* was originally published, I have discovered nothing that would substantially alter the picture presented in the first edition.

It has been a pleasure to the writer to note the ever increasing interest in the history of our Oklahoma Indians, not only among the natives but also among white people who now occupy much of the land formerly owned by these red men. The knowledge thus gained by the whites has made for a more sympathetic understanding of the Indian question. Intermarriage between the two races has largely obliterated the former bitter feeling of the Indians, whose children know no difference between the whites and themselves.

GRANT FOREMAN

Muskogee, Oklahoma
August 29, 1952

PREFACE

EMIGRATION of white settlers in the early part of the nineteenth century into the territory now forming the central and southern states, found the country occupied by tribes of American Indians who had lived there from time immemorial. Tentative legislation was enacted by Congress from time to time, and so-called treaties made with little comprehending Indians were used as instruments to drive them west and still farther west. How these things were done, the inevitable bloodshed and reprisals growing out of this conflict between the races, have been told many times and need no repetition here.

Indian removal, operated for some years in a haphazard manner, became established as a national policy with the election as president of its most powerful exponent, Gen. Andrew Jackson. From the Lakes to the Gulf the movement took form. Agents and commissions scattered through the country with reams of paper, quills, and ink with which to bind the Red Man. Indians were called into councils and gorged with pork and beef and plied with whisky; chiefs, warriors, and other influential men of the tribes by argument, persuasion, cajolery, threats, or bribes, the means depending on the exigencies of the occasion, were induced to agree to terms set down on paper called treaties. Indian removal by the government was thus formally inaugurated.

This book is the account of the removal of the southern Indians. In the North weaker and more primitive tribes yielded with comparatively small resistance to the power and chicane of the white man. A different situation in the southern states called into requisition different methods and resulted in a more complicated story. At least four of the tribes of southern Indians had so far advanced in learning and culture as to establish themselves permanently on the soil, build homes and farms, cultivate the land, raise herds and varied crops, including cotton which they carded, spun, and wove into cloth with which they clothed themselves. They laid out roads, built mills, engaged in commerce, and sent their children to schools conducted by the missionaries. And finally they established representative governments modeled on those of the states. Naturally, a people of such achievements, aware of their rights under prior possession and treaty guarantees with the national government, stubbornly resisted the aggressions of the whites. The forcible uprooting and expulsion of sixty thousand such people over a period of more than a decade, developed a story without parallel in the history of this country and resulted in a vast accumulation of manuscript material from which this account is mainly written.

It is not intended here to indict the people of the South for mistreatment of the Indians. Whatever may be charged against the white people in this regard is not sectional. The Indians have suffered at their hands throughout the country from north to south and from east to west. The author has undertaken here merely a candid account of the removal of these southern Indians, so that the reader may have a picture of that interesting and tragic enterprise as revealed by an uncolored day-by-day recital of events. Nor has he attempted an interpretation of these events or of the actions and motives of the people connected with them.

In the removal of these Indians, the magnitude of the undertaking was not comprehended, and the tremendous responsibility for the lives and comfort of the men, women, and children was never appreciated by Congress and the administration. Embarked on a novel enterprise, lack of experience should have requisitioned extraordinary ability and concern for the helpless objects of their decrees, which they were denied. Inadequate preparation by the government and the appointment of a horde of political incompetents to posts of authority, resulted in woeful mismanagement and cruel and unnecessary suffering by the emigrants. Much suffering, perhaps, was inevitable, but much would have been prevented by considerate and skillful preparation.

A conspicuous saving grace of this sorrowful story is the fidelity and skill with which the regular army officers and soldiers in the field discharged their unwelcome duties in connection with the removal. In nearly all instances they devoted themselves indefatigably and sympathetically to the sad task of removing the Indians with as much expedition and comfort as possible within the provisions made by their superiors in Washington. In this they contrasted sharply with the volunteer soldiers and a large class of political, civilian employees and especially those of local attachments and prejudices, and the contractors whose purpose was to realize as much profit as possible from their contracts, thereby excluding considerations of comfort for the emigrants.

Thousands of tragedies and experiences of absorbing interest marked this, one of the most dramatic chapters in our history, but there were no chroniclers at hand to record them. Only occasionally did the tragedy and pathos of some phase of this undertaking beguile a sympathetic officers to turn from routine and add a line or a paragraph—a stroke that might have been the beginning of a picture of this unhappy migration; but the finished canvas will never be seen by man; it can only be imagined. Little more than a suggestion of the realities is possible from the thousands of manuscripts that have contributed to this account.

While this book is not written to excite sympathy for the Indians, this tragic phase of American history is best understood if one will remember that for the most part the southern Indians were people of fixed habits and tastes. They were not nomads like some western Indians; they were less inclined to wander to strange places than white people. They loved their streams and valleys, their hills, and forests, their fields and herds, their homes and firesides, families and friends; they were rooted in the soil as the Choctaw chief Pushmataha said, "where we have grown up as the herbs of the woods." More than white people they cherished a passionate attachment for the earth that held the bones of their ancestors and relatives. Few white people either understood or respected this sentiment. The trees that shaded their homes, the cooling spring that ministered to every family, friendly watercourses, familiar trails and prospects, busk grounds, and council houses were their property and their friends; these simple possessions filled their lives; their loss was cataclysmic. It is doubtful if white people with their readier adaptability can understand the sense of grief and desolation that overwhelmed the Indians when they were compelled to leave all these behind forever and begin the long sad journey toward the setting sun which they called the Trail of Tears.

G. F.

Muskogee, Oklahoma.

CONTENTS

BOOK FIVE / Seminole Removal

ILLUSTRATIONS

MAPS

INDIAN REMOVAL

BOOK ONE / Choctaw. Removal

CHAPTER ONE / The Treaty of Dancing Rabbit Creek

As THE area of white population east of the Mississippi river expanded, intrusion into the regions occupied or hunted over by the Indians increased, and there was heard with greater frequency the demand that the government extinguish the Indian title to these lands. Numerous effective treaties to this end had been made with the Indians in the northern states, but in the South the stubborn resistance of the more permanent Indian residents blocked general removal of the tribes. Repeatedly had the whites attempted to invoke to their aid the terms of the Georgia Compact of 1802 wherein the federal government had agreed to extinguish at its own expense the Indian title within the reserved limits of Georgia as soon as it could be done "peaceably and on reasonable terms."

However, some progress had been made. A number of so-called treaties had been negotiated, nominally with the tribes, but usually by the well-established policy of appealing to the avarice of their corruptible chiefs. By these methods tracts of the Indian domain were cut off here and there, so that the whites by consolidating their gains and moving up again on the Indians, would improve their position for demanding more.

Since the Louisiana Purchase, no less than nine "treaties" had been made with the Cherokee Indians, by which they had been induced to release parts of their territory or agree to new boundary lines demanded by the whites; six with the Creeks, four with the Choctaw, three with the Chickasaw, and one with the Seminole. Events that followed each other in rapid succession were forcing the Indian situation to a crisis,[1]

1 American Historical Association, *Annual Report for 1906* (Washington, 1906), I, 235, "The History of Events Resulting in Indian Consolidation west of the Mississippi River," by Anna H. Abel.

a development due largely to the aggressiveness and bitter hostility of the State of Georgia. To please the white people of this state and his cousin Governor Troup, Creek Chief William McIntosh signed a treaty relinquishing the lands of the tribe, in violation of tribal law,[2] for which he was executed by his tribesmen in accordance with those laws. This roused the governor to fury, and gave fresh impetus to the efforts of the state to drive out the Indians.

Then there occurred the death of Path Killer, the chief of the Cherokee Tribe and delegates met on July 4, 1827, to elect a successor. Conscious of their advancement as shown by their possession of an alphabet, churches, schools, and laws, they sought a means of insuring stability and permanence in their home. They found it, they believed, in the adoption of a constitution modeled on that of the United States, which inaugurated a new era of Cherokee history. This threat of permanence stirred the State of Georgia to renewed efforts to drive

2 How did the white people compensate the bereft family of this chief whose betrayal of his tribe for them cost him his life? Years later his widow Peggie, a Cherokee, is seen at the office of Pierce M. Butler, agent for the Cherokee Indians in the West. "Some one casually observed she could not entertain a very friendly or partial feeling for those who had thus deprived him of his existence—the remark was repeated before she appeared to notice it; suddenly however, the shawl, which covered her shoulders and held together by her arm, partially enveloped her form, was loosed, and with a sparkling eye, and a voice full of tremulous emotion, she broke out into an indignant rebuke of that government, which had beggared her children and left her portionless and a widow to the cold, heartless, and uncertain charity of the world. 'No,' she exclaimed, 'no, I do not blame these people for these things—I do not blame the Creeks, the Creeks treat me well, the Cherokees treat me well—it was Government caused me to suffer, it was by Government my husband lost his life—Government say to my husband 'Go to Arkansas, go to Arkansas, and you will be better off.' My husband wished to please the Government—my husband he lost his life to please the Government—my home is burned, myself and children run—my children naked—no bread—one blanket, is all—like some stray dog, I suffer; with one blanket I cover my three children and myself—the Government say 'Go!' 'The Indians kill him; between two fires my husband dies; I wander—Government does not feed me—Creek does not feed me—no home, no bread, nothing! nothing! Till Gen. Ware gives me a home, I suffer like some stray Indian dog,' " (*Cherokee Advocate*, March 6, 1846, p. 3, col. 2; Draper Manuscript Collection, 29 cc 16, *Weekly Journal*, April 16, 1845). The act of this chief received belated recognition when a chapter of the Daughters of the American Revolution dedicated to his memory a bronze marker on the spot where he signed the treaty which the president found the whites procured by fraud and declined to enforce.

the Indians from within her borders. She countered by enacting measures extending her criminal laws over the Indians within the state.
Similar measures were adopted by the State of Mississippi in January
1830, over the Choctaw and Chickasaw,[3] and by Alabama over the
Creeks. The Indians sent delegations and memorials to Washington,
pleading for federal intervention to protect them in their treaty rights
against the states. The federal government was induced to send
emissaries to the Indians, and by approaching them publicly and
privately to attempt to break down their resistance against removing
west.

By the time Andrew Jackson became a candidate for president in
1828, the subject of Indian removal had become a national issue. Jackson's attitude as a strong partisan of the states that desired removal was
well known. He had appeared in the negotiations to procure many of
the Indian treaties of cession; his dominating personality impressed
the Indians, and he beguiled many into the conviction that he was
their friend; so that with the tremendous influence which he exercised
over them, he became the outstanding exponent of the white man's
relentless contest for the lands of the Indian. Logically one of the
first important measures to be urged by Jackson after his election was
what became known as the Indian Removal Bill. Missionary organiza-
tions and other influences in the North had been favorable to general
removal west of all the tribes, as the means best calculated to protect
the Indians; but when it developed that the people of Georgia were
interested only in driving the Indians from their state, active opposition
of most of the North was aligned against the measure.

After one of the bitterest debates in the history of Congress, this
bill was enacted into law on May 28, 1830. It did not itself authorize
the enforced removal of the Indians, and did not in terms appear to
menace them; but it announced a federal policy favorable to Indian

3   U. S. *Senate Document, No.* 512, Twenty-third Congress, first session, "Indian
Removal," III, p. 361. (This series of five volumes and more than 4,000 pages, compiled
in response to a resolution of the Senate, contains the correspondence in the war
department touching Indian Removal from November 30, 1831, to December 27,
1833. As it will be referred to frequently herein, for brevity it will be called "Document"). By this act the legislature "abolished and took away all the rights, privileges,
immunities, and franchises held, claimed or enjoyed by those persons called Indians
within the chartered limits of that state by virtue of any form of policy, usages or
customs existing among them."

removal, and placed in the hands of President Jackson the means to initiate steps to secure exchanges of lands with any tribe "residing within the limits of the states or otherwise." Knowing Jackson's views on the subject and the federal policy employed in dealing with the Indians, they were filled with foreboding.

President Jackson lost no time in taking steps to carry the new law into effect. At the adjournment of Congress, he and Gen. John H. Eaton, his secretary of war, planned to spend their holidays in Tennessee; and four days after the law was enacted they sent word by D. W. Haley that they would confer with delegates from the four tribes, who were favorable to removal.[4] The president, Secretary Eaton, and John Coffee arrived at Eaton's home in Franklin on August 11.[5]

Because of the strife between the factions of the Choctaw Nation, it was impossible to convene a meeting at which a representative and authorized delegation from that tribe could be selected to meet the president; therefore, only the Chickasaw delegates appeared. And after making a provisional treaty with them, Eaton and Coffee went to Mississippi to confer with the Choctaw Indians.

Some progress toward preparation had already been made in this nation, in a measure through the agency of Greenwood Leflore, a shrewd half-breed member of the tribe. As chief of one of the three districts into which the Choctaw Nation was divided, he exerted considerable influence; he was intelligent and ambitious, and was quick to realize the import of events and their bearing on his personal fortunes, if indeed, he did not rely on explicit promises made to him for his assistance. In March he called a meeting of some of the head men of the tribe friendly to him, who undertook ambitious and radical enterprises under his direction. He told them that in the face of the crisis confronting them, they must change the form of their government and in place of three chiefs must unite on one. As part of this plan, on the

4 *Document*, II, 3, 75, 240, "Journal of Proceedings."

5 *Jackson Gazette*, August 21, 1830, p. 3, col. 2. From his home in Franklin, Eaton addressed a long letter to the Choctaw chiefs in which he acknowledged receipt of their talk of June 2, rebuked them for their wish to examine the western country before entering into a treaty of removal and warned them of dire consequences if they neglected the present opportunity to remove with the aid of the government (OIA, "1830 Choctaws").

second day of the council, David Folsom, the rival of Mushulatubbe for chieftainship in the northeastern district, and John Garland, claiming against Nitakechi the same office in the Southern district, resigned in the council such tenure as they held. They then voted to make Leflore chief of the whole nation.

In the afternoon of that day, the sixteenth, Leflore assumed the rôle of chief of the tribe and addressed the council on the subject of the difficulties that confronted them and the necessity for immediate decision as to their future course.[6] After extended discussion the council voted in favor of emigration. The next day a treaty prepared in the handwriting of Alexander Talley, a missionary in the service of Leflore, was signed by the chiefs and two or three hundred warriors present; this document, for certain considerations, purported in the name of the tribe to give up their lands in Mississippi and agree to remove to the West. It was then delivered to Major Haley, the president's envoy, whose presence at the time explains much that took place there. Haley carried it to Washington, and it was soon followed by a protest from chiefs and leading men who were not in sympathy with the ambitious Leflore. When both documents were submitted to the Senate, the treaty was rejected,[7] and the subject was held in abeyance until commissioners appointed for the purpose could meet representatives of the whole tribe.

Leflore's conception of a government headed by one chief had much to recommend it; but he was not popular outside of his own district, particularly with the full-bloods, and the tribe as a whole was opposed to him as chief. The so-called election came to nothing in spite of the arguments and threats he wasted on Mushulatubbe, Nitakechi, and their followers. In fact, this attempted change which probably had the sanction of the administration at Washington, increased the jealousy and bitter feeling already existing between the chiefs and factions of the tribe and did more harm than good.[8]

6 *Jackson (Tennessee) Gazette*, May 11, 1830, p. 4.

7 *Document*, II, 4, 240.

8 *Ibid.* Mushulatubbe and Nitakechi, chiefs of two of the Choctaw districts, and a large number of other principal men of the tribe on June 2 addressed a memorial to the secretary of war, saying that LeFlore did not represent the sentiment of the tribe, and attacking the pretended treaty which Leflore, Folsom and Talley were instrumental in securing. They stated that there were two political parties in the

Leflore at first took a bold stand, and in April wrote to Mushulatubbe an arrogant letter which he signed as "Chief of Choctaw Nation," warning the full-blood chief that he must abdicate as district chief and conform to the views of the writer, or take the consequences.[9] Shortly after, Mushulatubbe and Nitakechi appealed to Agent Ward to prevent a threatened invasion of their districts by an army of a thousand men under Leflore and Folsom.[10] Bad feeling and excitement grew until, on July 14, a serious disturbance took place, where the Indians were gathered to hold a large council and to receive their annuity, at the factory in the Choctaw Nation, on the Tombigbee River, fifteen miles from Erie.

"The difference existing between Mushulatubbe and Leflore has existed for some time, which arose in the first place, from a disposition held forth by Leflore, to Christianize the Choctaw Indians, in which he

Nation; that theirs was the Republican, containing double the number of warriors of Leflore's, known as the Despotic. They wished "to establish, when we may be so situated as to allow it, a government similar to that of the United States, under which our people may flourish, and be perpetuated as a nation." They said that as they were ignorant of the country west of the Mississippi river, they desired to send an exploring party of sixteen men, which they wished the government to pay for; and on learning their report on the country to which it was proposed to remove them, they would gladly meet commissioners to discuss a treaty of removal (*Document*, II, 58).

9 Leflore to "Maj. Mushula Tubby," April 7, 1830, OIA, "1830 Choctaws (Agency)." Though a man of little education, Leflore was intelligent and had progressive views that might have been of benefit to his tribe but for the arrogant and autocratic bearing he assumed toward those possessed of more Indian blood than himself. Two years before, he had written to Thomas L. McKenny: ". . .I have made menny Laws one is that no more poles is set up for ded person second is no white man shall mary Indian woman without giting permission from chief then git licen from Agent then marry corden to white Law. this will show Indian white habits—wee have suffered by white man in marrying our woman then quit the woman when he please. Leve poor woman with half a dozen childrens then git yong wife this it is so bad for white man be gilty if should be Allow it wee cant advance in sivilized life I am determine to stop this two laws if it cannot my life. You may depend on my doing all good I can for my poor blind Brothers in this Nation I am true friend of Red men good will be with ous in our of Deingers in this troublesome world" (Leflore to McKenney, May 3, 1828, OIA). This manuscript letter purporting to be in the hand of Leflore, is not in the style of other extracts from the same author herein, which obviously had the benefit of an amanuensis of some education, probably Rev. Mr. Talley.

10 Mushulatubbe, Nitakechi, and others to Ward, April 17, 1830 (*Document*, II, 581).

erred, by exercising his authority to the utmost extent, which offended many of the people of the nation. Some of the opposition party burnt a large number of books, and one or two churches. Another difference arose out of the election of Mushulatubbe as chief of the Southern District of the nation and that of his opposing the views of Leflore in selling the lands to the United States, with a provision of reserving to himself, Folsom, and others, large and valuable tracts. To which Mushulatubbe and his party, was opposed.

"Mushulatubbe with his party, amounting to about 1000 warriors, (of this number between two and three hundred were armed), had encamped a short distance from the Factory, the agents were distributing to each his portion, with as little delay as possible, to let them depart to their homes.

"Information was received, that Leflore, with a party of about 1500 warriors had arrived, between eight and nine hundred of his men were armed, five hundred had muskets, and many of those who had not guns, had prepared themselves with war clubs, (the emblem of war), spears, knives, etc. In the mean time Leflore had sent a messenger to Mushulatubbe informing him, that if he did not consent to give up his commission, that he (L) would fall upon him, and would not desist while he retained life. Two hours were given for his decision. To this message Mushulatubbe paid the utmost contempt. Two or three messages of the same import, at different times, were given to M. and to all of which he gave answers of utter disdain, and defiance. His men were all anxious for a contest. Leflore's warriors were all painted, and expressed much anxiety to fight. This may be considered as an outrage, as Leflore must have come at least two hundred miles for the purpose of chastising Mushulatubbe, for his unbelief."[11]

Folsom had carried the ultimatum from Leflore to Mushulatubbe, and the latter replied in writing that he would never acknowledge as chiefs either Leflore or Folsom, let the consequences be what they might. "That evening the Hostile party came down to the House where we were and marched up in platoons to the old Mingo who was in the

[11] *Nashville Banner* and *Nashville Whig*, August 9, 1830, p. 2. col. 5; *The Democrat* (Huntsville, Alabama), August 26, 1830, p. 3, col. 5. The ". . .disturbance which threatened much bloodshed. . . was happily quieted by the timely interferance of Mr. Gaines and some other persons who had influence with them" (*Jackson (Tennessee) Gazette*, August 4, and October 9, 1830, p. 3).

middle of the yard within six paces and halted until all was formed, when the cowardly commander was told they were without arms but name the day and place and they should have a fight to his satisfaction; his reply was that he did not want to fight, only to restore peace and that he had nothing against him, the chief Nettuckegee, etc., etc. So he went away with his party and reported they made Mushulatubbe run which was faulse to my own knowledge, a greater Tyrent and coward I never have seen than this man Lefloure. He has now found that the Indians will not have him as King for life over them and he wants an excuse not only for his attempts upon their rights but is the first to oppose any Treaty. General Jackson has sent on Mr. Donnelly to try and get them to meet the Secy of War at Franklin Ten. and we are doing our best, but Lefloure will oppose every thing unless he can get all his everesious heart is set on."[12]

Mushulatubbe and Nitakechi and their full-blood following had thwarted Leflore's ambitious plan to present himself as the head chief of the Choctaw Nation in the forthcoming negotiations with the commissioners for the surrender of their lands in Mississippi. But he had exerted himself industriously and with some effect with the people of the tribe to facilitate those negotiations. Eaton and Coffee arrived at Dancing Rabbit Creek in the Choctaw Nation September 15 and began discussions with the head men of the tribe. The commissioners told the Indians that the government was unable to prevent the laws of the State of Mississippi from operating on them contrary to their rights guaranteed by federal treaties; that if they undertook to resist those laws, ten or a hundred times as many armed white men would compel them to submit; and warned them that their best interests required their removal to the West.

After providing for the issuance of rations to the Indians in attendance and other preliminaries, the council began on the eighteenth[13]

12 W. Ward, Choctaw agent, to R. M. Johnson, August 7, 1830, OIA, "1830 Choctaw Emigration." The beloved chief Pushmataha, who died in 1824, had warned his people never to select as district chief or permit to participate in the government of the nation any one having a drop of white blood in his veins. The inherent avarice of the white blood, he said, would prompt its owner to favor sale of their land. "His warning was unheeded, and to the influence of the mixed blood Greenwood Leflore, the Choctaws ascribe the loss of their lands in Mississippi" (H. A. Halbert in "Draper Collection," State Historical Society of Wisconsin, Tecumseh Mss. IV, YY).

13 The council was marked by the order of the commissioners excluding from the treaty premises the missionaries Kingsbury, Byington, Williams, and Cushman

with Peter P. Pitchlynn as chairman of the Choctaw participants and his father John Pitchlynn as interpreter. A bitter controversy arose over the contention of Leflore and his partisans that his district should have a larger representation in the council than the others; and it required much time, tact, and patience on the part of the commissioners to establish peace between the participants so that negotiations could proceed.[14] For nearly two weeks the Indians in the council were obdurate, and finally after agreeing that they would not sign a treaty, many of them left for home.

Then John Pitchlynn made a suggestion that won over the remaining Indians on the grounds, and dissuaded them from their threats to mob the chiefs and head men if they should sign the treaty: George S. Gaines of Demopolis was a merchant who had dealt honestly with the Indians and held their confidence and respect for his character and ability. The plan proposed by Pitchlynn and adopted by General Eaton was to promise the Indians that Mr. Gaines would be asked to conduct a party of them to examine the western country; if they found it satis-factory they were to remove and Gaines would be entrusted with the management of the removal, for the Indians said they knew that Gaines would not drive them through the mud like animals. Upon the request of Eaton, therefore, Gaines agreed to discharge the undertaking proposed, and the delegation of explorers was decided upon, which with the other inducements employed, resulted in securing the execu-tion of the treaty by the Indians on September 27.

The other means employed are obvious: the three chiefs of the three districts, who signed the treaty, Greenwood Leflore, Nitakechi, and Mushulatubbe[15] were each given four sections of land by the treaty.

(*Document*, II, 252; Eaton to Choctaw chiefs, September 18, 1830, OIA; *Journal of Treaty of Dancing Rabbit Creek*, "1830 Choctaws").

14   *Jackson Gazette*, October 9, 1830, p. 3, col. 1; *Document* II, 255.

15   An effort was made to win the old full-blood chief, Mushulatubbe, by launch-ing his candidacy for Congress; the *Port Gibson Correspondent* of April 1, 1830, con-tained his announcement. Press comment was calculated to impress the Indians with the fact that by a recent act of the legislature they had become citizens of Mississippi and subject to her laws (*Niles' Weekly Register*, XXXVIII, 327, 362). "Col. Leflore will realize $40,000 or $50,000 for his four sections. He received $6,000 or $7,000 for the section he received for signing the treaty of 1820. The Leflore connections in all will receive 17 sections, the Pitchlyns 10; Folsoms 8 or 9, Juzans about the same"

More than fifty other favored members of the tribe put forward by the chiefs, were given from one to two sections each for no apparent reason other than to win their approval and influence and remove their opposition. Medals and gratuities were passed about. David Folsom, besides receiving four sections of land, was later allowed one hundred dollars for the expense of each of his two sons at La Grange Academy, in Georgia, and Greenwood Leflore was given one hundred dollars to send his daughter to the Female Academy at the same place.[16]

This, the first treaty to be made and ratified under the Act of May 28, 1830, was known as the Treaty of Dancing Rabbit Creek.[17] The preamble of the treaty recited that "Whereas the General Assembly of the State of Mississippi has extended the laws of said State to persons and property within the chartered limits of the same, and the President of the United States has said that he cannot protect the Choctaw people from the operation of these laws."[18] By the terms of this treaty the Choctaw ceded to the United States the entire country owned

---

(Kingsbury to Evarts, November 17, 1830, *Andover-Harvard Theological Library*. "Missionary Records," LXXII, No. 27). Leflore received from G. W. Adams $6,300 for a section of land granted him for signing the treaty of 1825. He afterwards repented the transaction thinking he should have had more (OIA, "1828 Choctaw Agency, R. M. Johnson"). Folsom received $3,500 for each of his sections, but Mushulatubbe was swindled out of his by some white men for a few hundred dollars (*Document*, IV, 504).

16 General Eaton, secretary of war, wrote to Folsom: "You will not say anything of your boys going to that school at the expense of government, as others will expect a similar favor and I shall be pressed with applications" (Eaton to Folsom, December 2, 1830, OIA, "1830 Schools, Choctaws"). One of Folsom's sons, Allen, was earlier in the year at Miami University, Oxford, Ohio, at the annual expense of $210, paid by the government (Bishop, "Accounts" January 8, 1830, *ibid.*). Folsom wrote that he had just placed two daughters, nearly grown, in a school at Columbus, Mississippi, and he wished the government to allow him $150 annually for each of them (Folsom to McKenney, March 4, 1830, *ibid.*). At the same time William Bernard and Lee Compere, two Creek boys, were being educated at government expense at Georgetown; Col. Thomas L. McKenney was instrumental also in having educated at Georgetown James L. McDonald and Daugherty Colbert, a Chickasaw.

17 Charles J. Kappler [ed.] *Laws and Treaties* II, 221; *Document*, I, 240 to 263 "Journal of Proceedings with Choctaw and Chickasaw Indians." John Pitchlynn, interpreter, died in Columbus on the Tombigbee river.

18 When the Senate ratified the treaty it refused to ratify this admission by President Jackson that he could not protect the Indians in their treaty rights.

by them east of the Mississippi river and agreed to remove on the domain within the Indian Territory which the government promised to convey to them in fee simple; the Indians were given three years to emigrate. The treaty was not ratified and proclaimed until February 24, 1831. On May 26, the president proclaimed his grant conveying to the Choctaw Indians the lands described in the treaty, with boundaries, "beginning near Fort Smith where the Arkansas boundary crosses the Arkansas river, running thence to the source of the Canadian fork, if in the limits of the United States, or to those limits; thence due south to Red river, and down Red river to the west boundary of the Territory of Arkansas, thence, north along that line, to the beginning."[19]

There was much resentment against the treaty, as a majority of the tribe was opposed to it. Meetings were held where the Indians conferred on plans to memorialize the president and Senate to reject the treaty[20] but for want of leadership and ability to organize themselves this agitation came to nothing. Most of the leaders of the tribe had been aligned securely by bribery with the government and the treaty; but efforts were made to "break" or remove from office the chiefs who signed the treaty.

The attitude of the politicians in the tribe does not make a pretty picture. Familiar with the government's policy of bribing those in position to appear and bind the tribe, the desire to share in this largess is too apparent in their jealousies and contentions for official preferment at the time a treaty was to be negotiated and large sums of money expended in executing it. In the Northeastern or Mushulatubbe's[21] district, the partisans of David Folsom met and declared the latter chief of the district. His brother Israel Folsom and John Garland went in to Nitakechi's, or Southern, district, and by circulating among the Indians the charge that their chief had accepted money for signing the

19 *Document*, II, 304.
20 *Ibid.*, 184.
21 Mushulatubbe was deposed in 1826, and David Folsom was selected to replace him. According to his rival, the old chief was too much addicted to drunkenness, too tyrannical, and too likely to be influenced to yield their land to the United States. "We do not want a General McIntosh in our tribe," Folsom wrote, referring to the betrayal of the Creeks by their chief, who suffered death for signing a treaty giving up their lands (Folsom to McKenney, May 26, 1826, OIA, "1826 Schools, Choctaw").

treaty, got warriors of "Six-towns, Hajowanee and Chickasawhay" towns to meet in council and declare Joel R. Nail their chief.[22]

In Greenwood Leflore's district, the Western, the disaffected ones met on October 23 on Chufocto creek and elected as chief George W. Harkins,[23] who was then in the West. Harkins was the son-in-law of David Folsom and the nephew of Leflore. However, the government refused to recognize as chiefs any but those who had signed the treaty.[24] Meetings were held in a number of places where resolutions denouncing Leflore for his tyrannical conduct were signed by a large number of Indians and forwarded to the war department.[25]

22 "Captains in Council" to Eaton, October 16, 1830, OIA, "1830 Choctaw Emigration;" *Document*, II, 46.

23 *Ibid.*, 197. David Folsom who had been working with Leflore to promote the views of the government, wrote: "I am sorry to inform you, that nearly all the people of the Col. Leflore Dist. have forsaken him;" and said the followers of Nitakechi had abandoned him also; the reason given was that these chiefs had not kept their promise to oppose the treaty (Folsom to Eaton, December 24, 1830, OIA, "1830 Choctaw Emigration"). "Leflore is gone. He was obliged from over bearing, & tyrannical and cruel conduct to fly the country" (McKenney to Eaton, February 25, 1830, AGO, ORD, WDF).

24 *Document*, II, 46, 890. The tenure of these chieftainships was in the nature of a scrambling possession; Leflore had displaced Robert Cole, but when it became evident that he was using his position to promote the views of the government, it was attempted the year before to place Cole in power again. "At a collection of Leflour's District (the Northwest) to pay the annuities for this year, Col. Robt. Cole, a former chief of this district, attended with about one hundred men. It was believed that they were about to try to Brak Leflour the acting chief, and place Cole in power again. Leflour met him with about 400 men, 200 armed with Guns and marched round Cole and party's camp, took them prisoners and kept 10 or 12 tied all night under a strong guard; next day there was a kind of court over them and 14 were condemned to be whipped on their bare back. Cole was one who recd. sentence. But after whipping fore with 25 Strips well lade on, the ballance say two were reprieved by order of the Chief and council. Col. Cole was one of the number who recd. his lenient power" (Ward to Eaton, Choctaw Agency) July 14, 1829, OIA, "1829 Choctaw Agency"). In December Mushulatubbe called a council of 31 of whom twenty voted to reinstate him as chief; Folsom acting as chief, then called another meeting, removed five captains, and appointed others favorable to himself; the council then voted Folsom chief for life (*ibid.*, December 29, 1829). It was this tenure that Folsom undertook to resign in favor of Leflore.

25 Protest of thirty-nine Indians, November 3, 1830, OIA, "Choctaws, Wm. Ward."

CHAPTER TWO / *Indians Explore the Western Country*

A
s soon as the treaty was signed, long even before its ratification, white people began removing into the Choctaw
country in violation of the laws by which the land was
secured to the Indians.[1] Confusion reigned in the Nation
during the fall and winter of 1830 pending determination
of the question whether the treaty would be ratified by the Senate.
The tribe was torn by dissension; crops had been bad and some wished
to go at once to the West; others preferred to stay and be incorporated
into the state. Jealousy existed among the leaders of the tribe. They
distrusted each other; everybody was under suspicion. While numbers
were leaving and traveling independently of the government to their
new home in the west, others refused to go, and rallied around leaders
of like inclination.

Immediately after the execution of the treaty, arrangements were
made for sending west the exploring parties of Chickasaw and Choctaw.
Pursuant to the agreement made with General Eaton, George S.
Gaines closed out his business in order to finance and conduct the
expedition and made his preparations to depart with the company of
Choctaw explorers composed of the chiefs of the three districts, each
accompanied by four of his principal men.

Prior to their departure an independent exploring party conducted
by George W. Harkins and Robert Folsom, a brother of David Folsom,
set out for the western country and, returning the early part of December, made a favorable report on their new home on Red River.[2] They

1 *Document*, II, 42.
2 *Ibid.*, 197. Harkins's party left October 10. Besides Harkins and Folsom, it
included Josiah Doaks, A. Turnbull, and eleven warriors (Robert Folsom to David
Folsom, December 12, 1839; David Folsom to Eaton, December 24, 1830, OIA, "Choctaw Emigration").

crossed the Choctaw line at the salt works and later found "*good land enough on Little River to hold several thousand families. The second stream we come to was Clear Creek, and a beautiful stream indeed, the water is of the best quality, and no better mill seats in the world. The soil is good, plenty of timber, and stock range. This stream will afford a great many settlements. The third stream we come to was Gates Creek, and on this stream is where the old garrison* [Fort Towson] *was situated. The soil on this stream is also very excellent, well adapted for cotton, corn, and wheat; there is a great many fine springs to be found on this stream of the best quality, and game is plenty, such as deer and bear.*

"*The fourth stream we come to was the Kiamissa; this stream will afford fine navigation for boats; it is something like 80 yards wide. There is excellent prairies to be found on the Kiamissa, and salt springs in abundance; the timber is very good, and excellent stock range and plenty of game. The Kiamissa will afford fine settlement. The game is plenty on this stream, such as bear, deer, and turkeys, and on the west side of Kiamissa 15 or 20 miles there is buffaloe to be seen in great numbers. . . There is several Indian tribes living on our lands, such as the Cherokees, Creeks, Delawares, and Shawnees. They express a great desire that the Choctaws should permit them to live among them. We told them that no doubt but the Choctaws would receive them provided they would submit to the laws of Choctaws and become citizens.*"[3] On their return journey Harkins and Folsom met small parties of Choctaw who had already started to the west without waiting for the assistance of the government.[4]

Gaines prepared to start with his exploring party. He gathered up Nitakechi, Mushulatubbe and their captains, but when he reached Greenwood Leflore, that chief refused to accompany him. Gaines and his party, which was headed by Nitakechi, met the returning explorers Harkins and Folsom on the Arkansas river, and on November 28, 1830, crossed to the south side of that stream at Fort Smith where they camped several days. Here their conductor gave each member of the party a rifle, powder and lead, blanket and winter clothing.[5]

3   David and Robert Folsom, *Report of Exploring Party*, December 24, 1830, *ibid.*

4   Ward to Eaton, December 8, 1830, *ibid.*

5   The Choctaw captains were very poor and "so badly mounted and clad, that I have been compelled to aid them" in getting new horses, clothing, and blankets at

FROM AN EARLY PRINT

A characteristic river scene during Indian Removal

The party then ascended the Arkansas river to the Illinois, and camped at the salt works on that stream; from here Gaines sent some of his men with pack horses to Colonel Arbuckle at Fort Gibson with a request for supplies authorized by the war department and also for an escort of troops. The supplies were delivered at Webbers Falls on December 6 to the explorers, who then departed up the Arkansas and Canadian rivers. Colonel Arbuckle sent also an escort of twelve mounted men under Lieut. J. L. Dawson, accompanied by Army Surgeon J. W. Baylor, to afford the explorers protection against the roving Indians south of the Canadian river.

Dawson subsequently made an interesting report of the expedition.[6] His party went by way of Walter Webber's at the mouth of the Illinois river and then ascended the Canadian river to overtake the Indians. After passing two towns of Delaware Indians, one on each side of the Canadian, they ascended above the forks of that stream and discovered that the country had been burned off by the Indians returning from their fall hunt, leaving no grass to feed the horses of the explorers. They found the trail of the exploring party but on the eighteenth the weather turned intensely cold. At what was known as the South fork of the Canadian river, and afterwards called Gaines's creek, the Choctaw party was joined by the Chickasaw delegation. This party of sixteen in charge of Chickasaw Agent Reynolds, included the chief, Maj. Levi Colbert,[7] his brother, George, Pitman Colbert, Henry Love, and William D. King. They had arrived at Fort Gibson about the twentieth of November and from there on December 3 proceeded to the Canadian river.[8]

Fort Smith, wrote Gaines (*Document*, II, 193). These articles of apparel he purchased from Colville and Coffee, traders at Fort Smith.

6 *The Advocate* (*Little Rock, Arkansas*), March 9 and 16, 1831.

7 Levi Colbert was one of the party of Chickasaw who had made a hasty examination of part of this section in 1828 when with the Rev. Isaac McCoy's party, and returned home with a vague and unfavorable impression of the country (Grant Foreman, *Indians and Pioneers*, 307). The Chickasaw party included a warrior named Elaptinkbahtubbe, who "had long lived in the country west of Arkansas, and among the Pawnee and other wild tribes of the west and spoke the tongue of the Pawnees" (*Document*, II, 475).

8 Vashon to secretary of war, December 2, 1830, OIA; *Document* II, 401. Arbuckle furnished Reynolds and Gaines nine tents, six wagons, flints, powder, lead, and bullet moulds, flour, beef, pork, soap, corn, saddles, and rope.

Gaines wrote entertainingly of their travels; they packed and secured their flour, sugar, coffee, and salt furnished by Arbuckle with coverings of bear-skins and proceeded on their examination, backwards and forwards between the river and ridge, as they ascended northwestwardly. Game was abundant; hundreds of buffaloes, large droves of beautiful wild horses, deer, and turkeys were seen.[9]

"Every morning when I mounted my horse I was soon surrounded by the party all mounted to know the program for the day. Then the hunters would spread out to the right and left—always bringing into camp in the evening, plenty of game for the whole party, venison, turkeys, prairie hens and occasionally bear meat.

"Before reaching the mouth of the Canadian, the Lieutenant's command overtook us. The examination was intensely interesting; every-day novelties in country, an abundance of game, and fine weather to enjoy the chase, rendered each day and night joyous and happy. The Lieutenant and surgeon were both jolly soldiers and good hunters and entered into our hunts in the day and feasts and jollification at night with great spirit and zest. The buffalo now became plentiful and were daily killed for their humps and tongues. The rest of the carcass we found coarse and inferior to our beef.

"Above the mouth of the Canadian fork we were joined by Col. Reynolds and the Chickasaw delegation. Netuckeijah, invited them to join us and travel with us to enjoy our sports; wild horses were now plentiful and his invitation was accepted. The weather, now December, became quite cold. Large log fires at night, and longer nights, lengthened our social enjoyments. Our Choctaw hunting, war, love stories, and wit, were now seasoned by army stories and wit."[10]

Because of the cold and the burning of the prairies, and there being no cane on the Canadian river above the South fork, thus rendering it impossible to subsist their horses in that region, they abandoned further ascent of the Canadian and struck off on a southwest course across the headwaters of the Boggy and Blue, for the Washita river. Parties

9 *Mobile Commercial Register*, March 7, 1831, p. 4, col. 1.

10 "Gaines Papers," Mississippi State Department of Archives and History. George Strother Gaines was born in North Carolina and was reared in Tennessee. In 1805 President Jackson appointed him a Choctaw factor and in that year he settled on the Tombigbee river. He died at State Line, Mississippi, in February, 1873, aged 89.

of Osage, Delaware, Shawnee, Cherokee and Creeks were hunting in the fine game region lying on those streams. On one of the tributaries of the Boggy they met a party of Creek hunters who told them that another band of their tribe had been robbed of their horses by the Osage between the Blue and Washita rivers. A company of Delaware who had seen these Osage said they were in a starving condition when they came to their camp, and scarcely able to travel from hardship and fatigue.

The exploring Indians were very much pleased with the country between the Boggy, Blue and Washita, but the Chickasaw rebelled against going farther west. While they were camped on the Blue river, the delegations held a talk on the subject of a proposal by Major Colbert to purchase for his tribe part of the Choctaw domain; the Choctaw chiefs declined the proposal, but suggested that the Chickasaw could live with them—a proposition the latter rejected. On these streams was an abundance of cane, but a heavy rain and sleet had covered it with ice, so that when the horses ate it, it produced a colic that made the animals helpless. At one point the party was obliged to cut its way through the cane for half a mile, as the ice had matted it into an almost impenetrable jungle.

They had planned to explore the Washita to the mouth, but from fear of the prairie Indians and the cold weather the explorers determined to turn their faces eastward. On the Blue river they discovered the presence of a party of a hundred western Indians who, it was feared, contemplated an attack on them. To protect themselves the explorers, who numbered about sixty, agreed on Colonel Reynolds as commander and under his direction posted themselves on a high bluff for protection from that side. Tents were pitched in a half circle within which the horses were tied. While supper was being prepared, the men were busy cleaning their guns and moulding bullets. A log fire was kept burning all night in front of each tent and sentinels maintained their stations on the river bank above and below and in the rear of the semicircle of tents. But no attack was made during the night, somewhat to the disappointment of the younger men of the party.

The next morning after sending scouts ahead, the party departed from the Blue river. In the evening they discovered smoke ahead, and prepared for an engagement; the scouts penetrated the canebrake and found nothing but a pot, skillet, a parcel of beaver skins and traps.

"Just as we were listening to this report two men[11] rode up apparently well pleased by meeting us. They heard the tramp of our horses as we were approaching the ridge, and believing we were hostile Indians retreated from their camp, making a circuit to fall on our trail. Looking at the tracks of the horses they knew that they were shod, therefore they concluded that we were not wild Indians and hastened to overtake us;"[12] and from fear of the large party of wild Indians in the neighborhood joined the explorers. When they reached the Boggy river and had left the danger of hostile Indians behind them, Lieutenant Dawson and his party, on January 10, departed for Fort Gibson.

One evening, a week later when encamped on Red river, the explorers heard chopping and discovered some log huts occupied by Indians. The two trappers Mayes and Criner told them that the strangers were refugees from the Shawnee tribe who had been settled there since the British War of 1812. Some of the older men of the exploring party visited them; *"A half-breed woman looking at me said 'you are a white man—I hoped never to see the face of another white man.' I inquired her reason for such a hope. She answered, her husband and several members of her family had been killed by the whites. 'The remnants of my relations' said she, 'were compelled to leave their homes and we traveled to this country where we hoped to live in peace.' I replied, 'You should not entertain hatred for white Americans. It was not their fault your tribe joined the English who came over in their ships to fight us. In fighting them with your people among them, we could not help killing the Shawnees."*

A council was then held at which Nitakechi told the Shawnee they might remain where they were and be adopted into the tribe if they would conduct themselves properly and conform to the laws of the Choctaw Indians. The Shawnee chief gladly agreed to these liberal terms.

Maj. Levi Colbert, wishing to visit the Caddo Indians, crossed the Red river in company with Sheemacha and four other Chickasaw and examined the country between that stream and the Sabine, in April returning home by Natchitoches and the Red and Mississippi rivers.

11   Mayes and Griner who lived on Jack's Fork river.

12   "Gaines Papers," *ibid.*

After examining the Red river country, the Choctaw delegation departed for the east, arriving at Washington, Hempstead county, Arkansas, on January 29 "without a dollar in our pockets," Gaines and
Reynolds reported,[13] and reached their homes a month later after an
absence of four months.[14] Levi Colbert, who did not return from Texas
until April, had ". . .been heard to observe that he would not like to
live under Leflore, etc.; and I know his thirst for power is such as to
form an obstacle in his mind adverse to an union," reported Gaines to
the secretary.[15] On their return, the Chickasaw sent word to the
president that if he would purchase for them some of the land they
saw in Texas, they would be content to remove there. Nitakechi reported that they had suffered much with the cold, but he was pleased
with the western country in spite of the weather, and urged that
removal be started, as he found their new hunting grounds much occupied by bands of other Indians whom he wished the government to
remove.[16] The Indians had found much to please them; good streams
on which was fertile soil, an abundance of cane, and fine timber. The
favorable reports the two Choctaw exploring parties brought home
allayed somewhat the excitement and rancor caused by the treaty.

Reynolds and Gaines reported that *"The dividing ridge between the
waters of Red River and the Arkansas and Canadian, lies much nearer
the latter than the former; and in the event of the Choctaws becoming
disposed to sell a tract to the Chickasaws, this ridge would form a proper
boundary. The bottoms above mentioned (of Poteau, San Bois, and South
Fork rivers) would, in our opinion produce bread-stuffs, and as much*

13   *Document,* II, 401. In August Gaines writes to the secretary of war "That
arduous and unpleasant journey was performed by me cheerfully—although at much
sacrifice in my business; and I am sorry to remark that not a word in reply to any of
my letters or the joint report" by him and Reynolds has been received; and in particular his account rendered May 30 for expenses incurred by him in financing the
expedition has gone unnoticed (*ibid.,* II, 520). But the guileless Mr. Gaines was to
learn that the tawdry politics of the day had more shabby treatment in store for
him. Secretary of War Eaton left his post to become minister to Spain and he was
succeeded by Lewis Cass. Gaines's accounts were held up and his letters of inquiry
went unanswered; thirteen years later $2,500 of his claim was allowed and he was
remitted to Congress for the greater part.

14   *Document,* II, 401, 415, 475.

15   *Ibid.,* II, 420.

16   *Ibid.,* 415, 420.

cotton land and timber be left, as would support the Chickasaws, and grow as much cotton as they would likely plant for a century or two to come; but the uplands being poor, and affording little or no good timber, and but few good springs, and the want of cane above SouthFork [[Gaines's Creek]] *makes it unfit for a large Indian population.*"[17]

When Colonel Gaines reached the home of Greenwood Leflore and notified him that the exploring party was ready to leave for the west, his ". . .strange and unexpected determination . . .not to accompany the party, agreeable to his promise to you,. . . " placed Gaines in a most embarrassing position, the latter reported to Eaton. "Discontents have lately appeared in portions of all the districts, but most in this, and hence, I presume, is the true cause of Colonel Leflore's unwillingness to leave home; indeed, his friends think there is much possibility of his removal."[18] In spite of Leflore's remaining at home to guard against such action, this is exactly what happened when George W. Harkins, who was himself on an exploring tour to the west, was selected during his absence as chief in place of Leflore.[19]

But Leflore was occupied with other affairs more directly concerned with his personal interest, and had no time to waste in making investigation concerning the western country. Pending ratification of the treaty he was engaged on a consirable scale in negotiating with Indians whom he could induce to remove at once for the sale of their improvements to white men, whom he immediately put in possession of the land and improvements.

In this manner, though the treaty had not been ratified, he collected and started west a number of ill-organized and inadequately provisioned parties. Leflore boasted that he would remove the whole tribe if the president would back him, whether the treaty was approved or not; and Washington gave him free rein for his unauthorized activities.

About a week after the treaty was signed, Leflore wrote the war department: "*I find it impossible to prevent my people from emigrating immediately in considerable bodies. Many of them, in consequence of the disturbances in the spring, and the excessive dry summer, are without*

17 *Ibid.*, 401. Reynolds and Gaines wrote that the Choctaw spoke of the Chickasaw as their older brothers (*ibid.*, II, 421).

18 *Ibid.*, 184.

19 *Ibid.*, 197.

Greenwood LeFlore

provisions; and must seek them in the forest, go into the white settlements,
or emigrate at the risque of suffering in their new homes. I have advised
the latter as the most prudent course. . . .Dr. Talley will also go imme-
diately on to reorganize his churches, and afford such assistance as may
be in his power. . . Many of the people now emigrating, will leave the
aged and infirm together with their tools, in my neighborhood, in expecta-
tion that they will obtain a passage on steam-boats from my landing."[20]
Leflore furnishes another clue to his desire for haste: "*From the number*
and class of people who will leave the nation this winter, it is hoped that
the President will see the necessity of admitting such white families as may
purchase reserves . . .The motive for admitting them is quite apparent.
Many who emigrate will have hogs, and other things that they would
wish to sell. . ."[21]

The next month Leflore reported that seven or eight hundred
emigrants were on their way; he expected them to reach their new
home on the Kiamichi river about the first of January. "A considerable
portion of them are poor, and leaving with means hardly sufficient to
sustain them on the journey, will reach the place of their future
residence in a very destitute condition." This heartless improvidence
in the preparation of these poor people was excused by Leflore on the
ground that the Indians ought to be removed as fast as possible, "to
escape the evils of intemperance which are flowing upon the country
on all sides and have caused the death of a considerable number since the
administration of the Choctaw law was arrested" by the State of
Mississippi.[22]

Five or six of Leflore's most influential captains had departed with
the emigrants, "and I expect my Speaker will soon follow to take charge
of them." When the first party in charge of Alexander Talley arrived
at the Mississippi, they waited there bewildered until another party

20 *Jackson (Tennessee) Gazette,* December 4, 1830, p. 3.

21 Leflore to Eaton, October 5, 1830, OIA, "1830 Choctaw Emigration"; *ibid.,*
January 10, 1831; *Document,* II, 394; *ibid.,* I, 852. Haley who was an admirer of Leflore
and intermediary between him and the president, wrote: "All [emigrants] that are
entitled to reservations by the treaty, are selling them daily to the white people
under the inspection of Col. Leflore, and he gives the purchasers permission to come
in and take possession. This enables the Indians to sell their corn and all their loose
property" (*ibid.,* II, 465). They sold their stock for $4.00 a head; a cow and calf brought
$6.04 (*ibid.,* I, 453).

22 *Idem.* Leflore to Eaton, November 19, 1830.

came along under the leadership of a school teacher named Myers, also in the employ of Leflore. Myers helped them build a boat to cross the Mississippi and left them while he went ahead to arrange for ferriage on the Ouachita at Ecor à Fabri,[23] at the Saline, and Little river.[24] In January, ". . .the advance party of emigrants reached their place of destination after very great suffering from the unparalleled severity of the winter."[25]

Some idea of this terrible journey is conveyed by a letter written by the Rev. Mr. Talley after their arrival in the west: ". . .*The chief of the north-west district wished me to meet their people in the west, and as far as possible provide for them, but he could furnish no funds; the credit of the nation was to be used, if possible, in procuring corn, and a smith's shop, etc., for them. My own resources were four hundred dollars, the balance of an appropriation of the preceding year.*[26] *Myself, and my interpreter, and Mr. Myers and family (my Choctaw teacher sent on by the chief with the emigrants as an interpreter, and to open their way among the whites in all difficult cases) were to be provided for in a new*

23   "Ecore à Fabri (Fabri's Cliffs) 80 to 100 feet high. It is reported that a line of demarkation run between the french and spanish provinces, when the former possessed Louisiana, crossed the river [Ouachita] at this place; and it is said that Fabri, a frenchman, and perhaps the supposed Engineer deposited lead near the cliff in the direction of the line; we could not however obtain any authenticated account of this matter, and it is not generally believed; a little further is a small cliff called 'le petite cor à Fabri'(the little cliff of Fabri)." (*Journal of a Voyage by William Dunbar, Documents relating to the Purchase and Exploration of Louisiana*, American Philosophical Society, 60). The place was also sometimes called Côte de Fabri, Coafabri, and Coafabrica. Louis Le Blanc, a Frenchman made a settlement at Ecore à Fabri on 640 acres of land on the west side of the Ouachita river in 1780, and two years later he was killed by the Osage Indians. His widow and children remained there until 1806 (Affidavit of John Felhove, October 14, 1820, *Ouachita Land Office Records*, manuscript collection of Rebecca Bryan); the site of Ecore à Fabri is now included in Camden, Arkansas.

24   *Document*, II, 463; Talley to Eaton, November 10, 1830, OIA, "1830 Choctaws."

25   *Document*, II, 463.

26   The Rev. Mr. Talley was engaged the remainder of his life in trying to secure from the government a return of the meagre funds he had expended to keep his Indians from starving. In 1836 J. F. H. Claiborne wrote to the secretary of war: "I have the honor to transmit you the papers and acts of the late Alexander Talley precisely in the situation in which I received them. He died suddenly while preparing to present this claim and it is now offered for the benefit of his infant heirs" (Claiborne to Cass,

and expensive country, after a journey of four hundred miles, mostly wilderness and swamp. These were our prospects on leaving our comfortable cabins in the commencement of one of the severest winters ever experienced in the south or west. . . In December I reached the ruins of Cantonment Towson. In January my interpreter got on.

"The 10th of February brother Myers and his·family arrived, after encamping in forty-two places, and spending five weeks in preparing a boat to ferry the people over one stream [the Saline creek]. In a few days the first company of emigrants reached their destination. . . . One of the company perished with cold and hunger. To prevent a recurrence of such an appalling circumstance, I prevailed on friends to supply the future emigrants with corn at suitable points, from the Washita to the nation.

"Since September, the people have been partially employed in forming permanent settlements above the fort on Kiametia, and on Little River, east of the fort. . . . we are dividing into two Churches. During the crop season I had a house erected below the fort; but the people having left that part, I felt it necessary to go with them, and for the past three weeks, I have had my small family in the immediate neighborhood of the future camp ground on this river. Having no road, I only packed such articles as would enable us to occupy a tent, until a man that I had hired could put me up a cabin. Imagine a man and his companion in a deep and extensive forest, within two hundred yards of a dense cane brake in which the tracks of the largest sized panthers are found; living in a linen tent covered with ice and snow for a week, with but two blankets to cover a bed of grass and a common domestic tick."[27]

January 25, 1836, OIA, "Choctaw Emigration"). Three months later the secretary of war reported to the Senate against Talley's claim on the ground that his employment and disbursements to purchase food for his starving Indians had not previously been authorized by the government (U. S. Senate Files, Twenty-fourth Congress, first session, Report of the Secretary of War).

27 Nathan Bangs, An Authentic History of Missions of the M. E. Church (New York, 1862), 161 ff: a letter from Alexander Talley, September 5, 1831; Talley to Eaton, June 1, 1831 (Document, II, 463). George Harkins on his return from his exploring tour, "told me that he met upwards of one thousand Choctaws on their way to their new homes. He said they were driving their cattle and hogs, and packing horses with children, provisions, etc." (Choctaw Agent Ward to General Eaton, December 8, 1830, Document, II, 197). Prior to September 25, 1828 (the date of the agent's report), only fifty Choctaw had removed west of the Mississippi river under the provisions of the treaty of 1820, according to Ward (ibid., 52).

General George Gibson, commissary general of subsistence, on November 30, 1830, ordered Lieut. Lawrence F. Carter at Fort Gibson to proceed to the Kiamichi river where it was supposed the Indians sent out by Leflore would locate; and directed Carter to ascertain whether the resources of that section could furnish grain and meat for the emigrants. In the following February the emigrants not having arrived, Carter went among the settlers of Hempstead and Sevier counties in the adjoining part of Arkansas, and urged them to raise cattle to sell to the Indians.

In December President Jackson directed that the removal should be controlled by the commissary department of the army. Lieut. J. R. Stephenson of Fort Gibson was then ordered to proceed to the Kiamichi river to meet Leflore's emigrants; to procure and issue food to them as it was known that they had not been provided with any. He arrived at the Kiamichi on March 7, 1831, and found that of a thousand Choctaw emigrants reported to have been sent west by Leflore several months earlier, only eighty-eight had arrived; they were principally women and children and in all but a starving condition.[28] He thereupon entered into a contract with a Mr. Carter to furnish them with beef at three cents per pound until July 1. Fort Towson had been abandoned in June, 1829, and most of the buildings had been burned; Lieutenant Stephenson was obliged to build a log cabin for his official quarters about two miles from the site of the old fort and four miles from Red river. Such of the old log buildings as remained at the post were occupied by the starving and helpless Indians.[29]

The missionary, Alexander Talley, had gone out and contracted for all the corn within reach of the new emigrants, amounting to 1,000 bushels, at one dollar a bushel, for which he pledged the credit of the Choctaw Nation. He also engaged a smith, and with great difficulty secured enough tools and iron to start a blacksmith shop about the first of April, so that the Indians could prepare to put in some crops. After July 1, 1831, two small parties of emigrants arrived, making a total present by October 1 of 427.[30]

In March and April orders were given for the purchase of forty wagons, thirty to be drawn by oxen and the others by horses and

28 Stephenson to Gibson, April 1, 1831, OIA; *Document*, I, 852 ff.
29 *Ibid.*
30 *Ibid.*, 856.

delivered at Little Rock for the use of the emigrating Indians. Capt. J. B. Clark was ordered to Little Rock[31] to supervise the emigration it was expected would pass there. He advertised for sixty pairs or thirty teams of oxen and fifty horses, ten teams of five each.[32] He deprecated the purchase of heavy Pennsylvania wagons which he said would require three pairs of oxen to each, for drivers who knew how to handle teams of that size were hard to find.[33]

General George Gibson in February, 1831 ordered a detachment from Fort Gibson to the abandoned Fort Smith to repair the buildings for the reception of supplies intended for the emigrants. The floors, doors, and windows were destroyed; logs were torn out of the bodies of most of the houses which were sinking into the ground; the roofs of many buildings were falling in, and all were much decayed.[34] Lieut. G. J. Rains made some repairs during the summer so as to care for supplies of corn, meat, and salt.[35]

31 *Ibid.*, 8.
32 *Ibid.*, 9, 552. The people of Arkansas were preparing to profit by the emigration through their territory. Captain Clark lamented that "persons who have oxen for sale expect to receive for them from forty-five to sixty dollars a pair, and wagon horses are dear in proportion; indeed they seem to expect a high price for everything that will be required for Indians" (Clark to Gibson, Little Rock, June 4, 1831, *Document*, I, 553). They demanded $80 each for their little horses (*ibid.*). The settlers between Little Rock and the new home of the Choctaw Indians, in the spring of 1831 planted much more corn than usual in order to share in the prosperity promised by the Indian emigration (*ibid.*).
33 Clark to Gibson, July 10, 1831, OIA.
34 *Document*, I, 548, ff. Fort Smith, established in 1817 primarily to prevent hostilities between the Cherokee and Osage Indians, was abandoned in 1824 when the troops were removed up the Arkansas river to establish Fort Gibson. The departing troops carried with them the doors, windows, and other movable appurtenances; the post was reoccupied for a time from 1833 to 1834, and after 1838 was rebuilt and reoccupied; for accounts of this post see Grant Foreman, *Pioneer Days in the Early Southwest* (Cleveland, 1926); *Indians and Pioneers* (New Haven, 1930).
35 *Document*, I, 819, 821.

CHAPTER THREE / *Choctaw Emigration Begins*

THE year 1831 opened with the whole Choctaw tribe in confusion; though the treaty had been made it was not yet ratified. The Indians not knowing whether they were going to be removed or when, planted no crops; whisky peddlers, emboldened by the dominance of the laws of Mississippi to defy those of the United States,[1] plied their trade with the Indians. The latter in utter demoralization, were wasting their little substance in the purchase of whisky, and many of them became so impoverished that they were compelled to live on roots or starve.

William S. Colquhoun[2] of Dumfries, Virginia, wrote General Gibson on April 6, 1831, that as the high waters had washed away his mill dam, he was in hard straits and solicited employment in the service of Indian removal.[3] He proceeded to Washington where he was appointed a special agent by the secretary of war, and on July 5, was directed to go to the Choctaw Nation and there consult Leflore and the other Choctaw chiefs on the subject of removal. He was instructed primarily to get the views of Leflore on everything connected with the subject, and report to Washington. Ten days previously the department had addressed a long letter to Leflore, advising him what steps

1 The right of the Indians to the lands occupied by them had long been recognized, and from the formation of the government to 1871, 371 treaties were negotiated with them to acquire in a legal way the lands desired by the whites. Legislation was enacted for the regulation of intercourse and trade between the whites and the Indians and to protect the latter in the possession and enjoyment of their lands.

2 William Scott Colquhoun of Dunfries, Virginia, began his service in the army as second lieutenant in the Seventh Infantry, in 1819. He was stationed for a number of years at Fort Towson, where he was useful in securing information about the condition of the western Indians (Grant Foreman, *Indians and Pioneers*, 248). He was cashiered from the army in 1829.

3 *Document*, I, 545.

had been taken by the government, and asking him for information as to the number of Indians who would remove in the autumn, where they would assemble, what route he would recommend, where to cross the Mississippi river, about the transportation of the old and sick, the necessity and expense of opening roads, and whether provisions could be obtained in the Nation. The sending of Colquhoun into the Choctaw Nation was the first direct effort to act upon those Indians. And even at this time the department was undecided whether it should control the removal on the east side of the Mississippi river, or confine its operations to the west side.

It was then determined that the government would receive the Indians on the west bank of the Mississippi, and would convey them to Little Rock, and most of them overland from there in a southwestern direction through Washington, Hempstead county, Arkansas, and on to the Red river country, where it was understood the emigrating Indians desired to locate. Deposits of pork, flour, and bacon had been made on this route.

One of the inducements held out to the Indians to secure the performance of their treaty was that their friend George S. Gaines would have charge of their removal. They felt safe in trusting themselves, their wives, and children to his keeping as they believed he was honest and would not exploit them for profit. As plans for removal were being discussed the Indians referred to this promise and took the matter up with Gaines.

"At P. Jezan, May 22th, 1831. To Mr. G. Gaines: Dear Sir. This is to inform you that we the people of the Southern district wish you to do the business for us; although Chief Nithickachee himself will be at your house and see about the business which we want you to do for us. But he hase no interpreters for him—Therefore we think it proper to send the letter to let you know—He was about to take Capt. Pierre Jezan with him, when he goes. But himself is now unwell on the account of shoting himself by an excidence he was after the wild cow in the swamps and the cow was very Shy and danger therefore She ran up to him attempt to Stab with her horn—Then he was determine to shoot her But the pistle was unloaded then he began to load the pistle on the horse he just finish the loading she fire off and wound his right hand between thumb and little fingers, and one of the little fingers, bone is show. On this account he could not come there and interprete he could not use hand and write with.

"*I am directed by my own warriors and Captains to inform you they are determine to go west in next fall on this reason—they wish you to furnish them with Blankets, lead, Powder and the cloth to make tents with—which shall be paid on the other side of Mississippi—We wish to know whether you could furnish with provisions for us—And in fact we want you to let us know at where we shall get our provision according to the Sec. of War's promise—We are now still wish you to be our agent and do the things for us—you relect that John H. Eaton promised that he would furnish us with wagons and steamboats, and now we should like to know where we are to have wagons and steamboats at. We want you to inform us about all these things—We the people of the Southern district have appointed me to be their Chief in the spring year ago, and now they are still with me. Yours very sincerely Nitucka-chee, Chief of the Southern.*"[4]*

In June Nitakechi and Mushulatubbe for their districts reported that they were ready to migrate and requested the secretary of war to appoint their friend Gaines as conductor of the Indians to their new home in the west. They said[5] that Nitakechi having been west to see their new home, they had agreed that when they were removed, Leflore's district should be located "on the east side of Micquibisher[6] [Kiamichi], Netuchache on the west side, and Mushulatubbe on the Arkansas River."[7]

Their request was complied with only in part however; and on August 12 Gaines was appointed special agent to superintend the collection and removal of the Choctaw Indians as far as the west bank of the Mississippi river where they were to be delivered to Capt. J. B. Clark of the United States army. Politicians were early at work seeking places of profit in connection with the huge expenditure of funds about to be inaugurated. Among these was Wharton Rector who was appointed a special agent in connection with the removal from the

4   OIA, "1831 Choctaw Emigration."

5   *Document*, II, 476.

6   By Micquibisher, the Choctaw Indians meant Kiamichi River, near which Fort Towson had been located; literally Micquibisher means in Choctaw, a river on which government officials stay (authority of Peter J. Hudson, Choctaw, of Oklahoma Historical Society).

7   Mushulatubbe and Nitakechi to secretary of war, June 16, 1831, OIA, "1831 Choctaw Emigration."

west side of the Mississippi. Gaines's appointment was the first indication of a policy of taking charge of the movement within the Choctaw
Nation by the government. He accepted with much reluctance as he had
made other plans and said he could not spend much time "in the
woods"; but he immediately entered upon his duties. The next month
F. W. Armstrong[8] was ordered to Fort Smith to take charge of the
provisions stored there for the emigrants and to assume the duties of
agent for the "Choctaws West" until Congress made provision for
such employment.

The wagons descended the Mississippi river by steamboat to the
mouth of White river, where they were unloaded; the oxen and horses
were being assembled at Little Rock[9] and the first of September had
arrived without the formation of any plans for the movement of the
Indians beyond the Mississippi river. Embarked on a new adventure,
the government solicited information from all and sundry; many opinions were submitted, no two of them in agreement. Some proposed
crossing the Mississippi river in one place, some at another; some
favored movement by steamboats, others by land; roads must be cut
through on one route—roads were impossible at the same place.
Colquhoun made reports of conditions and opinions he found in the
Choctaw Nation. Leflore was solicited for advice, which he gave
freely.

The government was launched without compass or rudder into the
uncharted sea of Indian removal; for the first time it was about to engage
on a large scale in the removal of its aborigines from their homes in
which it was bound to collect and feed them, transport them across
the great Mississippi river, carry them part way by steamboats and
then overland through swamps and across streams, build roads and
bridges, cut banks down to the streams, and finally locate these expatriates, men and women, the aged and decrepit, little children, and
babes in arms, in their new country.[10]

8 *Document*, II, 341, 746. Armstrong had previously been United States marshal
of Alabama. He was appointed agent for the Western Choctaw, September 7, 1831.

9 *Ibid.*, I, 561.

10 A census taken in September, 1830, accounted for a total of 19,554 members
of the Choctaw tribe; in Leflore's district 7,505, Nitakechi's 6,106, and in Mushulatubbe's district, 5,943 (*ibid.*, III, 149, 581).

Gaines, Colquhoun and other agents notified the Indians that the government intended to remove at least a third of the tribe that autumn, as soon as their crops could be gathered. They were urged to organize at designated places, and from thence to proceed to the points where they wished to cross the Mississippi.[11] Rations were contracted for, muster rolls were prepared, and the agents went among the Indians to instruct them concerning the plans for removal. The Indians began to assemble at the rendezvous, gave their names and numbers in their families[12] to be entered upon the rolls. George W. Harkins who had been selected as chief in place of Leflore, was unable to secure recognition in Washington, or to obtain a contract for the removal of his people as proposed by him. He then announced that he could not remove until the next year and he induced his partisans to decline going until he was ready.[13]

Coffee urged the secretary in August, 1831, to start the Choctaw removal as soon as possible, "*so as to draw them off from their present country to the new one, and thereby carry with them many of the Chickasaws, who are intermarried with the Choctaws. We shall thereby get the influence of all who are thus connected with both nations, in bringing about an agreement for the Chickasaws to settle on the Choctaw lands, upon some terms or other.*"[14]

In October President Jackson appointed Eaton and Coffee commissioners to consult with the Choctaw chiefs and secure if possible a sale of 4,500,000 acres of their land in the West for the Chickasaw

11   *Ibid.*, I, 17, 19, 23, 26, 588; George W. Harkins was employed to help collect the Indians in Leflore's district. Colquhoun employed also "Mr. Robert M. Jones, an intelligent and educated Choctaw to act as assistant agent. . . The high character of Mr. Jones, given to him by Colonel Gaines, warrants the assurance of his efficiency" (*ibid.*, I, 588).

12   One method employed by the Choctaw Indians was to make a stick about the size of a quill to represent the man heading the family, a smaller stick tied to it with a string to signify each son over ten years of age; and notches in the middle of the large stick to represent females over ten years of age, and other notches cut near the end of the large stick indicated all younger children, boys and girls. The leader of each band collected these sticks, tied them together and gave the bundle to the agent from which he made up his roll of the party.

13   *Document*, I, 589.

14   *Ibid.*, II, 570.

tribe.[15] The commissioners accordingly gave notice that they would be in the Choctaw country in December to discuss the matter with them. This unseasonable proposal added further confusion to the situation, for many of the Choctaw people were then on their way to the west; and their head men who were within twenty miles of Vicksburg when the message reached them, sent word that it was impossible for them to stop. Leflore refused to attend the meeting, but Mushulatubbe and some of the head men of the tribe who had not departed, and a delegation of Chickasaw met the commissioners in a futile conference near the Choctaw agency on Oaka Knoxabee creek. One of the Indians addressed said the United States should let them put their feet on their new land before they asked for it.

Some of the Indians expressed a preference to go with their own horses and oxen under leaders of their own choosing, independently of the government officials. Armstrong favored this at first, but soon learned that this plan was promoted by mixed-bloods who planned to subsist the Indians on the way by hunting, and then collect from the government the allowance of ten dollars for each Indian. This speculation by the mixed-bloods on the unsuspecting full-bloods was extensively practiced. It resulted in organizing the Indians in political factions whose leaders employed the opportunity to aggravate the rancor and bitterness already existing between individuals and partizans of Indians.[16]

Vicksburg was selected as the gathering place for most of the Indians who consented to remove in the autumn of 1831; and nearly 4,000 of them arrived there between the fifteenth and the twenty-fifth of November.[17] All of these had determined to remove to that part of their new home on the Red river in the vicinity of the Kiamichi river. Before the end of the month more than twenty-five hundred of them had embarked on four steamboats.

It was decided to take the emigrants from Vicksburg by two routes, to avoid as much as possible congesting the limited facilities for handling them. Part were to be taken up the Arkansas river to Little Rock by

15   Ibid., II, 360, 624, 882; III, 17. Jackson said that "it is of importance that this should be speedily attended to in order that the Chickasaws may move with their elder brethren the Choctaws" (ibid., II, 624).
16   Ibid., I, 369, 379.
17   Ibid., 858.

boat, and from there overland southwest through Washington, Hempstead county, Arkansas, to the Red river section of their new home. The others were to go down the Mississippi river, up the Red river to the mouth of the Ouachita river, and up that stream to Ecore à Fabri, where they were to be landed. From here their course overland to Fort Towson, 160 miles away, took them through Washington where they joined the route of those coming from Little Rock. But for the Great Raft in the Red river, steamboats would have ascended that stream with emigrants, and landed them in the vicinity of the mouths of the Kiamichi, Boggy and L'Eau Bleu rivers.

The implacable full-blood chief Mushulatubbe and his full-blood followers had decided to locate and establish their district on the Arkansas river away from the other factions who had selected the country on the Red river for their home. He was bitterly opposed to the missionaries and their teachings, and was hostile to the Folsoms who were educated by the missionaries, and to their followers. He railed at the government for wasting their money by allowing the missionaries to disburse it for the education of their children: ". . .we have employed and payed Yankee Missionaries for twelve years; for which we have Recd. no compensation; we have never recd. a Scholar out of their Schools that was able to keep a grog shop book."[18] Mushulatubbe, Nitakechi, Joseph Kincaid, Pestambe and a number of other captains, joined in a letter June 15, 1831, requesting the secretary of war to direct that no more of their money be paid to the missionaries. "Neither do we wish for any of the present missionaries to go with us beyond the Mississippi; and Doctor Talley, who has already settled on our land, may be ordered out."[19]

Mushulatubbe on January 16, 1831, announced his abdication as chief to become effective when emigration began; and nominated Peter P. Pitchlynn as his successor to have charge of the emigration of his faction.[20] This selection was confirmed in council by his followers.[21]

18 Mushulatubbe and chiefs to Jackson December 23, 1830, OIA, "1830 Schools (Choctaw)"; *Document*, II, 205.

19 *Document*, II, 474.

20 Peter P. Pitchlynn was born in Mississippi in 1806. His father, John Pitchlynn, who died in 1835, was a white man and interpreter commissioned by General Washington. His mother, Sophia Folsom, was a Choctaw. Peter attended schools in Tennessee and became a useful and influential counsellor and chief in his tribe.

Mushulatubbe recommended "Peter P. Pitchlynn, Thomas Wall and Saml. Garland as the three conductors or agents to be employed; they are very intelligent, smart young men and can give any amount of security they inform me."[22]

Four hundred and six of Mushulatubbe's followers, under the direction of Pitchlynn, marched to Memphis,[23] where it was proposed to cross the Mississippi and proceed overland to their new home. But there had been such an excessive rainfall that no roads through the swamps west of that place could be traveled. Dr. John T. Fulton had given up his office as postmaster, his drug store, and practice of medicine at Little Rock for appointment as government agent in connection with the removal; he secured the steamboat *Brandywine*, five hundred tons, on which he embarked Pitchlynn's emigrants December 1, 1831, and proceeded down the Mississippi to the mouth of White River, and up to Arkansas Post, where he landed his charges. Their horses had been taken along in flatboats.[24]

On one of his trips to Washington on a steamboat he met Charles Dickens, who described him in his *American Notes*. He died in Washington, D. C., January 17, 1881, and was buried in the Congressional Cemetery. See part II *Handbook of American Indians*, 264, for an extended account of him.

Mushulatubbe was near sixty years of age at the time of the treaty of Dancing Rabbit Creek. In early life he won renown as a warrior. His name means *Determined to Kill* from his early exploits against the Osage Indians. He served in the Creek War under General Jackson and with a band of warriors he was present at the Battle of New Orleans. He had two homes with a wife at each; one in the western part of Noxubee county, Mississippi, gave its name to the present town of Mashulaville on the same site. He had large herds of horses and cattle, and when he signed the treaty of Dancing Rabbit Creek he owned eleven slaves and cultivated thirty acres of land.

Mushulatubbe was a man of powerful build. He carried himself very erect and affected a haughty, majestic gait. His face was large and square, with an intellectual expression. Though a brave man, he was more a politician in his later years than a warrior. He possessed much personal magnetism, and was one of the most brilliant orators the nation ever produced. He ruled over his people with justice, was very popular, but was never so greatly beloved as Pushmataha (H. A. Halbert to L. C. Draper, November 21, 1882, "Draper Manuscripts," State Historical Society of Wisconsin, *Tecumseh Mss.* YY).

21 *Document*, II, 393, 418. The selection of Pitchlynn was announced by E-yar-ho-kar-tubbe, speaker of the council and certified by Pierre Juzan.

22 Colquhoun to Gibson, September 4, 1831, OIA, "1831 Choctaw Emigration."

23 *Document*, I, 420, 394.

24 *Ibid.*, 591, ff., 420, 436.

Here they remained for about six weeks, waiting for the Arkansas river to rise sufficiently to be navigated to Fort Smith. In January they were taken aboard the *Reindeer*, a steamboat of one hundred tons, with a keel boat in tow, and arrived at Little Rock[25] on the twenty-second. After stopping there one day, the *Reindeer* departed for Fort Smith. However, the boat was arrested by low water about ninety miles below that post, and the emigrants were forced to disembark with their possessions, and remain in camp through one of the coldest periods ever known in the country.[26] It was nearly a month later that an increased stage of the water enabled the *Reindeer* again to ascend the river, take the emigrants on board, and land them at Fort Smith February 20, 1832.[27] The steamboat brought also a quantity of plows and other equipment for the Indians, promised them in the treaty. Several hundred horses belonging to this party of emigrants came over-land,[28] in charge of eighteen or twenty Indians, and passed Little Rock December 18, a month ahead of their owners.[29]

Another party of 594 Indians at Vicksburg in November boarded the steamboat *Reindeer* and her keel boat in tow, bound for Little Rock.[30] These Indians were from Mushulatubbe's district, and were in charge of Lieut. Stephen Van Rensselaer Ryan; they were adherants of David Folsom,[31] rival of Mushulatubbe for chieftainship, and were going to settle on the Red river; but when they arrived at Arkansas Post November 26, with prevailing lack of order and co-operation, an army officer there compelled the Indians to be put ashore so that one hundred troops bound for Fort Gibson could board the boat.[32] This contingent was added to the 1,500 that had previously arrived on the steamboats *Walter Scott* from Vicksburg and the *Brandywine* from Memphis. This gathering at Arkansas Post numbering 2,500 emigrants with 1,000 horses, completely swamped the facilities provided for

25 Ibid., 436; *Arkansas Gazette*, January 25, 1832, p. 3, col. 1.
26 *Document*, I, 438, III, 169.
27 Ibid., III, 191.
28 Ibid., I, 591, 420, 436.
29 *Arkansas Gazette*, December 14, and 21, 1831, p. 3, col. 1.
30 *Document*, I, 592, 595.
31 This party contained 126 families and traveled with 286 pack horses; among them was Edmond McKinney who had sixty pack horses (OIA, Muster Roll, December 31, 1831).
32 *Document*, I, 593.

them. "This error has thrown together Folsom's and Netuckachies parties—likewise the Memphis party."[33]

On their arrival at Arkansas Post many of Folsom's party were sick, and in order to contribute to the contentment of the emigrants during their detention, David Folsom, who had a reputation as a medicine man, was designated by the government agent as their official physician at two dollars a day, and his brother Israel was appointed official interpreter.[34] This party was obliged to remain at Arkansas Post until December 13, when they were brought away with forty-four wagons and 150 horses.[35] After excessive suffering from cold, they arrived at Little Rock on the twenty-second. Several days were consumed in transporting the Indians and their baggage and horses across the Arkansas river; they then went into camp at a place about three miles south of the village selected by Captain Brown[36] while they were being organized for their long and wretched journey to Red river.[37]

These Indians were in a desperate plight; they had left home in comparatively warm weather and were thinly clad; few of them wore moccasins. Capt. Jacob Brown at Little Rock, in charge of the movement, was touched by their distress: "This unexpected cold weather must produce much human suffering. Our poor emigrants, many of them quite naked, and without much shelter, must suffer, it is impossible to be otherwise." The thermometer reached zero December 10, and for a week had averaged twelve degrees; six inches of snow fell on the fifth, and for some days the river was impassable with ice. "*It is impossible to make any progress in movements to their destination; how very unfortunate the time for this operation! An overland journey just commenced of about three hundred and fifty miles, to be accomplished in*

33 *Ibid.;* Colquhoun to Gibson, December 10, 1831, OIA, "Choctaw Emigration."

34 *Document,* I, 425; Capt. Jacob Brown to General Gibson, November 20, 1831, OIA. The Folsoms were accompanied by their father Nathaniel Folsom.

35 *Document,* I, 428. ". . .They have no other means of transportation than the forty-five waggons and the roads are impassable. The situation is distressing and must get worse" (Colquhoun to Gibson, *ibid.,* 593). Nine hundred Choctaw horses crossed the Mississippi river that winter; 500 passed Little Rock, 300 going to the Kiamichi river, and 200 to Fort Smith; 400 went to the Red river country by way of Ecor à Fabri (Brown to Gibson, April 30, 1832, *ibid.,* 444, and OIA, "Choctaw Emigration").

36 *Arkansas Gazette,* December 28, 1831, p. 3, col. 1.

37 Brown to Gibson, December 22, 1831, OIA, "1831 Choctaw."

mid-winter, through a country little settled, and literally impassable to any thing but wild beasts."[38]

On December 29, Ryan's and Folsom's Indians began their march from Little Rock by way of Washington to the Red river. There were forty-five teams in the train, none with less than four oxen and horses, and some with six. The road to Washington was new, and was indescribably bad. A party preceded the emigrants, preparing the road as well as they were able; banks were dug and side cuts made to facilitate the crossing of streams and bayous. Between Washington and the Choctaw line on the military road much work was required; 815 yards of causeway was constructed through a particularly boggy stretch near the Choctaw line; rude bridges were built over Mine creek, the Big and Little Cossatots, Saline, and the cut-off of Little river.[39] A ferry boat was constructed on the Little river. The heavy wagons cut up the road traveled by them until it was almost impassable. At a number of streams they were obliged to wait for high water to subside.[40] They were at Antoine creek by the middle of January, and after four weeks of labor and hardship, reached the Red river country and were discharged by Ryan January 29, 1832, on the Mountain fork, Glover's fork, and the Kiamichi.[41]

38 *Arkansas Gazette*, December 5, 1832, p. 3, col. 1; *Document*, I, 427. From Little Rock to Washington the distance was about 130 miles and from there to the site of the old Fort Towson, one hundred miles (*ibid.*, 674).

39 Nine hundred ten feet of frame bridges at a cost of $2,576, and 145 feet of log bridges costing $89 were built (*ibid.*, 448). Arkansas citizens named Blankenship, Holeman and McWilliams contracted to construct these bridges for one to three dollars a lineal foot (*ibid.*, 49, 584).

40 *Ibid.*, 427. "The roads are horrid, horrid in the extreme," wrote Captain Brown. "I have large companies repairing the roads and making bridges on the route; but, notwithstanding all this, the roads will continue to be horrid." He said that for the emigrant parties to be caught in periods of high water on a certain stretch of road in southwestern Arkansas, "from Little river to the lick near the Choctaw line. . . was worse than a shipwreck among the Sandwich Islands;" for the inhabitants practiced barefaced extortions on the Indians and the government, and even created opportunities for imposition; bridges and ferryboats were mysteriously destroyed, so that while large parties of unhappy and suffering emigrants were necessarily delayed in cold and cheerless camps awaiting repairs or reconstruction of bridges, boats, or rafts, they were obliged to purchase food from the heartless conspirators at exorbitant prices (*ibid.*, I, 455). Between Vicksburg and Little Rock, eight children of Folsom's party died and they lost 150 horses.

41 David Folsom returned to the East in April, 1832 (*ibid.*, I, 604).

Corn for the emigrants and horses had been taken along the route to places of deposit called "stands." A herd of cattle was driven along to provide fresh meat which was issued to the emigrants every other day. The cattle purchased in Arkansas increased very much the difficulties of locomotion; they were small, averaging only about five hundred pounds each, and were so wild they could not be herded and driven along the route as ordinary live stock. The difficulty of confining them to the line of march, preventing their plunging into the timber and brush, and recovering them from muddy, path-less and endless expanses of timber, brambles, vines and jungles, added much to the labor and delays of travel.[42] Frequently when cattle got into the dense canebrakes, they were never recovered. Stragglers who stayed behind to hunt their horses also caused delays. Jackscrews were carried to lift the wagon wheels out of the bottomless mire. From the difficult roads the oxen became tender-footed and crippled, and as there was no one in the service or along the road who knew how to shoe them, delay resulted.[43] A traveling forge was constructed at the arsenal in Pittsburgh, and ordered sent to Arkansas in February, 1832.[44] Six oxen were driven to each wagon, which were none too many as the animals were very small. Advertisements for offers to furnish them to the government, provided that they should weigh at least six hundred pounds[45] each.

42   Ibid., 439, 881.
43   Ibid., 457.
44   Ibid., 58, 63.
45   Ibid., 552.

CHAPTER FOUR / *Suffering of the Emigrants*

NITAKECHI said that 3,000 of his people would be ready "to start the first white frost in October." He desired three conductors appointed, "Pierre Juzan for the Six Towns, William Juzan for Chickasawha, and Samuel Worcester, a native, for the Coonche settlement where he resides."[1] He asked that tents and blankets be furnished at Vicksburg for the use of the helpless old men, women, and children, and for the sick and decrepit; also a small allowance for medicine, sugar and coffee, and other hospital necessaries for the sick and infirm. ". . .Tents, perhaps, may be procured at Jefferson Barracks and at Cantonment Gibson. It is certain they will experience very inclement weather before they can be hutted, and the issue of blankets would be extremely provident to meet their certain exposure in their removal and afterwards."[2]

After the Indians had taken up their march, Colonel Gaines wrote: "The feeling which many of them evince in separating, never to return again, from their own long cherished hills, poor as they are in this section of country, is truly painful to witness; and would be more so to me, but for the conviction that the removal is absolutely necessary for their welfare."[3]

"Nitakechi and Nail (heathen chiefs)" rivals for chieftainship in their district arrived at Vicksburg with their combined parties amount-ing to 1,950 emigrants *"who expect to start for their new country in the morning, but if they get away in five days they will do well. George*

1 *Document*, I, 570; II, 429. "The *Kusha* and *Chickashopie* towns are equal in population, and the six towns are more than equal to both" (*ibid.*, 429).

2 Colquhoun to Gibson, September 1, 1831, *Document*, I, 570.

3 *Mobile Commercial Register*, November 12, 1831, p. 1, col. 1. Another observer told of seeing departing emigrants touching the tree trunks, twigs and leaves about their homes in token of farewell to these old friends.

Harkins came in last evening with a party of 500 more. All is confusion and uproar. They have taken their annuity for this year; much pulling and hauling, swearing and drinking. The Indians are in a great hurry to spend the little money they have, and the whites are quarreling for the privilege of cheating them."[4]

The steamboat *Walter Scott*, 200 tons, left Vicksburg the latter part of November with Colonel Gaines and about one thousand emigrants under the leadership of Nitakechi, who were landed at Arkansas Post to await with many others, boats that could ascend the Arkansas river. In January 1832, 1,000 of them in charge of Wharton Rector were embarked on the steamboat *Reindeer* and a 170 ton keel boat in tow, and disembarked at Little Rock January 16. The *Reindeer* immediately returned to Arkansas Post to bring up Mushulatubbe's party.[5]

The encampment of Nitakechi's people three miles south of Little Rock was called Camp Pope; here they awaited the arrival of their wagons from Arkansas Post. Four hundred more of this party in charge of Colonel Childress came overland from the Post with between 200 and 300 horses and on January 22 joined the remainder of the emigrants at Camp Pope.[6] This party in charge of Robert M. Jones, a Choctaw, had left Vicksburg with between 400 and 500 horses belonging to the emigrants to be brought through the Mississippi swamp to Arkansas Post, and there join the main body of emigrants. On the journey of nearly forty days through the swamp more than 200 of the horses died of starvation and exhaustion, which is not surprising in view of the fact that Jones was provided with only one hundred dollars to purchase forage for the horses and subsistence for the accompanying Indians.[7]

4 *New York Observer*, March 3, 1832, p. 2, col. 6.
5 *Arkansas Advocate*, January 18, 1832, p. 3, col. 4.
6 *Document* I, 437; *Arkansas Gazette*, January 25, 1832, p. 3, col. 1.
7 *Document*, I, 848. As these unhappy people were on the march to Vicksburg a distressing circumstance occurred: while in camp the night of October 28, "a severe storm of rain and wind had set in and just after comfortable quarters had been secured, a large tree was blown down among the camps, and two women, mothers of large families, were crushed to instant death, one girl sadly mangled, and several children severely injured. The darkness of the night, the severity of the storm, the frightful howling of the poor sufferers, and the noisy and extravagant demonstration of grief in which the whole camp indulged, presented a scene of distress altogether surpassing description" (Letter from George S. Gaines in *Mobile Commercial Register*, November

Maj. F. W. Armstrong, the newly appointed agent to the Choctaw, came to Little Rock[8] January 22, and shortly afterward a boat arrived bringing up a quantity of rifles, ammunition, hoes, and axes intended for the Indians, some of which Armstrong issued to Nitakechi's party of 1,400 at Little Rock.[9] On the twenty-fifth of the month 1,300 of this party under the direction of Wharton Rector[10] broke camp and left Little Rock with fifty wagons over the almost impassable road traveled by Folsom's party a month before, to Washington and the Red river. Two hundred more emigrants, who from the lack of wagons were unable to leave with the remainder of the party, followed on February 5 under the escort of S. M. Rutherford, who was instructed to pick up stragglers. This party included Nitakechi and his family who were quite ill.[11]

While the other boats at Vicksburg were loading for the Arkansas river, 564 emigrants with their effects led by Joel H. Nail[12] of Nita-kechi's district were embarked on the *Talma*,[13] 140 tons, in charge of

12, 1831, p. 1, col. 1). "It is said the lamentations for the dead, the groans of the wounded, and the noise of the storm, presented a most strange and horrific scene" (*New York Observer*, February 18, 1832, p. 2, col. 6). The dead were decently interred the succeeding day, and the wounded comfortably provided for. Before this party left home, the Christian Indians appointed a company of light horse to prevent the introduction of whisky into camp by white men which was accomplished with difficulty (*ibid.*).

8 Major Armstrong brought his family to the Choctaw agency September 11, 1833 (*Document*, I, 849).

9 *Ibid.*, III, 153.

10 Rector had resigned his post as subagent to the Quapaw Indians, to accept the position of special agent in connection with the removal of the Choctaw (*ibid.*, II, 573).

11 *Ibid.*, I, 427; *Arkansas Advocate*, February 1, and 8, 1832, p. 3, col. 1.

12 Joel H. Nail and Robert W. Nail were brothers; the latter was "an orphan and poor, but really a promising youth, having received a liberal education in Ken-tucky" (*Document*, III, 406). Nail returned to Mississippi in May to make plans for the next removal (Nail to Colquhoun, May 23, 1832, OIA, "1832 Choctaw Emi-gration"). Robert Nail acted as guide and interpreter for this party, and Joel H. Nail as commissary on the steamboat for seventeen days (*United States House Document No. 171*, Twenty-second Congress, first session).

13 The captain of the *Talma* said of some of the Choctaw people he took up the Ouachita river, "he never saw any people conduct better or appear more devout. They had morning and evening prayers and spent much of their time on board the boat reading and singing hymns; a part of this company belong to the Methodist Church." He said they were in good spirits in spite of the neglect of the agents (Alfred Wright

S. T. Cross a special agent; and 600 on the *Cleopatra*, 150 tons, headed by George W. Harkins of Leflore's district,[14] both bound down the Mississippi, up the Red river to the mouth of the Ouachita, and up that stream to Ecor à Fabri. Here they disembarked before the middle of December to organize for their march westward through Washington to the Kiamichi river. Two weeks later, still in camp on the river, Harkins wrote: ". . .*We sent our horses*[15] *and oxen by land, and about 250 head of horses have died on the road. We have had very bad weather. Since we landed at this place about twenty of Nail's party have died, and still they are continuing to die. Two of my party have died. We are about 200 miles from my country on Red river. It will be some time in February before we get to where we want to settle. There are 1,200 of us in company, and we are compelled to travel slow, as there are so many sick people. I am afraid a great many will die before we get home. Nail has 400 with him. He had been very sick but now is on the mend.*"[16]

After these had left Vicksburg, another party of 253 from Pearl river, under the leadership of Capt. Silas D. Fisher[17] a half-breed of Leflore's district, with fifty horses arrived there December 10, and were embarked on the steamer *Walter Scott* in charge of Lieut. W. S. Colquhoun. To reach the boat and escape the storm that was raging, they had been compelled to travel through sleet and snow for the last

---

to David Greene, January 10, 1832, "Missionary Records," *Andover-Harvard Theological Library*, LXXII, No. 137).

14 These followers of Nail and Harkins were more provident than some of the others. In preparation for this unprecedented undertaking, their women had been engaged for weeks in weaving on their crude looms cotton cloth to supplement the supply of shelter tents furnished by the government (Colquhoun to Gibson, January 2, 1832, OIA, "Choctaw Emigration"). Greenwood Leflore accompanied Nail's party to the West but he did not remain.

15 The horses and cattle belonging to the emigrants who left Vicksburg in November on the *Reindeer*, *Walter Scott*, *Talma* and *Cleopatra* were ferried across the Mississippi river and taken overland (*Vickburg Register*, November 25, 1831, p. 2, col. 3).

16 *New York Observer*, March 3, 1832, p. 2, col. 6; *Religious Intelligencer*, XVI, 649. Thirty-four of Nail's party died, most of them on the road (Wright to Greene, September 14, 1832, "Missionary letters," LXXII, No. 141).

17 Silas Fisher was educated at the Choctaw Academy in Kentucky; he married a woman whose father was a white man named Kelly, and lived at the home of his father-in-law just outside the Choctaw Nation. He was a captain in Leflore's district (*Document*, I, 609, IV, 530).

twenty-four hours without stopping, barefoot and nearly naked.[18] On December 17, the *Walter Scott* reached Monroe, Louisiana, which was as high as she could ascend the river.

At Monroe Colquhoun found forty-four Indians on the bank of the river and in the street. Their conductor had left them and hurried down the river with Captain Shirley to the rescue of others in the swamps. His abandoned charges were without provisions or shelter to protect them from the winter storm, and Colquhoun secured from Judge Byrd a large house with permission to burn the fence for firewood. The ground was covered with snow and sleet was falling. He placed the Indians in charge of Noel Gardner, a half-breed, and procured for them fifteen barrels of flour and 1,000 pounds of pork and bacon.[19] The suffering and destitution of the Indians excited the compassion of the good people of Monroe, who were very kind to them.[20]

Besides the large parties under government agents there were a number of others called commutation parties, as they received commutation certificates calling for ten dollars for each Indian on his arrival in the west in lieu of provisions that would have been furnished on the route if they had traveled with conductors. Of these Jeremiah Folsom and his son Robert in charge of a party of 200 from Mushulatubbe's district crossed the Mississippi river at Helena, and continued overland by Ecor à Fabri and Washington, reaching their new home on Red river in February.[21] Robert M. Jones was in charge of another party of one hundred who were traveling in the same manner.

18   "...They are generally very naked and few moccassins are seen among them. The snow has now been on the ground here [Vicksburg] without diminution since yesterday morning and the party just arrived and embarking on the *Walter Scott* for the Ecor à Fabri, are in the most wretched condition" (*ibid.*, I, 593). "...If I could have done it with propriety, I would have given them shoes. I distributed all the Tents and this party are entirely without. It would seem that Steam Boat hire was very high and indeed it is too true, but I assure you every exertion by advertisement and otherwise has been resorted to in order to procure them on better terms. The disgusting sight of a vessel loaded with human beings under no control or regularity, leaving their evacuations in every direction through the whole range of the Cabins and deck, would create in the mind of any one an additional allowance for the transportation" (Colquhoun to Gibson, December 10, 1831, OIA, "Choctaw Emigration").

19   *Document*, I, 937.

20   Colquhoun to Gibson, January 3, 1832, OIA, "1832 Choctaw Emigration."

21   Brown to Gibson, October 31, 1831, OIA, "1831 Choctaw Emigration;" *Arkansas Gazette*, January 18, 1832, p. 3, col. 1.

"*The weather for the last three weeks has been so excessively cold, that traveling of all kinds has been rendered nearly impracticable. The Mississippi river, though not completely frozen over at this place,* ⟦Memphis⟧ *has been and is still so obstructed with ice, that no flat boats, and but very few steam boats are able to make their way through it.*"[22] A number of small parties of Indians had been encamped at Vicksburg waiting to cross the river when the moderation of the weather would make it possible and forty-six of them departed January 3.

About a thousand Indians were traveling in these small parties entirely independent of the government and of each other, taking their time, camping and hunting as long as they wished. Some of them left home with directions to rendezvous at Point Chicot, Arkansas, where an agent issued commutation certificates to 388 who met him there. In all 873 went in this manner, 450 of whom crossed at Memphis with Thomas McGee. These people feared to trust themselves on steam-boats,[23] and endeavored to find their way by land, an undertaking in which they became involved in great difficulties and distress.

Among these was a party of 300 who separated from the Nail and Harkins party at Vicksburg and crossing the Mississippi river there, started west with their ox-teams through the swamp by Lake Providence. They were almost as helpless as children, and suffered incredible hardships from the cold; and, trying in vain to force their way through a swamp where there was no road, became bewildered to the point of complete surrender to the elements. However they were rescued by Cross who had gone with his party on one of the two boats up the Ouachita river to Ecor à Fabri. His charges compelled him repeatedly to stop the boat to see if news could be had from their brother emigrants, for whom they felt great anxiety because of the intense cold. And finally, after they were disembarked at Ecor à Fabri on December 9, they refused to proceed westward until their friends were found and brought to them. Cross then came down the river to Monroe, and learning the location of the emigrants, with Captain Shirley of the *Talma* penetrated the swamp within forty miles of Lake Providence until the suffering Indians were found.

22 Armstrong to Gibson, January 3, 1832, OIA, "Choctaw Emigration."
23 *Document*, I, 592.

They were in great distress, having been without food for six days and some of them had died from hardship and exposure.[24] They brought them out of the swamp to Monroe, where Cross rented a schoolhouse to shelter them. The steamboat *Talma* was chartered to return upstream and Cross placed the suffering emigrants with their surviving animals on board.

In the *Talma* they were carried up 210 miles to Ecor à Fabri, where they joined their friends. After long delay here in securing necessary equipment and supplies, with the three parties of Harkins, Fisher, and Nail they set out, reaching Washington about the middle of January,[25] and two weeks later the depot of provisions of Lieut. James R. Stephenson, "east of Fort Towson at McCann's old place on Clear creek." To accomplish this, the government agents were obliged to submit to extortionate charges for forty-six ox-teams and wagons; contractors were even charged with delaying the progress of the journey so that the Indians would be obliged to consume their corn at two dollars a bushel as long as possible, before reaching Washington where it could be had for fifty cents.[26]

These unhappy people thus driven from their homes were not allowed to depart in peace; many of them were outraged by citizens of Mississippi who carried off their property on fraudulent claims; but they found a measure of justice in the state courts that returned their belongings when they were able to hire attorneys and prepare a defense, though they suffered great inconvenience and loss through

24 *Ibid.*, 596. Cross learned "on the 22nd Inst that they were then in the Mississippi swamps suffering beyond description, both for provisions for themselves and forage for their stock. I immediately repaired to the Post of Washita, and went into the swamp myself and brought out the poor fellows with their few horses and cattle, many Horses having died and great numbers of the Indians much frosted. . . The number rescued from the deplorable situation amounted to 265 persons and 227 Horses and cattle" (Cross to Brown, December 28, 1831, OIA). The captain of the *Talma* told Mrs. Wright that he saw as many as one hundred horses standing up in the mud stiff and dead, and many head of cattle (Harriett B. Wright to David Greene, "Missionary Letters," *Andover-Harvard Theological Library,* LXXII, No. 138). The Indians "had been six days without food when they were taken into the steamboat *Talma*, Capt. Shirley, who deserves the thanks of the friends of humanity for his exertions to save them" (*New York Observer*, February 18, 1832, p. 2, col. 6).

25 *Document*, I, 434.

26 *Ibid.*, II, 459.

expenses attendant on delays and lawyers' fees. Many of these out-rages, however, were committed under color of the law, according to the testimony of A. Campbell, United States marshal for the district of Mississippi: ". . .*I was present in the Indian country at the departure of the Choctaw emigrating to the west of the Mississippi, and was an eye-witness with displeasure, when several of the Indians were harrassed in their progress by sheriffs and constables, acting under writs emanating from State authorities, causing interruption and delay to the officers conducting them.*"[27]

Their suffering and difficulties on the march excited the compassion of the people of northeastern Louisiana, who extended such aid as they could. One of them, Joseph Kerr, living at Lake Providence, sixty-eight miles from Vicksburg, within forty feet of the road along which the Indians passed, in great indignation addressed to the secretary of war a bitter arraignment of the inadequate provisions for caring for the Indians. He condemned the secretary for his responsibility for the shabby provisions in the treaty of one blanket to each family of Indians.

Provisions were issued to the Indians near Kerr's home to last over a distance of eighty miles, fifty of which were through an overflowed swamp "*in which distance are two large deep streams that must be crossed in a boat or on a raft, and one other nearly impassable in any way. This they had to perform or perish, there being no provision made for them on the way. This, too, was to be done in the worst time of weather I have ever seen in any country—a heavy sleet having broken and bowed down all the small and much of the larger timber. And this was to be performed under the pressure of hunger, by old women and young children, without any covering for their feet, legs or body except a cotton underdress gener-ally. In passing, before they reached the place of getting rations here, I gave a party leave to enter a small field in which pumpkins were. They would not enter without leave, though starving. These they ate raw with the greatest avidity.*"[28]

27 Ibid., III, 417.

28 Ibid., I, 719. Kerr's letter was referred to General Gibson who replied (ibid., I, 126) that this body of Indians were removing on their own resources in order to receive from the government $10 a head at the end of the journey and the government officials felt but little responsibility for their comfort. But he admitted "the fall and winter were unparalleledly severe; the Indians poorly provided." Kerr replied August

Kerr urged the secretary to provide food for the Indians on the long marches; suggested a blanket to each individual instead of one to a family, and that they be given shoes or moccasins, and stockings, or skins from which they could make them. This unhappy party of about 300 left Lake Providence and entered the swamp December 5, and the storm began on the sixth. It was some days later that they were rescued by Cross and taken to the river, where they were placed aboard the *Talma*.[29]

Another party that had not been able to keep up with the main body, in attempting to cross the swamp between the St. Francis and White rivers, became water- and ice-bound for more than forty days, during which it subsisted by hunting. In this plight the party suffered severely from cold, exposure, and hunger.[30]

The government had sent its agents with the Indians west of the Mississippi river with instructions to incur large expense in the purchase of supplies, horses, and oxen, and the employment of men; but

---

26 denying that these Indians were traveling on their own resources; he said they had with them from 1,500 to 2,000 horses and fifty yoke of oxen they were trying to take through to their western home by land, the only way these animals could be got there (*ibid.*, 721; OIA, 1832, "Miscellaneous, Emigration.")

29 Of a company of several hundred on the road to Memphis it was said by an observer: "There were very aged persons and very young children in the company; many had nothing to shelter them from the storm by day or night. The weather was excessively cold, and yet a neighbor remarked to me a few days ago, that he noticed particularly, and in his opinion not one in ten of the women had even a moccasin on their feet and the great majority of them were walking . . .One party came to us and begged for an| ear of corn apiece, to relieve for a season, their sufferings. Another party camped in the woods near us about three weeks ago, and that night a storm of hail and sleet commenced, which was followed in a day or two with a heavy fall of snow. For more than two weeks there was continued freezing and colder weather than I have ever seen in this climate. During the whole time these suffering people were lying in their camp, without any shelter, and with very little provision." (Letter dated December 24, 1831, in *Cherokee Phoenix* (New Echota, Georgia), May 5, 1832, p. 3, col. 2, from *New York Observer*, April 7, 1832, p. 2, col. 2).

Mr. H. V. Posey related to the author that his grandmother told him she was a girl living with her parents in southeastern Arkansas when the emigrating Choctaw Indians were passing; one party camped near her home were almost starving and her father taking compassion on their suffering gave them permission to enter his turnip patch and help themselves; they very gratefully did so and when they left there was not even a root of a turnip left.

30 *Document*, I, 449.

in the confusion attending the removal of the Indians, no money was given them for months after they were in need of it, though it had been appropriated by Congress for the purpose. In January, agents in charge of emigrating parties were clamoring for money needed to perform the duties imposed upon them. Maj. Francis W. Armstrong was appointed agent to the Choctaw West September 7, 1831, and on November 21, he was entrusted with $50,000 with which he then left Washington; thirty-five thousand for Captain Brown at Little Rock, and fifteen thousand for Lieutenant Stephenson at Fort Towson. He reached Little Rock January 22, and Fort Towson February 20,[31] after a journey of eight days from Fort Smith.

Armstrong had remained at his home, Nashville, until after January 1. He attributed the delay to the *"unexampled severity of the winter, such as has never been felt in the country before*[32] *. . . I have prevailed on my brother William to go to Arkansas with me. The truth is, I preferred confidential company, because the small sized notes, in the proportion directed by your letter, makes the money quite a bundle, and the rapidity of the Mississippi settling about the swamps makes me feel the risk greater then I thought it was when in Washington. You see a few days ago a set of villains boarded, while aground, the steamboat Favorite, and plundered and burnt her. Two Armstrongs are better than any insurance office."*[33]

"Four of my agents are now in charge of emigrants," wrote Captain Brown, superintendent of removal and subsistence of the Indians at Little Rock, *"and all are begging for funds. They tell me it will be impossible to sustain themselves and parties much longer. Drafts are coming in from all quarters; the holders are disappointed, they are clamorous; some have come two hundred and fifty miles and have had to return without their money.*

"Fifty days and over, have now passed since you informed me that funds had left a length of time, surely sufficient to have reached this. If I could only say 'I have funds in New Orleans, I can draw, etc.' it would greatly ameliorate my condition. . . but I have only to repeat what

31 Ibid., III, 289.
32 *Document*, III, 191.
33 F. W. Armstrong to Gibson, January 3, 1832, OIA, "1832 Choctaw Emigration;" *Document*, I, 368. Their brother Robert Armstrong was postmaster at Nashville.

I have said within the last ten days a thousand times, 'I have no money, but am expecting the receipt of an abundance every hour.' The consequences resulting from a much longer delay in the receipt of money will be terrible. . . .Three days ago I parted with the last five dollars of my own money."[34]

Major Armstrong set up his headquarters at the store of Josiah S. Doaks near Fort Towson. He called a meeting of the head men of the parties recently arrived, probably the first meeting of the emigrant Choctaw to assemble west of the Mississippi river. At least one chief, Nitakechi, was present. The Indians desired to organize their government and enact laws and wished to know the feelings of the government officers on the subject. However, Armstrong told them that as only one-fourth of the tribe had arrived in the west,[35] the government would not approve any laws enacted by them, and advised them to wait until a majority of the tribe was represented.

Armstrong issued an order notifying all fugitives from justice and all other persons not members of the Choctaw tribe to remove from within the confines of their country.[36] On March 4 he gave a formal appointment to Israel Folsom, making him the Choctaw interpreter for the United States, but requiring him to reside at the agency near the Arkansas river. A body of Shawnee Indians living in the Choctaw country on Red river had recently executed a Choctaw woman for being a witch, and Armstrong gave orders for the apprehension of the executioners, who were to be delivered to the military authorities.[37] The Choctaw had just executed two of their own people on charges of being witches. Armstrong then convened the chiefs in council and threatened the penalty of death upon any one instrumental in such executions in the future, and the lash for any one making a charge of witchcraft against a member of the tribe.[38] Armstrong delivered to the

34 *Document*, I, 429. The next summer Captain Brown was obliged to leave his post at Little Rock and go to New Orleans to procure money with which to pay expenses of removal (Brown to Gibson, October 18, 1832, OIA, "1832 Choctaw Emigration").

35 *Ibid.* Armstrong reported March 1, 1832, that there were 4,500 Choctaw Indians west of the Mississippi river (*Document*, III, 291).

36 *Ibid.*, 290.

37 *Ibid.*, 292.

38 The Choctaw had long cherished these weird superstitions. In 1819 the missionaries at the newly established mission of Eliot reported that ". . .today an

Indians 225 blankets (at the beginning of spring; they would have been much more grateful for them during the winter), 106 axes, 196 hoes, twenty-nine ploughs, fifty-five pounds of powder, 110 pounds of lead, ninety flintlock and 106 percussion rifles, 177 pounds of iron, seventeen pounds of steel. On his return to Fort Smith on the twelfth, Armstrong found a recently arrived party of Choctaw camped near by, and he rebuked the special agent in charge for leaving them in a place where the white men at Fort Smith had been able to supply them with whisky so that they were constantly drunk, and he ordered them removed to their permanent settlement.[39]

When Lieutenant Stephenson arrived at the Kiamichi river in March 1831, he began to prepare for the emigrant Indians as they should arrive. Money in that region was very scarce and after advertising for bids, he contracted for 250,000 pounds of beef at $3.90 a hundred pounds, to be delivered on the hoof, and 600 bushels of salt made at a lick near the line, at two dollars per bushel. Ten thousand bushels of corn, averaging $1.67 1-2 a bushel, was also engaged for the ten corn cribs he had constructed on the bank of Red river near the Kiamichi.

---

affectionate, industrious, inoffensive old woman named Ell-e-kee, more than sixty years of age who had lived in our family for sometime was murdered about two miles from us in a most barbarous manner on the superstitious notion that she was a witch." A young woman who had been ill for some time died; the members of her family concluded that some enemy had "witch shot her." The father and eight or ten of his friends armed with knives, went to the home of the old woman; coming up behind and seizing her by the hair the father said: "I have bought your life; you are a witch and must die;" and they cut her to pieces with their knives. These informal executions were common and in Yello-busho settlement alone twelve persons of both sexes had been killed as witches in the previous three years (Missionary Records, XV, No. 10, Eliot Mission Journal, April 14, 1819).

Later the Choctaw council undertook to regulate the subject by an act reading: "Council House, Sept. 18, 1829. Whereas it has been an old custom of the Choctaws to punish persons said to be wizzards or witches with death, without giving them a fair trial by any disinterested persons; and many have fallen victims under the influence of this habit;

"We do hereby resolve, in general council of the north, east, and southern districts, that, in future, all persons who shall be accused of being a wizzard or witch, shall be tried before the chiefs and committees, or by any four captains; and if they be found guilty, they shall be punished at the discretion of the courts" (Niles' Weekly Register, November 14, 1829, XXXVII, 181, from Alexander Gazette).

39 Document, III, 293.

He was to make lists of the emigrants as they arrived; and, to prevent duplication and fraud in issuing provisions, they were required to organize into companies of fifty to one hundred, and select from each company a captain or agent to receipt to the disbursing officer for their rations.[40] He was then to issue rations consisting of one and one-half pounds of beef or pork, one pint of corn, or an equivalent in corn-meal or flour to each, and two quarts of salt for every hundred rations. By October, Stephenson had under his supervision in the west 477 Choc-taw Indians all of whom had emigrated at their own expense.[41]

Stephenson established stations for issuing rations covenient to the places where the Indians settled. At Mountain Fork of Little river about forty miles southeast of Fort Towson, on April 30, 1832, he was issuing to 852 Indians; at Old Miller Court House on the bank of the Red river, southeast of Fort Towson, to 341; near Fort Towson he served 1205.[42] For Nitakechi's followers who settled in the country between the mouths of the Kiamichi and Boggy,[43] a depot was established on Horse Prairie[44] twenty miles west of Fort Towson, where 1351 Indians were served. Stephenson's equipment included two keel boats for carrying supplies up Mountain Fork to his depot, to prevent a monopoly by the owners of the boats on Red river.

Along the route and particularly after their arrival in the west the government agents encountered great difficulty in dealing with those who had supplies to sell for the use of the Indians. When bids for furnishing provisions were called for, the dealers frequently combined to compel the government to pay excessive prices. One dealer on Red

40   Ibid., I, 546, 857, 861, ff; III, 211, 291, 295. While at Doak's store near Fort Towson, the Indians came to see if Armstrong could secure for them an increase of their ration of one pint of corn; he agreed with them that their allowance was wholly inadequate, and so recommended to his superiors. With the increase subsequently allowed, Captain Brown later in the year felicitated General Gibson on the fact that they were able to ration the Indians enroute and in their new home at less than seven cents each a day (ibid., I, 481; III, 293).

41   Ibid., I, 54, 854.

42   Greenwood Leflore maintained a store near Fort Towson for a few years. On May 22, 1832 he wrote that he was on his way west to be gone two months.

43   Boggy creek or river was named by the French "Vazzures," meaning slimy or muddy (American State Papers, "Indian Affairs," I, 729).

44   Nuttall said in 1819, Horse Prairie "derives its name from the herds of wild horses which till lately frequented it, and of which we saw a small gang on our return" (R. G. Thwaites [ed.], Early Western Travels (Cleveland, 1906), III, 216).

river owned nearly all the keel boats on that stream that could be used in carrying supplies for the Indians; another who owned the salt works near the Choctaw line, hired the "proprietor of another saltwork to let his work lie idle" in order to prevent competition in the sale of salt for the Indians. Captain Brown denounced "the whole sordid and avaricious combination against the Government. . . and those speculative combinations which were. . . formed, and so strongly so, in some parts of the Territory, to overreach the agents, and prey upon the Government through their credulity."

After Lieutenant Rains had repaired some of the buildings at Fort Smith for the reception of supplies intended for the emigrating Indians, he reported September 6, 1831, that Capt. William McClellan, subagent for the Choctaw, had located a place about fifteen miles up the river which he called Choctaw Agency, and where he was about to erect some buildings to house Indian stores.[45] In May 1831, McClellan was issuing to fifteen emigrants at Fort Smith; the following January Rains was issuing rations to forty-seven Indians, while Pitchlynn's party was stranded ninety miles down the river. March 7 after their arrival, he had 536 to feed. ". . .They are settling widely apart, and of course wish their provisions carried to their section of country. . . My next place of issue will be at the Choctaw Agency (so called at present) eighteen miles from this place."[46] April 10 Rains was ". . .provisioning 519 Choctaw Indians, who have settled themselves in the neighborhood, and have gone to farming. They appear much pleased with the country, and satisfied. There are in the vicinity 541, but the year's provisions of some has expired. . . Every act of cunning is put in requisition to elude discovery of selling whisky by all the merchants here [Fort Smith] except one ((Colonel Mapes), and hundreds of gallons leave here almost daily for the Indian nations; the merchants making the Indian an agent for his illicit trade."[47]

A letter from Rains of June 10, reveals the government trying to compel the Indians to eat meat sent down from Fort Gibson because it was spoiled and unfit for consumption by the soldiers. Seventy-eight barrels had been condemned at the post and turned over to Lieutenant Rains; another lot of one hundred barrels had not been officially condemned, but as it had been stored at Fort Gibson for four or five years,

45 *Document*, I, 824, 856.
46 *Ibid.*, 828, 829.
47 *Ibid.*

officials took advantage of the supposed opportunity to salvage it by giving it to the Indians. However, the latter refused to accept it, and Rains found himself in difficulties, as he was charged with 178 barrels of pork. But ". . .after having it scraped and re-brined," he wrote in December, "I have issued some barrels of it, and am in hopes of issuing more."[48]

48   Ibid., 829, 837, 843.

PRELIMINARY to resumption of the removal in 1832, it was determined to construct a road from Fort Smith to the Choctaw settlements on the Red river. The Great Raft in that stream made navigation uncertain if not impossible. Freight was carried from Natchitoches to Fort Towson at a cost of five or six dollars a barrel, and required a passage of at least fifty days.[1] To reduce this excessive freight charge and find a better route, it was determined to carry supplies and provisions intended for those Indians up the Arkansas river to Fort Smith, and take them overland from there. It was planned to make this new road part of the mail route to Washington by which mail was carried "through from Fort Smith, through Missouri by or near Jackson, crossing the upper Mississippi near Cape Girardo, then passing to Golconda, and then crossing the Ohio."[2]

Fort Towson had been reëstablished in 1831 for the protection of the emigrating Indians and the frontier, despite the stubborn resistance

1 *Document*, III, 210.

2 *Ibid.;* The post route from Fort Gibson to Washington at that time was by way of Fort Smith, Memphis, Nashville, and Louisville, a distance in all of 1,388 miles (*ibid.*, I, 323). The mail "is generally carried in a small canoe, dugout; and I have on one occasion, seen it carried on a raft made of two logs lashed together. This was done for thirty miles on the Arkansas, and about eight miles on the Mississippi, when both of the rivers were high" (S. V. R. Ryan to Cass, April 24, 1833, *ibid.*, I, 842). This water route, the only one available when the swamps along the Mississippi river were overflowed, had been employed for a number of years. Nearly ten years earlier, it was reported from Little Rock that "The last eastern mail was received here completely drenched with water. We understand that the postrider, on the route from Memphis to Arkansas [Post] in descending the Mississippi, ran on a snag in the river, and upset his canoe, and he, however, true to his charge, succeeded in saving the mail bags and contents, and in doing so lost all the property which he had on board of the canoe, consisting of a number of articles of clothing (*Jackson (Tennessee), Gazette*, September 4, 1824, p. 2, col. 2).

of Greenwood Leflore, who had taken possession of the location when the buildings were burned and insisted on holding it.[3] Four companies of the Third Infantry under Major S. W. Kearny occupied the site of the old post in the summer of 1831, and called it Camp Phœnix; as the work progressed, it was later given the old name of Cantonment Towson, and then Fort Towson. The reëstablishment of the post created further demands for a road over the mountainous country intervening between it and the Arkansas river. In 1831, the citizens and Indians on the Red river were clamoring for the government to construct a road,[4] and in the autumn the secretary of war authorized Major Armstrong to call on the commanding officer at Fort Gibson to furnish troops to build it.[5]

After a route had been surveyed by Robert Bean and Jesse Chisholm, the road measuring 147 miles to Horse Prairie was constructed in three months by a force of men under Capt. John Stuart. The work was menaced at times by hostile prairie Indians and it was necessary for the troops to carry their arms ready for use on a gun rack mounted on a sled that was kept at the front of their work.[6] At one stage they met a party of Choctaw Indians traveling in great haste who said they had been run in by a band of Pawnee Indians who were in considerable force on the west side of Boggy river.[7]

3 Vose to Jones, June 5, 1833, AGO, OFD, 23 V33.

4 *Document*, I, 825.

5 *Ibid.*, III, 211, 294, 295.

6 Captain Stuart's interesting report and journal describing the construction of this, the first road in the Choctaw Nation, and the first but one in the new Indian Territory, is to be found in the war department (AGO, OFD, 130 A 32 and 185 S 32); it is copied with introduction and footnotes by Carolyn Thomas Foreman in *Chronicles of Oklahoma*, V, 333-347. This road ran from Fort Smith to near the present Spiro, Oklahoma, to reach the old Choctaw Agency; thence south approximating the route of the Kansas City Southern Railroad to Poteau, Oklahoma; thence Stuart's road, which paralleled the Kiamichi River most of the way was followed closely by the present St. Louis and San Francisco Railway to the Red river.

7 Three months before this Nail, Harkins, Nitakechi, Folsom, and other influential Choctaw Indians in council in the West addressed a communication to the secretary of war saying "that it is our wish that you would have troops stationed on the frontier immediately, as our people are settling up the Red river some distance; and unless we can have troops stationed on the frontier immediately, our people will be in great danger of these hostile Indians" (*Document*, II, 236).

Lieutenant Rains, disbursing agent for the Choctaw immigrants at Fort Smith, in January 1832, had thirty-three wagons, ox-teams and teamsters to transfer over this new road the guns, plows, and other property and supplies provided for the Indians on the Red river by the late treaty.[8] Six oxen were driven to each wagon, and though they were engaged for several months, they made but one trip to the Red river during the year. With the arrival of warm weather, the flies became so bad it was impossible to make more.

In the spring of 1832 ". . .*Owing to the law of the State of Mississippi passed at the last session, granting permission to the whites to settle in the Choctaw Nation, hundreds have come in and are squatting on the lands in all directions. Some of the settlers have bought reserves and are very rich. . . . .A great many complaints from the Indians are made at the agency against the whites, who are rapidly settling in every direction. I send you herewith enclosed, the copy of a communication addressed to Colonel Ward, the agent, to show the difficulties the Indians have to encounter in their intercourse with the worthless population squatted in the nation, particularly from Alabama. There are many exceptions, but, for the most part, every purchaser of cultivation reservations have made small advances to the Indians, with a promise to pay the balance when the Indians make a good title; which can hardly ever be effected, owing to the remote residence of the Indians when they remove to the west.*"[9] William S. Colquhoun wrote to the secretary of war about Daniel W. Wright charged with these frauds: "Wright is a popular man, and there are so many in Mississippi inculpated in fraudulent purchasers of Indian lands, that his conduct on that score does not in the least detract from his reputation."[10]

Upon application of Mushulatubbe[11] orders were given for a company of regular troops to proceed to the Choctaw country and under the direction of the agent remove the white intruders therefrom. A protest by Representative F. E. Plummer of Mississippi was lodged with the secretary of war about the time of the arrival in Washington

8   Ibid., I, 837, 839. Raines said the post office at Fort Smith was ". . .conducted in a very loose manner. It is now established in a dram shop."

9   Ibid., 605, 607.

10   Ibid., IV, 504.

11   Ibid., III, 193.

of the Choctaw agent, Ward. The agent who was charged with conniv-
ing with the whites against the Indians he assumed to protect reported
to Secretary Cass that the Indians had invited the whites into their
country. In this he expressed the views of Leflore, who assumed to
speak for the tribe, and opposed those of the full-bloods. "Upon this
information," Cass wrote to Plummer, "the president directed that the
contemplated proceedings should be stayed; and counter instructions. . .
together with orders to stop the movement of the troops, have been
given."[12]

To promote their designs the whites plied the Indians with whisky.
After the execution of the treaty Mushulatubbe and thirty-two of his
principal men in council addressed a memorial to the secretary of war,
seeking relief from a note giving white men a lien on several thousand
dollars of their tribal annuity, to satisfy some private claims. They
represented that Mushulatubbe was drunk when he was induced to
sign the note.[13]

In June, ". . .*Everything is in suspense, and the Indians constantly
holding councils and ball plays, where whiskey is openly sold, and drunkeness prevails to an extent beyond anything ever before experienced. Numerous parties of Indians pass the agency every week, with whiskey packed
on horses and on sleds from Columbus; and since the troops have retired,
the little intimidation they caused has ceased, and the most unrestrained
violation of the laws has resulted, with a perfect defiance of the authority
of the agent. The district judge, Nichols, held court in Columbus in May,
and expressly declared all laws of the United States in the Choctaw nation
null and void. . . . The sale of their reserves and stock keeps them amply
supplied with whiskey, which is kept for sale in every part of the nation. . . .
They are in a state of suspense. . .*" about their movements to the west.[14]

The emigration of the Indians in the autumn of 1832 profited by the
experiences of the preceding year. After the chiefs and head men had
their people located in the west, some of them returned in the spring
to their old home or to the Mississippi river to contribute their experience and aid to the emigration of that year. Warned by the terrible

12 Ibid., II, 837; III, 361.
13 Ibid., II, 196.
14 Colquhoun to Gibson, July 1, 1832, ibid., I, 619.

suffering of the last year's emigrants, of the danger of traveling in the winter, the Indians prepared to start earlier.[15]

The service was reorganized in the summer; in May a comprehensive set of regulations was prepared by the war department,[16] and in July a new staff of officers was created. On the second, William Armstrong was appointed[17] special agent and superintendent of the removal of the Choctaw from their homes to the Mississippi river. On the same day his brother, Major Francis W. Armstrong, was appointed special agent and superintendent of the removal of the Indians from the Missis- sippi river to their new homes west of Arkansas.[18] Assistant agents and disbursing officers, some of them taken from the army, were also designated.

It was planned to assemble the Indians at convenient points in the nation, to enroll and vaccinate them.[19] Instead of concentrating them at Arkansas Post or Little Rock as was done the year before, it was designed to have them all pass Rock Roe, a point on the White river east of Little Rock. The emigrants who left Vicksburg and Memphis by water were carried up the White river and disembarked at that point; the others who came overland from Memphis marched south- west from that city to Rock Roe; those destined for Fort Smith con- tinued to that post, their course leaving Little Rock on their left. The Red river emigrants passed from Rock Roe to Little Rock, and from there through Washington to the Choctaw country on the Kia- michi river.[20]

15 Ibid., III, 303.
16 Ibid., I, 343, II, 825.
17 Cass to Armstrong, July 2, 1832, OIA.
18 Document, I, 124.
19 Ibid., I, 372.
20 Thirty-four hundred Indians were removed from Choctaw Agency to Mem- phis, a distance of 200 miles, at a cost for rations and other necessities of $4.45 per head. Subsistence was furnished them by army officers, and the Indians kept well and were satisfied; but after they crossed the Mississippi river they were fed by private con- tractors and "there was constant complaint about their weight and measure, and frequently could not get their rations when they were due" (ibid., I, 796). Rock Roe, sometimes spelled Rock Row, is seen on an early map on the right bank of the White river at the mouth of Rock Roe bayou, a few miles below the present Clarenden in Monroe County, Arkansas. Near that location is the present village of Roe. Rock Roe was near a well known crossing over the White river just below the mouth of Cache creek. On the right bank of the river at this place was a good landing and here

About two thousand of Mushulatubbe's district fixed upon October 3, 1832, to assemble at their rendezvous at the Old Council House where they organized for removal; they divided about equally, one half following Mushulatubbe[21] to the country on the Arkansas river in the neighborhood of Fort Smith, and the other thousand under the leadership of David Folsom going to the Red river country. Armstrong had much trouble in starting the Indians: "The laws of Mississippi being extended over the Choctaws and their having had considerable dealings in disposing of their land and stock of various kinds, the constables and sheriffs were on the ground" to add to the confusion and aid in despoiling the Indians of all their property before they departed. In the confusion Armstrong had difficulty in getting the Indians separated and organized under their respective conductors.[22] The Folsom emigrants in charge of Mr. Irwin and another contingent in charge of Wharton Rector reached Memphis October 31, where they were thrown into a panic by the presence of cholera.

On all the steamboats coming down the Mississippi river deaths occurred from the disease. It was said to be progressing southward from St. Louis and Louisville, and on one boat, the *Express*, seven persons died between the latter city and Memphis.[23] The disease spread in Tennessee, and the next June F. W. Armstrong reported from Nashville that he and his wife had just recovered from it, and that business in the state had been entirely suspended in consequence

was an area of timbered land clear of the swamp and high enough to be dry, which afforded a good place for the Indians to encamp and organize for their land journey westward. The origin of the name Rock Roe is obscure, but one authority ascribes it to a French expression meaning "tough rock crossing of a river." It is said to have been an old Chickasaw crossing place on a trail leading from the Chickasaw Bluffs at Memphis over which the Chickasaw Indians traveled on their war expeditions. One officer quoted herein spelled the name "Racrat." "Roccroc" a French word meaning "lucky hit" pronounced "ra-kro" offers possibilities in connection with the well known fact that early French hunters and trappers bestowed names on streams and places familiar to them.

21   Peter P. Pitchlynn returned from the West to assist in preparing this contingent and conducting them west. He also secured a school teacher to accompany them and open a school in their district in the West (*ibid.*, III, 394).

22   *Ibid.*, I, 386.

23   *Ibid.*, 389. On "the *Constitution* two. The *Freedom* called here [Memphis] yesterday, five deaths since she left the mouth of Tennessee, and six now on board down, a lady said to be dying" (*ibid.*).

of it.[24] Though Armstrong endeavored to get the Indians to board the steamboat at Memphis for the passage to Rock Roe, the women refused to go themselves, or to permit their children. The result was that on November 1, less than six hundred boarded the steamer *Reindeer*, and a keel boat attached[25] in charge of Mr. Irwin; and four hundred of the party with their horses and wagons were ferried over the river and proceeded overland in charge of Lieut. J. A. Phillips.

The *Reindeer* discharged 455 Choctaw passengers at Rock Roe November 5.[26] Two deaths from cholera had occurred on board, and ten more during the next three days after the Indians landed and were waiting to begin their march. One hundred and fifty teams had been assembled by the drivers, but on the arrival of the cholera infected Indians such a panic resulted that many of the teamsters fled and seriously threatened the movement.[27] Heavy rains had recently fallen and the land contingent had a dreadful experience struggling through the great swamp between Memphis and the White river. They were nearly two weeks covering the ninety miles to Rock Roe.

After they were organized by William Armstrong and prepared for the next stage, in charge of Lieut. J. A. Phillips these followers of David Folsom together with a party from Greenwood Leflore's district conducted by S. T. Cross, that had come by boat from Vicksburg, in all numbering about 1,400, on November 14, camped four miles from Rock Roe.[28] There were several cases of cholera and the death of a child. They made an early start the next day and after traveling fifteen miles camped in the Grand Prairie at the "Creek Au Gree." On the sixteenth they made eleven miles and the next the unusual distance of

24 *Ibid.*, I, 411.

25 *Ibid.*, 394.

26 The agent at "Choctaw Camp, mouth of Rock Row, White River" reported only 450 disembarked from the *Reindeer*.

27 *Document*, I, 387, 737; Langham to commissary general of subsistence, November 8, 1832, OIA, "Choctaw Emigration." "The panic produced by the existence of this dreadful scourge was so great that while the Indians were marching through the swamp opposite Memphis, they neglected almost everything, even their families; at this time the Government had 150 wagons at Rock Row; eighteen teamsters ran away one night leaving their teams standing" (Armstrong to Herring, May 12, 1834, OIA, "Choctaws").

28 *Journal* of Lieut. J. A. Phillips, OIA, "Choctaw Emigration."

eighteen miles principally in the timber. Another child died of the cholera.

On the eighteenth "One new case of cholera. It commenced raining about one o'clock a. m. We started about 7 o'clock. The rain fell in torrents and very cold. The roads became very muddy and mirey. A part of the detachment reached the Arkansas river at night—the others were detained by some of the wagons that" had mired down in the mud. This was issue day, but the contractor failed them so that the Indians were not only wet, cold, and hungry but were without provisions. Lieutenant Phillips secured from Capt. Jacob Brown at Little Rock some hard bread and pork and issued it to the Indians who succeeded in reaching the Arkansas river late that night.[29]

"November 19th. The weather very cold. The wind blew hard, & rendered it dangerous to cross the river. Remained in camp today & issued rations to the Indians as they came up. Capt. Cross party & mine encamped together. Finding that the movement was retarded by the two detachments continuing together, Capt. C. & myself determined to separate, and to keep as far as practicable one day apart. Three new cases of cholera. Nov. 20th. The Indians still coming in. Capt. Cross commenced crossing the Arkansas River early today. The weather still very cold. Nov. 21st. Our party commenced crossing very early the Arkansas; finished today, & moved to Three Mile Creek, beyond the town. Here we received also one day's provision. Three new cases of cholera. The sick all got up. Clear and cold."

The party now numbering 700 departed early in the morning and at an afternoon camp "Mustered the Captains and had a talk relative to the movement, and I informed them of the duties I required them to perform." After several uneventful days they reached Ouachita river on the twenty-sixth "about nine o'clock and commenced crossing the baggage waggons at the Ford. The ponies were driven over and two or three of the Indian waggons. Crossed about 600 Indians in the Boat, & reached the encampment three miles beyond before dark." The health of the Indians continued to improve though there was one death on the twenty-eighth, the day they crossed the "Fourche de Caddo. Forded the river, except about 250 women and children, who were ferried across in the boat, and reached the camp before sunset."

29 *Arkansas Gazette*, November 21, 1832, p. 3, col. 1.

*Cypress swamp in Arkansas through which the Indians struggled for
thirty miles frequently up to their waists*

They crossed the Little Missouri river December 1, and reached Washington the evening of the next day.[30] One child died on the third and the next day a woman, who had dropped out from the Leflore party and whom they had picked up along the road. On the sixth a little Indian girl had her arm broken by the accidental upsetting of one of the transportation wagons. They reached the Great Cossatot river that day and the next left camp in the rain. On the eighth they reached "the line bounding the Choctaw Country before dark. Here many of the Choctaws, who had emigrated last year came to meet and welcome their friends to their new home. It was a night of great joy and re-rejoicing." The next day they arrived at the Mountain Fork river and reached the public crib where the Indians were discharged.[31]

Mushulatubbe's followers in charge of Thomas McGee reached Memphis November 3 and crossed the Mississippi river that day. This party was more alarmed about the cholera than Folsom's, and only a few could be induced to take the steamboat. William Armstrong who had tried in vain to secure a physician to travel with the Indians, accompanied the remainder and they were seven days making forty-two miles through the swamp; and during that time and afterward, many of the party died with the cholera. For thirty miles, Armstrong reported, they were compelled to struggle through a swamp from knee-deep to waist-deep in water.[32] On their arrival at Rock Roe, the sections were again consolidated into one party of 1,300 with a train

30 At Washington the party numbered only 690 (*Document*, I, 788; OIA, "1832 Choctaw Emigration"). Mr. Wright said there were more than fifty deaths in Nail's party; fifty or sixty in Folsom's; thirty in Leflore's and the same in Nitakechi's. Some of them were from cholera, but the great majority of those who died were little children, the aged and infirm, who could not survive the hardships of the journey (Alfred Wright to D. Greene, January 14, 1833, "Missionary Letters," No. 142).

31 *Document*, I, 632; Phillips to Gibson, December 22, 1832, OIA. At the end of their journey, Folsom's party numbered only about 700, according to the missionary Loring S. Williams, who wrote that they had lost fifty or sixty by cholera on the way. They settled on the north side of the Little river, near the place where rations were issued, which was close to William's station. The neighborhood, he said, was to some extent civilized: ". . .here is a native blacksmith, a shoemaker, a carpenter and joiner, a merchant, and two or three white settlers who are mechanics." But he deplored the arrival of many wicked people with the Indians (*Missionary Herald*, XXIX, 206).

32 *Document*, I, 398. Armstrong reported this party had "been sorely handled with sickness and very many deaths."

of thirty wagons carrying their heavy baggage: and under the leadership of Capt. John Page they departed for their new home above Fort Smith. December 6 they attempted to cross the Arkansas River in a flat boat at Dardenelle Rock, but a sudden rise of the river prevented all but five wagons and forty horses from being ferried across that day. Fortunately the steamboat *Volant* with a keel boat in tow, descended at that time and with her help the whole party was put across in twenty-eight hours.[33] They then proceeded and about 1,000 of them reached the neighborhood of the Choctaw agency west of Fort Smith the evening of December 14.[34]

A party of about 500 followers of Mushulatubbe who undertook to emigrate without the assistance of the government, but with the view of collecting the ten dollars *per capita* commutation on their arrival in the West, crossed the Mississippi river at Memphis and started their march to Fort Smith. After tremendous difficulties they struggled through the swamp to a point about forty miles from Memphis, where they abandoned further efforts; they built rude shelters against the elements, and scattered about trying to sustain life by hunting. Here they were found in the middle of December by William Armstrong; he had them brought into St. Francis, organized the party, and under the leadership of Wharton Rector started them to Fort Smith where they arrived January 20, 1833.[35]

33 *Ibid.*, 402.
34 *Ibid.*, 836, 401; Rains to Gibson, December 15, 1832, OIA.
35 *Document*, I, 403, 406.

CHAPTER SIX / *Experiences on the March*

I N LEFLORE's district the agent was endeavoring to enroll the
Indians for removal with the assistance of some of the leading
men of the tribe, who were in the government employ; but, as
was afterward discovered, while they were drawing pay from
the government, they were secretly advising the Indians to
follow Leflore's favorite plan, to be prepared to go without government
control, and collect the ten dollars commutation in the West. So that
while the agents had been assured of twenty-five hundred to three
thousand emigrants from Leflore's district at Vicksburg, at the appointed time there were only 617 ready to go with S. T. Cross, leaving
two thousand of the poorest Indians[1] who said they intended to remain
until the next year.

When these emigrants came near Vicksburg, on October 25, they
were greeted by the news that the citizens were flying from home
to escape the cholera. Though they were camped two miles from the
town and warnings were given the Indians and citizens to prevent
communication between them, the precautions were vain; the dread
disease made its appearance and caused many deaths among them. As
quickly as possible, on November 1, six hundred emigrants with their
baggage, oxen and horses were embarked on the steamer *Thomas Yeatman*, and the government snagboat *Heliopolis*. They were landed at
Rock Roe the twelfth, the *Heliopolis* having to transfer her cargo at
the mouth of the White river to the *Archimedes*, and *Harry Hill*,
boats of lighter draft.[2]

1 *Document*, I, 395.
2 Other arrivals at Rock Roe brought the total to 1,799; their 124 oxen were
"all worked by the Indians on the march," and their ponies were driven by a shorter
route through the swamps (*ibid.*, 400).

"Thirteenth Issued Rations to Indians for three days ending 15th.
Two deaths by Cholera—detailed 13 wagons for my detachment also an
order from Langham to call into Service two U. S. wagons to transfer
the sick with Cholera &c untill we met the ponies belonging to the
Indians making 15 teams in service to transport the baggage—sick &c.
Organized the party for the march and at 2 o'clock P. M. left Rock Roe
with the Detachment, travelled four miles and encamped, the Road very
bad—three deaths reported (by Cholera).

"Novr. 15. Left camp early in the morning, travelled 10 miles the
road being bad in the Prairie—encamped at night at Au Gree; this
morning the two U. S. teams came up and took in the sick, at least a part,
one death reported." The next day they encamped in the "Big Prairie"
and issued rations and forage for two days. Rain fell all that night and
another emigrant died on the seventeenth. The next day they traveled
in the rain and two more deaths occurred before the wet, cold, and
miserable emigrants reached the Arkansas river.

They spent the nineteenth and twentieth crossing the river and
traveled three miles before they encamped to wait for some of the
Indians who stopped at Little Rock to have their wagons repaired.
During the next week they advanced about seventy miles on their way
and crossed Caddo river. Sickness and deaths from cholera were increasing and thirteen wagons were filled with the sick Indians and
baggage. Day after day the routine was much the same; camp was
made in the afternoon to issue rations and give the Indians scattered
along the road time to catch up; or the conductor sent men back to
help them along so the whole party would be present for an early start
on the morrow.

The emigrants entered the Choctaw country December 8; they
"travelled 18 miles, encamped at McCanns, drew forage and provisions
for two days." The next day some of the emigrants dropped out and
decided to settle near; the remainder traveled thirteen miles and on
the tenth after they resumed their march they were cheered by the
sight of 300 of their friends, former arrivals, who came to welcome
them and marched with them to Clear creek. The next day the emigrants continued to the vicinity of Fort Towson where their journey
ended and they dispersed to select homes in the surrounding country.[3]

3 Cross's Journal, OIA, "1832 Choctaw Emigration;" Document, I, 632.

Lieut. Jefferson Van Horne, disbursing agent for the removal, conducted the contingent in charge of horses and cattle that were being
taken overland from Vicksburg to meet the main Leflore party on the
Fort Towson road. With the cattle and 244 horses of this party and
forty-seven Indians and negroes he crossed the Mississippi river on
the snag boat *Heliopolis* about eight miles above Vicksburg on November 2 and 3, 1832. The main party proceeded up the river by steamboat
as Van Horne and his party traveled overland through the swamps, for
a few days paralleling the course of the boat.

Though it rained the first three days, they made progress up the
river and by the sixth they were fifty-six miles from the river crossing.[4]
Then "*Made twelve miles, over a very deep and bad swamp where many
of the ponies (weak and exhausted when we started) were mired and we
had to pull them out. One or two that were unable to get along, were
knocked in the head by their owners. When we arrived at Bayou Macon
I called for some time for the ferryman. At length, a drunken old hag
bellowed from the cabin on the opposite side, that there was no man
about; and I must wait until he should come. Upon this, I commenced
crossing the horses. We drove in about twenty. They swam over, and
every one mired on the opposite shore. I induced an Indian to swim over
and bring the raft. About a dozen of us crossed and with some difficulty,
pulled all the horses out. I now crossed all the people & baggage on the
raft, and drove the remainder of the horses in lower down where they
crossed without difficulty.*"

They had trouble in keeping the horses together; some of the owners
were tardy in arriving in camp with their stock; horses strayed off
in the night and the search for them in the morning caused delays.
They had reached the house of one Morris, the last in the settlements
along the river and were about to enter the swamps again. Van Horne
had been ill and performed his duties with great difficulty. "*In the
evening one of my party called me aside and desired the prescription for
cholera. I gave it. As it was very cold this man and myself slept before the
fire, at Morris' house. The symptoms increased on me until near midnight, when the constant purging and vomiting, and terrible cramps &
pain in my stomach & bowels, induced me to take 20 grains of calomel,*

4 Journal of Lieut. Jefferson Van Horne, OIA, "1832 Choctaw Emigration";
Document, I, 632.

-{ 83 }-

& a large pill of opium. These I threw up. While vomiting through the floor, (from which Morris had torn up a plank) and bent double with pain, I was repeating the dose; I was ordered to leave the house. Morris said he had a large family, and that their lives and his own were at stake, that I had imposed on him in coming there in that condition, & that I must quit the house. The ground was already covered with frost, & was freezing severely. I rolled myself in my blanket, after begging in vain to remain, and walked three fourths of a mile to my tent."

Van Horne was better the next day but he continued very weak for some time. The following two weeks were uneventful, the party making from ten to twenty miles daily in the rains over bad roads through the swamps. They broke camp and started each day at seven to ten o'clock or as soon as their horses could be collected; and made camp at three or four in the afternoon when they could find a compara-tively dry place where there were wood, water, and cane for their stock. One day as they were traveling along a horse was killed by a falling tree. November 23 Van Horne's party intersected the road to Fort Towson traveled by Leflore's party. "The road was crowded with emigrating Choctaws. Some of my party anxious to join their wives and relatives, hastened on and united with them in the evening. Others joined next day".

A party of 1,800 Choctaw Indians from Nitakechi's district were approaching Little Rock from Rock Roe and Van Horne was directed to report to Major Armstrong at the former place for service in con-nection with these emigrants. *"At sunrise on the morning of the 29th I commenced crossing the party of Six Towns[5] assigned to me; consisting of 629 people, with 14 hired teams and 9 native teams. I counted the people as they crossed the Arkansas. We encamped about half past four o'clock, four miles from Little Rock, convenient to good water and wood. (4 miles).*

"30th. Proceeded at half past seven o'clock, over a good road to the stand on Hurricane Creek, where the party arrived at half past four

5 These Indians lived in and about Jasper county, Mississippi; they received their name of "Six Towns" from having formerly resided in six towns or settle-ments near together having the names of Chenocabee-tamaha, Inkillis-tamaha, Talla-tamaha, Okatalaia, Mishoweia, and Bishkun. As they lived remote from Dancing Rabbit Creek they were not present at the making of the treaty. They were the best ball-players and the fiercest and most warlike of all the Choctaw. They were generally of low stature and heavy build. It was easy to distinguish a Six Towns brave from any other Choctaw (H. S. Halbert, *idem.*).

o'clock. Issued two days provisions and forage in the evening. The whole party was comfortably encamped, and cooking their suppers early in the evening. (15 miles).

"Dec. 1st. Started at eight o'clock, and proceeded leasurely over a good road, until about half past two o'clock. We could easily have done much further; but Lieutenant Montgomery's party was not far ahead and deemed it best to keep a day's journey in rear of them. The party travelled with great cheerfulness and harmony; and were fast improving in health. When I joined the main party east of Little Rock, great numbers were sick, and considerable numbers dying. (11 miles).

"2nd. It rained powerfully last night. Started at eight o'clock. Issued two days supplies for the 3rd and 4th. Six people and twenty-four horses joined from the horse party. I rejected a quantity of beef presented at this stand. It had been slaughtered too long, and had spoiled. Other beef was furnished in its place. Encamped at half past three o'clock convenient to wood and water. (12 miles).

"3rd. Started at eight o'clock. I gave a certificate for crossing 584 of my people (small children not being counted) at the ferry over Washita river. Sixty-five of David Folsom's people, who had fallen back from Lieut. Phillips' party, being unable to get over, requested me to cross them. I did so. All the teams and horses of my party forded, but the river was too deep and swift for the people to do so. A man in the employ of David the Ferryman made several of my party drunk, notwithstanding I went into his shop before my party came up, and obtained his pledge that they should not have any liquor. Some of Lieut. Phillips' party whom I found here had been beastly drunk for many days. We encamped about 4 o'clock on the bank of a beautiful creek. (12 miles).

"4th. Started about eight o'clock. One birth since last issue. Issued to 634 people. Encamped about 4 o'clock on a fine stream. (12 miles).

"5th. All the captains called on me in a body and desired me to wait until the cart of their head man Etotahoma (which broke down last evening, and was unable to get to camp) should be brought up. I had sent back more than once, and had much trouble to get this old man and his cart along. His oxen were poor and worn out, and his cart badly constucted. But he was looked to and beloved by the whole party. He would not part with his cart, and although it might have been policy to go on and leave the wretched old establishment, I found it impossible to get his people along without him. He was old, lame, and captious, and gave me more trouble than all the rest of the party. Proceeded at half past nine o'clock, and crossed the Fournois. As the weather was cold and the water deep and swift, the teams, horses and young men forded, and the women, children and old men crossed in the boat. Etotahoma's cart was brought up & repaired. Encamped about 4 oclock (9 1-2 miles).

"7th. Rained all last night, and the whole day severely. Found it difficult to start the party at nine o'clock. Etotahoma's cart fell to the rear again. I sent back Mr. Ryan and the interpreter with a yoke of oxen and driver to bring it up. Encamped about four o'clock. The rain continued in the night. (12 miles)

"8th. Started at 8 oclock. The Little Missouri River had risen consider-ably, but I managed to get the teams and horses through it. . I crossed the people in the boat, counting only grown persons. I gave a certificate for the passage of 340. The road was quite muddy this day. We encamped at the stand at half past three oclock & two days of provisions & forage were issued. (13 miles)

"9th. Notwithstanding I had hired a yoke of oxen and driver to bring Etotahoma's cart with the party, he failed to bring it farther than Little Missouri river. Many of Etotahoma's people had stopped behind, and this morning all the captains called on me and requested that the party might lay to this day (Sunday) to allow all to get up with the party, and that they might wash, mend their mockasins and rest. They said Etota-homa was their chief, that they all loved him, that he old & lame, and that they were unwilling to go on and leave him behind. I remained, made a new axeltree for his cart, brought it up with a fresh yoke of oxen, and to prevent any more trouble, hauled his cart with this yoke of oxen all the remainder of the journey. Five people with five horses came to me here, stating that they had quit Lieut. Philips' party to hunt their horses which had strayed. As they were known to my interpreter, I took them on with my party."[6]

The journal for the following week contains little of interest. The party camped at Washington, Arkansas, on the tenth and reached Little river on the fourteenth. Van Horne began crossing his party at daybreak the next morning but some who were late in arriving at the river were not crossed until dark. Two days later they arrived at the "stand" established by David Folsom; here provisions for two

6 Van Horne's Journal.

days were issued to the emigrants who proceeded *"twelve miles farther, and encamped on a beautiful spot, convenient to excellent water and wood.*

"18th. Started at eight oclock. For the last few days we had been met by many Choctaw emigrants of preceeding years coming to meet their friends and relatives. My party had dressed themselves neatly for the occasion, and seemed in fine health and spirits. Agreably to the wishes of the party, and of Col. Nail their chief, I made a final encampment at half past one o'clock, four miles east of Clear Creek, where I fourthwith discharged all the teamsters, and mustered the people, who were enrolled by the issuing officer, numbering 648 persons."

In the autumn of 1832 about 3,000 of Nitakechi's people remained in his district, and they agreed to assemble at the rendezvous on October 1. To prepare for their removal, W. S. Colquhoun conductor, A. H. Somerville assistant, George W. Ward enrolling agent, and Robert Nail interpreter, left the Choctaw Agency September 13, 1832, and five days later arrived at "Cutchathlipee" creek, the main branch of the Chickasawhay where they began erecting a bullock-pen and cribs. These were completed in a week and then began the hauling of corn from a distance of twelve to twenty miles. Three days later Lieut. J. P. Simonton, disbursing agent arrived, and on October 1 began the arrival of wagons that had been engaged; they were dispatched in every direction to collect the Indians and their personal effects.

This work continued for a week and after most of the Indians had arrived at the concentration camp there followed a week of rain which made their situation very uncomfortable. However, on the fourteenth of October the baggage of the Indians was loaded in the wagons and on pack horses, the Indians were organized into bands of fifty to one hundred with a captain for each band to receive rations for his people; the next day they broke camp and proceeded six miles to Garland's Old Fields where they picked up more recruits.

There were now more than 1,700 Indians in the party traveling in two divisions; one headed by Opi-a-hooma (or Par-hoo-ma) brother of Nitakechi, who on his departure for the West had left his brother in command as second chief, and the other by his rival Joel Nail.[7] They were strung along the road for a great distance, men, women, and children, mounted on their ponies, or riding in their ox-carts, but most

7 *Document,* I, 376.

of the men traveled on foot. The Indians' wagons, those hired by the government, and the ponies were loaded to their capacity with an odd assortment of personal belongings of the Indians, loved possessions with which they planned to start life anew in a strange country. Ahead was a large number of cattle to furnish them fresh meat every other day. The countryside witnessed the astonishing spectacle presented by this caravan whence came the hallooing of the drovers herding the cattle along the route, the creaking and rattle of ox-carts, the commands of the ox-drivers and the cracks of their whips, the imprecations of teamsters to horses struggling to pull the wagons through the mud, the bawling of cattle and the whinnying of horses. After this little army had passed there were left only the patterns of thousands of hoof and footprints in the mud and a strange silence. These aborigines had departed forever from the land that for ages had been home to them and their ancestors.

On the seventeenth they traveled seven miles over roads so bad they found it necessary to hire more wagons to lighten their loads. The next day they were compelled to build a bridge, and passed through a swamp where they were in places obliged to hitch twelve oxen to a wagon. However, they made five miles by night and had 1,775 Indians enrolled, according to the journal kept by Colquhoun.[8] On the nineteenth—

"Left our encampment early; the oxen on one of the foremost wagons turned off a bridge to drink & capsized the wagon, causing a detention of 2 hours; another wagon broke; came to Crabtrees and issued Beef; detained by two Creeks and swamps, made only 7 miles. Indians well satisfied; 4 children born, one child died. Report says some of our party burnt an Indian house & destroyed his corn to force him to go & that he shot one of the party. A white man named T. C. Crawford took a $20 bill to get changed for an Indian into silver & went off with it; 1,788 Indians enrolled."

The next day they traveled nine miles and 15 more Indians joined the caravan. While camped at the corn cribs at Russel's Stand that night their cattle broke out of the pen and thirty-six of them were lost. They made thirteen miles on the twenty-first and the same distance the next day and the wagoners complained of fast driving. Good water

8   OIA, "1832 Choctaw Emigration."

was becoming scarce and large numbers of the Indians were suffering with dysentery. The next day when they went to issue beef they found the "stilyards" had been left behind and delay resulted. "Proceeded on through Brandon; court just adjourned, many drunken people in the place. The Indians of both sexes drunk. Forbid the sale of Whiskey without effect" . . They made but four miles.

Most of the Indians were drunk that night and when they broke camp in the morning, from whisky introduced among them by the whites. They soon reached the Pearl river and began crossing, an undertaking that was not completed for two days. The one ferry flat in use was so old it was constantly in danger of sinking. They were all across by the twenty-sixth when they were much alarmed by reports of the cholera at Vicksburg. This day their party was increased by fifty-three Indians under "Capt. Primettahaw."

On the 27th Chief Nitakechi went back to look for horses stolen from the party by whites. The party made five miles. The next day they met people flying from the cholera; one child died; passed Society Ridge and took the road to Dunn's ferry across the Big Black river. On the twenty-ninth William Juzan interpreter for the Six Towns Concha left the party. The next two days were spent in ferrying across the Big Black river.

For a few days the entries tell of alarm among the Indians and white wagoners from reports of cholera; Indians made drunk by whites. ". . .ten beeves broke out of the pen and were irretrievably lost; they were large and fat; I sent after them in all directions, but could not find them." A wagon falls over a bridge. Finally on the fourth of November they arrive at the Mississippi river and camp at a point above Vicksburg where it is hoped to escape the cholera raging in that city. Here they shiver in the rain and cold for a week.

"Netachache's party of Coonchees & Hoo-wan-nees with Capt. Lake's Company of Chukasawhays" numbering 565 were embarked on the steamboat *Volant* and a keel boat in tow bound for the mouth of the Yazoo river. The next day, November 13, Nail's party boarded the steamboats *Reindeer* and *Thomas Yeatman* with the same destination.[9] One hundred and forty horses and one hundred and fourteen

9 *Vicksburg Advocate and Register*, November 8, 1832, p. 3, col. 1. During this cholera epidemic and movement of the Indians, Washington Irving arrived at Vicksburg aboard the steamboat *Little Rock* bound from Fort Gibson to New Orleans. He

oxen were ferried across the river on the snag boat *Heliopolis* to begin their journey overland and rejoin the main party on the Fort Towson road.

On the fourteenth after ferrying across the Mississippi the horses of Mettahoma's company, the remainder of the Indians boarded the three boats which soon after midnight got under way. Colquhoun on the *Thomas Yeatman* records on the fifteenth: "*Held on till 6; landed at Tompkins Bend & Cooked. Overtook Volant and Reindeer at 2 o'clock; issued rations & pushed off. S. B. Volant towing a keel boat ran afoul of a snag which broke the keel boat loose & drifted her off into the bend of the river; this being at the hour of midnight, the lives of more than 300 Indians were in imminent danger. Reindeer detained by injury to her machinery arrived & landed opposite Lake Washington 16th in the morning at 8 o'clock & remained until 12 when we cooked and wooded.*"

Here occur some of the particulars of a feud developing between Colquhoun and Armstrong. The former was accused of being too liberal with the Indians. Armstrong complained that Colonel Gaines, Colquhoun's friend, the year before had spoiled the Indians; that he allowed them to carry their hominy mortars on the removal and per-mitted other indulgences that Armstrong did not approve of. "He [Armstrong] refused to permit the Indians to land on shore for indis-pensible purposes for more than 20 hours & when the boats stopped to get wood kept a fellow to beat them back from the shore where the propriety & necessity urged them to repair."

The steamboats arrived at the mouth of the White river November 18, and the Indians were put ashore while the vessels proceeded to different woodyards to replenish their supply of fuel. After the In-dians boarded the boats and they continued up the White river, Col-quhoun who thought they should have their blankets issued to them as the weather was rainy and cold, caused Nitakechi and Robert Nail to request them from Armstrong. He resented it and reproached Col-quhoun for his interference. The latter was intoxicated, shot and tried to kill Armstrong, was put off the boat and discharged from the service.[10]

---

declined a dinner invitation extended "by a party of gentlemen," but "attended a wine party in the evening given at Ball's" (*ibid.*, November 21, 1832.).

10 Armstrong to Cass, November 30, 1832, OIA, "Choctaw Emigration."

The weather was now cold and inclement and the half-naked Indians were in a wretched condition. They were *"the poorest in the Choctaw Nation. They live in huts, and with few exceptions, like the great majority of their race, exert no more industry than is necessary to procure a temporary subsistence. The climate is mild, and many, very many, do not think of clothing their children in the summer season until they have arrived at the age of seven or eight years. Many of these children came to the place of rendezvous and were enrolled to go west of the Mississippi, who had nothing under heaven to protect their naked bodies from the pitiless storm but a share of their parents' blanket, which served as a mantle by day and as a bed by night. In consequence of a change of food and exposure to much damp and rainy weather, which took place before we left the rendezvous, much sickness occurred."*[11]

Despite the efforts of the conductors the emigrants contracted the cholera and there were many deaths among them; and this made their difficulties enormous after they were packed like sardines on the river boats. "In some cases the people refused to come near us, or to sell us any thing we wanted. . . In ascending the river, the woodyards were abandoned; and they had cause of alarm, for scarce a boat landed without burying some person" wrote Armstrong to General Gibson.[12]

Armstrong ordered Lieut. Isaac P. Simonton on board the steamboat *Reindeer* on the seventeenth to take Colquhoun's place as conductor of the Indians. Simonton also kept a journal of events. A mile up the White river the Indians landed and went into camp. After a night of rain it cleared and turned cold so that the ground was frozen in the morning. The scantily clad "Indians were loth to leave their fires this morning, and we had much difficulty in getting them on board. Started 9 o'clock and stoped at sunset. Traveled 50 miles." Between nine in the morning and sunset of the next day they made 40 miles and camped again that evening. Twenty-six miles farther, on the twenty-first they arrived at Rock Roe, landed the Indians, got their wagons on shore and discharged the steamboats.

The next day they issued provisions and organized the Indians to resume their land journey. They continued in two parties, with the Concha in charge of Lieut. William R. Montgomery, and the Six Towns and Chickasawhays conducted by Lieutenant Simonton.

11 *Document*, I, 886.
12 *Ibid.*, 400.

Teamsters with their teams and wagons had been engaged to await the Indians at this place but a number of them had failed from fear of the cholera. Those who remained were placed in service and the emigrants set out from Rock Roe at eleven o'clock on the twenty-second bound for Little Rock.

THE roads were very bad. On the twenty-fourth they *"traveled 16 miles and arrived at Mrs. Black's farm. Found a party of twelve hundred Indians encamped here, under the charge of Capt. Page;*[1] *they suffered dreadfully with the cholera. The cholera which had been raging in our camp for some time past, now raged with increased violence; the woods are filled with the graves of the victims. Stop'd at sunset."* And so they continued their sad journey, making six, ten, twelve, and once fifteen miles in a day. They were delayed by rains, bad roads and an appalling amount of sickness and mortality among the emigrants. Additional wagons were required to haul the sick and dying. With 200 stragglers picked up on the way, this party began arriving at Arkansas river opposite Little Rock on the twenty-seventh and went into camp. Nineteen had died since leaving Rock Roe.[2]

"No man" wrote Armstrong, *"but one who was present can form any idea of the difficulties that we have encountered owing to the cholera, and the influence occasioned by its dreadful effects. It is true, we have been obliged to keep every thing to ourselves, and to browbeat the idea of disease, although death was hourly among us and the road lined with the sick. The extra wagons hired to haul the sick are about five to the 1,000; fortunately they are a people that will walk to the last, or I do not know how we could get on."*[3]

At Little Rock Armstrong divided the two parties into three which left that place at intervals of one day. One party of Conchas, numbering 600 and including Chief Nitakechi, in charge of Lieut. W. R. Mont-

---

1 This was the Mushulatubbe party, originally 1,300 in number.
2 *Arkansas Gazette*, November 28, 1832, p. 3, col. 1.
3 *Document*, I, 401.

gomery,[4] crossed the Arkansas river November 30 and arrived at the Kiamichi river near Fort Towson on December 16 and 17.[5] The second party of 629 Conchas under Lieutenant Van Horne, having also the horses of the emigrants, crossed the river on December 1, and with an increase of nineteen stragglers picked up on the way, reached Lieutenant Stephenson's place of issue near Fort Towson December 18.[6] The third contingent of 600 Chickasawhay and Six Towns traveled under the leadership of Joel Nail, the rival of Nita-kechi, conducted by Lieutenant Simonton.

Further accounts of this party after leaving Little Rock were recorded by Lieutenant Simonton. Frequent entries are made of additions from time to time of Indians from Folsom's detachment numbering from a dozen to fifty, who had become lost in the Mississippi swamps, or had been obliged from sickness to drop out along the way. Some of the nights were very cold and much difficulty was encountered in getting the half-naked Indians to leave the fires in the mornings and resume their journey. They crossed the Ouàchita river on the fifth and the Little Missouri five days later. Accidents to the wagons and carts caused occasional delays. Rations were issued every other day.

On the twelfth "*sent the party on with Maj. Summerville and returned with the Interpreter on yesterday's route to look for the Indians and cart that was missing. We ascertained that they had traveled but two miles and broke an axeltree. With the assistance of the Interpreter I got the stupid fellow's cart on its wheels once more, and started him to join the party. Nothing can exceed the tardiness with which an Indian performs any thing like manual labour. He forms no estimate of the value of time, and has no idea of what is to be gained by dispatch; he labors therefore only when necessity compels him. Whoever finds himself in the situation of an Indian Agent must treat them with paternal care. They look upon the Agents as the guardians of their wants, and expect assistance from them in the most trifling instances. So perfectly inefficient are they, that on one occasion my assistant Mr. Montgomery and myself were obliged to get off our horses and put a man into a cart, who was in the last*

4 Document, I, 401, 771. Nitakechi seems to have joined this party after it started west.

5 Ibid., 771, 405; Arkansas Gazette, December 5, 1832, p. 3, col. 2.

6 Document, I, 919; Van Horne to Gibson, December 18, 1832, OIA.

stages of the cholera, although there were more than fifty of his own people standing by. This was not the effect of the want of humanity, but a sheer want of energy. Having received assistance once, they would not bury their own dead afterward without asking help."

The party passed the Saline creek on the thirteenth and at a water-mill on Mine creek purchased meal for the teamsters. The Indians usually crushed their corn in holes they cut in logs along the road in lieu of the wooden mortar used at their homes. The next day they stopped at the salt works on the second Saline creek and issued provisions. On the fifteenth they crossed the Cossatot creek, passed through the Cossatot swamp, and began ferrying the Indians across the Little river. The service of the ferryman was very indifferent and the emigrants were not all crossed so that they could take up the march again until the seventeenth. The morning of that day they crossed the Choctaw line and rejoiced that they had left behind them "the dreary pine region through which we have traveled so many days past." After thirteen miles they went into camp and the next morning reached the home of Chief David Folsom, where some of Simonton's party remained. On the nineteenth they made fifteen miles and camped at Water Hole Prairie, sixteen miles from Fort Towson. Here they found encamped under their captains the advance contingents, which had been discharged the day before by Lieutenant Van Horne. Simonton there discharged his party and ended his responsibilities.[7]

About six thousand Choctaw Indians had been removed by the government, it was reported February 23, 1833;[8] and about one thousand more from Leflore's district, who crossed the Mississippi river at Chicot and Helena, had emigrated themselves, the leaders intending to claim the commutation of ten dollars each in the West. Another party was made up by Peter P. Pitchlynn and Garland of Mushulatubbee's district, with about fifty, chiefly slaves they had purchased with the proceeds of the sale of the land given them by the terms of the treaty.

During the winter of 1832-33, about seventeen hundred emigrants had arrived and settled on the Sans Bois creek near the Choctaw Agency, and on the upper waters of the Poteau river, reported Lieutenant Rains January 12: ". . .Consequently, on the application of the

7 Simonton's Journal, OIA, "1832 Choctaw Emigration."
8 Document, I, 498.

Choctaw agent, there have been established three depots for provisioning them; one at Pheasant Bluff, five miles below the mouth of the Canadian River, on the Arkansas, one near the Choctaw Agency on the Arkansas, and the third on the Porteau, about twenty-eight miles beyond the agency. . . . Emigrant Choctaws are arriving in detached parties of twenty to a hundred almost daily."[9] A party of sixty persons under Mr. Lensicum[10] reached Choctaw Agency February 10, 1833; in the early part of April, three hundred more came to Fort Smith. By January 7, a total of 3,333 had reached the Red river settlements during the winter, and straggling parties continued to arrive throughout the year.

While emigration under government auspices was progressing a considerable number of Choctaw Indians who were dissatisfied with the treaty and the plans of the government, refused to go to the country intended for them, and emigrated into Texas; Col. Peter Ellis Bean of Texas complained that more than seven hundred Choctaw Indians had passed from Nachitoches in the United States into that province, in February 1833, and settled within twenty-five miles of Nacogdoches and numerous bodies of Creeks and other Indians were preparing to follow them.[11] This was held by the Texans to be a violation of treaty rights.[12]

In the autumn of 1833, the government advertised for proposals to furnish meat and grain for the issues to the immigrant Indians. The average bid was seven and a third cents a ration, and one of the bidders was the Choctaw, George W. Harkins, who had been in the country less than two years, and yet Captain Brown at Little Rock said, he "has sufficient corn and stock of his own raising to fill the contract."[13]

The settlers of Mushulatubbe's following on Arkansas river were not so happily situated. Many of those expatriates, dejected and oppressed by their enforced removal from their homes and by their strange surroundings, lived on the year's allowance provided by the

9 *Ibid.*, 839; a few Chickasaw had removed and located with the Choctaw near the agency (*ibid.*, I, 843).

10 *Ibid.*, 498.

11 Bean to Cass, February 27, 1833, OIA, "Mexico (Choctaw)."

12 *Niles' Weekly Register*, XII, 317. Two hundred Choctaw Indians arrived in Texas in 1831 and 1832, and located west of the Sabine river and the alcalde complained to General Leavenworth (Gaines to Leavenworth, August 28, 1832, AGO, OFD, 76 S 32). He said that 400 more were coming.

13 *Document*, I, 531.

treaty and made no effort to establish themselves or raise crops for their future sustenance.

The more provident Indians were settling down to support themselves, and many had crops of corn along Arkansas river, when, in the first week in June, 1833, there came one of the greatest floods in the history of that stream. The government corn cribs at the Agency were swept away, and the Indians were suffering for food before the agent could reach them to issue rations. He was obliged to borrow some of the army rations, and "This even[14] I had boated up the Poteau River to the high land, as on the usual route was a sheet of water nine miles in extent." It was July 11, a month after the flood was at its height, before relief came in the form of a boat-load of corn from the Creek Nation, which the agent was obliged to purchase at $2.50[15] a bushel to keep his charges from starving and this supply was limited.[16] The government storehouse stood in water to the eaves and would have been swept away but for 6,000 pounds of iron and a quantity of arms that weighted it down.[17] Armstrong said the high water mark would be visible for years, and the Indians would have to hunt for the places where their houses had stood.[18] "Nearly all the people who lived upon the river have been ruined. . . on the bottoms near several of the creeks every house has been washed away. . . all the Fork of the Canadian was inundated. At the latter place a large amount of stock of almost every kind, was washed away."[19] The banks of the Arkansas above

14 *Ibid.*, 845. The Arkansas river "reached a height unparallelled in the memory of the oldest inhabitants. The corn crops are all killed and. . . there has been almost a total destruction of cows and calves, beef cattle, hogs, etc... the inhabitants will be in a starving condition, for the rise of the water was too sudden for removal" (*ibid*).

15 In 1831 Roley McIntosh, chief of the Lower Creeks, and Samuel Hopwood, another Creek Indian, contracted to deliver two thousand bushels of corn at Fort Gibson at forty-two cents a bushel (Clark to Jesup, *Quartermaster General's Records*, "Hall of Records," Book 13, No. 25). The year after the flood, dealers were asking $3.75 a bushel to deliver corn to Camp Arbuckle at the mouth of the Cimarron river (Richard Coody to Quartermaster, Fort Gibson, October 1, 1834, *ibid.*, Book 15).

16 *Document*, IV, 660.

17 Armstrong to Herring, September 17, 1833, OIA, "Choctaw Agency."

18 *Ibid.*, November 8, 1833.

19 Letter from Arkansas Territory, June 25, 1833, in *Cherokee Phoenix* (New Echota, Georgia), p. 3, col. 1; Arbuckle to Jones, June 12, 1833, AGO, OFD, 117 A 33; *Arkansas Gazette*, June 10, 1833; *American State Papers*, "Military Affairs," VII, 980; *Memoirs of Narcissa Owen* (Washington, 1907), 44; Grant Foreman,

the Choctaw Agency as far as Harreld's Bluff or Swallow Rock, after the flood waters receded, were "covered with mud, quicksand, and the carcasses of animals destroyed by the water."[20]

Much sickness followed the flood. *"Not a family but more or less sick; the Choctaws dying to an alarming extent. . . Near the agency there are 3,000 Indians and within the hearing of a gun from this spot 100 have died within five weeks. . .*[21] *the mortality among these people since the beginning of fall as far as ascertained, amounts to one-fifth of the whole number. The cause of so many deaths probably arises from the change of climate, the overflow of the Arkansas River, and having no physician among them except their own doctors, who are conjurors and mountebanks."*[22]

Resistance to disease was weakened by the destitution and under-nourishment of these unfortunate people. Many of them who depended on the year's subsistence provided by their treaty, neglected to plant crops for various reasons. Floods and sickness, unhappiness and discontent over their removal, bitter factional and political feuds and jealousies growing out of the treaty, inability so soon to readjust themselves to their new environment, and dependence on the government at the time for subsistence, had resulted in no provision for the future when the year's allowance of rations had expired. They were in a pitiable state. To keep from starving, they were begging for food and sacrificing their little annuity for one-sixth of its value to those ready to take advantage of their helpless condition. They were even reduced to eating the flesh of animals found dead in the woods and on the wayside.

Lieutenant Rains proposed to give them some of his pork, for ". . .though these people have refused it in their rations once, they

---

Pioneer Days in the Early Southwest, 21; Journal of Rev. W. F. Vaill, May 17, 1833 (manuscript), Missionary Records, *ibid.*, Vol. 73. No greater flood in the present Oklahoma has since been recorded and in the lower reaches of the Arkansas river it is believed to have been exceeded only in the year 1928.

20 *Document*, I, 845. The village of Van Buren, Arkansas was also flooded.

21 Armstrong to Herring, September 20, 1833, OIA, "Choctaw Agency." "One hundred died last month from various deseases" (Rains to Gibson, September 12, 1833, *Document*, I, 849.)

22 Rains to Gibson, November 4, 1833, *ibid.*, 851. The cholera continued through 1833. Eleven privates at Fort Gibson and thirteen passengers on one trip of the steamboat *Reindeer* to the post died from it (*Arkansas Gazette*, August 14, 1833).

would doubtless be glad to get it; for this is not putrid nor spoiled, except by age and salt, and gladly would they receive provisions of any kind to relieve their present necessities;"[23] and in April, 1833, he was happy to inform General Gibson that at last the Indians had been obliged to accept fifty barrels of his bad pork.[24] Destitution among this class was aggravated by recent arrivals during the winter of 1833 and 1834 who came too late to receive the aid of the government on their migration and reached their new home in a starving condition.

In February 1834, Armstrong requested from Colonel Arbuckle a loan of 500 bushels of corn to relieve their distress. "The situation of these people" said Armstrong to Arbuckle, "is worse than I really thought when I saw you. . . the women and children, many of them according to what they say, and from appearances have been from 4 to 6 days without any thing to eat; anything. Some of them have acorn meal and eat that. Lieut. Rains has a quantity of damaged Pork that he is issuing to them."[25]

The Indians remaining in the East were in a destitute condition in the summer of 1833; those of the Southern district, in full council on September 18, 1833, through their head men announced their unalterable intention not to remove to the West; the band of Captain Postoak determined likewise. Recent difficulties with the whites in which an Indian was killed was hoped to change their determination. October 15, the chiefs and warriors assembled, and "for several days it was thought that a party of 2,000 would emigrate. The misguided creatures decided otherwise, dispersed, leaving on my hands the supplies prepared for them."[26]

In August the agents estimated that in Leflore's district there remained about 4,000 Choctaw, some of whom wished to remain, and others proposed to go to Texas. In Nitakechi's district were 1,500, and in Mushulatubbe's about 700.[27]

William Armstrong and his assistants labored through September and October among the Indians in the old Nation, to break down their opposition to removal. A council was held in Leflore's district, where

23 *Document*, I, 842.
24 *Ibid.*, 843.
25 Armstrong to Arbuckle, February 25, 1834, OIA, "Choctaws West."
26 *Document*, I, 745, ff.
27 *Ibid.*, 412.

he made a favorable impression on some of the Indians present; then Armstrong with an interpreter went from house to house and en-deavored to start them to the rendezvous at the Choctaw Agency. In Nitakechi's district he held a council with two hundred warriors representing two thousand Indians; ". . .*and they positively refused to emigrate, and to avoid having any thing more to do with us, they actually have left their houses, and some of them have gone to Mobile;*[28] *and others through the state of Mississippi, picking out cotton in the different planta-tions. Every exertion to remove their prejudices, and to persuade them to emigrate, was urged by myself and Lieutenant Lane, but to no effect.*"[29]

By dint of much labor and patience, Armstrong had succeeded in securing the promise of about two thousand to depart with him, when a Choctaw Indian came from the West with the report that those who had removed the year before on their own resources were about to be paid by the government ten dollars each, which caused half of those already signed up to change their minds, and determine to go without government control so they could collect an equal amount on their arrival in the West. Armstrong said this information was sent by some traders among the emigrants in the West, who were desirous that the new arrivals should receive this money to be expended in trade with them. The prospect of a few thousand dollars in the hands of these Indians in this wilderness was a matter of tremendous importance to them, and to the traders. Here where furs and peltries were the usual medium of exchange, currency was little known. Few Indians had any money; that they were willing to live on the precarious fare gained by hunting on a journey of weeks to their new home for the privilege of possessing ten dollars each in actual currency indicates how highly they valued it.

"*The country is fast settling with the whites,*" wrote Armstrong, "*and whiskey very plenty through the country, and many of the whites who have groceries are detaining the Indians. I know that we have done all that could be done to get them off. I feel the disappointment, yet, I am confident that there will be three thousand remaining after we leave, and all those who will emigrate on their own resources.*" In Mushulatubbe's

28 Stragglers from the Six Towns and Chickasawhay Towns to the number of 200 were accustomed to living within the corporate limits of Mobile, "many families remaining through the summer to the annoyance of the citizens" (*ibid.*, 944).

29 *Ibid.*, 415.

district he succeeded in inducing nearly all to go except a party of two hundred headed by Little Leader, who were determined to remain.

With about one thousand emigrants, including many old, lame and blind, Captain Page set off from the Choctaw Agency October 12, and arrived at Memphis eighteen days later. Armstrong engaged two flatboats with which the wagons were ferried across the Mississippi. The steamboat *Thomas Yeatman* was employed to ferry the men and ponies across the river, and to convey to Rock Roe as many of the women and children as he could get aboard; she had a large keel-boat in tow, in which were loaded the Indian cariole and small wagons for Rock Roe, as it was impossible to pull them through the swamp to that place. Only about three hundred could be induced to board the steamboat which landed her passengers at Rock Roe a week later on November 9. The remainder, numbering about six hundred, were ferried across the river, and with the horses traveling by land arrived two or three days later.[30] Wagons and other provisions for three thousand Indians were waiting here; the 900 present were divided into two parties; they traveled together about twenty miles to Mrs. Black's, a sort of division point on the road, thence to within thirty miles of Little Rock, whence the Indians bound for the Red river continued to that village, and those for Fort Smith continued west and crossed the Arkansas river about seventy-five miles above. This latter division under John M. Millard, numbering 176 including three born on the route, reached the agency west of Fort Smith December 2, and the next day there were issued to them their arms, axes and other personal effects. The other division under Captain Page reached Fort Towson December 11.

Some of them must have deserted on the way, for when Page's party passed Little Rock it contained only 641, and the other contingent numbered only about 190; ". . .a meagre out it is for so much drumming," wrote Captain Brown.[31] A total of 3,215 had emigrated on their own resources since November, 1832,[32] and they and their conductors claimed the commutation of ten dollars each. On the eighth of the month, F. W. Armstrong completed the payment to the

30   *Ibid.*, 812. The 900 emigrants finished crossing the Mississippi river November 1 (Phillips to Gibson, November 2, 1833, OIA).

31   *Document*, I, 540.

32   *Ibid.*, 539.

commutation Indian on the Arkansas river, except those who were off hunting. The same class were paid at the Mountain Fork depot on the seventeenth and at Fort Towson on the nineteenth.[33]

On November 22, 1833, General Gibson promulgated the order of the secretary of war that no more Choctaw could be removed under the terms of the treaty which allowed three years for that purpose, and he discharged the large force of agents and employes in charge of the removal.[34]

A party of Choctaw Indians including many old and infirm persons was removed by S. T. Cross in 1838. They left their rendezvous in Mississippi on March 23 and arrived at Natchez the seventeenth of the next month; they continued up to Vicksburg, but as there was too much water in the swamps west of the Mississippi river to bring the horses through by land, the Indians with their live stock were carried by water. On the steamboat *Erin* they passed Little Rock May 8, and four days later, 177 in number, they were landed at the Choctaw Landing five miles above Fort Coffee and two from the Choctaw Agency. "*The party did not number as many as was anticipated, owing to several causes; some were prevented by the hands of their remorseless creditors, others by sickness and high water so they could not get in in time, and the greatest evil of all is the great influence exercised over the Indians to pursuade them from moving by those swarms of speculators who are trading on their claims to land under the 14th article of the treaty.*"[35]

There were about 7,000 Choctaw Indians remaining in Mississippi under the provision of their treaty permitting them to become citizens of that State. During the Creek disturbance in 1836 the white people of Alabama and Mississippi demanded that the Choctaw be removed so they would not become involved in the disorders; orders were given to organize them for removal, but nothing was done about it. The laws and environments of those states, intrusion of whites and introduction of whisky among them, were bringing the Indians every year into a

33 *Ibid.*, 425, ff.

34 *Ibid.*, 324.

35 Cross to Harris, May 23, and July 18, 1838, OIA, "Choctaw Emigration," C 688, 743, 744, 765, 805. These Indians were removed under the terms of an act of Congress of July 2, 1836.

more demoralized and destitute condition, and the government made several abortive efforts to get them away. The secretary of war made a contract March 3, 1843 with Alexander Anderson to remove them by water from Vicksburg to Fort Coffee, but the Indians refused to go on boats and the contract was cancelled. Another attempt was made September 4, 1844, with Anderson, Cobb, Forester, and Pickens. But the Indians still refused to remove until they could receive the script for their land, to which they were entitled from the government. The negligence of the government officials in failing to provide this script on time entailed considerable delay and loss to the Indians and to the contractors.[36] Others refused to leave without their oxen and horses and only 550 removed that year.[37]

In April, 1845, emigration was renewed when 1,280 Choctaw Indians from Mississippi joined their brothers in the Indian Territory; and the next year a thousand more came[38] who were peculiarly fortunate in their condition and were not at all like the destitute members of the tribe. Many years before, one of their number named Toblee Chubbee became converted to the Christian religion and exerted all the influence of a man of strong character to the uplift of his people. He converted them to Christianity, induced them to live sober, industrious lives, to abandon the habits of the Indians and to live like the better class of white people. For the most part they had comfortable homes and it was with difficulty they were induced to emigrate; in fact they would not consider moving until they had seen some of their western brothers and heard their accounts of schools, churches, and other improvements in the West.[39] When they did go, they not only

36 U. S. House Document No. 107, Twenty-eighth Congress, second session. White speculators exercised their influence over the Indians and agents to require the script to be delivered before the departure of the emigrants who were induced to part with it for a fraction of its value (Report of Commissioner of Indian Affairs for 1847).

37 Report of Commissioner of Indian Affairs (U. S. Executive Document No. 2, p. 571, Thirty-second Congress, first session).

38 Said to have been 1786 in number (Report of Commissioner of Indian Affairs for 1846; see also his report for 1851, p. 571).

39 When Superintendent Armstrong went to Mississippi to urge the emigration of the Choctaw remaining there, he took with him a delegation from that tribe living west of the Mississippi river, to present the inducements of life in their new home. Among them was the doughty old chief Nitakechi of Pushmataha district,

had more property, but were altogether superior in appearance to any other Indians in Mississippi. Unfortunately the change was not at first a happy one, for they suffered much from disease and many of them died in their new environment. In 1847 a total of 1,623 emigrated in eight parties and several hundred came yearly for the next few years. In the summer of 1849 a party of Choctaw emigrants were landed at Fort Coffee; they had contracted cholera and thirty of them died there.[40]

Near the end of the century when the Commission to the Five Civilized Tribes was engaged in alloting the lands of the Indians in severalty to the members of the tribes, the remainder of the Choctaw Indians still in Mississippi were invited to remove to the West, present themselves for identification and enrollment and apply for allotments of land. Applications were made for more than 24,634 persons the majority of whom possessed a large proportion of white blood; of these only 1,445 were enrolled and added to the tribe in the Indian Territory.[41]

---

who contracted pleurisy from which he died November 22, 1845, in Lauderdale county, Mississippi (*Arkansas Intelligencer*, December 27, 1845, p. 2, col. 1).

Nitakechi was a nephew of Pushmataha. He first rose into prominence about 1804 at a great battle between the Creeks and Choctaw; he served in the Creek war under General Jackson. After Pushmataha's death in 1824, Oklahoma, also said to be his nephew, became mingo of the district, but on account of his dissipation he was soon deposed and Nitakechi was elected chief in his stead. Nitakechi was a brave noble-minded Indian, upright in his intercourse with every one with whom he came in contact (Halbert to Draper, *ibid.*).

40 *Fort Smith (Arkansas) Herald*, July 4, 1849, p. 2, col. 1. Shuk-ha-nat-cha with eighty-two men, 116 women, and 162 children arrived at Fort Coffee on December 27, 1846. Punnubbee or Jim's party of Six Towns reached the Choctaw line below Fort Towson on April 22, 1847; the party included sixty-one men, ninety women and 191 children. Baptist's party of 123 Bay Indians reached the same locality May 4; the Big Black River band of 110 arrived by boat at Fort Coffee on June 10. Hacubbee's band landed there two weeks later. Another party of 25 Bay Indians from near Mobile arrived at the agency on July 14, 1847 (OIA, Muster Rolls).

In the early part of February, 1850, three parties of Choctaw Indians were brought up the Arkansas river on the steamboats *Choctaw*, *Phillip Pennywit*, and the *Dispatch*; eighteen died from the cholera on the latter boat between Little Rock and Fort Coffee. Within two weeks after they landed at Fort Coffee forty-three had died among a total of 160 emigrants (*Fort Smith Herald*, February 16 and March 2, 1850, p. 2, col. 1).

41 Reports of the Commission to the Five Civilized Tribes from 1899 to 1905.

BOOK TWO / Creek Removal

WHEN the president and Secretary Eaton planned their conference with the Indians directly after the signing of the Indian Removal Bill, the secretary sent word to the Creeks[1] that a crisis in their affairs wa s at hand; that the removal of small parties of emigrants to the West would cease until an opportunity could be afforded to ascertain the desire of the whole tribe; and advised them to send a delegation to Nashville to meet the president. But the Creeks and Cherokees were not ready to treat and did not appear.

Eneah Micco, principal chief, and other chiefs of the Lower Creeks on January 7, 1831, commissioned Tukabahchee Hadjo and Octe Archee Emathla with Paddy Carr and Thomas Carr as interpreters and Maj. John H. Brodnax as special agent, to proceed to Washington[2] where the next month and again in April they addressed memorials to the secretary of war, protesting against the operation of the laws of Alabama over them and the settling of white people on their lands, which resulted in frequent clashes between the men of the two races.[3] ". . .*Murders have already taken place, both by the reds and whites. We have caused the red men to be brought to justice, the whites go unpunished. We are weak and our words and oaths[4] go for naught; justice we*

---

1 *Document*, II, 6.

2 *Ibid.*, 411.

3 The year before, in February, 1830, the Creek chief Tuskineah stopped a United States mail stage and declared it should not pass through the Creek Nation. He was arrested by soldiers (*National Intelligencer*, March 8, 1830, p. 3, col. 4), and a thousand Indians gathered and would have released him, but he ordered them not to interfere. He was then taken to Mobile (*ibid.*, March 10, 1830, p. 3, col. 2).

4 Alabama had enacted a law prohibiting the word of an Indian from being received in court against that of a white man.

*dont expect, nor can we get. We may expect murders to be more fre-
quent. . . They bring spirits among us for the purpose of practicing
frauds; they daily rob us of our property; they bring white officers among
us, and take our property from us for debts that were never contracted. . .
We are made subject to laws we have no means of comprehending; we
never know when we are doing right."*

They told the secretary that they could not agree to remove to the
West. ". . .our aged fathers and mothers beseech us to remain upon
the land that gave us birth, where the bones of their kindred are
buried, so that when they die they may mingle their ashes together."[5]
Another objection to removal they said, was the report from their
tribesmen in the West of the unhealthfulness of the country and the
great number of deaths occurring among them.[6] Eaton assured the
Indians that the president could do nothing to prevent oppression by
the laws of Alabama, and that their only hope for relief lay in removal
to the west of the Mississippi river.

The poorer Indians were destitute and starving[7] and Eneah Micco
and other Creeks appealed to Cass for relief. The secretary again wrote

---

5   Eneah Micco and others to secretary of war, April 8, 1831, OIA, "Creek
Emigration;" *Document*, II, 424.

6   These reports were true; and yet while the government should have been,
and doubtless was in possession of this information, Secretary Eaton several weeks
before blandly denied it to a delegation of Creeks (*ibid.*, 290). A considerable number
of homesick immigrant Creeks abandoned the western country and returned to their
old homes bearing these reports and other discouraging accounts of conditions there
(*ibid.*, 933).

7   *Ibid.*, 305. "To see a whole people destitute of food—the incessant cry of
the emaciated creatures being *bread! bread!* is beyond description distressing. The
existence of many of the Indians is prolonged by eating roots and the bark of trees.
The berries of the Indian or China tree of last year's growth were ate by them as
long as they lasted—nothing that can afford nourishment is rejected however offensive it may be. . . but few of them on the borders of the state have planted
corn, because they had none to plant" (*Milledgeville Recorder* quoted in *Niles'
Weekly Register*, July 16, 1831, XL, 344). "They beg their food from door to door. . .
it is really painful to me to see the wretched creatures wandering about the streets,
haggard and naked" (Letter from Columbus, Georgia, in *Arkansas Advocate*, August
3, 1831, p. 1, col. 5). Governor Gilmer made a similar report to the president on
May 31: the Indians were "absolutely starving or subsisting upon the bark of
trees" (*Document*, II, 742). Their condition did not arouse the compassion of all
the whites however; a petition was sent by inhabitants of Mobile county to
their representative in the Legislature "praying the passage of a law to authorize

in November[8] reiterating that the president could not prevent the operation of the laws of Alabama over them, and urged them to agree to remove to the West, which he pictured as a happy home awaiting them. The favorite argument of government officials from the president down, was the impotency of the government to function where its power was invoked to protect the Indians from oppression by the whites. When appealed to by these unhappy people to keep the solemn promises to protect them and their lands against the whites,[9] promises based on valuable considerations given by the Indians, made by a powerful government to a weak and dependent people, time after time the disgraceful and humiliating response was a disclaimer of the power and intention to keep those promises. Occasionally the fraud was cloaked by a specious appearance of action; but usually the administration frankly defaulted in its solemn engagements.

Eneah Micco the resolute chief of the Lower Towns[10] and some of his head men addressed another memorial to John Crowell, the Creek agent, December 13, sending a list of the white intruders in their country. 1,500 whites including horsethieves and other criminals had squatted in the Creek country, and a large number of them were actively engaged in marking "out the situations they design occupying, by blazing and cutting initials of their names on the trees" around the homes of the Indians. "We expect to be driven from our homes. . . Yesterday in your hearing we were notified by a white man from Georgia that he had located himself in our country, and, should any

---

Justices of the Peace etc. to seize any meat found in the possession of Indians who follow hunting for a livelihood." This heartless proposal was soundly condemned in a sympathetic editorial that cited the long friendship of the southern Indians for the whites (*Mobile Commercial Register*, December 11, 1830, p. 4, col. 1).

8 *Document*, II, 365.

9 The year before, the grand jury of Pike county, Alabama, returned an indictment against Maj. Philip Wager, in command at Fort Mitchell, because in the discharge of his duties, he had issued a proclamation warning all white persons not having permits or Indians wives to remove from the Creek country within fifteen days, ". . .by which fear and confusion among the white settlers has been created, operating materially to their injury" (*Niles' Weekly Register*, May 8, 1830).

10 Eneah Micco was principal chief of the Lower Towns and Tuskeneah Thlocco of the Upper Creeks (*Document*, III, 469), meaning respectively the Fat King and the Big Fellow (*ibid.*, IV, 159).

thing of his be misplaced or interfered with, he should prosecute us under the law of Alabama."[11]

Another delegation was sent to Washington in December to intercede with the president and Congress for relief from oppression by the whites and the laws of Alabama recently enacted by the legislature, and to solicit a performance by the government of the provisions of their treaties. When the secretary of war refused to discuss anything with them except removal from their homes they told him they would have to appeal to Congress for relief.

At a conference held in the Creek Nation near Columbus in February[12] an additional number of chiefs was sent to join those in Washington with instruction to enter into some arrangement with the government relative to their present situation.[13] Accompanied by Crowell, the delegation departed March 1, and reached Washington a few weeks later.[14] They repeated their grievances to the secretary of war and received in reply his proposals for removal from their homes. They told the secretary *"We have made many treaties with the United States, at all times with a belief that the one making to be the last; but from the great assurance given us for protection, and the frequent solicitations of our great father, we have frequently given up large tracts of our country for a mere song; and we are now called on for the remnant of our land, and for us to remove beyond the Mississippi."*[15]

/ The delegates returned to Brown's hotel where for several days they considered the terms offered them by the secretary. Finally on the

11 *Ibid.*, II, 709. To add to their misery, small pox had broken out among them; Dr. W. L. Wharton, assistant surgeon at Fort Mitchell with an assistant was sent out in an effort to check the ravages of the disease, and from July 21, to December 5, 1831, vaccinated 7,126 Indians at the fort and in more than twenty Indian towns (Wharton to Crowell, December 5, 1831, OIA, "Creek Agency"; Crowell to Cass, December 8, 1831, *ibid.*; Wharton to Cass, January 1, 1832, *ibid.*).

12 *Document*, III, 220.

13 *Ibid.*, 225.

14 *The Democrat* (Huntsville, Alabama), March 22, 1832, p. 3, col. 4. The members of the delegation were Opothleyaholo, Tukabahchee Hadjo, Tukabahchee Micco, Benjamin Marshall, Effi Emathla, Tustenuc Micco, Billy McGilvery, and Thomas Carr.

15 *Document*, III, 259, 267, 275. The Creeks were the acknowledged owners of 5,200,000 acres of land in the State of Alabama (*U. S. House Document No. 452,* Twenty-first Congress, second session).

twenty-fourth of March, 1832, a treaty[16] was entered into by which the Creeks ceded to the United States all their lands east of the Mississippi river except their individual selections which they were to occupy for five years unless sooner sold by them; ninety principal chiefs were to have a section of land each, and every head of a family one-half section for which each would have a deed at the end of five years; the selections were to be made so as to include the improvements of the Indians. Twenty sections were to be selected for orphan children, and retained or sold for their benefit as the president should direct. Indians could sell their selections subject to approval by the president.

All intruders were to be removed from the Indian reserves for five years or until they were sold. The United States was to pay the expense of removal of the Indians to the West as fast as they were ready to emigrate, and subsist them for one year after they arrived there; but the Indians were free to emigrate or to remain on their land as they should elect. On removal each warrior was to be given a rifle, moulds, wiper, and ammunition, and each family a blanket. The Creek country west of the Mississippi river was to be solemnly guaranteed to the Creek Indians, "*nor shall any state or Territory ever have a right to pass laws for the government of such Indians, but they shall be allowed to govern themselves, so far as may be compatible with the general jurisdiction which Congress may think proper to exercise over them. And the United States will also defend them from the unjust hostilities of other Indians,*" and cause a patent or grant to be executed to the Creek tribe for their land.

Pursuant to the terms of the treaty a census of the tribe was taken. Benjamin S. Parsons completed the census of the Upper Towns, May 1, 1833; he showed a total of 14,142 members of that part of the tribe, including 445 negro slaves. The census of the Lower Towns was certified by Thomas J. Abbott May 13, 1833, by which he accounted for 8,552 members including 457 negro slaves.[17]

The census showed 6,557 heads of families, each entitled to reserve and at his option to sell a half section of land; these with other reserves for chiefs and orphans provided by the treaty, brought the amount so to be reserved to 2,187,200 acres, out of their total holdings of

16   Charles J. Kappler, *Laws and Treaties*, II, 247.
17   *Document*, IV, 239 to 294.

5,200,000 acres. These lands were to be surveyed by the end of the year 1833, so that the Indians could designate their selections, usually containing their homes, and have them entered by legal descriptions upon a record by a commissioner appointed for the purpose. After this was done it was assumed by the treaty, the Indians would be ready if they desired, to sell their selections in an orderly manner, and certifying agents would witness the execution and delivery of the deeds made by the Indians, the payment of the considerations, and then certify the deeds to the president for approval. As soon as the surveys were completed certifying agents were appointed in November, 1833 for this purpose.

Events following the execution of the treaty do not warrant a belief that the white contracting parties or the influences that controlled them were concerned with an honest performance of its terms for the protection of the Indians. If the government had deliberately sought to accomplish the complete ruin and demoralization of the Creeks, a more vicious measure could hardly have been devised than the provision of the treaty permitting them to sell their selections under the influence that existed, accompanied by the failure of the federal government to afford the Indians the protection promised in the treaty. It was said that the secretary of war had tried to prevent the incorporation of this provision, but other influences prevailed against his judgment.

As soon as the treaty was executed and before measures were taken to safeguard the Indians, a new flood of whites poured into their country to prey on them. The treaty promised $100,000 to pay the debts of the tribe. Immediately the country was overrun by white traders intent on securing that fund. Some brought merchandise, but more had whisky to sell. ". . .and a large business is going on as I am informed on credit, and the minds of the Indians are poisoned with whisky; and they (the Indians) are every day more and more embarrassed by debts, many of which debts will, I fear, be ante-dated, and, made by chiefs who are interested, to assume the character of claims against the nation."[18]

If the government had kept the treaty pledge that the white intruders would be removed from the Indian land, the situation would not have been so desperate; but the instant their removal was threatened,

18 Parsons to Cass, October 12, 1832, ibid., III, 483.

vociferous protests went up from the Alabamans, and the government supinely desisted. Having induced the Creeks to enter into the much desired treaty, the government agents gave themselves little concern for the promises made to the Indians. Their outstanding grievance—the presence of white intruders on their lands—the government had particularly bound itself in the treaty to correct. Yet not only was nothing done about it, but the situation was permitted to become much worse.

The next month after the treaty was made, the secretary of war directed Robert L. Crawford, United States marshal for the southern district of Alabama, to remove the intruders from the land of the Creeks. The failure to accomplish anything under this order is easily understood from its reading and the qualification that ". . .It is the President's desire, that this. . . be executed with as much regard to the feelings and situation of the persons, whose cases are embraced by it, as possible." As if that did not sufficiently emasculate the order of removal the secretary added: "In the execution of this delicate trust, I recommend to you to be as conciliatory as may be compatible with the object to be obtained." And further to save the feelings of these lawless intruders, Cass added in another paragraph: "Apply force only when absolutely necessary, and then only after having fully explained to the parties their own duties, the rights of the Indians, the obligations of the Government, and the instructions you have received."[19] Obviously no adequate results were expected and of course none followed.

In the following September the Creeks called a council at Wetumpka and on the twenty-seventh drafted a memorial to the secretary of war advising him that "*Instead of our situation being relieved as was anticipated, we are distressed in a ten fold manner—we are surrounded by the whites with their fields and fences, our lives are in jeopardy, we are daily threatened. . . We are prevented from building new houses, or clearing new fields—We have for the last six months lived in fear, yet we have borne it with patience, believing our father, the President, would comply on his part with what he had pledged himself to do.*"[20]

The month before, the government had made a feeble gesture through the United States marshal, who threatened to remove some

19 *Document*, II, 806.
20 *Ibid.*, III, 464.

intruders and actually did remove a few in Pike county; but as soon as the marshal had left the whites returned in force and ran the Indians away from their farms restored to them by the marshal. They were accompanied by the sheriff of the county who, armed with writs for the marshal and military officers with him, was prepared to defy the authority of the federal government.[21] Some of these intruders who had been removed by the marshal brought in the state courts actions of trespass against the Indians reinstated in their homes.[22]

A particularly attractive location on the west bank of the Chatta-hoochie river about forty-five miles below Fort Mitchell, was that occupied by a town of the Eufaula Creeks, known as Ola Ufala. These Indians were driven off, their houses burned, and in their stead the whites built a small village of log houses which the legislature in 1831 incorporated under the name of Irwinton.[23] The marshal reported in August that he found eighteen intruders on some choice land near this town. *"They had not only taken the Indians' land from them, and burnt and destroyed their houses and corn, but used violence to their persons. The Indians had fled from forty to fifty miles. Those persons who had been guilty of intrusion were ordered to leave the country; from threats and menaces used by them, I ordered a detachment of troops from Fort Mitchell, for the purpose of facilitating business, and my own security."*[24] The members of another little village who were driven from their homes, set out for the Cherokee Nation; ". . .After traveling a few miles,

21 Ibid., 410, 413.

22 Ibid., II, 932; III, 517.

23 Ibid., III, 453, 528, 561. The site of Irwinton is now occupied by Eufaula, Alabama.

24 Ibid., 410, 413, 440. The whites organized and armed a body of 140 or 150 and defied the marshal. Then the commandant at Fort Mitchell sent Captain Page with thirty-five men prepared for battle and demanded the surrender of the fortress and evacuation by sunrise. Consternation and alarm pervaded the village. It was a night of commotion and gloom. The morning came and found the town deserted and desolate. Some over-loaded wagons were stalled and the soldiers helped them along. Then the whites saw their devoted town fall a prey to the devouring flames. Thus terminated the storm, capture and burning of Irwinton. Short its existence, but *brilliant* its history. (Account from Columbus Georgia July 26 in *Arkansas Advocate* September 5, 1832, p. 2, col. 4.). These white intruders complained bitterly of this most just measure of retribution. This unhappy period of Indian history is treated in *Georgia and State Rights*, by Ulrich B. Phillips, American Historical Association, *Annual Report for 1901*, II.

they were stopped by a party of white men, who tied up and most inhumanly whipped some of them, and drove the whole party back."[25]

After driving them from their homes, the little corn fields of the Indians were raided, and this grain, their staff of life, was carried off by the whites while the Indians suffered from hunger and were even threatened with starvation. Crowell reported that most of the Indians were in the woods without the means of subsistence, hiding from the ferocity of the white intruders.[26]

Again the Indians met at Wetumpka December 20, and made another plaintive appeal to the secretary of war for a compliance with the promise of relief against the intruders. The futile gesture by which the marshal had removed a few intruders had been abandoned, the handful of troops withdrawn, and the whites were hilarious with their victory over the Indians and the federal officers. The Indians said: "We are without friends and surrounded by enemies. Our only alternative is protection from the United States. This is promised in the treaty; we claim it as a right."[27]

Enoch Parsons wrote to Cass, January 13, 1833[28] that the head chiefs were still opposed to going west; their influence prevented the common Indians from expressing a favorable opinion on the subject. "How the Indians are to subsist the present year, I cannot imagine. Some of them are sustaining themselves upon roots. They have, apparently, very little corn, and scarcely any stock. The game is gone, and what they are to do, God only knows. Nothing can preserve their property, or their existence, other than their immediate removal to the country designed for them."[29] He proposed to donate to the starving Indians thirty or forty barrels of spoiled flour at Fort Mitchell. He thought it would save the lives of many, and ameliorate the sufferings of others; "the Euchee people near the town, the women and children in particular, are most needy."

"Many desperate and unprincipled white men have, since the ratification of the treaty, entered our nation and have taken Indians wives, with

25 Document, IV, 148.
26 Ibid., III, 413, 485: ". . .They dare not return to their dwellings, being, like wild beasts hunted and driven from them."
27 Ibid., 565.
28 Ibid., IV, 14.
29 Ibid., 75.

the sole view of enjoying the privileges and securing to themselves the benefit guaranteed to our people in the treaty in the selection and ownership of reserves", wrote the chiefs to the secretary of war.[30]

As the white intruders had continued their aggressions with impunity and complaints continued to reach Washington, on March 14, 1833, nearly a year after the Indians had been promised relief, the office of Indian affairs at the direction of Mr. Cass, issued instructions to the marshal "to put an end to this lawless and disgraceful practice of intrusion."[31] Nothing was done under this order however and on June 3 the secretary himself directed the marshal to order the intruders off and to use the military to enforce his orders.[32] It was exactly a month later that deputy Marshal Austill reached Fort Mitchell to secure troops to remove the intruders. He reported[33] that there were three thousand white intruders, and that he would remove only such as the chiefs wished removed.

August 26, 1833 Mr. Cass wrote to Crawford: "*Mr. Austill has requested that instructions may be given to prevent the sale of whiskey upon the Creek lands, stating that the practice prevails to a great extent, and to the utter ruin of the Indians. However useful such a measure might be, it is not considered competent for the Executive to direct it. The only power vested in the President is to remove the intruders from the public lands. The State of Alabama has jurisdiction over that district of country, and her Legislature can only provide a remedy for this evil, and her courts of justice enforce it.*"[34]

Leonard Tarrant was appointed Creek agent to succeed Crowell; the bewildered Indians asked him[35] "how they are to seek redress when they have been beaten and abused by the whites, their property levied on for the debts of another (which, I am sorry to say, is frequently the case".) Though a federal officer, Tarrant was afraid to give advice to the distracted Indians and thus offend the people of Alabama.

Near West Point Austill was having a serious time in July in removing intruders, who were raising volunteers to resist the efforts of the

30 Ibid., III, 528.
31 Ibid., 612.
32 Ibid., 709.
33 Ibid., IV, 455.
34 Ibid., III, 758.
35 Ibid., IV, 457.

marshal and military. He was compelled to increase his force and threaten to take the intruders as prisoners to Mobile before they would yield.[36] Two weeks later Austill reported[37] that the condition of the Indians was most deplorable. Some of the white intruders he had not removed as they had a large number of claims against the Indians and threatened the latter that if they were removed they would sue every one without mercy. And as the agent knew they would be helpless in the state court of Alabama, where they could not be heard to defend themselves, he advised them to submit. Thus did the executive branch of the government decline to keep the promise made to the Indians less than a year before. Crawford, the marshal, protested against temporizing: ". . .Among those intruders were some of the most lawless and uncouth men I have ever seen; some of them refugees from the State of Georgia, and for whom rewards are offered."[38]

Intimidations continued; the Indians were in such fear of the vengeance of the intruders, and had such little confidence in the promises of the government that they asked that the former be not removed until their crops were gathered, if they would promise to pay for the use of their farms. *"Those who were driven off last season"* Austill wrote the secretary of war, *"had returned. . . and if they were put out, it would subject the Indians to greater difficulties than they are now in. They have compelled the Indians to give up their farms, and to consent to take rents; and although they are thus compelled into measures, there is no redress, for these people exercise the state laws over them to an alarming extent. The officers of the state have in some cases issued false precepts, and executed them upon the Indians. False accounts are made out; the Indians seized and put in jail, and compelled to surrender all they have, either their land claims or their property . . .how this species of fraud and villainy is to be obviated I am unable to say, unless the Indians leave the country. . . Certain men fleecing the Indians have obtained bonds for nearly all the valuable lands below here; and one half the Indians are not aware that it is for their lands, as many have already informed me. One case came before me, below: Several families were living on the same bluff, it being a desirable place to live, having fine water and lying convenient to rich river lands. Some Indians who lived there were driven off*

36 *Ibid.*, 469.
37 *Ibid.*, 486.
38 *Ibid.*, III, 454.

and their houses burned up; . . .and others. . . put a half breed upon the place to claim it, and for him to consent to their remaining there."[39]

39 *Ibid.,* IV, 487.

CHAPTER NINE / *An Emigrating Party in 1834*

IN THIS situation the secretary of war on May 2, 1833, commissioned Col. John J. Abert and Gen. Enoch Parsons to approach the Creeks with a view to making a new treaty, providing for their immediate removal to the West where they would be relieved from the wretched condition under which they lived in Alabama. They were instructed to discuss with the Indians removal under their own management with funds to be provided by the government. In Abert's reply to Cass he said of this proposal:

"They are incapable of such an effort and of the arrangements and foresight which it requires. Nor have they confidence in themselves to undertake it. They fear starvation on the route; and can it be otherwise, when many of them are nearly starving now, without the embarrassment of a long journey on their hands. A people who will sell their corn in the fall for twenty-five cents a bushel, and have to buy in the spring at a dollar, or dig roots to sustain life; a people who appear never to think of tomorrow, are not a people capable of husbanding the means, and anticipating the wants of a journey, with women, and children, of eight hundred miles. Every spot of good hunting ground, every storm, every trivial accident, will occasion days of delay; and join to these their listless, idle, lounging habits, their love of drink, which will keep them in its vicinity while they have a shilling to procure it, and what can be expected if the emigration is left to themselves? They need the unceasing exertions of a vigilant and intelligent agent, to urge them forward, and to supply their wants, to protect and encourage them.

"You cannot have an adequate idea of the deterioration which these Indians have undergone during the last two or three years, from a general state of comparative plenty to that of unqualified wretchedness and want.

"The free egress into the nation by the whites; encroachments upon their lands, even upon their cultivated fields; abuses of their person and

*property; hosts of traders, who, like locusts, have devoured their substance
and inundated their homes with whiskey, have destroyed what little disposition to cultivation the Indians may have once had. . . and the corn
crop of this season. . . will not feed more than a quarter of them. . .
Emigration is the only hope of self-preservation left to these people. They
are brow beat, and cowed, and imposed upon, and depressed with the
feeling that they have no adequate protection in the United States, and
no capacity of self-protection in themselves. They dare not enforce their
own laws to preserve order, for fear of the laws of the whites. In consequence, more murders of each other have been committed in the last six
months than for as many previous years; and the whites will not bring
the offender to justice, for he, like Iago, no matter which kills, sees in it
his gain."*[1]

The efforts of Abert resulted in a council of the Creeks on June 19.
Here it was proposed to the Creeks that they enter into a new treaty
providing for the sale by them of their land to the government for which
payment would be made in instalments so that the Indians would get
the full consideration for their land and thereby stop the swindling
and robbing of them by the white people. This excellent arrangement
might have been effective if the government had incorporated it in
the treaty of 1832, but the next year it was too late. The Indians were
so thoroughly cowed by the white people and so completely in their
control, that they were afraid to do what was for their best interest.
White men who held their contracts and bonds commanded the Creeks
to refuse the offer, and by their presence and intimidations controlled
the action of the Indians.

These whites had secured from the Indians who knew nothing of
the value of land, contracts for the sale of their selections, in most
cases for trifling considerations; for little or nothing, they had signed
contracts, and other papers they did not understand, or held the obligations of solvent purchasers which they surrendered for a trifle when
plied with liquor; bonds were taken from the Indians for title to be
made at the end of five years, for ten or twenty dollars in chattels for
which they had no use, and they gave receipts for several times the
amount.[2] They were oppressed by judgments for which they were not
liable; while the laws of the state prohibited an Indian from testifying

1 Document, IV, 423.
2 Ibid., 557, 570.

in court against a white man, with characteristic insincerity these same courts held that the contracts with the Indians for lands that had never been set apart to them were valid. Much of the time the Indians were in debt to the traders who were paid out of their annuities. In many cases the annuities were "paid, notwithstanding all the precautions of the officers. . . almost directly into the hands of the traders, sometimes without the formality of counting the specie of which they consist."[3] The council was continued in session for two weeks but the effort to secure another treaty finally was abandoned.

After the council broke up Abert and Parsons wrote to the secretary of war: ". . .*The abuses which these Indians suffer, under color of the law, in the way of damages, and of taxes for costs, equals, if it does not exceed the stories which we have heard in relation to their land sales, and are rapidly divesting them of their property, and reducing them to a state of abject poverty. Their helpless ignorance, their generally good character, (for they are a well disposed people), instead of establishing claims upon good feelings, seem rather to expose them to injuries. Their weaknesses receive no compassion, and their very helpless ignorance but renders them more liable to wrongs. We see no remedy to their condition but in emigrating west; and it would be better for them to abandon their lands for nothing (as they are now said to be doing) and to move, than to remain under their present circumstances.*"[4]

The feeble efforts of the federal government to keep its promises to the Indians provoked the increased hostility of the white people. A man named Hardiman Owen who had cruelly beaten the Indians, driven them from their lands and killed their hogs and horses, defied and threatened the marshal. When arrested in July, 1833, about twenty miles from Fort Mitchell, he promised to leave and was released. He then went into his house, mined it with gun powder, invited the marshal in and disappeared through the back door. The marshal was about to enter when he was stopped by the warning of an Indian, and

3 *U. S. House Document No. 2, p. 290,* Twenty-fourth Congress, first session.
4 *Document,* IV, 451. One Eli S. Shorter of Columbus, Georgia fought Abert's efforts to make a new treaty; he said in that matter he represented himself and others; for himself and Dr. John S. Scott jointly he had employed the latter who had purchased 171 reservations for which he had paid "an average of something over ten dollars each" the balance to be paid when the titles were perfected. Another man he repesented in the fight against the treaty was one Benjamin P. Tarver who had acquired 160 reservations (*ibid.,* 465).

in a few seconds the house was blown up. The soldiers pursued Owen, surrounded him and killed him when he attempted to shoot one of them.[5]

The killing of Owen created great excitement[6] and the governor of Alabama demanded that the federal government withdraw the marshal and commit the Indians to the tender mercies of the state courts for redress of their grievances; also claiming for the white people of the state title to most of the Creek land by virtue of the notoriously larcenous contracts which the Indians had been induced to sign.[7] In September Mr. Cass replied: "*Since the ratification of this treaty, repeated representations have been made to this department by the public agents, by respectable individuals, and by the Indians, that gross and wanton outrages have been committed upon the latter, by persons who have intruded upon the ceded lands. It has been stated that the houses of the Indians have been forcibly taken possession of, and sometimes burnt, and the owners driven into the woods; that their fields and improvements have been wrested from them and occupied by white persons; that aggravated injuries have been committed upon the persons of the Indians; and that their horses, cattle, hogs, and other property, have been forcibly taken from them. The appeals of the chiefs to the Government to carry into effect and to afford their people protection, have been repeated and forcible. They represent that their crops have been taken from them, and they look forward to a state of starvation, unless some decisive step is adopted in their favor. And, in addition to all this, the deputy marshal reports that there are four hundred persons selling whiskey to the Indians on the ceded lands.*" In conveying the president's rejection of the proposal, Cass mildly reminded the governor that "it would be vain to expect that the protection promised" by the federal government could be obtained in the State courts.[8]

5 *Ibid.*, 493.

6 *Ibid.*, 539.

7 Gayle to Cass, August 20, and October 2, 1833, *Alabama State Department of Archives and History*, "Executive Letter Book G" 131, 133. The Alabama legislature had laid off the Creek country into the counties of Benton, Talledega, Randolph, Coosa, Tallapoosa, Chambers, Russell, and Mason, and Governor Gayle proposed that the Indians look to the state courts in those counties for their remedies against white intruders on their lands.

8 *Document*, III, 765.

The grand jury of Russell county on October 14 returned indict-
ments against the soldier James Emmerson who was supposed to have
shot Owen, charging him with murder, and the other soldiers and the
officers and Jeremiah Austill the deputy marshal, as accessories.[9]
Austill was arrested, and an attachment was issued for Maj. James S.
McIntosh in command at Fort Mitchell who was cited for contempt
of court, because he would not deliver up the soldier under his command. Excitement increased and a clash between the militia of Alabama
and the marshal and the federal military force impended. The marshal
called on Major McIntosh at Fort Mitchell for a detachment of fifty
troops to accompany him to Pole Cat Springs where he proposed to
remove some intruders. McIntosh declined for the reason that he
feared the marshal's action would precipitate bloodshed, and there
was not enough ammunition at the garrison to enable the soldiers to
defend themselves against the citizens who were arming for combat.[10]

On October 31 the president employed Francis Scott Key to go to
Alabama, investigate the conditions in connection with the killing of
Owen and assist the United States district attorney in defending the
indicted officers and soldiers.[11] Key arrived in Alabama in the early
part of November and reported that the evils of the intruders were
caused by the weakness of the United States government in the face
of the aggressive action of the white people of Alabama. He said that
had the first orders for removal been backed up and rigidly enforced
the present situation would not have existed. Key explained to the
governor and the members of the legislature the government's recession
from its demands and the proposition that the most flagrant violators
of the rights of the Indians would be removed and others permitted to
remain, to which the state officials expressed their approval. The
speculators in Indian titles, he said, hoped to sustain the leases by
which they held Indian lands by force of the state laws. The dread of
the Indians of being sued in the courts in which they could not testify
and then taken to jail would make them submit to every oppression.
Land speculating companies in Columbus, he said, had bought up
between three and four thousand Indian reserves advancing in each
case about ten dollars. They relied on leases to put them in possession

9 Ibid., IV, 616 (copy of indictment).
10 Ibid., 622.
11 Ibid., III, 810.

until the time when they could demand a deed for a consideration based on fraudulent accounts that were run against them for whisky and other items calculated to deceive the Indians.

The condition of the Indians was deplorable Key wrote; most of them were almost starving, few of them had made any corn and nearly all had sold their land two or three times over for any trifle that had been offered them. "I met crowds of them going to Columbus with bundles of fodder on their heads to sell, and saw numbers of them in the streets there where they exchanged everything they carried for whiskey."[12]

Key reported on November 14 that the officials in the office of the Russel county district court refused to let him see the indictment against the government officers.[13] That the whites undoubtedly would have lynched the men and officers for the killing of Owen if they could have got possession of them. They declared that resistance to the federal authority was legal and justifiable, and that they were going to prosecute the officers and deputy marshal in the state court for murder. Key said it would be impossible to induce the Indians to send a delegation to Washington to treat for removal and sale of their land to the government as the speculators and their agents had the Indians completely in their power.

The state authorities proposed[14] that in consideration of permitting the whites to remain on the lands where they were the least obnoxious to the Indians, prosecution of the officers charged with killing Owen would be dropped. Key said there were ten thousand whites living in the Creek country. By December he had arrived at an understanding with the Alabama authorities by which the latter agreed to pass measures to help enforce the federal laws and prevent speculators from harrassing the Indians under the state laws in consideration of

12 Ibid., IV, 665.

13 Ibid., 701. Key said that a majority of the whites of Talladega county "are well disposed and treat the Indians with kindness." Nor were they all cruel in Chambers County where a meeting was "called by the factious and violent, and a lawyer from Columbus attended, and attempted to excite them by a speech. He was replied to and put down by an old gentleman. . . and no resolutions were passed" (ibid., IV, 704).

14 Ibid., 741.

concessions to be made by the government.[15] Key then returned to Washington by way of the Ohio river steamboats, and stage-coach.

All this turmoil, excitement, and bitterness had resulted from the premature and illegal activities of the whites. For it was not until November 1833 that the surveys were completed so that the individual Indian reserves could be designated, the certifying agents could begin their work and legal conveyances could be made. In the meantime some efforts had been made to induce the Indians to remove from Alabama. In January 1833, former governor George M. Troup of Georgia asked the secretary of war to appoint his cousin Chilly McIntosh an agent for the removal of the Creeks.[16] McIntosh and Benjamin Hawkins of the western Creeks were in the old Creek Nation in a pretended effort to adjust the differences between the two factions of the tribe. The eastern Creeks granted five sections of the twenty-five at their disposal under the treaty to the western Creeks.[17] This grant was made to bind a treaty of amity between the two factions by which they "mutually pledged themselves to the observance of a lasting friendship."[18]

The western Creeks gave McIntosh and Robert Tiger a power of attorney to sell the five sections[19] but later became suspicious of McIntosh and revoked the authority.[20] McIntosh employed every artifice to induce the Creeks to enroll for removal but he was mainly interested in securing from them powers of attorney authorizing a swindling land company of Columbus, Georgia, with which he was associated, to dispose of their lands; when this was discovered his commission was rescinded on May 4, 1833.[21] The result of the efforts of McIntosh was about sixty emigrants all told, forty of whom were brought to Fort Gibson in the early part of September and twenty by Benjamin Hawkins a few months earlier.[22]

The necessity of emigration was everywhere obvious. Benjamin Marshall and McIntosh reported to Colonel Abert that the starving

15 Ibid., 766.
16 Ibid., III, 575.
17 Ibid., 680.
18 Ibid., IV, 57, 161.
19 Ibid., 471.
20 Ibid., 471, 473, 627.
21 Ibid., III, 691, 703; IV, 426.
22 Ibid., IV, 400, 541.

Indians were worked upon and furnished whisky by the whites, and everything they had, even the corn issued to them, was carried to the grog shop. In September the heads of the families of "Sche-se-ho-ga" Town with a total population of 236, received permission from the Chickasaw Indians, to remove to their nation. They .petitioned the government for assistance in making the change as they were heavily involved in debt to white people where they were living. They said they desired to join the Creeks living in the Chickasaw Nation, who were their family connections, so that they could all travel together, when the emigration began.[23]

In November Abert wrote to the secretary of war that all those who had sold "*are ready to move west as soon as the sales are approved, and the balances due paid them. The difficulties to which they have been exposed by intruders, and by the laws of Alabama, have had no small share in promoting this spirit. They linger, however, about their homes with great fondness, and arrest any disposition to move on the slightest evidence of adequate protection where they are. A deputation had been nominated to visit the Arkansas, and select a place for those disposed to emigrate. It was not sent, however, as the marshal appeared to move off intruders at the time it was ready to depart, which was considered and acted upon as evidence that they might remain unmolested where they were.*"[24]

In the summer of 1834 extensive arrangements were made by the commissary general of subsistence for the removal of the Creeks from Alabama. A superintendent and two assistant agents were appointed from among the citizens of that state and Capt. John Page, an experienced disbursing officer was associated with them.[25] The government officials were expecting a large number of Creeks to come forward for emigration, but their hopes were not well founded as the Indians refused to go with the Alabamans. Only 630 Creeks enrolled for removal under the humane Captain Page, and they began their march in December. They traveled by way of Tuscaloosa, the capital of the State.[26] These Indians were poor and almost destitute of clothing, and

23   Ibid., 546.
24   Ibid., 663.
25   *U. S. House Document No. 2*, Twenty-fourth Congress, first session.
26   While waiting at the Capital, the chief Ufala Hadjo, a man of the most dignified appearance, with some of his people visited the gallery of the House; here he made an address to the members on the subject of the removal of his people to

the winter was unusually severe.[27] It rained, snowed, and froze nearly every day; they began the day's journey at four o'clock in the morning and traveled until night to make as much as six to ten miles.

The cold weather was "so severe on the little children and old persons and some of them *nearly naked* that they would perish if they were not attended to," wrote Captain Page from Columbus, Mississippi.[28] These pitiful children and sick people were compelled to lie on wet or frozen tents in the wagons, for there was not time to dry them after a night of rain or snow. "*I have to stop the wagons to take the children out and warm them and put them back again 6 or 7 times a day. I send ahead and have fires built for this purpose. I wrap them in tents and anything I can get hold of to keep them from freezing. . . Strict attention had to be paid to this or some must inevitably have perished.[29] Five or six in each wagon constantly crying in consequence of suffering with cold. I am sometimes at a stand to know how to get along under existing circumstances.*" Their distress wrung the heart of this compassionate officer who wrote again: "there was continued crying from morning to night with the children. . . I used to encourage them by saying that the weather would moderate in a few days and it would be warm, but it never happened during the whole trip."

When they reached Memphis the steamboat *Harry Hill* was engaged to convey the Creeks to Fort Gibson; but the boat was delayed several days by high winds on the Mississippi river, and two or three days by the ice on the Arkansas river. On the twenty-fourth, twenty days from Memphis, they arrived at Little Rock, where shallow water prevented further progress. Here the Indians were put ashore to join

---

the West (*Mobile Commercial Register and Patriot*, January 7, 1835, p. 1, col. 1). Ufala Hadjo later served the United States as interpreter and ambassador to the Seminole Indians during the war in Florida.

27 "These emigrants in going west so late in the season, it is understood, suffered many privations," reported Commissary General Gibson; but he solaced himself with the observation that "this office is perfectly satisfied that the able and intelligent army officer who conducted them did all that humanity could demand to alleviate their condition" (*U. S. House Document No. 2*, Twenty-fourth Congress, first session).

28 Page to Gibson, April 25, 1835, OIA, "Emigration."

29 *Ibid.*, January 6, 1835. During this time influenza was raging in Arkansas and numbers in the same family were dying from it.

another contingent in charge of their two hundred ponies.[30] Owing to the near-naked condition of most of them and the great number of sick in the party, they remained in camp for a week, during which time a number died. March 1 with a hint of spring in the air, the party with their few small wagons resumed their land journey.[31]

"*On the 9th March when we were about 150 miles from Fort Gibson, we had a very severe snow storm and the roads were impassable for all carriages of every description. Except those employed in the emigration I do not recollect of meeting anyone but two or three horse carts, and they gave it up when they struck the road that we came over, there was nothing but prying out wagons from morning to night.*" This wretched journey lasted three months and it was March 28, 1835, when Page delivered 469 survivors of his original party at the western Creek agency near Fort Gibson. Included among them was Sampson Grayson who had with him thirty-four slaves, besides twenty-three slaves belonging to "the Widow Stidham."

Most of this party settled around a leading man named Neahola about five miles west of the crossing of the Verdigris river. This was in the section settled five or six years before by the McIntosh Creeks who retired in advance of the newcomers and hastened to appropriate other choice lands higher up the Arkansas river, some of them locating in the vicinity of the present city of Tulsa. The improvements vacated by them were gratefully occupied by the members of Captain Page's party.[32]

30 *Arkansas Gazette*, February 22, 1835.
31 Brown to Gibson, March 1, 1835, OIA, "Creek Emigration."
32 Van Horne to Gibson, April 2, 1835, *ibid*. The next January Commissioner Armstrong directed Capt. R. A. McCabe, Creek agent, to rent from Chilly McIntosh his home in this settlement two or three miles west of the Verdigris river to be used by him as the Creek Agency in place of the location on the east bank of that stream (Armstrong to Superintendent of Indian Affairs, January 15, 1835, OIA).

CHAPTER TEN / *Frauds on the Creek Indians*

M ANY Creek heads of families died after the treaty of 1832, offering rich plunder to white vultures in Alabama and Georgia; the courts permitted white men to administer on the estates of these people and by devious means they secured for a trifle title to the half section of land to which the deceased was entitled, leaving nothing for his family or heirs. But these people soon evolved a simpler method for robbing the Indians of their lands.

Agents were appointed in November 1833, to witness the execution and delivery of deeds by the Indians, and the payment of the considerations, and then to certify them to the president for approval. The work of locating the Indians was completed in January 1834, and the certification of conveyances began.

The Indians knew nothing of the value of land or of business transactions; they spoke only their own language, and the temptation, to corrupt men to take advantage of their helpless condition was so alluring that almost from the first complaints of fraudulent practices were made. Reports of "manifold instances of fraud and injustices" were conveyed in March 1834, by the certifying agents, J. W. A. Sanford and Dr. Robert W. McHenry, but Abert in a private letter warned them of the confusion that would result if their charges reached Washington.[1]

Sanford then admitted his error and said: "I am now sensible of the *utter* futility of any attempt to prevent their occurrence, and agree with yourself that the proper redress is with our own tribunals."[2] In spite of their efforts to cover them up, information of these frauds did

1 Abert to Sanford, March 26, 1834, *Alabama State Department of Archives and History.*
2 *Ibid.*, Sanford to Abert, April 5, 1834.

reach Washington, but Secretary Cass comforted Sanford and other residents of Columbus with the assurance that the frauds "were clearly beyond your reach as they are beyond the reach of this office."[3]

As these reports reached Washington from time to time, the agents were cautioned to exercise greater vigilance to protect the Indians; but nothing adequate was directed or attempted. This infamous business was permitted to run along until it seemed well established that the swindlers had little to fear from the government. They then prepared for a drive that would yield a speedy and lucrative harvest. So bold had they become that there was fierce competition among the rival companies, and men engaged in this business said that as so many others were in it, each intended to have a share.

"*Artful schemes and devices gave impunity and success to bold bad men, whose profligate and wanton conduct not only extended their operations, but became utterly regardless of public observation and opinion, until at length, in the spring of 1835, every prudential restraint was set at defiance, and acts which should make men cover their faces and shun daylight, came to be the boast of these despoilers of Indian property.[4] . . .I have never seen corruption carried on to such proportions in all of my life before. A number of the land purchasers think it rather an honor than a dishonor to defraud the Indian out of his land.*"

In the neighboring town of Columbus, Georgia, a few score of enterprising citizens banded themselves into rival companies to plan and to carry into effect the most detestable and heartless frauds upon the Indians to be found in history. These men associated with them Luther Blake, a former Creek agent, and Paddie Carr, an intelligent educated half-breed Creek Indian.

They organized themselves and set out systematically to steal the land from the Indians; and by force of their numbers and influence in the country they were very successful. Their method was to "*drill or coach an Indian who had sold his land or never owned any, to represent another who was the holder of a reservation; he learned his name and that of his tribe and town where he lived, the situation of his dwelling, and of the town-square and council-house, and such other circumstances as the agent would be likely to inquire into, with the view of identifying the*

3   Ibid., Cass to Sanford, April 28, 1834.
4   Crawford to Poinsett, May 11, 1838, *U. S. House Document No. 452*, p. 10, Twenty-fifth Congress, second session.

reservee; and, thus prepared, he was presented before the agent, and, answering readily the usual questions, the officer was deceived, the contract certified, and the proprietor of the land defrauded. The wages of this combined iniquity were generally $5 or $10."

Another method employed was "taking the true Indian before the agent, and in his presence paying the consideration money, which was afterwards obtained from him by fraud or force by the pretended purchaser."[5] The swindlers gathered the Indians in parties sometimes numbering several hundred near the office of the certifying agent but out of his sight where they were fed and given whisky while awaiting to be called before the agent.

When commissioners were later directed to investigate these frauds, they said: "It is shocking to reflect on the disclosures elicited. They embrace men of every degree. Persons, heretofore deemed respectable, are implicated in the most disgraceful attempts to defraud those incapacitated from protecting their own interests." In some instances it was found that nineteen out of twenty deeds certified had been procured by fraud. Evidence taken disclosed "acts that make the blood of a just man mount to his cheeks for shame that he and the perpetrators of them belong to the same community."[6]

"Near the town of Cusseta, in which Dr. McHenry certified, Indians were collected in large bodies, amounting to 400 or 500; and from that to 1,000 were encamped in the woods, which, in the language of one witness, 'appeared to be full of them', and were fed by and under the direction avowedly of the agents of those to whom the largest number of contracts was certified; that all regard for appearances even was abandoned, and no attempts at secrecy in their movements was made; and that threats and menace were used by some of those engaged in this business against the persons who exposed their unprincipled proceedings.

"That early in March, 1835, 'the land stealers were crowding into the office by droves, and certifying contracts very fast, and it appeared as though they would steal all the Indians' land; they seemed to carry on the business in sport'; that a toast was given in a crowd by one of those concerned in these nefarious practices, 'Here's to the man that can steal the most land to-morrow without being caught at it;' and that such a

5 Ibid., p. 11.
6 Ibid., p. 15.

flood of fraud inundated the agency that Dr. McHenry closed his books." This business "exhibited scenes at which principle revolts and the heart sickens."

March first, 1835, Eli S. Shorter, one of the leaders in this business wrote from Columbus to some of his associates at Tuscaloosa: "*I left at the agency, Hayden and his son, General Woodward, Stone, McBryde, Collins, the whole Columbus company and a host of others, with, I believe, 400 Indians hid out all around the hill. Certifications commenced last (yesterday) evening and about sixty were taken through. The agent will be at home certifying the whole of next week; and in that time, most if not all of the land will be swept that is worth a notice. I have the agent's promise to meet us at any place of our appointment on the Monday afterwards.*" They were directed to gather up their Indians and bring them to the vicinity of Chambers, to use them over again as needed. "*Camp your Indians out of sight of the road. You need give yourself no trouble about the value of the land; I will arrange all that. Stealing is the order of the day; and out of that host of Indians at the agency, I do not think there were ten true holders of land.*"[7]

Finally, on March 7, 1835, after the harvest was nearly over, Secretary Cass undertook to limit the frauds by directing that contracts should be certified only in the towns in which the Indian grantors lived. But he was too late and this order did no good. On March 16 and again a week later the Indians protested to the certifying agent: "*We have borne with oppression until further forbearance has ceased to be a virtue, and we are now determined to speak out, let the consequences be as they may. While we have been at home preparing something for our dependent families to subsist on, other Indians have sold our homes, our all, the only means for our support; and when we have applied to you for redress, what has most frequently been the result? Why, sir, that you would enquire into it. You place the burden of proof upon us. . . but worse than all this, and more to be regretted, is the fact, through fear of the merciless hordes who surround your office, our people cannot speak to you in defense of their just rights without subjecting themselves to punishment.*"

A better class of white people of Chambers county, Alabama, indignant at these outrages, judiciously conscious of the chaotic condition of titles to follow, and predicting the Indian hostilities, suffering, and

7   Ibid., p. 64.

bloodshed that resulted, protested to the president April 8, 1835, against what had become in less than two months "a regular business, not more distinguished for its baseness and corruption than for the boldness with which it is carried into execution."[8] In the same month a grand jury in that county indicted a justice of the peace for promoting these frauds by signing in blank a large number of affidavits of owner-ship to be filled in by the swindlers at their convenience.

Finally the frantic appeals of the Indians supported by the protests of decent resident white people began to have some effect and more than a year after it had been first apprised of these frauds, the adminis-tration at Washington reversed its attitude of indifference and futility, and on April 28, 1835 orders were issued to stop certifying sales and to investigate all those already approved.

Directions were given to General Sanford to make an investigation. Accordingly he gave notice that he would proceed to hear complaints from the Indians at Columbus in June, 1835. This proposition to make the investigation in the city in which these infamous schemes were conceived and promoted, and where most of the land thieves lived, was foredoomed to failure especially as Sanford himself was not trusted by the Indians.

In spite of this handicap a number of those whose lands had been fraudulently conveyed by others, gathered at the home of Eneah Micco, a Hitchiti chief, for the purpose of going to Columbus to present their grievances to Sanford. Agents of the land thieves frightened the Indians by telling them that the direction to come to Columbus was a device to get them in Georgia where they would be arrested for old debts and enrolled and sent off to Arkansas. The result was that none went to see Sanford. Eneah Micco then sent word of the situation to Sanford and asked him to meet the Indians on the Alabama side of the Chattahoochee river, but Sanford refused. The Indians then on August 25, 1835, again wrote the president about the situation and told him that they would like to begin their movement to the West but they were unable to sell their land and get the proceeds; they could not depart until they had the money with which to remove and begin life anew in the West, which was promised them by the terms of the treaty, from the sale of their land.

8 *American State Papers*, "Military Affairs," VI, 648.

The president then appointed John B. Hogan, a friend of the Indians, to make an investigation; he traveled about among them taking testimony touching these frauds. On January 22, and February 14, 1836, Hogan wrote interesting accounts of his investigation: "*A greater mass of corruption perhaps, has never been congregated in any part of the world, than has been engendered by the Creek treaty in the grant of reservations of lands to those people. I am followed from place to place by gangs of from twenty to forty 'speculators,' as they are termed; and nothing but my long residence in Alabama and known character has prevented me from coming into collision with these people, who occasionally break out, but generally behind my back, when I do not hear them.*"

In some sections it was discovered that nine-tenths of the supposed sales were procured by "personation," the term used in official correspondence to describe the methods employed, and more than one-half of all were fraudulent. The investigation was slow, and where fraud was established it seldom helped the Indian as he could not sell his land until the cloud had been removed by the action of the president, or a release was secured from the swindler. Thus sales by those who desired to sell and enroll for removal to the West were delayed and removal was hampered. This situation opened new fields for land swindlers who induced those who had actually sold their land to embarrass rival purchasers in good faith by claiming to have been defrauded. With this slight vantage ground, land purchasers combined in the autumn to protest clamorously to the president against all investigations; better, they said, for the Indians to lose their land than for the whites to be delayed in getting their titles confirmed; and besides it was unthinkable that an Indian's word should be received to contradict that of a white man; it could not be under the laws of Alabama, and ought not to be under the laws of the United States.

Removal of the Creeks was seriously embarrassed by the frauds practiced on them which at the same time demonstrated the hopelessness of their situation among the whites. The Lower Creeks were opposed to removal and their chief Eneah Micco[9] obstinately refused to

9 Eneah Micco removed from Florida to the country of the Upper Creeks in November, 1824 (*Louisiana Herald*, January 28, 1825, p. 2, col. 2). Opothleyaholo charged that "Neah" Micco and Tuskeneah were responsible for much of the evil influence exerted on the Creeks (*Niles' Weekly Register*, September 17, 1836, p. 38).

consider it. The Upper Creeks, on the other hand, who comprised about two-thirds of the tribe, recognized the necessity of removal, but their chief Opothleyaholo objected to the country provided for them west of Arkansas.

They were led to believe they could find a congenial home in Texas on a tract of land one hundred miles square, which speculators hoped to secure from Mexico and sell to them for money they believed the chiefs could obtain from the government.[10] A conditional grant of land had been made by the Mexican government to General Felasola and it was planned to secure and transfer this to the Creeks. The half-breed Benjamin Hawkins was engaged in the enterprise and he induced Opothleyaholo, Jim Boy, Tukabahchee Micco and Dave Burnett, conducted by a white man of Albany, New York, named Barent Dubois who was married to a Creek woman, to meet him in Nacogdoches in the winter of 1834-35 to examine the land under consideration. From Nacogdoches they commenced a tour of exploration towards the sources of the Sabine and Trinity rivers; they were much pleased with the country they saw and concluded to purchase it if possible. The tract commenced fifteen leagues north of Nacogdoches and extended north and west.

Hawkins then negotiated with Archibald Hotchkiss, agent of a "New York company engaged in colonizing the grants made to Burnett, Veihlen, and Zavala under the name and title of 'Galveston Bay and Texas Land Company.' "[11] In March, 1835, at Nacogdoches, the Creek chiefs signed a contract by which they agreed to meet Hotchkiss and Hawkins in New Orleans and pay them $20,000 and the latter were then to proceed to Mexico and purchase the land from Felasola; when the purchase was completed the Creeks were to pay an additional consideration of $8,000. The Indians returned home and in April went to New Orleans where they made the payment of $20,000.[12] Hotchkiss then went to New York to see Felasola instead of going to Mexico.

10   After paying the white people of Georgia for their slaves who had escaped to Florida, there was an apparent balance owing to the Creeks under the terms of their treaty of 1821 by which they gave up their lands in Georgia for a pittance.

11   Peter Ellis Bean to Lewis Cass, February 24, 1835, in *Columbus Inquirer;* Hogan to Gibson, April 8, 1835, OIA, "Creek Emigration."

12   *American State Papers,* "Military Affairs," VI, 723, 781.

When information of these negotiations reached Mexican officials, Peter Ellis Bean, colonel of cavalry of the Mexican republic, from his post at Nacogdoches addressed a vigorous protest to the secretary of war of the United States. The Mexican authorities were particularly exercised about the matter as several hundred Choctaw Indians had recently located about twenty-five miles from Nacogdoches.[13]

On the return of Opothleyaholo and his associates the Indians held a conference on the subject of removal to Texas, and during that time they declined to talk to the agents about emigrating west of Arkansas; Ben Hawkins went to Washington to ascertain whether the government would favor the purchase of land in Texas for the Creeks; but he returned in June and reported that negotiations had failed.[14] A "committee of vigilance and safety for the Department of Nacogdoches" in September addressed a protest to President Jackson asking that the Indians be prevented from entering and settling in Texas.[15]

White citizens of Macon county, Alabama assembled at the home of James Abercrombie May 19, 1835 and adopted resolutions reciting that "*great fraud has been recently committed in obtaining title to lands, belonging to Indians without their knowledge or consent in any way whatever; the person committing such frauds or rather stealing the lands of the Indians has some other Indian who he has drilled with the description of locations and other matters in relation to the land; the Indian when thus drilled and a new song put into his mouth goes before the certifying agent and passes his land by certificate as being the real Indian owning that tract of land to the stealer or white man, who immediately sends such certificate to Washington City for the approval of the President; the Indians who are the rightful owners of the lands knowing nothing of this foul and dishonest transaction until nearly all their lands have been swept from under them,*" and begged the president to withhold his approval of certificates except upon a re-examination of the facts.[16]

13 Hogan to Gibson, April 8, 1835, OIA, "Creek Emigration;" *ibid.*, John Page to Gibson, May 6, 1835; *ibid.*, Tarrant to Cass, March 27, 1835.

14 Hogan to Gibson, April 8, 1835, *ibid.*

15 John Forbes, Sam Houston, Henry Ragen, D. A. Hoffman, L. L. Peck, Wm. P. Logan, George Pollitt to Jackson, September 11, 1835, OIA. Hawkins was soon after killed by the Cherokee Indians (H. Yoakum, *History of Texas*, I, 328). He was a brother of Sam Hawkins who was executed with his father-in-law, William McIntosh, by the Creeks in 1825 (*American State Papers*, "Indian Affairs," II, 768).

16 J. H. Howard, *Chairman*, OIA, 1835, "Creek Reserves."

The Indians were restless and undecided about their future; and the large number of agents who traveled among them trying to induce them to prepare for emigration, made but slight impression. The whites were permitted to dispense whisky among them without let or hindrance, and drunken Indians went through the country creating alarms among the people. The Indian chiefs and other Indian officials had been stripped of their power of control over the members of the tribe by the state laws of Alabama and Georgia that threatened them with dire punishment for attempting to exercise their own laws. The frauds committed on them had led to some reprisals and one or two white people had been killed. The whites in turn drove the Indians from their fields, settlements, and towns on the Chattahoochee river and compelled them to seek refuge in the pine forests ten or fifteen miles away.[17] In this situation, some of them had reached a starving condition and in order to live had killed live stock belonging to the white invaders of their country; and the whites were becoming alarmed for their safety.

Uneasiness had become acute in the vicinity of Fort Mitchell, but *"this may be attributed to the known dissoluteness of the Uchees; they have ever been known and stigmatized as a bad and rogueish set of Indians; their language is different from the Creeks and they are said to be great thieves and rascals; these Indians inhabit these two counties but bad as they may be, if half the reports be true, that is asserted of the conduct of the land-buyers towards these people, it is not to be wondered that those ignorant savages resort occasionally to revenge and take the law in their own hands, and redress their grievances."*[18]

Gov. John Gayle of Alabama wrote Secretary Cass that the Indians in Macon and Russell counties were terrifying the whites and he asked for military protection. But he called the attention of the secretary to the *"infamous and unprincipled frauds which organized bands of speculators have practised and are practicing on the Indians in first obtaining their lands, and then, the small and inconsiderable sums they may have paid as a consideration for their purchases. These impositions have acquired great notoriety, and are subjects of unusual complaint."* He said citizens had hailed with great satisfaction a report that the president had refused to ratify any of the land sale contracts; that "a rigid scrutiny into each case would doubtless result in restoring to

17 Hogan to Gibson, May 14, 1835, *ibid.*, "Creek Emigration."
18 Hogan to Gayle, June 2, 1835, *ibid.*, "Creek Emigration."

these miserable people property of which they have been wrongfully deprived."[19]

The next day Governor Gayle wrote on the subject of the disturbances caused by the starving and destitute Indians and called on the state officers to protect the whites. But with a proper sense of responsibility, he added that "*The grog shops, which I understand are the most common establishments throughout the country, should receive your prompt and decided reprehension. They are generally established as I learn, for the accommodation of the Indians, and can any one doubt that to these fountains of crime and immorality are to be ascribed many of the difficulties which our citizens have to encounter.*"[20]

Besides their other difficulties the Creek tribe was torn by dissensions and cross purposes: While Opothleyaholo's faction, Tukabahchee and kindred towns wished to go to Texas, Tuskineah had a plan to colonize his part of the Nation on a tract of land in Alabama which some white speculators wished to sell to them. This chief was under the ban of others who proposed to "break" him. Sampson Grayson who had emigrated to the West the previous autumn, sent back letters to his relatives making serious complaints against conditions in his new home, which did much harm to the cause of emigration. A grand council of the tribe was called for June 11, at which it was proposed to reach a determination on the subject of removal.[21]

This council was held at Setelechee; and when the Creek agent Judge Tarrant, announced that on this occasion he would make the last annuity payment to be disbursed to the Creeks before their emigration, the news "flew like wildfire among the whites, for nearly every second man on the ground had his pockets filled with accounts against the Indians and these scamps are the very men that retard the emigration although they make great professions in favor of their removal."[22] When the annuity was paid to the chiefs it was divided into two lots between the Lower and Upper towns; for the further division of the money "the broken days was given out (14 days from this time) but the

19 Gayle to Cass, May 27, 1835, *Alabama State Department of Archives and History,* "Executive Letter Book," p. 166.

20 *Ibid.,* p. 168.

21 Hogan to Gibson, June 3, 1835, OIA, "Creek Emigration."

22 *Ibid.,* June 18, 1835.

Indians have so many claims set up against them that they have concealed the place of meeting; there was two Jack legged lawyers on the ground, threatening to sue if the Indians did not pay the claim they held."[23] However the Cherokee Indians, Ridge and Vann who stood high in favor with the administration, came to the council with a claim of $5,000 against the Creeks and a letter from the secretary of war urging them to pay it. Feeling ran high and *"one Indian stabbed another on the council ground; the relations of the dead Indian immediately took the murderer, tied him to a tree and stabbed him to death and left his body hanging to the tree; there was a great many white persons on the ground but neither them or the chiefs took any notice of the affair."*[24]

23 Ibid.
24 Ibid.

W ITH assurances that the fraud investigation and all difficulties involving their lands would be adjusted by autumn, large numbers of the Indians, even the recalcitrant chief Eneah Micco of the Lower Creeks, agreed to prepare for emigration. This compliance was induced by the supposition that they were to be removed by John B. Hogan, the agent appointed for that purpose, whom all the Indians trusted; hundreds were being enrolled and the agents were enthusiastic over the prospects for removal when the government agents, with a singular genius for bungling, destroyed all that had been accomplished: A contract for the removal of the Indians was let to a company made up principally of the men who had been most active in stealing their lands, and for whom the Indians cherished implacable hatred. They declared they would never consent to be delivered into the hands of these men whose primary interest would be to save as much as possible out of the twenty dollars a head allowed by the contract for removal. The movement collapsed.

However Opothleyaholo continued to make preparations to emigrate. He announced in September that his town, *"The Tucabachies, with that of the Kialachies, Thloplocko-Clewalas, Autaugas, and Ottosees, who all burn the same fire and talk with the same tongue, forms all the Tuckabaches, and is the great leading town of the nation. . . have set apart the 15th day of next month for our final departure. . . We shall at that time take our last black drink in this nation, rub up our tradition plates, and commence our march."*[1] He said he had prepared "his marching physic" and was "preparing his traveling clothes, and will put out his old fire and never make or kindle it again until he reaches west of the Mississippi, there never to quinch it again."[2]

1 *American State Papers,* "Military Affairs," VI, 643.
2 Hunter to Gibson, September 3, 1835. OIA, "Creek Emigration."

However new difficulties arose; suits were filed by white men against the Indians. The chiefs and head men who were solvent feared that if they attempted to leave, the whites would attach their negroes, horses, and other property. Many influences worked against removal; the Indians could not understand why they, the heirs of dead members of their families, were not entitled to possess or convey the lands inherited by them, which the white courts insisted on administering and selling. Any Indian who had anything of value, land or money, was the victim of white greed until he had been thoroughly despoiled of every thing; many were embarrassed by debts to speculators and they were threatened with attachments if they attempted to remove; others were detained by white land buyers who induced them to believe they could recover land or money from competitors who had already paid for their land; and a large number would not consent to leave until the fraudulent complications over their land were adjusted.

Many of the Creeks had sold all their provisions, corn and cattle so they would be ready for removal; numbers had become destitute having sold their land and dissipated the proceeds; or having been evicted by fraudulent purchasers, they became wanderers, wretched and miserable, and a menace to the whites. Finding no refuge among the latter, they began drifting into the Cherokee country in Alabama and Georgia until in February, 1836, 2,500 destitute and hungry Creeks of the Sakapatayi, Kan-tcati, Tallase-hatchee, and Talladega towns found shelter among their red brothers who were themselves soon to be evicted.[3]

A company of Georgia militia attacked and fired on fifty of these Creeks who were encamped on the Georgia side of the Coosa river, killing and injuring a number of the Indians. The Georgians afterwards killed some defenseless old Indians who were picking cotton along the Chattahoochee river. Because the Indians attempted to defend themselves the Georgia general of militia ordered 1,000 men to assemble

3 Statement of Opothleyaholo, *Niles' Weekly Register*, September 17, 1836. In January it was claimed that there were 2,000 Creeks settled near Turkey Town on the east side of the Coosa river in that part of the Cherokee Nation in Alabama (Garrett to Clay, January 25, 1836, *Alabama State Department of Archives and History*).

for the purpose of crossing the river and attacking the Indians in Alabama.[4] Thus, said an army officer,[5] the Georgians had started the "war." The Creeks who were driven from Georgia back into Alabama, took refuge among the Cherokee living in that state. Gov. Clement C. Clay requested of the secretary of war permission to drive them by force to the banks of the Tennessee river and compel them to take boats there for the West; but the secretary reminded him that under the terms of the treaty, the Creeks were free to leave Alabama when and as they pleased.[6]

However, removal was not entirely abandoned. Opothleyaholo promised that he and his people would be ready to remove by the next April. Benjamin Marshall, a half-breed Creek, a member of the emigrating company that had the contract for the removal of the Creeks, was anxious to take his family and slaves to the West that autumn. He was an influential member of the tribe and largely through his efforts an emigrant party of 511 was organized on the Tallapoosa river near Wetumka December 6, 1835. The party was made up of members from Fish Pond, Kealedji, Hilibi, and Asilanabi towns. They were accompanied by Marshall who had with him his family of eight, and his nineteen slaves.[7] The party was conducted by Lieut. Edward Deas of the army detailed to see that the conditions of the contract for caring for the Indians were observed by the contractors, represented by Doctor Ingersoll.

The agent attempted to enroll the Indians of his party in Tallapoosa county, but he "found it impossible to get a correct roll in the Nation in the vicinity of so many grog shops," and he was obliged to take them across the Coosa river before he could count them. Traveling about twelve miles each day they passed through Montevallo, and forded the Cahawba river on the eleventh; passed Elyton, crossed two forks of the

4 To the annoyance of the Alabamans the Georgia militiamen established themselves in their neighbor state where their commanding officer undertook to police the country and instruct the governor of Alabama as to measures he should take (Howard to Clay, April 2, 1836, *Alabama State Department of Archives and History*).

5 McCrabb to Jones, January 27, 1836, *New York Observer*, February 13, 1836, p. 2, col. 5.

6 Cass to Clay, March 12, 1836, *Alabama State Department of Archives and History*, "Executive Letter Book," p. 180.

7 Muster Roll, October 15, 1835, OIA, "Creek Emigration."

Black Warrior river, the west fork of Flint creek, Moulton on the nineteenth, and arrived at Tuscumbia the twenty-first. Hearing discouraging
reports about the condition of the roads, Deas decided to take the
Indians from here by boat. Sending their horses in charge of the contractors to be driven through by volunteer Indians, the remainder of
the party, their wagons, beef, and corn were embarked December 23
on a small steamboat and two keel boats that carried them down the
river to Waterloo; here they were placed aboard the steamboat *Alpha*
and two large keel-boats in tow for the passage to Fort Gibson, and
departed the twenty-sixth.

They stopped every evening before dark to clean the boats and
enable the Indians to camp on shore, and started again after daylight;
temporary hearths were constructed on the decks of the keel-boats
which the Indians employed to cook their food and warm themselves;
fresh beef and meal were issued to them daily.[8]

The emigrants reached the mouth of the Tennessee river December
28, and Memphis the thirty-first, at the same time their ponies arrived
there. The Indians had been allowed only two quarts of corn for each
horse a day on the road which proved wholly inadequate for horses
driven as rapidly as they were, twice as fast as the rate specified in the
contract; and the Indians had been obliged to exchange horses for feed
along the way until out of a total of 154 that left Tuscumbia December
23, only 132 reached the Mississippi river.[9]

Leaving Memphis the day of their arrival, the boats soon entered the
Arkansas river, and after a passage averaging forty miles a day reached
Little Rock on January 9, where they were anchored for an hour
in the stream, the Indians not being permitted to go ashore.[10] Deas
made every effort to prevent introduction in the party by white men of
whisky, which in spite of all they could do gave Deas and the conductors much trouble.

After delays occasioned by having to go ashore and cut wood for
the boilers, where the wood yards had been depleted, and by repeatedly running aground on sand-bars, or running on snags and

8   Deas to Gibson, December 21, and 28, 1835, *ibid.*

9   *Ibid.*, January 9, 1836; Journal of Edward Deas, February 4, 1836, OIA,
"Creek Emigration" 61 J.

10   *Arkansas Advocate*, January 15, 1836, p. 2, col. 1; *Army and Navy Chronicle*,
II, 70; *American State Papers*, "Military Affairs," VI, 773.

springing leaks in the boats, at times obliging all but the sick to walk while they worked the boats over the shallows, they finally reached a point two miles above Fort Smith on January 22, when low water prevented further progress of the boats. The emigrants were obliged to wait here a week until messengers sent to Fort Gibson could secure the return of their ponies that through bad management had been driven ahead. They then loaded their household utensils and other personal effects in ten wagons, three with six oxen to each, four with four oxen, one with four oxen and one horse, one with four horses, and one with six mules, besides a number of small wagons and carts belonging to the Indians. Then mounting their ponies and wagons the Indians began the last stage of their journey; they traveled the military road, crossed Sallisaw creek and on the thirty-first camped at Mackey's eighteen miles from Fort Gibson; forded the Illinois river and reached the post February 2.[11] Then they continued to the west side of the Verdigris river where they desired to locate.[12]

With the passing of winter the Indians in Alabama were voluble with promises to remove; not now—but as soon as the interminable investigation of the frauds would clear their titles so they could sell their lands and take the proceeds with them. Sanford's company was predicting that as many as eight thousand would remove in the spring and it was making arrangements accordingly. But conditions did not justify the hope. Thousands of the Indians were destitute, dispossessed of their lands, some legitimately, but most of them by fraud. Of this class were the Yuchi, nearly all of whom were compelled to leave their homes and wander over the surrounding country, stealing and killing stock to keep from starving. The white people in the vicinity, panic stricken abandoned their homes.

Early in May, 1836, removal agents with much labor induced nearly two thousand more Indians to assemble ready to depart for the West. While they were in camp Opothleyaholo was arrested and held under a bail writ for a debt for which he was "as much responsible as he is for the national debt of Great Britain," according to Sanford.[13] The chief sent word to the Indians not to leave until he was released and could accompany them. From their lack of confidence in themselves

11 Deas Journal; Deas to Gibson, February 5, 1836, OIA, "Creek Emigration."
12 Deas Journal.
13 Sanford to Gibson, May 14, 1836, OIA, "Creek Emigration."

and in the white contractors, and their reliance on Opothleyaholo, they declined to attempt the journey until he was ready to go.

The secretary of war on March 11, directed J. B. Hogan and two other commissioners named by him to make a new investigation of the frauds on the Creeks and to push it vigorously. They had begun their work and were making progress, when early in May hostilities were begun by the Indians; the opinion was general that they were planned and promoted by the white despoilers of the Indians in order to inter-rupt and prevent investigations of their villainy and thereby cover it up, and hasten the validating of the bogus titles procured by them. Roving bands of Yuchi, Hitchiti, and Chiaha towns of the Lower Creeks situated on the Chattahoochee river suddenly began attacking white people and destroying their property.

These hostilities and depredations took place near Columbus where they were certain to receive the greatest amount of publicity. And the Indians entered into the destruction of property with greater fury in the vicinity of the city in which the wrongs perpetrated upon them had been planned and promoted. Between Tuskegee and Columbus a number of whites were murdered and the rest fled and abandoned the country to the Indians who robbed and burned houses, barns, and cribs, burned the toll bridge across the Chattahoochee river, fired upon and captured two steamboats on that stream near Columbus. As that town had harbored the swindlers who had done the most to drive the Indians to desperation, it was but natural that the citizens should have feared reprisals.[14]

May 16 a company of fifty or sixty Indians attacked a mail stage about twenty miles west of Columbus on the road to Tuskegee, robbed and burned the stage and killed some of the passengers. To this act they were incited by a white man who was later tried and on November 21 of that year sentenced to hang for his par-ticipation in this affair. Panic stricken white people fled to Columbus with such of their worldly possessions as they could carry, until the place was crowded with them, their horses, oxen and wagons.

14 Colonel Sanford wrote on May 14: "Our town is under military law, ex-pecting an attack every minute" (Sanford to Gibson, *ibid.*,). The next day A. Aber-crombie, another citizen of Columbus wrote to the governor of Alabama, "For God's sake, send us some help" (Abercrombie to Clay, May 15, 1836, *Alabama State Depart-ment of Archives and History*).

Indians who were not involved in these excesses, starving and fearful of the cruelty of the whites, came flocking into Fort Mitchell where they were fed. "We have men, women, and children more than can get inside of the picketts" wrote Captain Page of the post.[15] Hostilities between the Seminoles and whites in Florida had intensified the fears of the people, and the war department directed the issue of arms and ammunition in Alabama, but on March 19, the secretary wrote Governor Clay that no occasion existed for organizing a regiment in his state and directed the discharge of all troops that had gathered.[16]

Citizens of Barbour and Russell counties, from Wetumka and Montgomery were sending to Governor Clay alarming reports of depredations and killings committed by the Indians which, it was claimed, indicated a concerted plan of the Lower Creeks to go to war. The governor then made another call on Secretary Cass for authority to raise a force of troops to act against them. He also ordered Gen. Gilbert Shearer, at the head of the state militia to prepare to carry on the war against the Creeks whenever it became necessary. But Shearer advised the government that there was *"nothing to apprehend from the Indians unless the daily intrusions committed on them by the whites should drive them to desperation; I also find this same view of the subject taken by the Editor of a Montgomery paper and also by that of the Georgia Journal. These prints convey that many persons are interested in producing an alarm and provoking hostilities, with the hope of diverting a scrutiny into their own fraudulent transactions with the Indians."*[17]

The truth of the situation is probably to be found in the account in the *Montgomery Advertiser* which presumably was not prejudiced in favor of the Indians: *"We must speak plain on this question. It is meet that every thing relative to it should be properly understood. We do not censure the Executive of Alabama for making preparations to resist the aggressions of a hostile foe; on the contrary, we approve of his motives,*

15 Page to Gibson, May 12, 1836, OIA, "Creek Emigration." Gov. William Schley of Georgia wrote May 12: "The Creeks are in a starving condition and must be fed where they now are, by the United States, or they must be killed or driven out of the country (*American State Papers*, "Military Affairs," VI, 446).

16 *Alabama State Department of Archives and History*, "Executive Letter Book." pp. 172, 174, 178.

17 *Ibid.*, p. 194, Shearer to Clay, May 2, 1836.

but we do deprecate the conduct of those who are continually sounding the cry of danger, when there is none to be apprehended.

"Is this country never to enjoy a season of repose? Are interested land speculators from Alabama and Georgia longer to palm off their deception on the public? Who believes that the Creeks are about to assume a hostile attitude towards the whites? We answer, no one.

"The war with the Creeks is all a humbug. It is a base and diabolical scheme, devised by interested men, to keep an ignorant race of people from maintaining their just rights, and to deprive them of the small remaining pittance placed under their control, through the munificence of the govern-ment. We do trust, for the credit of those concerned, that these blood suckers may be ferreted out, and their shameful misrepresentations exposed.

"We have lately conversed with many of the settlers of the nation, and also the Superintendent of Indian Affairs, and the unanimous opinion is, that there is nothing like a system of hostility meditated by the Creeks; that the chiefs are utterly averse to a war fare with the whites; that it is foreign from their intentions to resist the Treaty; that they are now preparing to remove, and will, in a short time, commence emigrating west of the Mississippi.

"The Red Man must soon leave. They have nothing left on which to subsist. Their property has been taken from them—their stock killed up, their farms pillaged—and by whom? By white men. By individuals who should have scorned to take such mean advantages of those who were unprotected and defenseless. Such villainy may go unpunished in this world, but the day of retribution will most certainly arrive."[18]

Alarming reports of the situation reached Washington and on May 19 the secretary of war issued orders to abandon forthwith the efforts to rectify the frauds committed on the Indians. Assuming that the action of the few in turning on the whites in futile reprisal for their wrongs, divested all, of the rights guaranteed them by the solemn treaty with the United States, orders were given to remove the whole tribe as a military measure. The secretary ordered Gen. Thomas S.

18 *Montgomery Advertiser*, quoted in *The Southern Advocate* (Huntsville, Ala-bama), May 17, 1836, p. 3, col. 4.

Jesup to put an army in the field in Alabama, inaugurate an operation of war against the Indians, subdue and remove them to the West.[19]

A company of unorganized armed white men from Lafayette, Chambers, and Troup counties went to Lutcapoga Town, drove the Indians into the swamp and burned their town. The whites induced Opothleyaholo to raise a company of 300 friendly Indians and pushing them to the fore, scoured the country and drove the Indians suspected of being hostile from their homes which they burned; but before the end of the month the Indians tired of this service and not realizing the promises made them that white soldiers would soon join and share their exposures and hardships, they returned to their homes. However Opothleyaholo killed one of the leaders of the recalcitrants, put thirteen in irons, and did much to prevent others from joining the hostiles. The next month, June, he organized 1,150 warriors from the Kialedji, Eufaula, Fish Pond, and Nuyaka towns, and with himself at their head, enlisted[20] under command of General Jesup to put down the "war." Besides these there were several hundred other warriors under Jim Boy, Tukabahchee Hadjo, and Tukabahchee Micco serving with Jesup. Out of a total of more than 11,000 organized and unorganized troops put in the field to suppress hostilities, 1,806 were Creeks.[21]

By the first of June Governor Clay estimated that there were 1,000 hostiles under Eneah Micco between Montgomery and Columbus and 500 under Eneah Emathla, chief of Hitchiti Town on the Hutchechubbee river. *"Opothleyaholo thinks the present war has been produced by the retailers of spirituous liquors and by the 'Sandshakers.' My own opinion is, decidedly, that it has been mainly brought about by the latter. I have already seen some evidence, unquestionably genuine—going far to sustain my opinion; and have strong hopes of obtaining more, that will be perfectly conclusive. Opothleyaholo represents that many of the people of the Upper Towns are suffering for the means of subsistence—almost if*

19 Cass to Jesup, May 19, 1836, OIA, "Creek File."

20 Clay to Jesup, June 12, 1836, *Alabama State Department of Archives and History; American State Papers*, "Military Affairs," VII, 347; *Army and Navy Chronicle*, III, 60.

21 *American State Papers*, "Military Affairs," VI, 807. Besides these there were 776 Creek volunteers serving in Florida on the side of the government (*ibid.*, p. 807).

not quite, in a state of starvation—and that they are anxious to emigrate."[22]

Citizens of Alabama and Georgia living near the boundary line, in fear and panic of the Indians, and outraged by the whites who had precipitated the trouble, in June forwarded a memorial to Congress praying for relief; they said that an investigation would lead to the exposure of "the most revolting facts known to the annals of history, disclosing scenes of turpitude and rapine. . . clandestinely opening the flood-gates of savage assassination upon the defenseless women and children of this late prosperous country;" that there was sufficient grounds for the immediate arrest of various individuals contiguous to the disaffected Indian districts; that they were surrounded by "the devastating horror of a savage war brought into existence by an abandoned and heartless association of white men" who were entrenching themselves by influencing *"some of the public presses of the country by their ill-gotten wealth, making them the servile organs of misstatement and falsehood. But the principal grounds for a judicial investigation your memorialists believe are summed up in the public expose of the late swindling transactions, together with the determined purpose of the before said Land Companies to create an Indian war at the time when the governmental investigations should commence into the fraudulent contracts."* This memorial signed by over 700 persons, was forwarded to Washington,[23] and the House of Representatives on July 1 referred it to the president with the request that he investigate and prosecute those guilty of the crimes charged by the memorialists.[24]

Congress and the president were finally spurred to do something about the situation and a commission was appointed to inquire into the causes of the recent hostilities. The commissioners first asked the governors of Georgia and Alabama to give them such information as they cared to submit. Gov. William Schley of Georgia responded October 7 that he knew nothing about the cause of the "war"; but gave it as his opinion that the Indians were "idle, disolute vagrants, many of whom had for a long time, been subsisting on provisions stolen from the people of Georgia living on and near the Chattahoochie"

22 Clay to Cass, June 3, 1836, *Alabama State Department of Archives and History.*
23 OIA, "Creek Emigration."
24 OIA, "Creek File" J 22.

and that when the whites resisted their depredations, they would add murder to their other crimes. Many of them he said were in a state of starvation. As to the fundamental causes of their situation and the responsibility of the white people for the troubles that grew out of them, the governor showed little interest or disposition to help the commissioners and declined any information.[25]

Governor Clay of Alabama was more frank and helpful in his reply: *"So far as I am able to judge from the communications of individuals, or from indications of public sentiments, as expressed at public meetings, and otherwise, it seems to me that the opinion prevails extensively, if not universally, that the frauds and forgeries practiced upon the Indians to deprive them of their lands, were amongst the principal causes which excited them to hostilities. Some of those with whom I have conversed have ascribed the war to the combined influence of several causes; to the frauds and forgeries above mentioned; to the vice and intemperance introduced amongst them by a class of white men; and to the destitute, and almost starving condition to which they were reduced, mainly by the operation of the two former. With the means of information in my power, I am inclined to believe the latter opinion most correct."*[26]

Several thousand white troops were ordered into the Creek country,[27] and Gen. Winfield Scott whose Seminole campaign[28] had fared so badly reached Columbus on May 19. The hostiles were operating, or depredating, in three parties; one, headed by Eneah Emathla, who was regarded as the active leader of the uprising; one by Eneah Micco, and one by Jim Henry. "The latter party have been endeavoring to cross the Chattahoochee River to get to Florida. . . I sent to Ne-he-Mathla, the other day, to try to find out what his strength was" wrote Captain Page; "but he is too great a general for me; no information could

---

25   Schley to Balch and Crawford, October 7, 1836, OIA, "Creek Reserve File."

26   Clay to Crawford, October 27, 1836, *Alabama State Department of Archives and History;* OIA, "Creek Reserve File"; General Jesup wrote: "I have no doubt the war was brought about by interested white men and by half breeds and by Indians who were their dupes" (Jesup to Clay, July 18, 1836, *Alabama State Department of Archives and History.)*

27   1,103 regulars, 4,755 Georgians, and 4,300 Alabamans, not all armed however were enlisted (*American State Papers,* "Military Affairs," VII, 354).

28.   By order of the president a military court of inquiry was held in November, 1836, in Frederick, Maryland, to inquire into the causes of the failure of the campaigns in Florida under General Scott and General Gaines (*ibid.,* 129).

be gained; his men are too well drilled to communicate anything."[29]
Some of the hostiles stole a number of stage horses and mules and
joined the Seminole in Florida.

With the aid of Jim Boy and his followers, in the early part of June,
Eneah Emathla was captured and brought in irons to Fort Mitchell;
a few days later about a thousand of his people surrendered and were
also brought to the fort which was filled to overflowing with wretched
humanity. They made an interesting and pathetic spectacle as they
were brought in; the body composed of men, women, and children of
all ages from infancy to nearly a hundred, were mostly mounted on
ponies, and were of all complexions shading through white, red, and
black.

29 *Ibid.*, 953. Washington Irving became interested in Eneah Emathla from
information given him by Governor Duval and wrote a sketch which he called "The
Conspiracy of Neamathla" (*Wolfert's Roost and other Papers*, New York, 1863).
This was an account of the chief in the early twenties while he lived and fought with
the Florida Indians and ruled as the chief of the warlike Mikasuki. After Duval
deposed Eneah Emathla as a Seminole chief he "left the country in disgust and returned to the Creek Nation who elected him a chief of one of their towns." Eneah
Emathla had always been active in the "depredations on the frontiers of Georgia
which had brought vengeance and ruin on the Seminoles. He was a remarkable man;
upwards of sixty years of age, about six feet high, with a fine eye, and a strongly
marked countenance, over which he possessed great command. . . Though he had
been prevailed on to sign the treaty [of 1823] his heart revolted at it. In one of his
frank conversations with Governor Duval, he observed: 'This country belongs to the
red man; and if I had the number of warriors at my command that this nation once
had, I would not leave a white man on my lands. I would exterminate the whole'."
Irving's original notes of what Duval told him and his manuscript of "The Conspiracy
of Neamathla" are in the Huntington Library. Eneah Emathla and his family left
Tallahassee on November 26, 1824 for the country of the Upper Creeks (*Louisiana
Herald*, January 28, 1825, p. 2, cols. 1 and 3). Eneah Emathla resorted to drastic
measures to prevent his people from emigrating; some years before he cut off the ears
of a man and a woman who had consented to remove to the West (*U. S. House Report
No. 227*, Twenty-first Congress, first session).

THE troops captured most of the Eufaula and Chiaha recalcitrants by the first of July, the Hitchiti and Yuchi holding
out to the last; the leader of the latter was the wily Jim
Henry, who escaped when his followers were taken.[1] But
he was finally captured early in July,[2] and with his leadership removed, the military declared the "war" ended. Blacksmiths had
been at work making handcuffs for the prisoners. Sixteen hundred Indians, men, women, and children, guarded by three companies of armed
soldiers, left Fort Mitchell July 2, for the West; near Tuskegee the
body was augmented at the encampment of Echo Hadjo by a considerable number of prisoners including the chiefs Eneah Micco[3], Cheemalee, and Jim Henry. The latter had been demanded by the State of
Georgia for trial and execution, but as he was a citizen of Alabama that
state refused to surrender him.[4]

1 "Jim Henry got off, but it was a hair breadth escape. This fiend in Man's shape
is said to be badly wounded in one of his shoulders" (*Army and Navy Chronicle*, III,
26). In later years in the Indian Territory Jim Henry was known as McHenry. He
joined the Methodist church became a minister and for years was a devout and
influential religious leader among the Creek Indians. On October 10, 1855, he was
admitted to the Indian Mission Conference at Asbury Mission in the Creek Nation.
He died May 1, 1883, and was buried at Broken Arrow (G. G. Smith, *Life and Times
of Bishop George F. Pierce*, Nashville, 1888).

2 *American State Papers*, "Military Affairs, VII, 361, 368."

3 One hundred and forty-five members of Eneah Micco's party held out and were
captured north of Tuskegee the middle of July. "The war is entirely at an end" wrote
General Jesup. "And so far as regards Indian hostilities, the inhabitants might return
to their farms in perfect security; but their houses have been burnt, their means
of subsistence destroyed and their crops on the ground will yield them nothing"
(*Army and Navy Chronicle*, III, 86).

4 "The notorious Jim Henry has given himself up to the friendly Indians, and
is to be brought to Fort Mitchell today; the Creek war may now be considered as

*Jim Henry when he lived in Indian Territory and when he had entered
the ministry and was known as Jim McHenry*

It was "very slow moving them in irons, chained together, and Montgomery is the nearest point we could take water," wrote Capt. John Page.[5] The sullen warriors, manacled and chained, marched in double file. The venerable chief Eneah Emathla was not exempt from this humiliation. An observer relates that this chief ". . .*is 84 years old, but his eyes indicate intelligence and fire and his countenance would give the impression that he was a brave and distinguished man. . . They were all handcuffed and chained together; and in this way they marched to Montgomery, on the Alabama, 90 miles. Old Eneah Mathla marched all the way, hand-cuffed and chained like the others, and I was informed by Capt. Page, the agent for moving the Indians, that he never uttered a complaint.*"[6] On July 9 and 10, nine hundred more of Eneah Emathla's people were captured and sent west after the other prisoners.[7]

In the wake of the manacled warriors followed a long train of wagons and ponies conveying the children and the old women and sick who were unable to walk.[8] As they approached Montgomery where they were to be placed aboard the boats, their despair led them to commit numbers of excesses: One warrior who was being brought through the

---

ended. Jim Henry and Eneah Mathla were the principal instigators and actors, and they are now both in irons. Henry is a half-breed about twenty years of age, a smart and intelligent fellow; for three years past he has been employed in one of the principal mercantile houses in Columbus as a clerk. Upon the breaking out of hostilities he joined his tribe, and with Eneah Mathla planned the system of operations which they have been disappointed in executing, and headed the party which attacked and burnt the village of Roanoke. Eneah Mathla is a veteran in the wars; he says he is eighty-four years of age, and a noble, fine looking fellow he is. He was a conspicuous actor in the Seminole wars, and has been, and ever will be, the enemy of the whites; this he declares openly, and who can but respect him for it? He, his son, and three hundred hostile warriors were marched from Fort Mitchell yesterday for the Mississippi, escorted by two companies of artillery under the command of Major Churchill. They were handcuffed and divided into three squads, with a chain communicating from one to another. Some two or three thousand women and children followed, shedding tears and making the most bitter wailings. It was a deplorable sight, but the wretchedness and destruction they have caused, and the diabolical cruelty which has characterized them during this warfare, demands the most ignominious punishment, and chains are worse to them than death" (*Army and Navy Chronicle*, III, 57).

5 *American State Papers*, "Military Affairs," VII, 953.
6 *Army and Navy Chronicle*, III, 126.
7 *American State Papers*, "Military Affairs," VII, 361.
8 *New York Observer*, July 23, 1836, p. 3, col. 3.

streets in a wagon, drew a knife and cut his throat; another killed a guard with a hammer and was shot dead; another was bayoneted by a guard. At Montgomery "The spectacle exhibited by them was truly melancholy. To see the remnant of a once mighty people fettered and chained together forced to depart from the land of their fathers into a country unknown to them, is of itself sufficient to move the stoutest heart."[9]

On July 14 2,498 of these unhappy people including 800 warriors, and forty to be surrendered to the civil authorities for punishment[10] were crowded aboard two little river steamboats, the *Lewis Cass* and the *Meridian*, and two barges in tow of each, and conveyed down the Alabama river to Mobile.[11] "From the inauspicious season of the year and the crowded condition on the boats" the *Montgomery Advertiser* predicted the Indians would suffer much from disease.[12]

This body included 900 Yuchi and 500 Kasihta; they were in charge of Lieut. J. Waller Barry, and guarded by the Alabama artillery, a Mobile volunteer company. They arrived at Mobile on the sixteenth, and were landed below the city to give them opportunity to prepare their food and arrange the little bundles containing their meager personal effects for the long sad journey ahead of them. Twenty-three hundred of them were embarked aboard two boats that evening for the Mississippi river; the next night a severe storm was encountered and the terrified Creeks were battened in the holds of the vessels for safe keeping.

These Indians reached New Orleans on the eighteenth; "One of the barges was retained for the purpose of taking the sick, infirm, children and baggage up the Canal, and was towed by the Indians themselves to their present encampment near the basin."[13] "*Until the departure of the boats which are to convey them to the place of destination, west of the Mississippi, they have made a temporary lodgment along the bank of the new canal, below the basin at the foot of Julia street. The excessive rains of Monday night, and which continued nearly without interruption all of*

9 Montgomery Advertiser copied in Southern Advocate (Huntsville, Alabama), July 19, 1836, p. 2, col. 5.

10 American State Papers, "Military Affairs," VII, 361.

11 Army and Navy Chronicle, III, 72; Grayson to Gibson, July 15, 1836, OIA, "Creek Emigration."

12 New York Observer, July 30, 1836, p. 3, col. 4.

13 Barry to Gibson, July 19, 1836, OIA, "Creek Emigration."

yesterday, have proved peculiarly unfortunate to these poor savages. . .
With the aid of a few staves and boards, some tattered canvass and soiled
blankets, they have put up a few rude tents, which afford them, however,
but feeble protection against the driving rains."[14]

The emigrating company, headed by J. W.. A. Sanford, embarked
the Indians on the steamboats *Lamplighter, Majestic* and *Revenue*, and
on July 21 they started up the Mississippi river,[15] landing on the twenty-
ninth at Rock Roe.[16] Here they remained eight days while the necessary
wagons, oxen and horses were collected for their overland trip to Fort
Gibson.[17] Lieutenant Barry, reporting when they reached Little Rock,
lifts the curtain slightly on this unhappy enterprise: "*Indians peaceable
and entertaining themselves in camp by ball playing, fishing, etc. The
chains and handcuffs taken off the Indians were packed in barrels and
brought up to Racrat [Rock Roe] on board the* Revenue *steamboat. They
were put on shore with some thirty or forty barrels of meat and provisions,
and during the night rolled into the river by the Uchee Indians. The barrels containing them were not heard of and the chains are lost irrevocably.*"[18]

The weather was so intensely hot in the daytime that the contractors
obliged the emigrants to travel at night. Their limited equipment of
twenty wagons was crowded with old women and children and the
sick, while many old and infirm people were compelled to walk; small

14   "From a New Orleans paper" in *New York Observer*, August 6, 1836, p. 3.

15   *Niles' Weekly Register*, August 27, 1836, p. 425; aboard the *Majestic* were
500 Kasihta Indians. "The party is accompanied by Eneah Micco, principal chief,
and Eneah Mathla the leader in the late hostilities. They came from Montgomery,
Alabama, *via* New Orleans across Lake Ponchartrain, being less than fifteen days
from Montgomery to White River" (*Arkansas Advocate*, August 5, 1836, p. 2, col. 2).
"Jim Henry was detained at Montgomery, by order of Governor Clay, to answer for
his crimes. Several of his accomplices in cruelty were also detained as prisoners. The
wife of Jim Henry was among the emigrants, and the parting between them is represented as being truly affecting (*Army and Navy Chronicle*, III, 88). Eneah Micco died
near Fort Gibson about the middle of December (*Niles' Weekly Register*, February 25,
1837, p. 416; *Arkansas Gazette*, January 10, 1837).

16   *Army and Navy Chronicle*, III, 140; *Arkansas Gazette*, August 6, 1836, p. 2,
col. 2; Brown to Gibson, July 31, 1836, OIA, "Creek Emigration."

17   Abadie to Gibson, August 14, 1836, *ibid.*

18   Barry to Gibson, August 10, 1836, *ibid.* John Waller Barry, son of W. T.
Barry, ex-postmaster general and minister to Spain, was graduated from the United
States Military Academy in 1830, and died at Lexington, Kentucky, June 2, 1837,
aged twenty-seven (*Army and Navy Chronicle*, V, 313).

children were carried on the backs of their mothers and sisters. From August 8 they traveled by land from Rock Roe on the White river, and reached Fort Gibson September third; crossing the Verdigris river they stopped on the west side of that stream in the Creek settlement.[19] To prevent depredations by the emigrants along the road, a law was passed by the chief inflicting "the punishment of fifty lashes upon any person who shall be found guilty of theft. The day after the promulgation of the law, two Uchee girls suffered the penalty of its violations; they were whipped before the whole camp. This has already operated beneficially."[20]

The crowded condition of the boats, the salt rations to which they were unaccustomed, the muddy drinking water from the Mississippi river, and the unbridled indulgence in green fruit after they left the boats resulted in much sickness among the emigrants. The prevailing diseases were bilious and congestive fevers, dysentery, diarrhea, and cholera infantum. A total of eighty-one deaths occurred in this party, including the Indian shot by a soldier in Montgomery and the one who was bayoneted and who died on the boat two days after the party left New Orleans. Of those who died of disease, thirty-seven "were children under five years of age, thirteen under ten, the balance being old and infirm and but a few in the prime of life," according to Dr. Eugene H. Abadie, the surgeon who accompanied them.[21]

A woman was killed near the camp shortly before they reached Fort Gibson. She had climbed a tree to procure grapes from a vine clinging to it, when she fell and broke her back. One of the steamboats

19 After they took up their march from Rock Roe Barry reported: "We have experienced more trouble and difficulty from the white men in this part of the country than from all the Indians; they are the most depraved, lying, cut-throat scoundrels I ever met with. They would come into camp with offers of service to assist us in seizing whiskey and other liquors, and at the same time be selling it to the Indians behind our backs. No serious difficulty occurred, but the people of the neighborhood where we landed are entitled to all the credit for having done everything in their power to bring it about" (Lieut. J. Waller Barry to Gen. George Gibson, August 14, 1836, OIA, "Creek Emigration"). No provision was made to transfer the meager personal effects of the Indians which they were obliged to carry on their backs or leave behind. Barry said the 900 Yuchi had but little baggage, having been driven away from their homes almost destitute.

20 Ibid.

21 Abadie to Gibson, October 20, 1836, OIA, "Creek Emigration."

towed a barge-load of these Indians up the Mississippi river. As they were passing Columbia, Mississippi, and a large number of them were watching the town, the decayed deck collapsed under them, several being injured and a little girl killed.

As the hostile Creeks approached their new home with their chiefs, to be followed by the great majority of the tribe, the small faction of McIntosh Creeks who had emigrated in 1829 became uneasy and restless. A council was held by the Western Creeks August 14 to consider the situation, and from threats made there, General Arbuckle feared disorder and violence if the coming majority of the tribe attempted to establish a government for the whole tribe; and as there was much bad feeling on the part of the early emigrants against those who were approaching, Arbuckle called on the governor of Arkansas for ten companies of volunteers.[22]

However, General Arbuckle and Captain Armstrong arranged a meeting at Fort Gibson between Roley McIntosh the resident chief, Eneah Emathla and Eneah Micco recently arrived, and other chiefs and head men. The new arrivals who had lost everything they possessed were warned that their annuity would be withheld from them unless they met the wishes of the government officials. Under the stress of their great destitution, they agreed to recognize McIntosh as their chief and to live under the government already in operation in the West.

Armstrong said that he had *"never seen so wretched and poor a body of Indians as this party of Creeks; they have really nothing; and at the urgent request of Genl. Arbuckle, together with the Indians, I supplied them with four dozen felling axes; the whole party had not a dozen with them and them worth nothing; and in order to scatter them and get them employed in building houses, I ventured to assume the responsibility of getting them the above mentioned axes. . . I hope the Department will be satisfied that the total destitution of the Indians, together with the object effected of getting them employed and thereby enable them to protect themselves from the approaching winter, will be considered a sufficient excuse. I also put the public blacksmith to making a few frows to rive boards, and some iron wedges, which appeared to satisfy the Indians very*

22 Arbuckle to Jones, August 16, 1836, OIA, "Creek Emigration," File A 31; *Army and Navy Chronicle*, III, 204. These Arkansas volunteers rendezvoused at Fort Towson where they were outfitted and prepared to march to Fort Gibson.

much. . . I do not see how these people are to get along unless they have a portion of the annuity. . . they have but very few ponies, not exceeding a dozen in the whole twenty-three hundred."[23]

The remainder of the "hostiles" in charge of Capt. F. S. Belton of the artillery, principally women and children, aged and infirm, departed from Montgomery August 2 aboard the streamboat *Lewis Cass* and arrived four days later at Mobile where they were transferred to the *Mezeppa*. Outside the Keys they found the passage very rough but arrived safely at Lake Pontchartrain where they were transferred in the rain to a railroad train that carried them to the old barracks at New Orleans. By this time much sickness had developed in the party but regardless of that on the tenth they were all loaded on the steamboat *Mobile* and began the ascent of the Mississippi river. Before they reached Montgomery's Point sickness increased and numbers died.

Amidst lamentations, weeping, and protests against the separation of families, the sick were carried aboard a keel-boat here for passage up the Arkansas river; those able to walk were started overland through the swamps in the hope of finding means of transportation at Arkansas Post. At the first camp of the land party near the river, a flatboat was landed at midnight by the white owners who secretly sold a quantity of whisky to the Indians. In the morning at marching time they were all drunk and the conductors destroyed the liquor concealed about them.

Upon their arrival at Arkansas Post August 25, Captain Belton was discouraged with the prospects of securing transportation. All the vehicles in the vicinity were "miserable ox (cotton) carts, many without tired wheels or indeed without iron of any kind." Owing to the war scare in Texas[24] most of the able bodied men of the country had volunteered and departed for Fort Towson and Fort Gibson to replace the troops from those posts who had been sent to the Texas border. These volunteers had taken with them all the wagons and horses which might have been used for transporting the sick Indians, Lieutenant

---

23 Armstrong to Harris, September 17, 1836, OIA, "Creek File." Nearly two years later General Arbuckle wrote from Fort Gibson that the "poor of the Creek Nation and perhaps other tribes in this vicinity. . . cannot at present obtain furs or deer skins sufficient to enable them to provide themselves and families with clothing" (Arbuckle to Jones, June 19, 1838, OIA, "Western Superintendency").

24 For an account of this disturbance see Grant Foreman, *Pioneer Days in the Early Southwest*, 271.

Barry with his large party having engaged all of the best wagons and teams in the country.

However, by waiting several days at Arkansas Post they were able to secure a few wretched carts and the emigrants departed September 6. *"Moved early and reached Robins, 15 miles. The flies are most distressing; a horse can hardly be controlled from lying down to roll, such is the torment. The heat is excessive and the water of the worst description; some forty-five sick, and constantly dropping; the ox-teams breaking and carts tumbling to pieces."* In four days they reached Mrs. Black's[25] where they secured two more wagons and continued over the roads filled with rocks and roots, that jostled the wretched sick passengers and broke down the carts.

"During the passage of the prairie, it has, with the exception of two days of scorching sun, rained almost all day and night; the situation of the Indians is deplorable; the sick exceed fifty of the small party, and death occasionally carries off the weakest; the wagons or carts have been overloaded and great difficulties surmounted; to reach settlements, forced marches have been necessary. Paid off and discharged the carts engaged at Post Arkansas; three additional wagons are engaged—for Indians one, and for officers transportation; these are miserable small and old vehicles, poor teams and harness, but better cannot be done. The charges too are high indeed, the people taking advantage of an obvious necessity, and having heard of larger parties in the rear, very indifferent about engaging at all. What better can be done? The sick require attention to their situation and weakness & the very elements against us. There is nothing better in prospect, the best wagons being with the large hostile party in charge of Lt. Barry and the Volunteers marching from the neighboring settlements for Fort Towson have engaged every good thing of the kind at enormous prices; the country is sparcely settled; we are at the mercy of circumstances."

25 Mrs. Black's was a public house on the Big Prairie, half way between Rock Roe and Little Rock. The house was a log building "called in the West 'two pens and a passage' which means two rooms from ten to twenty feet apart, the whole under one roof. One of these was the dining room, the other the sleeping room, in which there were four single beds. The kitchen and other apartments occupied by the family, built likewise of logs, were in the rear. I found in Mrs. Black a widow of goodly proportions: I have seen fatter women but not many. She has several sons and daughters growing up" (Description by Captain George A. McCall in 1835, *Letters from the Frontier* (Philadelphia, 1868), 278).

A wheel collapses and the party is delayed while repairs are made. Torrents of rain fall incessantly, day after day, and the wretched emigrants toil and flounder through mud and water in what by courtesy were called roads, but were "mere cut-outs without draining or causeways."

On September 19 the party reached the old home of Maj. William L. Lovely and crossed the Illinois Bayou on the ferry below the site of old Dwight Mission. Normally small streams that had become raging torrents, delayed the party from time to time; arrival at a country smithy was the signal for other delays while much needed repairs were made.

The conductor and journalist Captain Belton was failing under fever and the tremendous hardships of the journey, and on the twenty-seventh he was too ill and weak to note in his journal just where he lay down on the wayside while the Indians struggled on under the direction of his assistant Dr. J. Jones. Only 165 of the original party of 210 put in charge of Captain Belton at Montgomery were finally delivered to Captain Stephenson on October 3. Seventeen had been taken by the civil authorities of Alabama, nineteen had died on the way and nine were missing and unaccounted for.[26]

The "war" was now over except for minor disturbances by a party of Eufaula warriors under Nuthcup Tustenugge and other detached parties that had been driven into the swamps. Now began the enforced removal of the friendly Indians no longer needed to help the whites fight the hostiles. August 1, 2,700 Indians under the leadership of their faithful chief Opothleyaholo began their march.

This contingent in charge of Lieut. M. W. Batman left Tallassee August 31 but proceeded slowly owing to the difficulty of organizing and the demoralization occasioned by the arrest of a number of their principal men by whites to extort from them the little property they had been able hurriedly to salvage from the disaster that had overwhelmed them; the difficulties were so great that General Jesup began to fear the movement would fail entirely. "Suits were multiplied against the Indians—their negroes, horses, and other property taken—themselves driven almost to desperation by the difficulties which surrounded them—the greatest dissatisfaction prevailing among them, there seemed

26 F. S. Belton's Journal, November 28, 1836, OIA, "Creek Emigration."

-{ 160 }-

*to be no means of getting them out of the country peaceably, but by
enabling them to pay the just demands against them and defending
them against those which were doubtful or unjust.*"[27]

The chiefs insisted upon having pay for the land they were leaving,
or advance payment of their annuity for 1837. They had been denied
the proceeds of the sale of their lands by the frauds committed upon
them, and their enforced departure before the time specified in their
treaty, and saw no way to begin life anew in their western home
without the assistance of their annuities. At this time when the women
and children most needed their men to help them on their journey, to
begin new homes and put in crops for sustenance, the president conceived the amazing policy of calling upon them for a force of their
warriors to fight the Seminole Indians in Florida; this incomprehensible
course was calculated to contribute to their helplessness and destitution.

Taking advantage of their necessities, General Jesup made the furnishing of the force required by the president one of the conditions
upon which he would comply with their demands. A contract was
therefore executed August 28, 1836, between John A. Campbell
appointed by Jesup as a commissioner on the part of the United States
and Opothleyaholo, Little Doctor, Tukabahchee Micco, and Yelka Hadjo for the Creek Nation by which the Indians were enabled to ransom
themselves from the whites. By this contract the United States agreed
to advance the Creek Indians their annuity of $31,900 to be applied
to the payment of their alleged debts. This money was paid them in
consideration of their agreement to "furnish from their tribe 600 to
1,000 men for service against the Seminoles, to be continued in service
until the same shall be conquered, they to receive the pay and emolu-
ments and equipment of soldiers, in the Army of the U. S. and such
plunder as they may take from the Seminoles." The offer of "plunder"
was understood to authorize the Creek warriors to keep such slaves
as they could capture in Florida.[28]

After these negotiations were completed and the rapacity of the
whites temporarily was abated by the payment to them of the Indians'
annuity advanced by the government, Batman's emigrants resumed

27 Jesup to Cass, August 30, 1836, OIA, "Creek File" J 22.
28 Jesup to Harris, September 24, 1837, OIA, "Seminole Emigration."

their march September 2[29] and reached Tuscaloosa on the twelfth. As this sad cavalcade of people passed through the town, a sympathetic observer remarked on their appearance: "*They all presented a squalid, forlorn, and miserable condition, and seemed to be under the influence of deep melancholy and deep dejection. They are said to have left their homes with great reluctance, but they are becoming more reconciled to their destiny. Their condition excited much sympathy and commiseration in the hearts of our citizens, and many a heartfelt regret was uttered at the necessity which compelled us to remove them to the far West.*"[30]

Batman reported no further interruption or trouble except that many of the Indians got drunk on whisky furnished by white people in every town or village through which they passed. They arrived at Memphis October 7, and on the thirteenth 1,200 of them boarded the steamboat *Farmer* and after four days reached Rock Roe where they began their land journey.

More than three weeks later on November 8,[31] the first division of this party in charge of Batman had traveled only forty-eight miles and arrived at the crossroads at Irwin's Stand twenty miles north of Little Rock. "The roads are most horridly bad" said their conductor; "Rains have been falling almost every day."[32] They arrived at Fort Gibson December 7 and the remainder of the party four days later. "*The march has been long, laborious, and tedious. The roads and weather have been indescribably bad. The Indians have suffered much, especially the old and infirm and children. Two of the rear parties, say about 5,000 souls arrived within the last two days. Two parties are still in the rear, say about 6,000. I am fearful that they are detained by high water.*"[33]

The second detachment composed of 3,022 Indians headed by William McGillivrey and conducted by Lieut. R. B. Screven departed from Wetumka August 6; it crossed the Coosa river September 3, and on reaching Memphis six weeks later, there were 3,142 in the party. From here they went by water to Rock Roe whence they resumed their land journey. They arrived at Little Rock on November 20 and

29 Batman to commissary general of subsistence, September 2, 1836, OIA, "Creek Emigration," File B 535.
30 *Arkansas Gazette*, October 11, 1836.
31 *Ibid.*, November 8, 1836.
32 Batman to Harris, December 12, 1836, OIA, "Creek Emigration" File B 112
33 *Ibid.*, December 12, 1836.

GRANT FOREMAN

Old road at site of Cherokee Camp on bank of Arkansas River at mouth of Cadron Creek

went into camp across the river a mile and a half from the village; a stop here was necessitated by the fact that several hundred of their horses had been lost and the Indians suffered from a failure of the contractors to provide adequate supplies of corn and other provisions; what they succeeded in procuring was obtained at exorbitant prices.[34]

Hungry, straggling bands of this party dropped off here and there, killing hogs and stealing food to keep from starving, and only about 2,000 were delivered at Fort Gibson by Screven.[35] Some of those who were left along the road were later placed on board the steamboat *John Nelson* which went aground near Fort Coffee and the Indians were put ashore to walk to Fort Gibson.

Another party of 1,170 from Talledega district in charge of Lieut. Edward Deas, began their sad journey on August 6.[36] These people were collected from Randolph, Benton, and Talledega counties, and included 400 Creeks captured by the troops in Tennessee. When they reached Gunter's Landing on the Tennessee river November 18, accessions there increased the number to 2,000. Deas then returned to Talledega and brought another party of 2,320 over the same route. The first party crossed the Tennessee river at Deposit Landing September 25 and proceeded by way of Huntsville to Memphis,[37] while the second accompanied by Deas passed through Decatur and Courtland, arrived at Tuscumbia October 2,[38] and on the twenty-fifth reached Memphis where its members found their neighbors who had preceded them. Both parties camped half a mile below Memphis on the bank of the Mississippi to await transportation across the river.

By early November it was reported from Memphis: "*Our town and vicinity have been filled and no little annoyed for the past two weeks by the emigrating Creek Indians; 8,000 of them have crossed the Mississippi. . and 5,000 more are around us. In about two weeks the whole tribe, about 15,000, will be west of the Mississippi. Lieut.Sprague leaves today with*

34 *Army and Navy Chronicle*, December 5, 1836, III, 382; *Arkansas Gazette*, November 22, 1836, p. 2, col. 2.

35 *Army and Navy Chronicle*, III, 412.

36 Of this party 413 were under ten years of age, 247 between ten and twenty-five, and eighty-one over fifty; six hundred and twenty-six of them were females (OIA, Muster Roll).

37 Deas to Gibson, September 27, 1836, OIA, "Creek Emigration" File 73.

38 *Ibid.*, October 2, 1836.

his party accompanied by the chief Tukkabachee Hadjo in steamboats to Little Rock, the Arkansas bottoms being excessively muddy. They are generally in good health. Most of the chiefs opposed taking water, fearing sickness, but their greatest dread was being thrown overboard when dead."[39]

The Mississippi swamps in Arkansas were found to be impassable for wagons and Deas secured transportation by water for his people as far as Rock Roe, the horses to be driven through the swamps. Deas's Indians on November 5, were the last to cross the Mississippi river.[40] They left Memphis on two steamboats one of which reached a point two miles below Rock Roe in four days and the other in seven, having been delayed by running aground. On their arrival at Rock Roe, Deas found that the contractors had failed to assemble provisions for the emigrants as their contract required, and much delay and suffering resulted while their conductor scoured the surrounding country for food.

A large number of the Indians had refused to board the boats at Memphis and undertook to make their way by land. A sub-agent of the contractors was directed to conduct them through the swamps but he neglected his duty and arrived at Rock Roe with only a small fraction of the party; the remainder he left strung along almost impassable roads through the swamps without food, no adequate provision having been made to care for and feed them. Deas went back over the road and found several hundred Indians in wretched camps, sick, exhausted, and hungry with no means of transportation, and "the whole road from Rock Roe full of dead horses and Indian ponies." Deas started his main party from Rock Roe on November 20 and then went back to pick up the stragglers and get them in motion again.[41]

Most of his Indians who were traveling by land reached the vicinity of Little Rock in about a week, but they refused to go any further until the hundreds of sick left behind along the road, could catch up. They remained several weeks in camp in the vicinity, and their consumption of supplies brought a measure of prosperity to those who had

39 *Memphis Enquirer*, account copied in *Arkansas Gazette*, November 15, 1836, p. 2, col. 6.

40 Deas to Gibson, November 5, 1836, OIA, "Creek Emigration."

41 *Ibid.*, November 22, 1836.

them to sell, but greatly increased the price of provisions. This exasperated the residents and exaggerated complaints were made of depredations committed by the Indians on corn fields, hogs, and rail fences which they used for fuel; Gov. J. S. Conway made an imperious demand on Lieutenant Deas to remove his Indians from the vicinity immediately, and to make no more unnecessary stops within the state; and he announced the law for all other government agents in charge of emigrating Indians.[42] Deas in a respectful reply explained to the governor the necessity for the stops in the interest of humanity and efficient emigration, and his authority from the government to determine when such stops should be made.[43] The colloquoy was an indication of the hostile feelings entertained by the whites toward these unfortunate people who by no desire of their own were obliged to pass through the state.

42   Conway to Deas, December 6, 1836, *ibid.*, File D 17.
43   Deas to Conway, December 8, 1836, *ibid.*

T HE fifth detachment of Creeks numbering 1,984 left Tallassee September 5 in charge of Lieut. J. T. Sprague of the marine corps. He had been directed by General Jesup to proceed to the Kasihta and Coweta towns and prepare the Indians for immediate removal. He arrived there the tenth of August, he relates in his interesting journal of events; there he had "*an interview with the principal Chief, Tuck-e-batch-e-hadjo, and urged upon him the necessity of taking immediate measures to prepare his people for emigration. To this, after using every argument against it, he reluctantly consented. His principal reasons were, that his peoples crops were not gathered. . . their cattle were not sold, and that the time specified for their departure was earlier than he anticipated.*

"*The following day, I assembled all the chiefs and explained to them the necessary arrangements to embody their towns, in order to transfer them to the charge of the Alabama Emigrating Company upon such a day as might be designated by the Commanding General. They gave no other than a silent acquiescence to my wishes, but expressed among themselves strong feelings of dissatisfaction. I promised them every assistance in disposing of what little they had, but assured them that upon the day fixed for their departure they must be ready.*

"*The necessity of their leaving their country immediately was evident to every one; although wretchedly poor they were growing more so every day they remained. A large number of whitemen were prowling about, robbing them of their horses and cattle and carrying among them liquors which kept up an alarming state of intoxication. The citizens of the country had no security, for though these Indians had professed the most friendly feelings, no confidence could be placed in them, as the best informed inhabitants of the country believed them to be allied with those who had already committed overt acts of hostility. Some families which had* fled for safety were afraid to return until the country was rid of every Indian. Public indignation was strong against them, and no doubt the most serious consequences would have resulted, had not immediate measures been adopted for their removal.

"In this state of things, however indignant their feelings or however great the sacrifice, it was but justice to get them out of the country as soon as possible. On the 23rd. inst. I received orders from the Commanding General to move the Party on the 29 inst. The time, however, was prolonged five days, to the 3rd of September. On the 1st of September I had in Camp near two thousand ready for removal. This number comprised the whole of the two towns, excepting a few who had been secreted in a swamp from the commencement of the Creek War. These sent an express to know if I would receive them as friends, should they come in. I assured them they would be treated like the rest. I heard no more from them until the ninth night of our march, when they joined the train with their women and children. Their number I could never learn, as they kept themselves aloof lest they might be treated as hostiles; but from other Indians, who were silent on the subject, I learnt there were from one hundred to one hundred and fifty.

"The 3rd of September I placed all the Indians under my charge in care of Mr. Felix G. Gibson and Charles Abercrombie, members of the Alabama Emigrating Company, and on the morning of the 5th the Party started for Arkansas, arranged to waggons according to the contract. The train consisted of forty-five waggons of every description, five hundred ponies and two thousand Indians. The moving of so large a body necessarily required some days to effect an arrangement to meet the comfort and convenience of all. The marches for the first four or five days were long and tedious and attended with many embarrassing circumstances. Men, who had ever had claims upon these distressed beings, now preyed upon them without mercy. Fraudulent demands were presented and unless some friend was near, they were robbed of their horses and even clothing. Violence was often resorted to to keep off these depredators to such an extent, that unless forced marches had been made to get out of this and the adjoining counties, the Indians would have been wrought to such a state of desperation that no persuasion would have deterred them from wreaking their vengeance upon the innocent as well as the guilty.

"As soon as time and circumstances would permit, proper arrangements were made to secure to the Indians, regularly, their rations and transportation. A large herd of cattle were driven ahead of the train which supplied the Party with fresh beef. Two days rations were issued every other day, while corn was issued every day. The Party moved on without any serious inconvenience, other than the bad state of the roads and frequent drunken broils, until the 22nd, when from the warmth of the weather and the wearied condition of the Indians, I deemed it expedient to halt for a days rest. Tuck-e-batch-e-hadjo, the principal chief, had been desirous of stopping sooner, and had expressed his determination to do so. The situation of the camp at the time was not a desirable one for a halt, nor was I inclined to indulge him. I ordered the train to proceed. He with reluctance, came on.

"From the first days march, I saw a disposition in the Indians, among both old and young, to remain behind. From their natural indolence and from their utter disregard for the future, they would straggle in the rear, dependent upon what they could beg, steal or find for support. I used every entreaty to induce them to keep up but finding this of no avail I threatened them with soldiers and confinement in irons. This had a salutary effect, and was the means of bringing most of them into camp in good season. On the night of the 24th inst. the party encamped at Town Creek, Al., after twenty days march averaging about twelve miles a day. I waited on the contractors and requested them to halt the party the following day. To this they expressed their unqualified disapprobation and denied my authority to exercise such a power. Their expenses they said were from six to seven hundred dollars per day, and if such authority was given or implied in the Contract, their hopes of making anything were gone. I assured them, that from the condition of the Indians, the common calls of humanity required it, and that one of the stipulations of the Contract was that they should treat the Indians with humanity and forbearance. I ordered the Indians to halt, and told the Contractors they could act on their own pleasure; either go on with their empty waggons—or remain. The party halted and resumed the journey on the following morning, the 25th. The Indians and horses were evidently much relieved by the days rest.

"From this period to the fifth of October our marches were long, owing to the great scarcity of water; no one time, however, exceeding twenty miles. The Indians in large numbers straggled behind; and many could not

get to Camp till after dark. These marches would not have been so bur-
densome had proper attention been paid to the starting of the Party in
the morning. It was necessary that their baggage, as well as their children,
should be put in the waggons, and the sick and feeble sought out in the
different parts of the Camp. But this was totally disregarded. I reminded
the Contractors that the party now required the utmost attention, that
unless they were strictly seen to, we should not at night have more than
half the Indians in Camp. To this they were indifferent, saying, that
'they must keep up or be left'. Early in the morning the waggons moved
off, the Agents at the head, leaving those behind to take care of themselves.[1] Its an absurdity to say, that the Indians must take care of themselves; they are men it is true, but it is well known that they are totally
incapable of it, and its proverbial that they will never aid each other.

"To this course of proceeding I remonstrated, and the tenth article
of the Contract which authorizes the officer to make any expenditure con-
tributing to the comfort and convenience, etc., I put in execution, which
relieved the Indians from the destitute situation in which they would otherwise have been placed. My letters to the Contractors accompanying this
report embrace this period and will explain to you more fully the course
I was compelled to adopt. It, however, affords me pleasure to say, that upon
a better knowledge of their obligations, they very readily consented to pay
the expenses which accrued in keeping up the rear.

"On the 5th of October I again halted the party and rested one day.
To this the contractors objected and seemed determined to drive the
Indians into their measures. The 7th the party again moved and on the
9th inst. encamped near Memphis, Tenn. Great inconvenience was
experienced upon this entire route for the want of Depots of provisions.
There was no time when the proper rations were not issued, but from the
frequent necessity of gathering and hauling corn, the Indians were often
obliged to take their rations after dark. This caused great confusion and
many were deprived of their just share. Though the neglect of these Agents
in not bringing up the rear of the party deserves the severest reprehension,
yet, I must in frankness acknowledge that there were many who would not

---

1 "The lame, sick, and blind were left behind, dependent upon the charity of
the country; I remonstrated against such a manifest violation of the contract. They
[contractors] denied all that I alleged and treated my complaints with contempt. . .
hired waggons and brought up such Indians who from various causes were unable
to get up" (Sprague to Gibson, October 16, 1836, OIA, "Creek Emigration").

come up under the most favorable circumstances. This, however, was no apology for not bringing up those who would, or at least making an effort. If liquor could be found upon the road, or within four or six miles of it, men and women would congregate there, and indulge in the most brutal scenes of intoxication. If any white-man broke in upon these bacchanals he did it at the imminent hazard of his life. Often in this state they would come reeling and singing into camp late at night, threatening the lives of all who came within their reach—alarming the citizens of the country, and not infrequently creating the most indignant feelings among the sober Indians towards all the white-men who were about them. They would taunt them as cowards and dare them to join them in some nefarious act. Without the means of quelling such restless spirits by the strong arm of power, the most kind and conciliatory feelings should have been evinced towards them. But unfortunately for me, these Agents entertained no such sentiments.

"At Memphis I met a number of the contractors and before them I laid my complaints and convinced them that if no remedy was provided, I was determined to relieve the company of their charge of the Indians, and take the arduous responsibility of taking them to Arkansas myself. The President of the Company in a highly honourable manner declared that nothing should be left undone to meet the wishes of the Officers of the Government. These Agents I either wanted dismissed or taught the first lesson of the obligations they had assumed. One of the Agents left the party, and it was afterwards in charge of Mr. Gibson and Gilman. Here, I think, Mr. Gibson for the first time read the contract, and I found in him ever after a willingness to comply with what I considered expedient for the comfort and convenience of the Indians. With such indications of a proper interpretation and understanding of the contract, and upon the assurances of the most respectable men belonging to the Company, I could have no hesitation in giving them an opportunity to redeem their pledges.

"At Memphis we remained from the 9th of October until the 27th. The Mississippi was here to be crossed, and the Company were much disappointed in not finding their steam boats as they anticipated. The boats, however, arrived on the 11th; Captain Batman's party were the first to cross, Lieutenant Screvens was the second, and my own the third. Lieutenant Deas' and Mr. Campbell's parties were in the rear. The assembling of thirteen thousand Indians at this one point, necessarily made our movements slow. This detention was of advantage to the Indians as it gave them rest and afforded the sick and feeble an opportunity to recover. The required rations were furnished them regularly within this time, and they all conducted with the greatest propriety. The Common Council of the City passed an ordinance prohibiting the sale of liquor, which added greatly to their comfort, and to the peace and security of the citizens.

"The Mississippi Swamp at this season was impassable for waggons and it was agreed that the horses should go through while the women and children with their baggage took steam boats to Rock Roe. This place was attained by descending the Mississippi, about one hundred miles to the mouth of White River, and ascending this river about seventy miles, and thereby avoiding a swamp about fifty miles in breadth.

"Finding that the embarkation of the parties that proceeded mine would cause much delay, a mutual agreement was effected between the Chiefs, the contractors and myself, to take the party up the Arkansas river to Little Rock. The advantages to be gained by this were evident; it put us ahead of all the other parties, secured us an abundant supply of provisions, and avoided a tedious journey of one hundred and fifty miles on foot. A commodious steam boat was procured and upon this and two flat boats I put as near as could be estimated fifteen hundred women and children and some men, with their baggage. The men amounting to some six or seven hundred passed through the swamp with their horses, in charge of my Assistant Agent Mr. Freeman. I received every assurance that upon this route the necessary provision was made for them. On board the boats, an abundance of corn and bacon were stored for the party to subsist upon until we should reach Little Rock. On the 27th the boat started. The Indians were comfortably accommodated, sheltered from the severity of the weather and from the many sufferings attending a journey on foot. The boats stopped at night for them to cook and sleep, and in the morning, resumed the journey.

"The current of the Arkansas being so strong at this time, it was found expedient to leave a part of the Indians until the boat could go up and return.[2] These were left in the care of an Agent with the necessary supplies. On the 3rd of November we arrived at Little Rock. The larger

2 They were brought up by the steamboat *John Nelson*. They left Little Rock by land on November 4 and 5 while the steamboat returned down the river to Arkansas Post to bring up the remainder numbering 900. Some of those who had gone

portion of the party which passed through the Swamp, joined us the 4th. Many remained behind and sent word, that 'when they had got bear skins enough to cover them they would come on.' Here, they felt independent, game was abundant and they were almost out of the reach of the white-men. At first, it was my determination to remain at Little Rock until the whole party should assemble. But from the scarcity of provisions and the sale of liquor, I determined to proceed up the country about fifty miles and there await the arrival of all the Indians. Tuck-e-batch-e-hadjo refused to go. 'He wanted nothing from the white-men and should rest.' Every resting place with him was where he could procure a sufficiency of liquor. The petulant and vindictive feeling which this Chief so often evinced, detracted very much from the authority he once exercised over his people. But few were inclined to remain with him.

"The 12th we encamped at Potts,[3] the place designated for the concentration of the whole party. My Assistant Agent, together with three Agents of the Company, returned immediately to bring up and subsist all in the rear. Some of them went as far back as the Mississippi Swamp. They collected, subsisted and transported all they could get to start by every argument and entreaty. . . . A body of Indians under a secondary Chief, Narticher-tus-ten-nugge expressed their determination to remain in the swamp in spite of every remonstrance. They evinced the most hostile feelings and cautioned the white-men to keep away from them. The 14th the steam boat that had returned from Little Rock to bring up those left on the Arkansas, arrived at our encampment with Tuck-e-batch-e-hadjo and his few adherents on board. On this boat the following day, I put all the sick, feeble and aged, placed them in charge of Doctor Hill, the surgeon of the party, with instructions to proceed to Fort Gibson, and then be governed by the proper officer at that place. This party arrived at their place of destination on the 22nd instant and were received by the officer of the proper department. The Agents bringing up the rear, arrived at camp on the 17th. Those in the Swamp still persisted in their determination to remain.[4] Neither the Agents or myself had any means by which we could force them into proper measures, most conducive to

---

overland through the swamps overtook them at the Dardanelle (*Arkansas Gazette*, November 8, 1836, p. 2, col. 1).

3 Near Lewisburg, Arkansas.

4 More than a month later these destitute Indians were still in camp near Potts, trying to keep from freezing. On December 26 the governor of Arkansas ordered 100

their comfort and progress. The season being far advanced and the weather daily becoming more severe, I ordered the party to proceed the following morning.

"The sufferings of the Indians at this period were intense. With nothing more than a cotton garment thrown over them, their feet bare, they were compelled to encounter cold, sleeting storms and to travel over hard frozen ground. Frequent appeals were made to me to clothe their nakedness and to protect their lacerated feet. To these I could do no more than what came within the provisions of the Contract. I ordered the party to halt on the 22nd and proceeded again on the 23rd. The weather was still severe, but delay only made our condition worse. The steam boat, on its return from Fort Gibson, fortunately found us encamped near the river Spadra. On board of her I succeeded in getting nearly the whole party, amounting now to some sixteen hundred souls.

"The boat started again for Fort Gibson on the 24th. Those that determined to go up by land were all mounted or in waggons and I directed them to proceed as fast as possible. On the 30th we learned that owing to the rapid fall of the Arkansas the boat had grounded. We soon came in the vicinity of her; waggons were procured and this body from the boat soon joined those on shore. The Indians here were frequently intoxicated. They procured liquor from other Indians residents of the country, and the artifices of both combined no man could detect. On the 7th of December, when within eighteen miles of Fort Gibson, I again halted the party, and agents were sent back to bring up all that could be found in the rear. This being done, we started the following morning, and arrived at Fort Gibson on the 10th inst. By the order of Brigadier General Arbuckle I encamped the party in the vicinity of the Fort.

"Many reports were in circulation that the Creeks settled in the country were inimical to the emigrants, and it was deemed advisable to have a perfect understanding among all parties previous to entering their new country. This was effected to the satisfaction of all, but how long it will last the future can only tell. Two agents belonging to my party, who had remained behind, arrived on the 15th, bringing on all they could find or all that were willing to come; a few they said were behind. As soon as I was satisfied that all were present that could be brought up, I had

---

troops of the militia to drive them out of their camp, and the Indians fled towards Fort Gibson (*Arkansas Gazette*, January 17, 1837, p. 3, col. 1).

the number counted as correctly as circumstances would admit. The number present was twenty two hundred and thirty seven. The number for which I required of the Company rations and transportation, was two thousand and eighty seven; leaving one hundred and fifty that were not enrolled. This number, no doubt, were the hostiles who joined the train on the march. I could never obtain from the Indians, nor from any one identified with them, any satisfactory information respecting their number or how they subsisted. Their friends, doubtless, shared their rations with them, to prevent their being enrolled lest they might be treated with severity. I gave them every assurance of friendship but it had no avail.

"On the 20th inst. the officer of the Government appointed to receive the Emigrating Creeks, acknowledged the receipt of my entire party. . . After the Indians had received their blankets in compliance with the treaty, I proceeded with the larger portion of them to the country assigned them. Thirty five miles beyond Fort Gibson I encamped them upon a prairie and they soon after scattered in every direction, seeking a desirable location for their new homes. . .

"The excessive bad state of the roads, the high waters, and the extreme cold and wet weather, was enough to embarrass the strongest minds. The distance traveled by the party from Chambers County, Alabama, to their last encampment, was eight hundred miles by land, and four hundred and twenty-five by water; occupying ninety-six days. The health of the Indians upon the entire route was much better than might have been anticipated.

"Twenty nine deaths were all that occurred; fourteen of these were children and the others were the aged, feeble and intemperate. The unfriendly disposition of the Indians towards the whites from the earliest history of our country, is known to everyone. To what an extent this feeling existed in the party under my charge, I cannot with confidence say, for it was seldom expressed but when in a state of intoxication. But if this be a fair criterion, I have no hesitation in saying it was the most vindictive and malignant kind. To say they were not in a distressed and wretched condition, would be in contradiction to the well known history of the Creeks for the last two years. They were poor, wretchedly, and depravedly poor, many of them without a garment to cover their nakedness. To this there was some exceptions, but this was the condition of a large portion of them. They left their country, at a warm season of the year, thinly clad and characteristically indifferent to their rapid approach to the regions of a climate to which they were unaccustomed, they expended what little they had for intoxicating drinks or for some gaudy article of jewelry.

"So long a journey under the most favorable auspices must necessarily be attended with suffering and fatigue. They were in a deplorable condition when they left their homes, and a journey of upwards of a thousand miles could not certainly have improved it. There was nothing within the provisions of the contract by which the Alabama Emigrating Company could contribute to their wants, other than the furnishing of rations and transportation, and a strict compliance with the demands of the officer of the Government; these demands, unquestionably, must come within the letter and spirit of the contract. All these they complied with. The situation of the officers of the Government, at the head of these parties, was peculiarly responsible and embarrassing. They were there to protect the rights of the Indians and to secure to them all the Government designed for them. These Indians, looking up to the officers as a part of the Government, not only appealed for their rights, but their wants. They could sympathize with them, as every one must who saw their condition, but could not relieve them. They had nothing, within their power, for in a pecuniary point they were scarcely better off than those they were willing to assist. All that the contract granted was secured to them. But all this could not shield them from the severity of the weather, cold sleeting storms, and hard frozen ground.

"Had a few thousand dollars been placed at the disposal of the officer which he could have expended at his discretion, the great sufferings which all ages, particularly the young, were subjected to, might have been in a measure avoided. But as it was, the officer was obliged to listen to their complaints without any means of redress. Captain Batman's was the first party to arrive at Fort Gibson, my own was the second, Mr. Campbell's the third. Lieutenant Screvens' the fourth and Lt. Deas' the fifth. . .

"Many exaggerated reports are in circulation, respecting the miserable condition of these emigrating Indians. Let these be traced to the proper source and it will be found that the white-men with whom they have been associated for years past have been the principal cause. There is enough in support of this opinion. It is only necessary to advert to the allegations in many instances, well established, of the lands of the Indians having been purchased by some of these citizens at prices much below their real value, or of the purchase money having been in whole or in part, withheld, the prosecution for valid or fictitious debts, commenced at the moment of their departure for the west, and thereby extorting from them what little money they had.

"Had they been permitted to retain the fair proceeds of their lands they would have had the means of procuring any additional supplies for their comfort. The stipulations of the treaty were fairly executed; all that was to be furnished the Indians was provided, and if these were inadequate to their comfortable removal and subsistence, no blame can be attached to the agents of the Alabama Emigrating Company or to the officers of the government."[5]

On their arrival at Fort Gibson[6] a number of this company belonging to Kasihta Town addressed a letter to their conductor: "You have been with us many moons. . . you have heard the cries of our women and children. . . our road has been a long one. . . and on it we have laid the bones of our men, women, and children. When we left our homes the great General Jesup told us that we could get to our country as we wanted to. We wanted to gather our crops, and we wanted to go in peace and friendship. Did we? No! We were drove off like wolves. . . lost our crops. . . and our peoples' feet were bleeding with long marches. . . Tell General Jackson if the white man will let us we will live in peace and friendship. . . but tell him these agents [emigrating contractors] came not to treat us well, but make money and tell our people behind not to be drove off like dogs. We are men. . . we have women and children, and why should we come like wild horses?" The letter contained expressions of keen appreciation of the kindness of Lieutenant Sprague for his efforts to ameliorate their misery and afford such comfort as he could.[7]

5   Sprague to Harris, April 1, 1837, OIA, "Creek Emigration." This emigration denuded the country through which the Indians passed of cattle, hogs, and corn; all who sold demanded specie and as Arkansas money was discounted twenty to thirty per cent in New Orleans banks, contractors who engaged to furnish provisions to the immigrants in their new home were obliged to go to Missouri, Illinois and other states for them.

6   Ibid., December 20, 1836.

7   Letter to Lieutenant Sprague, December 21, 1836, ibid.

N° PORTION of our American history can furnish a parallel to the misery and suffering "*at present endured by the emigrating Creeks. They consist of all ages, sexes, and sizes, and of all the varieties of human intellect and condition, from the civilized and tenderly nourished matron and misses, to the wild savage, and the poorest of the poor.*

"*Thousands of them are entirely destitute of shoes or cover of any kind for their feet; many of them are almost naked, and but few of them anything more on their persons than a light dress calculated only for the summer, or for a warm climate. . . In this destitute condition, they are wading in cold mud, or are hurried on over the frozen ground, as the case may be. Many of them have in this way had their feet frost-bitten; and being unable to travel, fall in the rear of the main party, and in this way are left on the road to await the ability or convenience of the contractors to assist them. Many of them, not being able to endure this unexampled state of human suffering, die, and are thrown by the side of the road, and are covered over only with brush, etc—where they remain until devoured by the wolves.*

"*How long this state of things will exist, it is hard to conjecture. It is now past the middle of December, and the winter, though cold, is by no means at its worst stage, and when the extreme of winter does fall upon these most miserable creatures, in their present suffering and desperate condition, the destruction of human life will be most deplorable.*"[1]

Capt. John Stuart reported from Fort Coffee January 15 that among the thousands of Creeks crossing Arkansas, many were unable to keep up with the main parties, and, falling in the rear, received none of the food

---

1 Letter from Little Rock, December 25, 1836, in *New York Observer*, February 11, 1837, p. 4.

issued by the contractors; and they would kill a hog or take a bushel of corn to keep their families from starving. A great clamor was made by the whites on account of these depredations; Stuart did not think the loss amounted to much in the aggregate, but the whites were preparing to file claims for a large amount of money. *"The condition of the Creeks yet on the road to Fort Gibson, is most terrible. It is said they are strewed along the road for a great distance, I know not how far. Many of them are almost naked and are without shoes. The snow for five days has been from 4 to 8 inches deep and during the first and second days of the storm, women and children were seen bending their way onward, with piteous and heartrending cries, from cold, etc. I have not heard anything from them for the last three days and whether any of them have perished, I know not."*[2]

Their trail was easy to follow: *". . .Numerous square holes cut in the fallen trees showed where the squaws had pounded their maize to make bread. More melancholy traces were visible in the bones of human beings and animals which were strewed about. Many a warrior and squaw died on the road from exhaustion, and the maladies engendered by their treatment; and their relations and friends could do nothing more for them than fold them in their blankets, and cover them with boughs and bushes, to keep off the vultures, which followed their route by thousands, and soared over their heads; for their drivers would not give them time to dig a grave and bury their dead. The wolves, which also followed at no great distance, soon tore away so frail a covering, and scattered the bones in all directions."*[3]

By November a large part of the emigrating Creeks amounting to nearly fourteen thousand were crossing the State of Arkansas, making almost a continuous line from Little Rock to Fort Gibson as with aching hearts and bitter reflections they toiled wearily over the rough roads. On December 18 of that year General Arbuckle was moved by the sad state of recent arrivals, and he reported to Washington that Opothleyaholo and six thousand other Creeks were camped near Fort Gibson in a wretched condition; they had no winter clothes, as their baggage had all been left behind by the contractors who had promised to send it along with them but had not kept their agreement. From

2 Stuart to Jones, January 15, 1837, OIA, "Creek Emigration" File A 110.
3 Frederick Gerstaecker, *Wild Sports in the Far West* (London, 1854), 276.

November 22 to December 22, 1836, 9,833 Creeks had been delivered at Fort Gibson and the Verdigris river by the contractor, the Alabama Emigrating Company, and by spring 15,045 Creek emigrants were being subsisted in their new country.[4]

While the great majority of the Creeks were emigrated in 1836, a considerable number for various reasons did not remove[5] until the next year. Believing the Seminole war would be of short duration, 776 Creek warriors under their chief Jim Boy[6] had enlisted for service in Florida[7] with the assurance that they would be discharged on the first

4   In all, 14,609 Creeks were removed in 1836 including 2,495 enrolled as hostile (*American State Papers*, "Military Affairs," VII, 952).

5   A considerable number escaped to Florida where they joined the Seminole; but "several hundred Indians who escaped from Echo Hadjo's camp, in this neighborhood [Tuskegee, Alabama, 8th September, 1836] and attempted to force their way into Florida, were attacked in the most gallant manner by the Georgia troops, and, with few exceptions, were destroyed, captured or driven back to their swamps" (*Army and Navy Chronicle*, III, 189).

6   Two of the sons of Jim Boy served with him in Florida (*Mobile Daily Commercial Register and Patriot*, January 23, 1837, p. 2, col. 1). Much credit was given Jim Boy for the successful termination of the Creek "war" (Account from *Montgomery Journal*, in *Arkansas Advocate*, August 12, 1836, p. 2, col. 4). Some of the Creeks escaped "down Chocktahatchie River" into Florida, committing depredations. "These Indians are not disposed to emigrate to Arkansas; hence their women have murdered their own small children and fight as the men" (Letter from Archibald Smith, Indian Agent, Blackwater Bay, March 4, 1837, to *Pensacola Gazette*, in *Mobile Daily Commercial Register and Patriot*, March 15, 1837, p. 2, col. 1). There is other authority that these women who engaged with their men in grim war to the death, killed their young children; experience had shown that they must inevitably have succumbed anyway to the cruel warfare in which their parents were engaged, and their infant voices might betray them when secrecy and silence were vital.

7   One of the Creek officers was David Moniac who was graduated from the United States Military Academy with the class of 1822; this Indian was first commissioned second lieutenant in the Sixth Infantry, but resigned from the army in December of the same year. When the Creeks entered the service against the Seminole, Moniac volunteered, and on August 17 was made captain in the Mounted Creek regiment; November 15, 1836, he was promoted to major. Six days later in the battle of Wahoo Swamp, while crossing a difficult morass in the face of Seminole fire, he was killed. He was thirty-four years of age at the time of his death (G. W. Cullum, *Biographical Register of the Officers and Graduates of the U. S. Military Academy*, I, 239). His grave was added to the two large burial places containing the men of Dade's company massacred by the Seminole on December 28, 1835 (*Manuscript Diary of Major Ethan Allen Hitchcock*, Library of Congress). Echo Hadjo was another influential Creek enlisted against the Seminole (*Army and Navy Chronicle*, III, 285).

of February, 1837, so they could begin their journey to the West with their families in time to put in a crop in their new country that would sustain them the following year. But finding the Seminole problem too difficult for solution in a few months, General Jesup detained them seven months beyond that time, against their wishes, while they suffered much from sickness. To reconcile them to remaining longer, he told them the government would subsist them for a year after their arrival in the West and until they could gather their first crops.[8]

While the regiment of Creek warriors were engaged under the officers of the United States in fighting the Seminole, their families remained in Alabama in concentration camps under the supposed protection of federal officers. Here they were assured they would remain in peace until their men came home to take charge of them for removal to the West. In December, 1836, one of them was killed by some white men.

A few hundred of the hostile Creeks who had been driven into the swamps in a starving condition were still in hiding with their chief Tuskeneah. During December a party of them looking for food attacked the plantation of Doctor Battle on Cowigee creek, burned some houses and killed a negro man. The next month they attacked the plantation of Lewis Pugh higher up the creek, where they killed Pugh and some negroes. A company of white volunteers then went to the neighborhood and killed a number of Indians. While this seemed to be the end of the Indian hostilities, the whites claiming to be alarmed for their safety, induced the government agents to take away the firearms from the friendly Indians who were located near their agent Lieut. John G. Reynolds about thirty miles from the hostiles.

In the early part of February a considerable number of men from Russell county, Alabama and Franklin county, Georgia, appeared in the settlement of these friendly Indians concentrated around Reynolds, who was expected to afford them the protection promised them by General Jesup. By way of introducing themselves, they first "halted at the house of Anne Curnell, a half-breed Indian, secured and carried away

8 *American State Papers*, "Military Affairs," VII, 522, 866. "Had they left me on the first of February," wrote General Jesup, "according to the assurances given to them, I must have called into service at least two regiments of militia or volunteers to have taken their places, at a heavy expense" (Jesup to secretary of war, March 7, 1837, OIA, "Creek Emigration" J 72).

two free Negroes and an Indian boy, besides setting fire to and wholly destroying all her houses, fodder stacks, and moveable property generally, including three hundred dollars in bank bills. This sir, I have from the suffering woman herself, who is now on the Point. . ."[9]

About ten days later these citizen companies again entered the camp of the agent and proceeded to make prisoners of some of his charges. The agent protested against the outrage and explained that "the faith of the government had been pledged to the Creek warriors then helping the United States in Florida, that those remaining behind should be wholly unmolested by the citizens, and placed under the protection of the United States." This made small impression on "General" Welborne, who was accompanied by a force of men much larger than the handful who attended the agent. That afternoon the Indian men and boys appeared at the agency as they did every other day for roll-call and to receive their rations; when the 253 peaceable males answered to their names, they were surrounded by a cordon of four companies of white ruffians who proceeded to make them prisoners.

After nightfall, while these men were prisoners and separated from the women and children, the agent heard shots in the direction of Thlobthlocco, Jim Boy's town[?]. An investigation disclosed that Loche Yahola, a ninety-year-old man "who had been excused, owing to the infirmities of age and deafness, from attending muster at the issuing-house. . ." had been killed. ". . .found him lying in one corner, shot in the breast and his head literally stove in with, as I supposed, butts of muskets." A fifteen-year-old girl was shot in the leg. ". . .She stated the men wished to ravish her; she refused, and ran towards a thicket which was near by, when she was fired at . . . .Upon prosecuting my inquiries further, I learned that the same men had in several instances accomplished their diabolical views upon the frightened women, and in many cases deprived them by force of finger-rings, ear-rings, and blankets. Many of their women and whole families, under a state of alarm, ran to the swamp, where the major part of them are still, and no doubt viewed as hostile. I have used every possible means to draw them out without success. . . . The marauders belonged to a Mr. Park's company of citizens, of Russell County, Alabama. . . ."

9 Report of Lieut. John G. Reynolds, March 31, 1837, ibid.; American State Papers, "Military Affairs," VII, 867.

The whites proposed to carry the Indian men away to Tuskegee and the agent was helpless to protect them. He obtained permission to submit to the Indians the option of being separated from their families or all leaving their Nation together. "There was no hesitation; they preferred the latter; and in thirty-six hours afterwards with but five four-horse teams, my party of upwards of 1,900 strong, were on the march."[10]

The whites surrounded the camp of another agent and drove the Indians indiscriminately up around his quarters and "*there guarded until twelve o'clock the next day, without provisions, and in most instances without a blanket to shelter them from the inclemency of the weather. . . . I protested against their conduct as inhuman, uncalled for, and contrary to the solemn pledges of the government, and that it would be more honorable and soldier-like to punish the aggressors than to harrass a few unarmed friendly men, women, and children. After pillaging several of the Indian houses of property, and in one case of money, they determined to remove the Indian men and boys to Tuskegee, and place them within the stockade under a strong guard, and permit the women and children to remain immediately around my quarters.*"

So wrote Lieut. T. P. Sloan, the agent, who says the white mobs returned at intervals and carried off horses, mules and ponies. Finally they ordered this helpless agent to prepare his people to be removed. ". . . *On the morning of the 23rd I ordered the Indians to prepare to remove to Tuskegee, and in half an hour the whole camp was on the march. In consequence of having no means of transportation, I directed them to deposit their effects in my quarters etc, until wagons could be procured to remove them to Tuskegee; but in the meantime the house was broken open and plundered of most articles of any value.*" This officer inventoried some of the property of his party that was lost in their flight, as 145 ponies, 60 head of cattle, 200 hogs, 100 bushels of corn, 100 bee-hives, cooking and farming utensils and crockery ware; 63 guns, "sacrificed in hurried sales of property, $1,200; money stolen from Tal-lo-war-harjo, $250."[11]

10 Ibid.
11 Ibid. General Jesup wrote the secretary of war that he "had seen an account in the newspapers of the removal of the Creek families, but was not aware of the brutal treatment which those families had been compelled to submit to, until I received the reports of Lieuts. Reynolds and Sloan to Major Wilson, whom I had

Several hundred members of the state militia under the command of Welborne then proceeded to hunt out of the swamps the Indians who had sought refuge there. On March 24 they attacked a body of these half starved creatures. "Upward of forty were found dead on the field, and the prisoners say that more of their dead were thrown in the river than were left on the battle ground. The rest fled in every direction. Of the whites two were killed and several wounded."[12]

It matters little whether indignation most condemns the ineptness of the government officials or the cowardly brutality of the white mobs, the result is the same: The government's promise to protect the families of the Indians as a part consideration for their service in the army in Florida, had a familiar realization. Like many another promise to the Indians, it served its purpose when made; its fulfilment later was forgotten in the welter of intrigue against the helpless Red People.

Governor Clay had secured the sanction of the secretary of war to the removal of these friendly Indians to Mobile Point in violation of the promise made them. Other authorities and the press were in harmony with this eviction of the Indians; their little farms, houses, and other improvements were highly desirable acquisitions at that time of the year, just at the beginning of the crop season. Before the end of February Captain Page was engaged in gathering in the remnants of the Creeks who had not been removed in the two main parties.[13]

By March 8 nearly four thousand of these Creeks were concentrated near Montgomery preparatory to being sent down the river on their way west. *"The spectacle exhibited by them is truly heart rending; with all their cruelties, they are human beings and no man of feeling can look upon their present destitute condition. . . while our citizens are rolling in ease and luxury, those who are natives of the country are in the most*

---

sent to Mobile Point to inquire into the circumstances preceding the removal, copies of which are enclosed. . . The Creek families were plundered of the greater part of their property, and it is no more than justice that they be remunerated" (Jesup to Poinsett, April 11, 1837, OIA, "Creek Emigration" J 72).

12 Skinner to Clay, March 25, 1837, *Alabama State Department of Archives and History.*

13 *Mobile Daily Commercial Register and Patriot,* February 10, 1837, p. 2, col. 3; *ibid.,* February 27, 1837, p. 2, col. 2.

abject poverty, dependent for their sustenance on the charity of the govern-ment."[14]

Sixteen hundred Creeks were herded on two steamboats, the *John Nelson* and the *Chippawa*, and on March 20 started down the river to Mobile Point,[15] where they were soon joined by the remainder of the exiles in Alabama; here they were concentrated in a sickly camp, awaiting the arrival of their husbands, brothers and fathers serving in Florida, and the boats to take them to New Orleans.[16]

The warriors on their return to Alabama were incensed at the breach of faith on the part of the government officials in not protecting their families in their homes until their return, when they could be present to assist in the removal, look after their wives and children, and preserve their property.[17] Jim Boy and some of the other chiefs with 200 friendly Creeks joined the party here in July having been brought on the steam-boat *Merchant*.[18]

About 500 of these Indians, men, women and children, in April, arrived in New Orleans where they were quartered in the old barracks during their stay.[19] In charge of Lieutenant Deas, they ascended the Mississippi river the next month, on the steamer *Black Hawk* and June 2 reached Little Rock, whence they continued their journey to Fort Gibson by water.[20]

The remainder of the friendly Creeks to the number of 3,500 at Mobile Point suffered much with disease. There were so many deaths among them that the Indians became panic stricken. Captain Page then directed them to select a delegation of about fifty persons taken from the different towns represented in the camp, and these men after examining a number of places, decided that Pass Christian would be

14 *Montgomery Advertiser*, March 8, 1837, copied in *Jacksonville (Alabama) Republican*, March 30, 1837, p. 2, col. 3.

15 *Mobile Daily Commercial Register and Patriot*, March 20, 1837, p. 2, col. 1.

16 Collins to Harris, May 14, 1837, OIA, "Western Superintendency."

17 *Army and Navy Chronicle*, V, 10; *Jacksonville (Alabama) Republican*, July 13, 1837, p. 1, col. 5. Jim Boy rejoined his family who had been exempted until then from the general enforced removal, and accompanied by his two wives and twelve children came down the river from Montgomery, arriving at Mobile July 21 (*Mobile Advertiser*, July 21, 1837, p. 2, col. 1).

18 *The Bee (New Orleans)*, April 25, and 26, 1837, p. 2, col. 1.

19 *Army and Navy Chronicle*, IV, 409.

20 Page to Harris, July 27, 1837, OIA, "Creek Emigration" P 171.

a healthier location. Page then employed a boat to remove them and the last detachment reached Pass Christian July 18. Page had "*Great difficulty in getting them on board the boat, there were such a number sick; many of them died on the wharf before they could get on board and some died immediately after they embarked and we had to bury them; this detained the boats some time.*

"*On the return of the boats for a second load, I directed the Indians to break up their camps and be on the wharf ready to embark the same night; all the sick were brought to the spot in litters; a storm came up and the Boats could not lay along side the wharf; the storm lasted for two days; this rendered the situation of the Indians very unpleasant. Every thing was done to secure the sick from the storm that could be. I endeavored to get them to return to their old camps, but they positively declined, saying it would spoil their physic; they have so many superstitious notions in cases of this kind it is very difficult to get along with them.*"[21]

Between March 20 and the end of July, 177 deaths occurred in this party; ninety-three at Mobile Point and eighty-four at Pass Christian. Thirteen persons died on July 20 and twelve the next day; and part of the time at Mobile Point every officer and agent engaged in the emigration was ill. After their removal to Pass Christian the officers had much difficulty in keeping dispensers of whisky away from the Indians. They attacked some peddlers who were bringing whisky into the encampment, and destroyed several barrels of it. For the assault the civil authorities at Bay St. Louis arrested Reynolds and Lieutenant Sloan, tried them for riot and fined them $100 each, but approved the action of the officers in destroying the liquor.[22] After the destruction of the whisky conditions improved; there was less drunkeness and the Indians enjoyed better health.[23]

21 Reynolds to Harris, September 2, 1837, OIA, "Creek Emigration" R 124.

22 August 21 two schooners brought from Tampa Bay 216 Creeks, some of them being part of Echo Hadjo's volunteers and others were Creek refugees to Florida of all ages. Many of them were very sick with dysentery and fevers (Reynolds to Harris, August 27, 1837, *ibid*).

23 *New Orleans True American*, account copied in *Niles' Weekly Register*, August 5, 1837, p. 356. Many of them were afflicted with dysentery and a number had died (*Army and Navy Chronicle*, V 158). Another detachment of 208 Creek volunteers after a years service, left Tampa Bay September 14 for Pass Christian to be mustered out of the service and join their families (*ibid.*, V, 216, 236).

The Indians were to remain in camp at Pass Christian through the summer until joined by their men from Florida, and until the arrival at New Orleans of boats and high water that would carry them to Fort Gibson. While in camp they were objects of considerable curiosity to the people who had fled from the yellow fever epidemic in New Orleans and were stopping at the summer hotel recently erected near by. One observer gives some of his impressions: "*Their tents are rude and slight, though some of them betray a neatness almost amounting to elegance; for even with these children of nature there are evidently classes or grades. There is too, an aristocratic or 'West End' of the encampment, where the squaws are better dressed—where the papoose swings in a neater cradle—and where the lodges are furnished with cleaner beds and culinary utensils than in any other quarter. Jim Boy is a fine looking savage, and has a certain air of importance in his appearance and bearing that marks him out as a 'great chief.' A fair lady who visited him on Sunday was about to leave his lodge without the ceremony of leave-taking, as her pretty lips, though admirably formed for the soft caresses of the Greek, had never been twisted out of beauty by uttering the barbarities of the Creek dialect; but the proud chief told the interpreter that the white squaw had forgotten herself in forgetting him, and she accordingly returned, took his huge paw and bade him a courteous good day. . . The men for the most part are a fine race of beings, but idle, careless and mendicant as usual. The squaws are unusually good looking; their persons cleanly and decently attired, while their hair is dressed with peculiar neatness. . . The greatest objection to the proximity of the Indians arises from the nefarious acts of some debased scoundrels, who, for the profit of a few paltry dollars, continue to supply them surreptitiously with liquor in defiance of the law and the vigilance of the officers.*"[24]

The warriors who had served in Florida arrived in small parties through September, many of them to swell the number of sick and dead in the camps at Pass Christian. It was not until October that they were taken to New Orleans to board the steamboats; the conductors had been apprehensive of their contracting the yellow fever then raging in New Orleans and the Indians were hurried through the city. Jim Boy and some of the other chiefs arrived in New Orleans October 16,

24 *The Courier* (New Orleans), October 16, 1837, p. 3, col. 1.

··{ 186 }··

"on the *Mazeppa* from Pass Christian. Jim Boy is a perfect model of his species, being every inch a man, very large and well formed."[25]

Near the end of the month they were embarked on nine steamboats. A party of 1,600 in charge of Lieutenant Sloan left on October 29 aboard the steamboats *Farmer, Far West*, and *Black Hawk*. Echo Hadjo, John Chupco, Jim Boy and Tuskeneah and their people departed a few days before.[26] Some of them were soon involved in a pathetic tragedy: The steamboat *Monmouth*, with 611 Indians on board, was proceeding up the Mississippi river, when through the negligent handling of the boat she was taken through Prophet Island Bend on a course forbidden to upbound vessels; in this place at night she collided with the ship *Trenton*, towed by the *Warren*: The *Monmouth* was cut in two, and sunk almost immediately with a loss of 311 Indians.[27]

"The fearful responsibility for this vast sacrifice of human life rests on the contractors for emigrating the Creek Indians. The avaricious disposition to increase the profits on the speculation first induced the chartering of rotten, old, and unseaworthy boats, because they were of a class to be procured cheaply; and then to make those increased profits still larger, the Indians were packed upon these crazy vessels in such crowds that not the slightest regard seems to have been paid to their safety, comfort, or even decency. The crammed condition of the decks and cabins was offensive to every sense and feeling, and kept the poor creatures in a state unfit for human beings."[28] The *Monmouth* had been "freighted on exceedingly

25 *Mobile Daily Commercial Register and Patriot*, January 24, 1838, p. 2, col. 1; *New Orleans Free American*, October 27, 1837.

26 *New Orleans Bee*, account quoted in *Commercial Bulletin* (St. Louis), November 12, 1837, p. 2, col. 1.

27 *Army and Navy Chronicle*, V, 314. In this disaster four of the twelve children of Jim Boy were drowned (McKenney and Hall, *History of the Indian Tribes of North America*, II, 25). "The Monmouth was broken in two—the after part of the boat drifted some distance and sunk". Many of the survivors were badly injured (*The Courier* (New Orleans) November 2, 1837, p. 3, col. 1; *ibid.*, November 7, 1837, p. 3, col. 1).

28 *New Orleans Free American*, account copied in *New York Observer*, November 18, 1837, p. 3, col. 4. It was considered by steamboat owners that no more than 400 or 500 Indians should be transported on a boat, allowing "seven superficial square feet to every Indian, embracing men, women, and children" (Woodfin to Reynolds, September 22, 1837, OIA, "Creek Emigration" R 124).

moderate terms, as it had been condemned on account of its great age."[29]

These Indians were at a great disadvantage to resume their journey at the end of their water trip. They had been driven from their homes without notice or preparation, and had been robbed and compelled to leave behind their ponies, wagons, carts and household utensils; many were ill or convalescent and too weak to travel on foot. And when called on by Lieutenant Reynolds to furnish them additional land transportation to meet this situation, the contractors objected and delay of the departure from Pass Christian resulted while Reynolds consulted his superiors in Washington.[30]

Several hundred Creeks fled from their Nation after the execution of their treaty of 1832, and took refuge among some of their tribesmen who were intermarried with Cherokee; when their surrender was demanded, the Creeks begged the Cherokee to give them sanctuary. "We came here to escape the evils of war. In time of trouble we came to the Cherokees as to the home of a brother. . . While living here we planted corn in the season, but the white man destroyed it, and took away much of our other property. In this bad treatment two of our men were killed, one man was shot through the thigh and arm, and three children lost in the flight of their mothers." Many of them were related to the Cherokee by blood and marriage, and their hosts refused to give them up.[31]

"Some check" wrote General Wool, "ought to be put to the course now pursued. Humanity revolts at such a course. Many of these Creeks have not participated in the late hostilities, but have lived many years in the Cherokee Nation, and are now connected with that people by the ties of blood and marriage. They ought not to be hunted and dragged like so many beasts to the emigrating camp. . . What possible objections can the government have to their being permitted, if the Cherokees are willing, to come in and remove under the treaty with them to the west?"[32]

To escape capture, these unfortunate people had fled from their homes to the forests and hills of a thinly settled tract of country, and the officers found them "in a most destitute and wretched condition. Many

29 Abbe Emmanuel Domenech, *Seven Years Residence in the Great Deserts of North America*, I, 433.

30 Reynolds to Harris, September 25, 1837, OIA, "Creek Emigration," R 124.

31 *New York Observer*, April 21, 1838, p. 2, col. 2.

32 *American State Papers*, "Military Affairs," VII, 557.

Jim Boy (Tustennuggee Emathla), Creek Chief

Mouth of the Arkansas River in 1846

of those captured by Colonel Byrd had subsisted for several days on the sap of the timber."[33] In time however they were hunted out of their hiding places by the hundreds of soldiers, and concentrated in guarded camps near the Tennessee river. "Miserable and impoverished," they were later assembled at Gunter's Landing, 543 in number, and embarked on the Tennessee river in charge of the Alabama Emigrating Company and military guards accompanied by Lieut. Edward Deas who kept a journal of events of the expedition.

They began their journey May 16, 1837, on nine flat boats four of which were about eighty feet in length and the others little more than half as long. Their voyage was uneventful except that on several occasions when storms compelled them to land at night, numbers of the prisoners escaped from the guards. On the twenty-first with the aid of pilots they successfully passed through Muscle Shoals, covering the fifteen miles between ten in the morning and four in the afternoon. Two days later they reached Waterloo where the party was placed aboard the steamboat *Black Hawk* and one large keel-boat and two large flatboats in tow. They made about eight miles an hour down the Tennessee, Ohio, and Mississippi rivers and reached the mouth of White river the morning of the twenty-eighth.

There was a high stage of water in the Arkansas river and the passage up that stream at the rate of three or four miles an hour, was without incident. Each day a stop of two or three hours was made to gather wood for the boilers, which was generally cut by the Indians who were paid for their labor; those who were not so employed used this opportunity for much needed exercise. Before they had left the Tennessee river, there occurred deaths of infants and very old people, and Lieutenant Deas reported one nearly every day. On June fourth the boats entered the mouth of the Verdigris river and the Indians were landed about four miles above, near the Creek agency; as they went ashore they were counted and mustered and found to number 463; the difference, eighty, being accounted for by deaths and escapes.[34]

And still not all of the Creeks were emigrated; some were hanged for their participation in the recent disorders, and a number of others,

33 *Army and Navy Chronicle*, IV, 301.
34 *Journal of Edward Deas*, OIA, June 5, 1837, "Creek Emigration," D 97; Collins to Harris, May 31, 1837, OIA, *Western Superintendency*, "Emigration File" C 260.

mostly children, were held by whites of Alabama in bondage as slaves.[35] Eight hundred Creeks who had fled to the Chickasaw Nation in Mississippi, were hunted out and found there "in a sick and helpless condition and dispersed situation" and gathered up when the Chickasaw started west. Several hundred of them were placed aboard the steamboat *Itaska* at Memphis, November 19, 1837, and delivered at Fort Gibson on the thirtieth. Another party of them reached this post on December 28.[36]

Jim Henry and David Hardage "*after remaining in jail one year had their trial and were acquitted last January. I was compelled to keep them in my own room until such time as I could turn them over to Benjamin Marshall, U. S. Interpreter for the Creek Tribe, who happened to be in Montgomery, Ala., at that time. I requested him to take charge of them and transport them to their new country west. . . There was so much excitement about their being acquitted that if they had been turned loose in the country they would have been murdered.*"[37] Captain Page requested the war department to pay Marshall his expenses incurred in removing Henry and Hardage to the West.

35 Davis to Commissioner of Indian Affairs, June 20, 1840, OIA, "Creek" D 522. Six Creeks were executed November 25, at Girard, Alabama (*Army and Navy Chronicle*, III, 361). Among a small number of Creeks yet remaining in Alabama was a son of Jim Boy named Ward Co-cha-my who did not remove west until about 1845. Three years later he returned to Alabama to aid some of his people in emigrating to the Indian Territory. He arrived at Fort Smith June 24, 1848 with a party of sixty-five Indians, but despite his earnest efforts he was unable to secure a number who were held as slaves by white people. "I think" he said, "there yet remains in Alabama not less than 100 Creeks, and most of them in a deplorable condition; a man by the name of Dickerson in Coosa County has one family, a woman and her children, 7 in number. A Mr. Floyd and a Rev. Mr. Hays both of Autauga County have each a number of Creeks. I tried to get these but was prevented doing so by threats of their would-be masters. I shall get them yet—but not this season; when the waters are in good boating order next season you will hear from me again" (Ward Co-cha-my to Commissioner of Indian Affairs July 16, 1848, OIA, "Creek Emigration, File C 163-206").

36 Clements to Harris, December 31, 1837, OIA; *Army and Navy Chronicle*, V, 412. Among those Creeks living with the Chickasaw were a number who had committed murder in their own nation, and had fled to escape the punishment of death by the relatives of their victims (Clements to Harris, November 18, 1837, OIA, "Creek Emigration" C 465).

37 Page to Harris, May 14, 1838, OIA.

BOOK THREE / *Chickasaw Removal*

P RESIDENT JACKSON's meeting in the summer of 1830 was attended by a delegation of twenty-one Chickasaw principal men. Accompanied by their agent Benjamin Reynolds, they reached Franklin August 19 and shook hands with the president. Three days later in the Presbyterian church they held a council with the commissioners, Eaton and Coffee, who submitted to them the president's "talk."[1] He warned them that they would be compelled to remove to the West or abandon their tribal laws and customs and submit to the laws of the state, which, he said, he was powerless to prevent; and white people would occupy their lands though the government had bound itself in previous treaties not to permit it.[2] He told them that "By an act of Congress, it was placed in his power to extend justice to the Indians; to pay the expense of their removal; to support them for twelve months; and to give them a grant of lands which should endure 'as long as the grass grows, or water runs'."[3]

After several days' negotiation and the offer by the commissioners to give four sections of land to each of the Chickasaw chiefs in the conference, Levi Colbert, George Colbert, Samuel Sealey, and William McGilvery, a provisional treaty was agreed to and signed September

1 *Jackson (Tennessee) Gazette*, September 4, 1830, p. 3, col. 1.

2 *Document*, II, 240. Benjamin Love acted as interpreter in this treaty conference for thirty-three days for which he received $100 (*U. S. House Document No. 171*, Twenty-second Congress, first session.)

3 *Document*, II, 240: "Journal of Proceedings with Choctaw and Chickasaw Indians." Superficial writers have erroneously stated that the grants to the Five Civilized Tribes contain this poetic assurance. Whether they do or not, and whether Jackson invented the phrase for the occasion is not important, for other guaranties more definite and enforceable were included in the treaties and disregarded without compunction.

1;[4] Tishomingo was similarly favored, though his name is not included among those participating, probably because of his great age. Provision was made also for sending an exploring party to examine the western country.

The performance of this treaty was conditioned upon their being provided a home in the West on the lands of the Choctaw. The joint exploring expedition in the autumn of 1830 was arranged with that end in view; the delegations of the two tribes however, could come to no agreement on the subject and it was abandoned for the time and the treaty became void. The Chickasaw were opposed to sharing the western domain or entering into a joint arrangement with the Choctaw Indians who outnumbered them three to one.

No solution of the problem having been reached, the secretary of war the next spring directed Isaac McCoy to examine the Osage reserve in the present Kansas, and ascertain whether there was sufficient desirable land there for the Chickasaw tribe. From this examination made in the summer McCoy thought the Indians could be accommodated there.[5] A little later the secretary proposed to locate this tribe between the Canadian river and the North Fork of that stream.[6]

In June the secretary wrote an interesting letter to Greenwood Leflore, to enlist his influence for a division of the Choctaw land with the Chickasaw. A tempting picture was drawn of a union of all the tribes under a common government, in which, naturally, he would assume a prominent position. "*Should the Cherokees and Creeks and Chickasaws remove, matters may be so arranged as to bring the whole of the tribes under one great federative government. Thus united, and the wandering tribes turned to agriculture, with a population of sixty or eighty thousand souls, they cannot fail to become a great and powerful people; and, with a good well established government, a prosperous and happy people; and then Congress might be disposed to admit one or more delegates to represent their wants and wishes. . . . The United*

4 *Niles' Weekly Register*, September 18, 1830. This treaty was never ratified. February 27, 1832, the House committee on public lands asked the president to submit the treaty for its inspection that they might examine a clause in it said to grant four square miles of land to each of two white men, but the president refused to let them see it (*Document*, II, 296, 786).

5 *Document*, II, 276, 562.

6 *Ibid.*, 292.

States might, and I doubt not would be disposed to give you a Territorial Government.

"It is a matter of some concern that the Chickasaws were not able to find a suitable country. If one cannot be found, of course they cannot remove; but against their wishes and inclinations, will be constrained to remain where they are, under the laws of the State of Mississippi. . . . They and your people are old friends and ancient neighbors; you ought to lend your assistance to take care of them. The Choctaws should invite them to take a portion of their country on the northern boundary; for which they will be able to pay you a fair price from the annuities which are secured to them by the United States. . . . The Choctaws west of the Mississippi have an extensive country, amounting to at least fifteen or seventeen million acres, fully as large, or larger than the country which both the tribes now occupy on this side of the river. The Chickasaws so long accustomed to self-control, would dislike to have merged their national name and character. They would prefer their ancient usages and their own self-government; but upon the federative plan I have spoken of, both nations would presently become the same people, and dwell under the same principles of government. The strength of each nation would be greatly increased. Admit them to a part of your territory, the Creeks and Cherokees will ere long follow, and then you may succeed in establishing a government to be entitled 'The Indian United Tribes.'

"Every patriot and every man, should desire to see the Indian name and character preserved and perpetuated; but this cannot be done, except through some rational and inspiring system and rule of government, by which each individual may feel himself to be a component part of it. I intreat you think seriously of these suggestions, for in them is much of future promise for the red man's happiness."[7]

After the Choctaw removal got under way, John H. Eaton and John Coffee with commissions from the president, addressed delegations from both tribes at Oaka Knoxabee creek on December 7 and endeavored to secure their consent to amalgamate on the lands of the Choctaw in the West.[8] They explained the plan of the government to divide their domain into four districts, three of which should be

<hr/>

[7] Ibid., 300. See "Proposals for an Indian State" by Annie H. Abel, Annual Report of the American Historical Association for 1907, II, 89; plans for an Indian confederacy west of the Mississippi, Grant Foreman, Indians and Pioneers, 213.

[8] Document, III, 17.

Choctaw and the fourth Chickasaw, this tribe numbering about one-fourth in population of the two tribes. No progress was made however, with the few delegates who were present, all of whom were opposed to the project, and the matter was postponed for future consideration. Eaton and Coffee said the "Chickasaws are reluctant to part with power, and hence will be unwilling to become merged with their. . . brothers."[9]

The Commissioners again pressed the matter on the Chickasaw Indians three weeks later. After thinking it over for another two weeks the Chickasaw meet at their council house January 15, 1832 and agreed to co-operate with the government in the attempt to locate them in the West, but declined the proposition to consolidate with the Choctaw.[10] The Colberts were men of importance in the Chickasaw Nation, and were reluctant to enter into another form of government where they would be compelled to surrender their influence. Levi Colbert, an ambitious man, was particularly averse to submitting to the dictates of the arrogant Leflore.[11]

On the twenty-third of the next month Colbert addressed the president, taking exception to his statement that the Chickasaw were ready to emigrate; reminding him that their treaty of Franklin was effective only in the event that they could find a satisfactory home in the West. He said the available land *"which the Choctaws perhaps might let us have, is most of it big prairies, mighty little wood, water, or good land; it will be mighty hard for my people to live there. . . it was the words in your message which alarmed and roused the fears of my people; you speak of this treaty as final, this is not the sense of it; we have not got as yet any home in the west, . . . you can see the strong and marked difference of our condition here and in the wild distant regions of the west, surrounded by none but distant and deer trade and warlike tribes thrown together."*[12]

On their western tour of exploration in 1830, Levi Colbert and four companions left the main party to examine the lands of the Caddo Indians on the south side of the Red river, between that stream and

9 Ibid., II, 360, 690, 697, 700. Eaton and Coffee reported: "The country is full of speculators on Indian titles" (*ibid.*, 697).

10 Ibid., III, 11.

11 Ibid., II, 420.

12 Ibid., III, 216.

the Sabine river with which they were much pleased; and they reported that if the government would purchase it for them, they would be glad to remove there.[13] Levi Colbert believed that a sufficient tract could be secured there for twenty thousand dollars, but the government officials were opposed to considering this location. In July, 1833, William K. Hill came to the Chickasaw Nation with a power of attorney from Chambers and Padilla authorizing him to sell them four million acres of Mexican land in what is now the Panhandle of Texas.[14] The Indian commissioner said the Indians could buy it if they wished but that the government would have nothing to do with the transaction.[15]

While the Chickasaw treaty of 1830 was never ratified by the Senate, it served as an entering wedge for the white people who began pressing into the Chickasaw country in Alabama and Mississippi. The government was impatient to meet the wishes of the white people of those states and to convince the Indians that their best interests required their immediate removal to some place west of the Mississippi river. Accordingly in 1832 commissions were issued to John Coffee and John H. Eaton to negotiate another treaty with the Chickasaw Indians wherein they would agree to remove. Eaton did not take part in the treaty conference which was conducted by Coffee on the part of the government, from September 20 to October 22. It was held at the council house on Pontotoc creek[16] and resulted in the treaty of October 20, 1832.[17]

By the terms of this treaty the tribe ceded outright all of its land to the United States, to be put on the market and sold as public lands, the proceeds of which were to be held by the government for the Indians. The government was to proceed at once to survey its land and the Indians were to decide on a location in the West. It was provided that the Indians were not to be disturbed in their homes while considering the matter of a new location. They were to be allowed to

13 "Oto-cho (the king)" and forty-two others to Jackson, May 28, 1831, *Document*, II, 479.

14 *Ibid.*, IV, 489.

15 Hill to Commissioner of Indian Affairs, July 14, 1833, OIA.

16 *Document*, III, 510. Pontotoc, a Chickasaw word meaning "cat tail prairies."

17 Proclaimed March 1, 1833 (Kappler, *op. cit.*, II, 259).

make liberal selections of land containing their improvements, for which they were to be paid when the land was surveyed and sold.

After the treaty was signed and before its ratification, Levi Colbert as chief and a large number of full-blood head men of the tribe held a conference at the home of Colbert where they addressed a long and bitter memorial to the president protesting against the terms of the treaty and the means by which it was executed. They said that General Coffee was overly solicitous for the interests of mixed blood Indians and white men who had intermarried in the tribe, and he insisted on the provision in the treaty for the reservations to these individuals, of large tracts of land which they might sell. The full-bloods said that they could not compete with the mixed bloods and intermarried whites who would get all the best lands and would engage in speculations to the prejudice of the remainder of the tribe; that they had decided in council they did not wish reservations to be made and had so informed Coffee; that they wished the lands sold by the government as a whole and the proceeds divided equally among all the individuals. An annuity was due them and they charged that Coffee would not permit it to be paid until they had agreed to the treaty prescribed by him; that he browbeat and abused them and in the end coerced them into agreeing to the treaty at the time Chief Levi Colbert was ill and unable to attend the conference.[18]

At this conference, a delegation composed of Tishomingo and others were commissioned to go to Washington with the memorial and attempt to have the treaty amended before it was ratified. Tishomingo was not able to go, but the remainder of the delegation arrived in Washington in January, 1833. The other members were Col. George Colbert, Pitman Colbert, Captain Greenwood, J. L. Allen, assistant Chickasaw agent, and John A. Bynum, the son-in-law of Maj. James Colbert.[19] Counter charges were made that the delegation were acting under the influence of Colbert and white men who hoped to handle the funds arising from the sale of their lands, and their request for a change in the terms of the treaty was refused.[20]

18 Levi Colbert and others to the president, November 22, 1832, OIA, "Chickasaws."

19 *Document*, III, 556, 557.

20 *Ibid.*, IV, 15, 56.

The year 1833 was passing without any effort on the part of the Indians to remove to the West or to decide on a location. White people in defiance of the laws were moving into the Chickasaw Nation, occupying the lands of the Indians, overrunning their country and producing much unhappiness among them.[21]

The government did next to nothing to prevent this unlawful intrusion, which it had promised in the treaty to prevent, nor did it do anything adequate to assist the Indians in locating a home in the West. The Indians were more than apathetic on the subject of leaving their ancestral homes—a subject they considered with bitter sorrow in their hearts. Having lived in one place for many generations, the problem of moving was new and perplexing, and they were lacking initiative, a state of mind with which the government had long been familiar; yet it was assumed the Indians would take the steps to carry the treaty into effect, an assumption wholly unwarranted by experience and knowledge of their habits.

Because of the cholera then raging, the Indians refused to go in the summer, but Reynolds finally succeeded in securing an exploring party of twenty-one chiefs[22] including Levi and Pitman Colbert, Henry Love, William McGilvery, and others who set out with him from Tuscumbia October 16, 1833. They crossed the Mississippi river at Memphis on the thirty-first, and proceeded by way of Little Rock[23] to Fort Towson where they arrived December 4. Here they sought a council with the Choctaw chief on the subject of purchasing part of their land. The meeting could not be arranged until the twenty-first when about two-thirds of the Choctaw chiefs and head men met the Chickasaw delegation.

21 Two white peddlers named John Walker and Marshall Goodman entered the Chickasaw country in violation of the law and opened a trading store; on the complaint of old Chief Tishomingo in January, 1831, John L. Allen, United States sub-agent seized the goods of the intruders and sold them, turning half the proceeds over to Tishomingo for his tribe. The white men then went into the Monroe county circuit court of Mississippi, had Tishomingo and Allen thrown into jail, and secured judgment against them for $493.09; the United States government carried the case to the supreme court of the state which affirmed the judgment of the lower court ("Mingo and Allen v. Goodman," I *Mississippi High Court of Errors and Appeals,* p. 552; for transcript of case see OIA, "1833 Chickasaws.")

22 *Document,* IV, 609.

23 *Ibid.,* IV, 182, 700.

Choctaw Agent Armstrong and Reynolds made speeches urging the delegates to reach some agreement by which the two tribes could live together, and then retired from the meeting. Levi Colbert then spoke for the Chickasaw, and David Folsom for the Choctaw, and the council adjourned.[24] The conference was futile, the Indians remaining unchanged in their attitude. The Choctaw refused to sell any land to the Chickasaw but offered to make a home for them on the Choctaw domain; the Chickasaw spurned the offer and said they would move on the land only if they could buy and own it.[25]

During their expedition the members of the party impressed the agent with the general desire of the tribe that their treaty be amended in some particulars. Accordingly another delegation[26] was invited to Washington where on May 24, 1834, another treaty[27] was made. Among the principal features of this treaty especially desired by the Chickasaw was the promise by the government contained in section one, that if the Indians removed to the West they would be protected against the hostile tribes of the prairies of whom they stood in great fear. The fourth article of the treaty contained a novel provision to protect the members of the tribe against their own incompetence in handling their property, evidence of sagacity of a high order on the part of their chiefs. It provided that Ish-ta-hota-pa, the king, Levi Colbert,[28] George Colbert, Martin Colbert, Isaac Alberson, Henry Love, and Benjamin Love be constituted a commission to pass upon the competency of members of the tribe and that none could sell any of his land without the recommendation of this commission.

The white people continued to overrun the Chickasaw country and destroy the peace and happiness of the Indians long before the survey was completed, or plans were made for their removal, or other lands

24 Reynolds to Herring, December 27, 1833, OIA, "1833 Chickasaws."
25 Colbert and others to the president, December 27, 1833, Ibid.
26 The Chickasaw council on March 7, 1834, named a delegation to Washington composed of Levi Colbert, Isaac Alberson, Henry Love, Martin Colbert, and Benjamin Love. They had proceeded no farther than the Chickasaw agency when Levi Colbert became too ill to go farther and he named his brother Col. George Colbert to go in his place. Levi died soon after, at the Buzzards Roost.
27 Kappler, op. cit., II, 309.
28 Levi Colbert having died, the chiefs in council on August 24, named James Colbert to fill the vacancy (Certificate of chiefs August 24, 1834, OIA, "Chickasaws").

were found for them to occupy. The United States marshal for Mississippi posted notices warning white squatters to remove from the Chickasaw Nation by November 15, 1833. Not one obeyed the command and as no steps were taken by the government to enforce the order, the whites regarded this inaction as a license to remain, with the result that many more continued to move in.[29] The circuit court for Monroe county, Mississippi, with jurisdiction extending over all that part of the Chickasaw tribe living in Mississippi, late in 1832 ruled that the laws of the United States regulating intercourse and trade with the Indians had been nullified in that state by the extension of the laws of Mississippi over the Indians. "The consequence is that whiskey traders and peddlers with other intruders are overrunning the country to the manifest injury of the Chickasaw tribe."[30] This action of the state court assuming to nullify a law of the United States, characteristic of the time, was all that was needed to encourage the whites to invade the Chickasaw country. And the federal government did nothing to protect the Indians in the rights guaranteed to them in the recent treaty.

After the survey had been completed so that the Indians' lands could be described and conveyances made, the customary campaign of larceny of their holdings was soon launched by the conscienceless horde of whites who invaded the country. James Colbert tried to induce the secretary of war to protect the Indians: *"The fate of the Chickasaw people requires that some person should interpose in their behoof and unless you will interpose and require a strict compliance with the treaty their ruin is inevitable. A host of Speculators are going over the country and have hired all the half breeds to interpret for them and give them five or ten dollars for each contract they make; they use every stratagem they can devise and practice every imposition on their ignorance; these half-breeds tell them the agent says you must sell and they believe every thing the agent tells them must be done and there is not one out of a hundred that has sold knows what they are to receive for their lands nor when nor who has purchased; they have signed deeds most of them blank ones and receive from five to ten dollars in advance. It is thought those large companies will purchase the approbation of some of the*

29 Allen to Herring, January 4, 1834, OIA, "Chickasaw Subagency".
30 Reynolds to Cass, December 9, 1832, *ibid.*

Commissioners of the nation and that the agent is interested. The Surveyor Genl. has with his Company purchased seven or eight hundred sections and have advanced from ten to twenty dollars; five hundred dollars is about the average price agreed on per section and some of them worth ten times as much. With the exception of the Creek nation I expect there never has been such frauds imposed on any people as the Chickasaws, but we look with confidence to the President of the United States to see that every treaty stipulation is complyed with."[31]

"I beseech you to have a care over our red children; the white men are cheating them out of their lands and they do not [[know]] what they are to git for it nothing can save us but your parental care; instruct the agent to reject all of those fraudulent contracts for if he sanctions them our leading men will perhaps do the same; to see justice done to us and not let us be robbed of our rights we will be the poorest miserable people on earth if such contracts are tolerated." So wrote Ton-e-pia to Secretary Cass. The customary and efficient method of robbing the Indians was in full swing: *". . .immediately over the line, but off the Office section, a number of Shops have been established whither the Indians resort, and drink Spirits to an intoxication of almost unparallelled extent, presenting scenes of brutality revolting to every principle of humanity and consequences ultimately to the Indian truly appalling. Indeed unless this practice can be stopped it is impossible to say the difficulties that will be thrown in the way of the successful prosecution of the public business,"* wrote the register and receiver of the land office at Pontotoc on May 29, 1835.[32]

A second exploring party was sent west of the Mississippi river in the effort to purchase land from the Choctaw on which these unhappy people could find relief from the persecution of white people, which the federal government seemed unwilling, and admitted itself unable, to prevent. This party, consisting of Martin Colbert, Pitman Colbert, Thomas Colbert, and others under the leadership of John K. Balch of Tennessee, held councils with the Choctaw first on Arkansas river, then on Red river in November, and returned to their homes in January, 1836.[33]

31 Colbert to Cass, June 5, 1835, OIA, "Chickasaw Reserves."
32 OIA, "1835 Chickasaws."
33 *Arkansas Gazette*, December 29, 1835.

A third effort was made and on November 12, 1836, George Colbert, James Colbert, Henry Love, Benjamin Love and other chiefs at
Pontotoc issued credentials to James Perry, Maj. John McClish, Maj.
Pitman Colbert, Maj. James Brown, and Capt. Isaac Alberson to
negotiate for a sufficient tract of Choctaw land for a price not to
exceed one million dollars.[34] The Chickasaw delegation met delegates
from the Choctaw tribe at Doaksville, near Fort Towson, where meetings were held from day to day and their proposals were considered and
discussed until an agreement[35] was reached on January 17, 1837. By
the terms of the contract between them, for the sum of $530,000 the
Choctaw Nation sold to the Chickasaw a large tract off the western
part of the Choctaw country and admitted them into most of the
privileges of citizenship in the Choctaw tribe.

The Chickasaw chiefs reported to the president on February 17[36]
that they were satisfied with the report of their commissioners sent to
purchase "a new and, as they hoped, a permanent home for their
people, now almost destitute and homeless." They said a considerable
portion of the tribe would be ready to start by May 1, and asked the
president to lend his aid to their removal. They discussed the business

34 Record of proceedings and letter to commissioners, November 12, 1836, OIA.
35 Articles of convention and agreement, January 17, 1837, OIA, "Chickasaw
File P 199." This agreement was signed for the Choctaw Nation by Thomas Leflore
as chief of Oklafalaya District, Nitakechi chief of Pushmataha District, and Joseph
Kincaid as chief of Mushulatubbee District; and commissioners P. P. Pitchlynn,
George W. Harkins, Israel Folsom, R. M. Jones, Silas D. Fisher, Samuel Worcester,
John McKinney, Eyach-a-ho-pia, Nathaniel Folsom, Lewis Brashears, James Fletcher,
and George Pusly. And by the Chickasaw commissioners Pitman Colbert, John
McLish, John Brown and James Perry.

By this grant the Chickasaw Nation acquired all of the Choctaw domain bounded
and described as follows: "Beginning on the north bank of Red River at the mouth
of Island Bayou about eight or ten miles below the mouth of False Washita, thence
running north along the main channel of said Bayou to its source; thence along the
dividing ridge between the Washita and Low Blue river to the road leading from
Fort Gibson to Fort Washita; thence along said road to the line dividing Mushulatubbee and Pushmataha Districts, thence eastwardly along said District line to the
source of Brushy Creek, thence down said creek to where it flows into the Canadian
River, ten or twelve miles above the mouth of the South Fork of the Canadian;
thence west along the main Canadian River to its source, if in the limits of the United
States or to those limits, and thence due south to Red River and down Red River
to the beginning."

36 Chickasaw Memorial to the president, February 17, 1837, OIA.

and detail of the undertaking in a manner that showed a much better grasp of the subject than the government officials had displayed, and an understanding based upon the experiences of other emigrants that should have guided the action of the government to more humane and efficient plans; begged the president not to deliver them to contractors whose only interest lay in making as much money as possible out of the business; made pertinent suggestions about steamboats and the purchase of provisions at points enroute and asked the president to appoint in charge of the removal either Henry B. Carter or Captain Chase of Little Rock.

A. M. M. Upshaw of Pulaski, Tennessee, was appointed by the president on March 9 as superintendent of the Chickasaw removal. Upshaw employed William R. Guy and Francis G. Roche as enrolling agents and notified the Indians to meet in council to discuss plans for removal. The superintendent told them they "*ought to remove as soon as possible, as there are a great number of your people who are spending all their money and making no crops. They get drunk and lose their money and white men make them drunk to cheat them of their property and their wives and children are suffering for something to eat. They should go soon so that they may have time to build houses before winter to keep the cold from their wives and children.*" The chiefs of the four districts into which the Chickasaw Nation was divided, conferred and agreed that on June 7 they would meet at the rendezvous designated by Upshaw, prepared to start on their long journey.

Upshaw established three camps in the Chickasaw Nation, but by July 13 only 300 prospective emigrants had appeared, instead of the thousand he had been led to expect. McGilvery was obstinate and there was much opposition to removal in his district. The greatest difficulty had its origin with designing merchants who sought to keep the Indians in their debt as long as they had any money or property.[37] During these difficulties a white man named Jones killed Emubby, the chief counsellor to the Chickasaw king. Emubby was described as a brave and generous warrior who served with General Jackson in most

37 Upshaw to Harris, OIA, "Chickasaw Emigration" File U 5 to 14; *Army and Navy Chronicle*, I, 75.

of his wars. Indignation over this murder made the officers apprehensive of further trouble which, however, did not materialize.[38]

Finally Upshaw set out with the nucleus of his party. They traveled slowly through the Nation and other families living near the line of march joined from time to time. The rattle and creaking of the wagons and carts, and the voices of the drivers of the approaching caravan were melancholy heralds of the sad journey they were about to begin. Giving a last look at the familiar hearth, home and dooryard, trees and fields, they turned towards the moving company and loaded their belongings into the wagons; their women and children mounted their ponies, and with heavy hearts the families joined the procession headed for a strange and distant country.

38 *New York Observer*, August 5, 1837, p. 3, col. 5; "Emubby was very active and influential in hastening the march of his tribe . . .he had been murdered without any provocation. . . When Jones presented his rifle at him, he leaped from his horse, opened his breast, and said 'Shoot! Emubby is not afraid to die.' The wretch did shoot and the Indian fell" (*Memphis Gazette*, July 11, in *Jacksonville (Alabama) Republican*, August 24, 1837, p. 4, col. 1).

U PSHAW's party of 500 passed through Memphis July 4 where they were delivered to another conductor. "*They presented a handsome appearance, being nearly all mounted, and, with few exceptions, well dressed in their national costume. It has been remarked by many of our citizens, who have witnessed the passage of emigrating Indians, that on no previous occasion was there as good order or more dispatch. Not a drunken Indian we believe, was seen in the company; and the whole after traveling eight miles crossed the Mississippi on the same day.*"[1]

From Memphis this party was conducted by John M. Millard with W. R. Guy as assistant; Capt. Joe A. Phillips was United States disbursing agent, and Dr. C. G. Keenan directing physician.[2] After crossing the Mississippi river they went into camp to await for three days the arrival of their rations delayed by the neglect of the ferryboat proprietor. "*After some little delay occasioned by the loss of some Indian horses, we struck camp and commenced march at 10 o'clock, A. M., and continued without any interruption until half past four o'clock when we were compelled from the severity of the rain to stop and camp for the night. Our march today was 13 miles and we could have gone farther but for the inclement weather.*" Two or three sick Indians were sent on the boat conveying rations up to the crossing of the St. Francis river.

---

1 *Army and Navy Chronicle*, V, 75; *New York Observer*, August 5, 1837, p. 3, col. 5.

2 Some of Upshaw's other assistants were D. Vanderslice, G. Langtree, W. J. Welborne, F. G. Roche, W. S. Henderson, and James Williamson.

"8th July, Black Fish Lake. We moved this morning at 8 o'clock and after having traveled five miles came to the termination of the newly constructed road; we found the Swamp almost impassable. All the wagons but two arrived at the lake; these were left on the road two miles distant from camp.

"9th July, West side Black Fish Lake. This day was passed in crossing the lake, bringing up the wagons, horses, and Indians that were left on our yesterdays march. We also found it necessary to rest the horses after the fatigueing drive of the previous day (12 miles) through the swamp. Black Fish is distant from Memphis twenty-five miles, its width is about 150 yards. The water is clear and its surface smooth, although there is a tolerably strong current, which empties into the St. Francis.

"10th July, Camp Guy. Left Black Fish at 8 o'clock A. M. and travelled over boggy roads and through mud and water, frequently up to axeltrees of the wagons. The distance we came today is about eight miles and by every person acquainted with the roads, considered a good drive.

"11th, Camp Marietta, 3 miles west of St. Francis. This has been a laborious drive today, but thanks to good fortune has taken us through the great Mississippi swamp, without any serious accident or ill luck but some slight injury to the wagons, which, as we remain here tomorrow can be easily repaired. The sick who were sent by water to this place, are convalescent; one yet remains on the sick report.

The next day after emerging from the great swamp they spent in resting their horses and oxen and adjusting their baggage. During the following week they made from six to fifteen miles a day, sometimes delayed by Indians who lingered behind along the road. On the seventeenth they reached White river at the mouth of Cache creek and consumed two days in ferrying the river with their horses and wagons and proceeded four miles to Rock Roe bridge. They then continued four miles through the White river bottom and reached the prairie.

"All the Indians, now, more than five hundred in number are in camp and impatient for their march through the great prairie." The next few days were uneventful. To avoid the heat the caravan departed from Rock Roe at six o'clock on the evening of the twentieth and before daylight arrived at Mrs. Black's. Here they remained in camp all day, resumed their march at two o'clock that night, and after traveling nine miles camped again for the day. This program was repeated until they reached the Arkansas river opposite Little Rock on the twenty-fourth. The party now contained 516 emigrating Indians, 551 ponies, and thirteen wagons.[3] Thirty other Indians not enrolled were in the rear.

"26th July. Remained in camp all day and made preparations for an early start in the morning. At a late hour today Lt. Morris came to our camp and informed that rations had not been thrown on the roads, on account of the impossibility of procuring wagons. This being unexpected, caused some little delay, also some difficulty having arisen with the Indians as to the road they would go. They were told by Emubby[4] a chief of the nation that they should go by the Red river route and some of them are determined to do so, though contrary to the positive directions of myself and all concerned in the emigration.

"8 o'clock P. M. The Indians after being twice in council concluded to disobey the wishes of the conductor and go as they had been directed by their chief. After much persuasion however, they, by way of compromise, agreed that their women, children, and infirm should go on board the steamer Indian and proceed to the Choctaw Nation by water, and that the young men with the chief Sealy should go by land with the horses.

"27th July. We now believed that all difficulty was settled to their satisfaction but we were deceived; the baggage was scarcely on board the boat, when Sealy the chief came and informed me that about 300 of his men would go with him by way of Fort Towson and would go no other way; they could not be persuaded from this intention by all the arguments and instructions of the conductors and such citizens of Little Rock as were acquainted with the Indian character and the country through which they were compelled to pass. They were told the comparative distance of the routes and the impossibility of procuring food on any but the Fort Coffee road, as the rations purchased for them were deposited at that place, but they could not be shaken from their determination.

"At 3 o'clock this day Capt. Morris Dis. Officer, Doctor Keenan Direct Phys., and myself in the Steamer Indian with all the baggage and one hundred and fifty Indians for Fort Coffee; W. R. Guy Ass. Con-

3 Arkansas Gazette, July 25, 1837, p. 2, col. 1; Phillips to Harris, June 30, 1837, OIA, "Chickasaw Emigration" File P 127.

4 The old and respected chief who was killed by a white man as they were preparing to start on their emigration.

ductor left at the same time with a party of thirty Indians, about one hundred horses and two wagons for the same place by land. The party headed by their chief Sealy were determined to go by Red River and stop, when and where they pleased."[5]

The party on the steamboat arrived safely at Fort Coffee August 2, without incident except that a fourteen-year-old girl fell from the boat on July 29 and was drowned before help could reach her. The party went into camp near a good spring about a mile from the Choctaw agency.

After this detachment was established in camp, the conductor J. M. Millard, accompanied by Lieut. Gouverneur Morris and the Choctaw interpreter Daniel McCurtain descended the Arkansas river to Little Rock to look after the remainder of the emigrants, and Millard records their experiences from that time: "*Aug. 10. Left Little Rock and overtook seventy or eighty Indians about five miles from Town, found many of them very sick. Provisions having been provided on the other route, and my instructions being positive on that subject, efforts were again made to induce them to return and take that route, but to no purpose; they declared they would sooner die than change the way which they had determined to go, whereupon a wagon was procured to transport the sick, and these Indians traveled about five miles before night and camped.*

"*Aug. 11. Proceeded six miles, came to a small Brook, near which about twenty Indians were encamped; found one woman dead and another woman and a small child prostrated with the bilious fever. Capt. Morris procurred medicine and prescribed for the sick, employed a team to transport the sick and baggage up to the main party.*

"*Aug. 12. The scarcity of provisions and the difficulty of procurring them on the route, renders it necessary to transport almost all the supplies from Little Rock; accordingly this day was taken up in bringing the sick and scattering Indians to the principal party and procuring wagons to send to Little Rock for provisions.*

"*Aug. 13. This is the first time that the sick and scattering Indians could be collected together, notwithstanding the unremitted efforts of Capt. Morris and myself; a little Boy died this morning. The whole company encamped thirty-five miles from the Rock.*

5   Journal kept by J. N. Millard, emigration agent, OIA, "Chickasaw Emigration" File M 101; *Arkansas Gazette*, August 1, 1837, p. 2, col. 1. Morris became a captain September 6, 1837.

"*Aug. 14. The Indians felt no desire, nor could they be moved today;
they gave for an excuse that they could not find their horses, that most of
their men were engaged in hunting them, and that they had reason to
believe a great many were stolen by the whites, which I think was very
probable. The deer moreover, abounded in great numbers at this place,
and the hunters were very successful in killing them, which rendered them
more reluctant than otherwise to remove.*

"*Aug. 15. Found all the horses but five which had their bells cut off,
and from the appearance and direction of their tracks had been driven off
and stolen in the night. Some citizens in spite of our exertions and re-
monstrances for a few days past, in particular, and indeed, during the
whole route from the Rock, had for a little base lucre, succeeded in selling
ardent spirits to the Indians, occasioning dissatisfaction, riot and disorder
among them. They only went two and a half miles today; a heavy shower
of rain fell this afternoon, and they could not be made to go any further.
The sick were generally convalescent. In consequence of the extreme illness
of two of the Indians, we had great difficulty to transport them. They
would neither ride on the wagons, nor on horse, and were obliged to be
carried on a litter by hand.*

"*Aug. 16. The Indians only went three miles today and camped,
fine venison stopped their progress; they went early in the morning to hunt
up their horses, and came in loaded with deer.*

"*Aug. 17. The teams and a few of the Indians went to the Ouachita
River, distance twelve miles. The principal part only went two and a
half miles and camped, where they remained all the next day, without
making any effort to proceed. On the afternoon of the 19th Capt. Morris
and myself with the interpreter returned in pursuit of them; found many
of them on our arrival out hunting. Those in camp were assembled (among
whom were most of the principal men) and a talk was held to them by
myself, in which was stated in the most positive manner and plainest
terms, their unaccountable and singular conduct, and the rule and duty
they should in future perform, and as an Agent of Government I was
determined to exact; after which Capt. Morris read the following letter
to them: 'Ouachita Crossing, Aug. 19, 1837. Sir; I deem it my duty to
report to the officer U. S. Army commanding at Fort Towson, that a
party of three hundred and fifty Chickasaw Indians now emigrating to
their District under John M. Millard Conducting Agent and myself
as Dis'g officer, have refused to proceed; they throw their baggage out of*

the Teams which have been provided for their transportation, say they will have their own time and manner to get to their country, and seem to take great satisfaction in disregarding all directions and orders they receive from us.

"These Indians crossed the Arkansas River at Little Rock on the 25th of July, to go to Fort Towson, contrary to the orders of Maj. Upshaw the Supt of Chickasaw Removal and the Agents in charge of them, and have only progressed to this place, a distance of forty-five miles. They hunt and loiter about the habitations of the citizens and create serious apprehensions and complaints among them. They have not shown the least disposition to be hostile, but there is behind their action some thing I cannot account for.

"Under all the circumstances I believe it would be very proper to use military force to complel them to remove, and accordingly request you to dispatch to this place with as little delay as possible Two Companies of Infantry to conduct these Indians out of the State of Arkansas to their proper Territory. . . Gouverneur Morris. . .(To) Commanding Officer, U. S. Army, Fort Towson."

This threat to remove the Indians at the point of the bayonet was effective and as they agreed to follow instruction thereafter, Lieutenant Morris did not send his requisition to Fort Towson. The whole company came up to the Ouachita river on the twentieth and encamped on the right bank; "the ponies and horses recruited themselves by feeding on the young cane growing on the bottom lands." The next morning "an infant died; the Indians went only five miles and stopped to bury the child."

"Nearly all day the weather was extremely hot and the country very broken." At Prairie Bayou "one of the wagons broke down; it was unloaded and discharged. The weather and country same as yesterday. Nearly all the camps were provided with venison and turkeys, it being the best hunting ground on the whole route. The Indians had several very fine horses stolen." At Caddo Crossing the conductor hired a team "to send back for the sick and the load which had been left at the Bayou Prairie yesterday."

On the twenty-fourth there was great difficulty in collecting the "Indian Ponies and Horses. Some were lost in consequence of which we started very late in the day." The next day they reached "Antoine Bridge; at this camp several valuable Horses were stolen. It appeared that there was a gang of Horse thieves who followed the Indians and robbed them when ever they could get an opportunity, notwithstanding all the precautions the Indians took to guard their camp."[6]

"*Aug. 27. Travelled to [Little] Missouri River, Eleven miles, weather very hot and water scarce; at this camp the cane was excellent for the ponies. There was no house on the way for seven miles to Murphresborough, the seat of Justice of Pike County. The citizens of this place evinced great desire to sell ardent spirits to the Indians. They followed the train three miles to the River, with a large supply of whiskey and introduced it in camp the next morning at the very moment the Indians had mounted their horses to start, and in fact after about one half of them had taken the road.*

"*Aug. 28. The wagons and perhaps the third of the Indians went to Brier Creek, Eleven miles. Ehi oche tubby (the principal leader) and the remainder of the Indians tarried at Missouri River the whole day indulging in dissipation.*

"*Aug. 29. The party all came up, several of them much intoxicated. The country for several miles around this place is a scrub oak barren, affording little or no grass, and as many horses had previously been stolen from the Indians, I directed them to keep their horses up, and fodder to be procured for them. It may be proper to suggest in this place the necessity and propriety for the Government to issue forage to the Horses of Emigrating Indians while on their route. By this means the horses would not stray from Camp. They would be always strong and in good condition, enabled to perform long marches every day, actually prevent great delay and expense in the Emigration, and at the same time the Indians would not loose their animals by being stolen or broken down from famine and fatigue.*"

The next few days were uneventful except for delay occasioned by the illness of Samuel Sealy's son who died on the third of September on Rock creek and was buried there the next day. "Sept. 5. Capt.

---

6 Mr. Kingsbury, assistant agent for removal, later undertook to recover the stolen horses. On September 23 he reported from Murfreesborough that he had recovered six. "The thief is in confinement here under sentence of death. The people in the vicinity have been very active in their exertions to apprehend the thief and recover the horses" (Kingsbury to Harris, OIA, "Chickasaw Emigration" File K 24, 35, 46).

Morris and myself proceeded to David Folsom's[7] twenty-two miles west of the line, to make arrangements to furnish the Indians with Rations and Enroll them. There being no agent present to receive them, we remained until the 9th Inst to enable the whole party to get up." A contract was made by Capt. Morris with "David Folsom for eight cents per ration[8] and on the Eighth and Ninth I completed the enrollment, a copy of which I left for Mr. Kingsbury the acting agent. On the tenth Inst. Capt. Morris and myself proceeded via Fort Coffee on our way to join Maj. Upshaw at Pontotock Mi."[9]

When Superintendent Upshaw saw his emigrants safely across the Mississippi river, he returned to the Chickasaw Nation to recruit the remainder of the tribe. And by November 9 he had assembled at Memphis 4,000 Indians whom he proposed to remove by water.[10] A contract was made with Capt. Simeon Buckner of Kentucky to transport the Indians from Memphis to Fort Coffee in steamboats at the rate of $14.50 each. For that purpose Buckner assembled six vessels at Memphis; as the Indians approached the Mississippi river however, they began to hear accounts of the sinking of the steamboat *Monmouth* in the river below Memphis with the loss of over three hundred Creek emigrants. The Chickasaw became panic stricken, and many refused to board the boats.[11]

Upshaw had started four boats with Indians, by November 25, and was preparing to send another. "*Those that are going by land have been*

7   At Eagletown near the military road thirty-seven miles east of Fort Towson (Collins to Harris, September 2, 1837, OIA, "Chickasaw Emigration" File C 271).

8   Soon afterward a contract was made with Doak and Timms white contractors to supply the Indians at thirteen cents a ration.

9   Journal of J. N. Millard, *op. cit.; Arkansas Gazette,* September 2, 1837. The Indians remained here until the next year. Morris issued rations on the route as follows: Little Rock, August 10; Benton, August 13; Hot Springs, August 16; Ouachita river, August 19; Caddo river, August 22; Antoine bridge, August 27; Brier creek, August 31; Ultima Thule, September 3; Rolling Fork, September 4 (*ibid.,* File 221). The great emigration from Arkansas to Texas had made such a demand for food supplies along the Arkansas river that by autumn corn brought from one to two dollars a bushel (Armstrong to Harris, October 4, 1837, OIA, "Chickasaw Emigration" File A 261). Corn and beef were brought from Illinois and Missouri by the contractors.

10   OIA, "Chickasaw Emigration" File U 25.

11   *U. S. House Report, No. 454,* Twenty-seventh Congress, second session. Out of a total of 5,338 brought to the river that autumn, only 3,001 could be induced to travel by water.

crossing the river for several days, and it is likely they will be crossed in three or four days. The Chickasaws have an immense quantity of baggage. A great many of them have fine wagons and teams. They have also some four or five thousand ponies. I have used all the influence that I had to get them to sell off their horses, but they would about as lieve part with their lives as part with a horse."

Fortunately there was a rise in the Arkansas river that enabled the boats to ascend at good speed; the *De Kalb* passed Little Rock on the twenty-second with 500 Indians on board, the *Kentuckian* on the twenty-eighth with 800, and the *John Nelson* the next day; and they all completed the journey and discharged their passengers at Fort Coffee in from eight to ten days.[12] Those who went by land were divided into three parties under conductors Langtree, Welborne, and Millard.

Upshaw left Memphis December 3 with 227 more emigrants on the second trip of the steamer *Fox*, arrived at Little Rock four days later, and Fort Coffee on the twelfth.[13] Captain Millard left the west bank of the Mississippi river about the same time with a large number of Indians traveling by land with their ponies. They encountered tremendous difficulties: on the eleventh it was reported from St. Francis that "*Capt. John Millard, conductor of a party of Chickasaw Indians, reached Strong's last evening with about 800 Indians, 38 wagons and 1,100 ponies. The balance of this party, supposed to be from 700 to 800 in number, is still in the swamp, and will not reach here for some days owing to the desperate condition of the road. Capt. Millard thinks that not less than 70 or 80 ponies have been bogged and left dead in the mud. This party will remain here until the balance of the party come up.*"[14] They later proceeded, and at Little Rock Millard induced some of those who were weary of land travel to board steamboats for the remainder of the journey. Most of them however, with their horses and oxen continued overland, in charge of Captain Phillips.[15]

12 *Arkansas Gazette*, November 28, 1837, p. 2, col. 1; Armstrong to Harris, OIA, "Chickasaw Emigration," File A 294.

13 Upshaw to Harris, January 26, 1838, OIA, "Chickasaw Emigration" File U 29; *Commercial Bulletin* (*St. Louis*), December 12, 1837, p. 2, col. 1.

14 *Arkansas Gazette*, December 19, 1837, p. 2, col. 1.

15 Upshaw to Harris, August 1, 1838, OIA, "Chickasaw Emigration" File U 54.

COURTESY COL. JOHN R. FORDYCE

View of the Arkansas Swamps through which thousands of Indians labored on their westward march

Mrs. Rebecca Neugin at the age of ninety-six years (1931), a member of the Cherokee nation

Another land party of emigrants under Conductor Welborne having a large number of ponies, lay in camp for several days on the north side of the Arkansas river opposite Little Rock; two or three hundred of them were induced to embark on the steamboat *Cavalier* and leave that place on December 17, the remainder of them with their ponies continuing by land.[16] During this movement the steamboat *Itaska* carried up the river 800 Creeks in charge of R. B. Crockett who had gathered them up in the Chickasaw Nation and delivered them at Fort Gibson about the end of the year.[17] Another party of Chickasaw known as the Bear Creek Indians boarded a boat at Memphis December 28 in charge of Captain Phillips, bound for Fort Coffee.[18] Another came by land with their live stock and arrived at Fort Coffee about January 20 having lost between five and six hundred horses and oxen on the way.[19]

16   *Ibid.*
17   *Army and Navy Chronicle* IV, 412; *St. Louis Commercial Bulletin*, December 6 and 12, 1837.
18   Phillips to Harris, December 28, 1837, OIA, "Chickasaw Emigration, File P 254.
19   Armstrong to Harris, January 19, 1838, *ibid.* File A 316.

FTER the principal body of emigrants had left the East, a company of 175 Chickasaw Indians, followers of Kin-hi-cha, known in the Nation as the Cleanhouse Indians, departed with 206 horses and oxen, and arrived at Memphis on January 18, 1838.[1] They were then enrolled by Mr. Crockett, who, finding that the Mississippi swamps were impassable, placed them on the steamer *Itaska*, and their live stock on flatboats towed by her, and disembarked them at Arkansas Post. By this arrangement no horses or oxen were lost in the swamps. They then proceeded by land as far as Little Rock, where they were divided; the main party including the women and children under Conductor Vanderslice, were placed aboard a steamboat and delivered at Fort Coffee in February. The remainder with their chief Kin-hi-cha, their horses and oxen, conducted by Capt. J. A. Phillips, went overland and reached Fort Coffee March 16.

When Colonel Upshaw returned from Fort Coffee on his way to Memphis, he found 450 Chickasaw Indians at Helena, Arkansas, and he directed Mr. Crockett, who was returning from Fort Gibson after delivering his party of Creek Indians, to enroll the Chickasaw and conduct them to Fort Coffee.[2] However they refused to be enrolled and refused to have any whites with them. They said they were paying their own way, and they were determined to cross the Arkansas river at Arkansas Post; they intended to spend the winter in hunting, take their own time about traveling, and reach Fort Towson in the summer. Upshaw was therefore forced to leave them to their own plans. Still another party of nearly 200 who had been loitering on the way for

1 Upshaw to Harris, August 31, 1838, OIA, "Chickasaw Emigration," File 54; Grant Foreman, *A Traveler in Indian Territory*, 170, 254.

2 Upshaw to Harris, January 16, 1838, OIA, "Chickasaw Emigration," File U 29.

some months, arrived near Little Rock late in May, crossed there and proceeded to Fort Towson.[3]

Altogether nearly a thousand Chickasaw traveled to their new home without assistance or direction by the government. They were arriving in small parties from time to time through the winter and spring, having been compelled by sickness and cold weather to stop and camp for a considerable time along the road. Among these Col. George Colbert at his own expense removed a number of people and their slaves, who arrived early in the winter. Another party of 171 was removed by Pitman Colbert and located near Doaksville; it included James McCoy, Edmond Perry, John Craval, Daniel Harris, Mesho hogo, Anderson Frazier, Adams Perry, Pockopachee, Ish-to-fe-la-chee, Cooper, Captain Mehatah, Robert Colbert, and others with their families and slaves. Sixteen arrived at Fort Coffee on the steamboat *Liverpool* and twenty on the *Itaska* in May, 1838, and a little later a party of 150 who were paying their own expenses on the route.

A picture of the Chickasaw removal is furnished by Colonel Upshaw: "*As for the expense of moving the Chickasaws being so great, I have to account for it in this way. In the first place, they had a great deal of money, that is, their own private funds which they spent very freely. They bought a great many valuable articles for themselves to take west, believing that their wants could not be supplied after getting to their homes. In fact, some of them bought as high as a thousand dollars worth of goods of various kinds which it was impossible for me to prevent, even had I been present. Every merchant was pressing off on them every article he could. In fact, sir, I saw two women purchase seven hundred dollars worth of goods in the course of two hours. And sir, in getting these Indians to Memphis I did not get one more public waggon than I could possibly help. But a great number of them had waggons of their own. Some had three or four waggons. In fact Col. James Woolf sent to Memphis, besides two waggons of his own six waggons loaded with baggage. Besides the waggons that they brought loaded, they brought about seven thousand ponies and horses, all packed as long as an Indian can pack them, and they can pack more on a horse than other people I ever saw. Well sir, all this came to Memphis. What had I to do? I complained; told them they could not take so much baggage. What was*

3 *Arkansas Gazette*, May 30, 1838, p. 2, col. 1.

the reply of the chiefs and head men to me? It was this: 'We are moved out of our own money. This is our property. We want it. It is valuable to us. Were we to attempt to sell it, we could not for a hundred dollars worth get five dollars. Will you make us burn or throw our property in the River? We are the friends of the Whites; we have ever been and wish ever to be. In our treaty with our Great Father, it does not say that we shall not carry our baggage with us.' Under these circumstances what could I say? I tell you what I did say: 'Put your baggage in the boat.' If I was wrong, it was in not obeying the Regulation. Feelings of kindness and justice compelled me to take the course I did."[4]

The Chickasaw Indians were paying for their removal out of their tribal funds arising from the sale of their lands under their recent treaty with the government. It was fitting therefore that they should have some voice in the arrangements for their subsistence and comfort; and they accordingly made requests and suggestions for purchase and issuing their rations. They particularly requested that their superintendent be authorized to purchase such provisions as they required and have them distributed along the route. These it was estimated would cost them something over $100,000.

Instead of this, influences at work at Washington induced the authorities there to direct the agents at New Orleans and Cincinnati to purchase flour and pork by the hundreds of thousands of dollars worth for the anticipated use of the Creeks as well as Chickasaw. And in the summer of 1837 steamboat after steamboat ascended the Arkansas river and unloaded on the banks of that stream at Fort Coffee and Fort Gibson thousands of barrels of flour and pork, to stand in the sun and spoil. After it was too late, notice was taken of the fact that the Indians in the West as well as the white people were producing quantities of provisions suitable to the demands of the emigrants. Desperate efforts were made to re-ship these provisions down the river, but navigation was over for the season and there was no help in that direction. The government officers found themselves at the mercy of the contractors who agreed to take over at their own price the most of these provisions and enter into contracts for rationing the Indians. The result was that the Indians were imposed upon unmercifully, and the Chickasaw fund in the hands of the government was depleted to the extent of several

4 Upshaw to Harris, August 1, 1838, OIA, ibid., U 54.

times the amount first agreed upon. This situation was one reason for the desperate efforts to divert the first party from the route of their choice, from Little Rock to Fort Towson, and compel them to proceed to Fort Coffee, where the prodigal supply of provisions awaited consumers.[5]

After the first party had arrived at Fort Coffee on August first, some consideration was given to the next move, though no plans had been formulated. The Chickasaw desired to settle "near the mouth of False Washita River where General Leavenworth in 1834 established an out Post." But they feared they would be exposed to the depredations of the wild Indians who would steal all their horses in a short time. There was no road from Fort Coffee to the country where they wished to settle, and there were no facilities for subsisting them when they should arrive there. Captain Collins wrote that "*The obstacles which they may have to encounter (and which for the present I think will prevent their removing there) will be fully made known to them by the Choctaws, many of whom appeared anxious that the emigrants might be induced to stop among them, and at places and under circumstances, that would give them an opportunity of preying upon their necessities.*"[6]

January 2 Colonel Upshaw had delivered to Capt. G. P. Kingsbury at Fort Coffee 3,538 Chickasaw emigrants, and more were coming. They had a great amount of agricultural implements and baggage and were supplied with good tents. Before that time the Chickasaw who were in camp became restless for some settled plan to get them to their future home and they were extremely anxious to have a road made,[7] so that they could remove in time to prepare the ground for a crop of grain to sustain them the following year. Accordingly, four men selected by the Chickasaw[8] accompanied Captain Kingsbury from Fort Coffee on December 21, 1837 to mark out a road.

5 Grant Foreman, *op. cit.*, 193, 253.

6 Collins to Harris, September 2, 1837, OIA, *ibid.*, C 271.

7 G. Colbert and others to Armstrong, December 13, 1837, *ibid.*, A 299; *ibid.*, Armstrong to Harris, December 26, 1837.

8 These four men were "Tush-coon-tubbee, William Barr, Ish-te-ki-yo-pa-tub-bee and I. L. Myzell" (G. Colbert, Isaac Alberson, James Perry and others to Armstrong, December 13, 1837, OIA). The Indians complained that too many agents were employed at their expense, but they wished Colonel Guy retained. They also requested

They followed the road leading to Fort Towson for about twenty-five miles, then took a turn to the right and proceeded for twenty-five miles to the second branch of the Fourche Maline river; then twelve miles to Gaines creek; twenty miles farther to Brushy creek, from there twenty-five miles to Little Boggy creek, and twelve miles farther to Clear Boggy creek. They found an abundance of cane on all the creeks crossed, to sustain their stock while on the move, but there was very little cane on Blue[9] river.

"*Upon Clear Boggy, a distance of about 120 miles from the Agency we found one of the finest ranges for horses and cattle I have ever seen at this season of the year. There is a large quantity of cane upon both sides of the river, and at intervals in the cane brake there are large patches of green grass. The range is sufficiently extensive to subsist all the Chickasaw horses during the winter. This point moreover being about equal distance from several points of the Chickasaw line, the land adjoining being fertile and well watered, and the water being good, are considerations that induce me to recommend this point as the place for a depot of provisions. The Indians can draw their provisions at this point, go out and select their locations and return again when their provisions are exhausted; and I have no doubt from the many advantages that the country adjoining possesses, that numbers of them will settle near this point. As the Chickasaws are very desirous to get to their district as early as possible, I would respectfully recommend that their emigration commence immediately as the route possesses much greater facilities for their transportation than I had heretofore imagined. The teams will require but little forage as there is large quantities of cane at a distance of from 10 to 15 miles upon the whole route. We were out fifteen days, most of the time our horses were without corn, and they returned from the trip but little worsted.*"[10]

---

that a military post be established near their new home to protect them from the wild Indians (*ibid.*).

9 Blue river was frequently called by the name given it by the French, "De L'eau Bleu" and usually written "Low Blue" or "Loe Blue." The Indians called it "Oak-she-me-la" (Armstrong to Harris, October 4, 1837, OIA, *ibid.*, A 261).

10 Kingsbury to Armstrong, January 11, 1838, *ibid.*, A 316. Captain Kingsbury died near Fort Towson July 24, 1839 and was buried "with military honors; his wife was a daughter of Governor Dodge and a niece of Senator Linn of Missouri" (Armstrong to Crawford, July 29, 1839, OIA).

Capt. William Armstrong, acting superintendent for the western territory, at his post at the Choctaw Agency, sent out a force of men to cut and prepare the road located by the exploring party to the depot on Boggy creek. Of their thousands of horses and oxen the emigrants started with from the East, they had lost so many as seriously to handicap them in removing their great quantity of baggage that had been brought to Fort Coffee by steamboats. Their removal therefore to their new home in Pushmataha district of the Choctaw Nation was tedious, laborious, expensive, and slow.

Five hundred emigrants with twenty-eight wagons and teams in charge of J. M. Millard left Fort Coffee February 18, but the cold, high water and bad roads made their progress so difficult that they were more than five weeks in reaching the station on Boggy river; an equal number were for the time located on the Canadian river, 400 were at Folsom's near Fort Towson; the remainder were at Fort Coffee waiting for the weather to permit them to move. It had been unusually cold, so that the Arkansas river was closed with ice that sustained traffic. "The Chickasaws are inclined to be very idle, and it requires driving to get them off; they have been doing nothing but drinking since the treaty, and are very much indisposed to work;" a result of the unsettled condition growing out of their unwilling removal, and to the Fort Smith and Van Buren dispensers of whisky.[11]

By spring five depots for rationing the Chickasaw emigrants were established convenient to their temporary encampments; at Eagletown, Doaksville, Brushy creek, Boggy river, and one on the Canadian river. The emigrants on the steamboats Itaska had contracted smallpox on the way through Arkansas, and on their arrival spread the disease among the earlier arrivals. Between four and five hundred deaths occurred, principally among the Choctaw residents near the Arkansas river; among them was their chief Mushulatubbe who died on August 30, 1838, near the Choctaw Agency.[12] Doctors were sent among the Indians to vaccinate them and as the Chickasaw emigrants were somewhat concentrated in their encampments these measures

11 Armstrong to Harris, February 16, 1838, OIA, "Chickasaw Emigration" File A 305.

12 *Army and Navy Chronicle*, VII, 240.

met with greater success there than among the Choctaw people, whose schools were broken up and their crops neglected.[13]

By the middle of April about 750 Chickasaw had arrived at Boggy creek and some of them were building and planting; another large party were on their way and a third party of 800 were planning to start as soon as their issue of corn was made to them. About 1,500 remained near the Choctaw Agency on the Arkansas river to make a crop, as the season was too far advanced to reach their own district in time to plant for that year.[14] 600 were located on the Fourche Maline river and 500 on Brushy and Gaines creeks.

The Indians soon began to suffer from the negligence of the contractors: "Owing to difficulty of transporting provisions to a country so remote from civilization as the Chickasaw District, the Contractors failed to have their corn there in time for the last issue, and the Indians have been about a month without bread. The Contractors however started 14 wagons about 12 days since."[15] Three weeks later Mr. Upshaw reported from Mississippi: "*I have this day received a letter from Mr. William R. Guy, the issuing commissary for the Chickasaws that emigrated last fall, which statement has been more than confirmed by Col. Benj. Clements and Major Felix Lewis, who arrived at this place on yesterday and today. Their account is truly distressing, and I have thought it my duty to inform you of it. Their suffering, I have no doubt originates from neglect from some quarter, but I am not prepared to say from where. Mr. Guy writes as follows:*

"*'I am here starving with the Chickasaws by gross mismanagement on the part of the contractors, and when our situation will be bettered is hard for me to tell, for it is one failure after another without end.*

13 Captain Stuart "sent Fredson (a soldier) into the Choctaw Nation with directions to vaccinate the whole nation, commencing with those near where the Chickasaws have settled—by this means a large quantity of vaccine matter can be collected by the time you return for use of the other tribes" (Kingsbury to Armstrong May 4, 1838, ibid., K 100). By the end of the year the disease was diminishing among the Chickasaw and Choctaw Indians but was "still raging amongst the Creeks, Seminoles, and Cherokees, and has spread to some considerable extent amongst the troops at Fort Gibson" (Collins to Crawford, January 26, 1839, "Western Superintendency," OIA).

14 Kingsbury to Harris, April 20, 1838, OIA, "Chickasaw Emigration," File K 93.

15 Ibid., May 18, 1838.

You or Col. Armstrong are very much needed here at this time for there is such a propensity to play Farrow at Fort Coffee that I begin to think we will have to starve to death or abandon the Country. There has been corn within forty miles of this place for four or five days without moving a peg to relieve the sufferings of the people of Blue or Boggy.' This letter was dated the 14th of May.

"I am also informed that the Small Pox is still raging between Fort Coffee and Blue and Boggy, and that provisions are very scarce. I have nearly come to the conclusion to take the party that I shall start with in the course of two or three days by the way of Fort Towson, where, I am informed, provisions can be had in abundance on the road, and it is free from desease."[16]

Alarming reports from the West of smallpox and lack of provisions frightened the Indians and seriously interfered with Upshaw's efforts to enroll the remainder of the tribe in the East. He was able to induce only 129 under their king Ish-ta-ho-ta-pa to leave Pontotoc with him on June 9. They arrived at Memphis on the twenty-fourth, and left July 2, arriving at Little Rock on the fifteenth, whence they departed southwest, reaching Fort Towson[17] in August. After they left Little Rock so much sickness developed among them that about one hundred miles on the road they were obliged to remain in camp for two weeks. Of 130 in the party, there were at one time seventy prostrate with fever; however only two died. "One of the two was the King's wife, who was the Queen of the Chickasaw Nation; the other was a child about two years old." They were unable to continue until after the middle of August. Upshaw then turned them over to Millard and Vanderslice while he returned to the East to prepare others for removal.

It was not until autumn that Upshaw could induce the remainder of the Chickasaw people to start. He left his encampment forty miles southwest of Pontotoc October 10 with 200 and reached Memphis twenty days later. Here he was joined by 100 more recruits who came

16 Upshaw to Harris, June 7, 1838, OIA, ibid., U 48. Between 500 and 600 of the Chickasaw immigrants died of smallpox contracted on the way through Arkansas (Report of Commissioner of Indian Affairs for 1838; Armstrong to Harris December 26, 1837, OIA).

17 Upshaw to Harris, June 24, 1838, OIA, ibid., U 51; Arkansas Gazette, June 18, 1838, p. 2, col. 3.

in two parties, one of them from Tuscumbia. The *North Alabaman* published at Tuscumbia reported early in November that the entire Chickasaw tribe had left that place and added the following tribute: "*In taking leave of our red brethren and neighbors we render them no more than a just tribute to their merit, when we say that they have always stood deservedly high as a nation of Indians. They have been, both in profession and practice, the friends of white men. In war, they have always been found enlisted in the cause of Government, and not infrequently their blood has been spilt in support of the cause of civilized man.*"[18]

These people were engaged nearly a week in crossing the Mississippi river which was so low and the banks were so bad that they had much difficulty in boarding and landing from the ferry-boats. Late in November these 300 Indians with their baggage wagons, ponies, and cattle consumed several days in crossing the Arkansas river; they then took their course for Red river in the neighborhood of Doaksville[19] where they arrived December 22, 1838. Most of them later continued up to their new district on Boggy creek. This party included many of the wealthier members of the tribe who had delayed moving until the last. Among them was a small band headed by Jackson Kemp[20] who brought thirty slaves with him. George Colbert had used his influence to bring the party as far as Memphis, and from his own means had provided them with corn and meat, slaughtering twenty beeves for that purpose.

The late arrival and the prevalence of smallpox and fevers among them prevented their planting much and the crops that were started were burned by a serious drought so that but little grain was produced. This condition, complicated by the neglect of the contractors and the great amount of sickness and the excessive death rate caused much suffering and distress among the emigrants.

James Colbert, Isaac Alberson, Sloan Love, Greenwood, George Colbert, James Perry, and other head men, in behalf of their people still located on Brushy creek, on September 9, 1838, petitioned for help;

18 *Army and Navy Chronicle*, V. 347.

19 *Arkansas Gazette*, November 28, 1838, p. 2, col. 1.

20 In 1835 Benjamin Reynolds, Chickasaw agent, wrote that he had appointed Jackson Kemp a native Chickasaw as his interpreter. "I found him in office when I came to the agency in 1830, and he has acted as interpreter ever since, and in all cases I have found him competent and unexceptional in his moral character."

"Many of our people have died and the general drought through the Indian country has been particularly felt through ours; for these reasons together with the fact that many of our people arrived too late to make a crop, makes it our duty to apply for further subsistence." Late in December Captain Kingsbury reported from Fort Towson that he found many of the Chickasaw emigrants living near there in a very destitute condition, their year's subsistence having expired; some of them he said were almost starving. No adequate relief having been authorized from Washington, the Indians continued to beg for food. Captain Armstrong wrote the commissioner in February: "*The situation of the Chickasaws required immediate action to save them from starvation; I saw myself their distress; the season of the year for putting in a crop is near at hand; if they were left without further aid nothing could be done. The Chickasaws settled on Blue and Boggy are in danger of great suffering; there is neither Cattle or hogs in the country; a small drove of forty or fifty hogs was driven in while I was on Blue which commanded the enormous price if twenty-five cents a pound, but few of the Indians have money; and if they had they are one hundred and twenty miles from the line; such was their pressing wants that they hung around me, stating their situation, and without either corn or beef, they must starve. . . The petition of the Chickasaws set forth their wants; without the provisions but few could have remained at their new homes, they would have come into the settlements and abandoned their homes.*"[21]

The Chickasaw Indians were not yet all removed.[22] Benjamin Love of Holly Springs, Mississippi, came out in the summer of 1840 and selected a location for himself and his relations. Before leaving Mississippi he prepared a roll of these people who wished him to conduct them, and forwarded it to the commissioner of Indian affairs, with the request that funds be sent him with which to defray the expense of removal. In the autumn he brought his party by water as far as Fort Coffee. The roll listed ninety-two whites and 340 slaves, ninety-five of whom belonged to Love, fifty-one to Delila Moon, forty-four to

<hr />

21 Armstrong to Crawford, February 22, 1839, OIA, "Chickasaw Emigration" File A 521; Collins to Crawford, January 26, 1839, OIA, "Western Superintendency." Because of the destitution following this epidemic and inability to raise crops that year, Congress authorized a seven months additional issue of rations to these Indians.

22 In September, 1839, there were 5,947 Chickasaw Indians enrolled in the West (Armstrong to Crawford, September 9, 1839, OIA, *ibid.*, A 522.

Simon Burney, twenty-nine to Susan Colbert, twenty-two to Samuel Colbert, twenty-six to James Colbert, eighteen to David Burney, and the remainder to other members of the party.[23] In 1842-43 two hundred eighty-eight more Chickasaw Indians removed and joined their tribesmen in the West; sixty-four more came in 1846, and forty-four the next year.[24]

Chickasaw removal was a comparatively tranquil affair, and there is little to be found about it in the contemporary press, which gave much space to the Seminole war then raging. In the newspapers of the day, items about the war in Texas, Mexican and Texan emissaries seeking recruits among our southwestern Indians were interlarded with accounts of adventures in railroading; of experiments with improved paddle wheels on ocean steam boats; reviews of Irving's latest book, *The Adventures of Captain Bonneville;* the death of Black Hawk; messages of President Jackson; of the court-martialing of Maj. Gen. Winfield Scott; movements of sloops of war; advertisements for bids to furnish ash and live oak timber for the construction of naval vessels; a voyage of "Old Ironsides" to Constantinople; stories from the Sandwich Islands; the amazing feat of traveling from Florida to Washington in six days; fulminations against abolitionists; advertisements of nostrums to cure kings-evil and other ailments; accounts of "rencountres" and anti-masonic agitation.

23 Love to Crawford, September 13, 1830, OIA, "Chickasaw" File A 882; Upshaw to Armstrong September 13, 1840, *ibid.*
24 Reports of the Commissioner of Indians Affairs for 1843, 1846, and 1847.

BOOK FOUR / Cherokee Removal

THE legislature of Georgia passed an act December 19, 1829 appropriating a large area of the Cherokee Nation, incorporating it in the territory of the state, and adding it to the counties of Carroll, DeKalb, Gwinnett, Hall, and Habersham. The act extended the laws of the state over this section of the Cherokee Nation and provided that from and after the first of the following June all persons living therein should be subject to the state laws.[1] It provided further that after that date all laws, ordinances or regulations enacted by the government of the Cherokee Nation should become null and void, and made it illegal for any person to justify under any of the tribal laws. Not content with the destruction of the means by which the tribe regulated its own affairs, the State enacted further that any member who sought to influence another not to emigrate to the West should be punished by imprisonment in jail or the penitentiary. And, as if to achieve the depths of infamy, it was also provided "that no Indian or descendant of an Indian residing within the Creek or Cherokee nations of Indians, shall be deemed a competent witness in any court of this state to which a white person may be a party."[2] June 3, 1830 the governor of the State issued his proclamation[3] declaring all the provisions of that law to be in effect, and warning the Indians that it would be enforced.

On the same day the governor issued another edict: Gold had been discovered on the lands of the Indians and the executive gave notice that all the Cherokee lands including the gold mines, belonged to the State;[4] and warned the Indians and all persons engaged with their

1 Alabama and Mississippi did the same (*Document, ibid.*, II, 290).
2 *Ibid.*, 235.
3 *Ibid.*, 232.
4 *Ibid.*, II, 231.

consent or otherwise to cease operating the mines. Much disorder in the gold district resulted and the government sent troops to protect the Indians, but at the instance of the state authority withdrew the soldiers and yielded to the possession of the State.

While President Jackson's bill for the removal of the Indians was pending, Gov. George R. Gilmer of Georgia sent to the president his two proclamations and demanded that the national government keep its promise contained in the Act of 1802, to remove the Indians from the State. He was seconded by Gov. William Carroll of Tennessee, who offered to attempt the bribery of some of the influential Indians to lend their support to the movement upon the passage of the bill: *"I cannot but hope that I can induce both the Creeks and Cherokees, as directed by the Secretary of War, to agree to hold treaties; in which event the means of success will be found in assailing the avarice of the chiefs and principal men. . . I think I can move among the Cherokees without exciting their suspicion."*[5]

James Rogers, an influential mixed-blood member of the tribe who had emigrated to the West and located on the Arkansas river in 1816, was secretly employed by the secretary of war to go among his Indian brothers in the East and influence them to remove under the terms of the treaty of 1828.[6] Promises were made to Rogers inducing him to believe that for his help he would secure "a liberal reward which would place myself and family in easy circumstances for the ballance of my life."[7] Small parties of Indians left Georgia from time to time to join those removing from Arkansas under the recent treaty, to their new home in the present Oklahoma. For their transportation seventy keel- and flatboats were delivered to their agent in the latter part of 1829 and the first of the next year.[8] Most of the emigrants boarded the boats at Gunter's Landing; from there the Indians worked and steered the craft down the Tennessee, Ohio, and Mississippi rivers to Montgomery's Point at the mouth of White river where they embarked on steamboats for the passage up the Arkansas river to their new home.[9]

5 Ibid., 76.
6 Kappler, *op. cit.*, II, 206.
7 OIA, "Cherokees East, Claim of James Rogers for secret service."
8 *Document II*, 171.
9 *Ibid.*, 85. The lower part of the White river connected with the Mississippi and Arkansas rivers, making a short route between them.

About 200 emigrating Cherokee on the steamboat *Industry* passed Little Rock January 28, 1830 on their way up the river. An observer said that few of them looked like Indians as most of them were inter-married whites with their Indian families and negro slaves. The next day the steamboat *Waverly* passed up and besides 100 cabin and deck passengers she carried nearly 200 Cherokee emigrants among whom white and black blood predominated.[10]

Two months later the steamboat *Reindeer* with a large keel-boat in tow, both deeply laden, and thirty-five or forty cabin passengers, about the same number of deck passengers and between seventy and eighty Cherokee emigrants arrived at Little Rock; she departed on the twenty-third for Fort Smith and Fort Gibson. After they left the mouth of White river "a half breed woman named Vann about 60 years old" fell from the keel-boat in the night and was drowned. The steamboat *Industry* the next month carried up the Arkansas river 250 cabin and and deck passengers including 150 white emigrants mostly from East Tennessee, and principally bound for Washington county, and about 80 emigrating Cherokee.[11]

"The Five hundred Cherokees who reached here this year," wrote their agent George Vashon in August, 1830, *"have been under the necessity from a want of supplies, of selling their claim on the govern-ment, for provisions, to any one who would furnish something to relieve their sufferings. It is greatly to be regretted that the long continued delay of payment has operated to place these unfortunate people so much in the pitiless power of speculators."*[12] More than a year later Vashon wrote again that they "complain most feelingly of the loss sustained when compelled by necessity to trade off their claims, continuing to inquire of me, incessantly and solicitously, how much longer they will have to wait for the money."[13]

In 1830 after the removal bill was passed, the president directed the agent to suspend the enrolling and departure of small parties, which in the aggregate were inconsequential; but at the same time he warned the Indians that the government was powerless to prevent

10   *Cherokee Phoenix*, March 10, 1830, p. 2, col. 1.
11   *Arkansas Gazette*, April 27, in *Jackson (Tennessee) Gazette*, May 3, 1830, p. 3, col. 3.
12   *Document*, II, 90.
13   *Ibid.*, 606, 608, ff.

the State of Georgia from exercising sovereignty over them and that if they insisted on remaining in the state, they did so at their peril, and that they need expect no help from him.[14] Secretary Eaton commissioned John Lowery to attend the Cherokee council in October and undertake to induce the whole Cherokee Nation to leave Georgia. He submitted to the Indians in writing the propositions he wished considered. He told the council that the State of Georgia would probably enter their territory and survey it and that the president would not interfere. The council through its president John Ridge and Going Snake, the speaker of the council, and the officers of the national committee directed Chief John Ross to say that they would not be coerced by the threat to withdraw from them the protection guaranteed by their treaties made with the government; and that they intended to hold the domain secured to them by those treaties.

The council appointed a delegation composed of Richard Taylor[15] John Ridge, and William Shorey Coodey to go to Washington and present their grievances against the State of Georgia for seizing their gold mines, and for establishing a boundary line between the Cherokee domain and a tract claimed to have been acquired by the state from the Creeks by the treaty of 1826. It had been in the possession of the Cherokee for over thirty years, but Georgia claimed that as it had once been Creek land, it had passed to the state by the Creek treaty. It had been given to the Cherokee by the Creeks for assistance against the whites many years before, but the Georgians claimed the Cherokee won it from the Creeks "in ball play" wherein it was wagered by the Creeks on the result of the play.

When the Indians reached Washington the secretary of war refused to recognize them as a legally constituted delegation as they had not come with authority to discuss a treaty of removal. But the Indians were not without friends in Congress. The next month on February

14 Ibid., II, 14.
15 Taylor, fifty-six years of age, was described as a "large, portly man, of a bland, open countenance, which seemed shaded with an expression so deeply pensive, if not sad, as to indicate that but little hope for the fortunes of his country lingers around his heart. . . [He] . . .smokes a silver pipe of elegant workmanship with a silver charm attached, presented by General Washington to one of their chiefs. [Ridge was twenty-eight and Coodey] twenty-four years of age, and both of them intelligent and dignified men" (Account in *New York Observer* quoted in *Religious Intelligencer* (*New Haven*) January 15, 1831, p. 520).

15, 1831, the Senate of the United States adopted a resolution requesting the president "*to inform the Senate whether the provisions
of the act entitled 'An Act to regulate trade and intercourse with the
Indian tribes and to preserve peace on the frontiers' passed the 30th
of March, 1802, have been fully complied with on the part of the United
States Government, and if they have not, that he inform the Senate
of the reasons that have induced the Government to decline the enforcement of said act.*" On the twenty-second President Jackson delivered
to the Senate his special message in answer to the resolution.[16] He
frankly announced himself as the champion of Georgia in her controversy with the Indians and as frankly disclaimed any intention to
enforce the treaties made by the government with these Indians for
their protection, wherein they conflicted with the pretensions of
Georgia.

After the passage of the removal bill the Cherokee and their friends
brought an action in the supreme court of the United States to restrain
the operation of the laws of Georgia upon them but on March 5, 1831,
the court dismissed the proceeding[17] for want of jurisdiction on the
ground that the Cherokee Nation was not a foreign state within the
meaning of the Constitution and therefore could not bring a suit in
the supreme court. Chief Justice Marshall in announcing the opinion
of the court said that if courts were permitted to indulge their sympathies, a case better calculated to excite them could scarcely be
imagined; but apparently much against their inclination the court was
obliged to hold against the right of the Indians to maintain the action
against the State of Georgia. While this bill was pending a Cherokee
named Corntassel who had been sentenced by the Georgia authorities
to hang, sued out a writ of error to the United States supreme court.
The writ was issued by the Chief Justice to the proper authorities in
Georgia and by the governor conveyed to the legislature which resolved
that the supreme court of the United States had no jurisdiction over
the subject and in defiance of that court advised the immediate execution of the prisoner, which was carried out. J. W. A. Sanford
had been appointed to command the guard stationed among the
Cherokee to enforce the new Georgia laws against the Indians. He

16 James Richardson, *Messages of the Presidents*, II, 536.

17 "Cherokee Nation vs Georgia," *U. S. Supreme Court Reports*, V Peters, 1.

reported following the decision of the supreme court[18] that universal gloom corresponding to the former elevation of their hopes, prevailed throughout the nation. The Indians were distracted and did not know what to do.

But part of the decision by the supreme court gave some comfort to the Indians; it found that the tribe was a political entity capable of managing its affairs, and that it had rights under the law which in proper proceedings should be protected. For this small comfort extended the Indians, the chief justice was denounced by Governor Gilmer[19] as interfering with the administration of the criminal laws of the state. This part of the decision was used by the influential men of the tribe to encourage the Indians to believe that they still had rights that could be maintained against the efforts of Georgia to destroy them. With this vain hope held out to them the Indians refused to consent to remove.

The sympathies of the missionaries burned with a sense of the injustice put upon the Cherokee and they probably went outside their legitimate field as teachers and spiritual guides, to give encourage-ment and advice to sustain them in the unequal fight they were waging. On March 12, 1831, Isaac Proctor, the Rev. Samuel A. Worcester, and the Rev. John Thompson, teachers and missionaries at Carmel, New Echota, and Hightower were seized by twenty-five members of the Georgia guard, and one of them was carried before the Georgia superior court in Gwinnett county, charged with a violation of the state law for remaining among the Indians without securing a permit and sub-scribing to an oath of allegiance to the state. He was discharged by the court on the ground that the missionaries were in a sense agents of the government and not subject to the state law. Governor Gilmer then demanded to know of the government whether it claimed such immunity for them. Secretary of War Eaton promptly disclaimed any protection for the missionaries, informing Gilmer[20] that only the Moravian and Baptist missionaries could claim to be agents of the government as it was through them the ten thousand dollars appropria-ted annually since 1819 for civilization of the Indians was expended.

18 *Document*, II, 451.
19 Gilmer to Jackson, June 20, *ibid.*, 479.
20 *Ibid.*, 281.

The latter part of May the missionaries were warned that if they did not remove within ten days they would be arrested.[21] As they did not falter in their devotion to the Indians, Worcester and Rev. Elizur Butler were arrested by armed soldiers; July 7[22] they were carried before the court, tried and convicted of violating the law of the state against white persons remaining in the Cherokee country without subscribing to an oath of allegiance to the state and securing a license to remain; and as punishment, were sentenced to serve four years in the penitentiary at hard labor. An appeal was taken from this judgment to the supreme court of the United States and this being a proper case for determination by that court, the wrongs perpetrated by the State of Georgia upon the Cherokee Indians were characterized and denounced. Chief Justice Marshall in one of his great opinions[23] held that the acts of the state were unconstitutional and violated the rights of the petitioners and of the Cherokee Indians under the solemn treaty made with them by the United States; the conviction rendered in the State of Georgia was reversed and set aside and the missionaries were ordered released from imprisonment. However, officials of Georgia refused to obey the mandate of the supreme court and did not release Doctor Worcester for many months after the judgment of the supreme court was announced.[24] It was said that President Jackson in commenting on the decision in favor of the rights of the Cherokee Indians remarked: "John Marshall has rendered his decision; now let him enforce it."

In August Governor Gilmer thought the state had oppressed the suffering Indians sufficiently to induce them to be glad of the chance to remove.[25] He accordingly wrote the president that he thought the

21   One of the missionary teachers was warned by a Georgia officer to cease teaching a black boy which was a violation of the laws of the state (*Cherokee Phoenix*, March 17, 1832, p. 2, col. 2).

22   *Document*, II, 645.

23   "Worcester vs Georgia," *U. S. Supreme Court Reports, VI Peters*, 512.

24   During his incarceration on January 14, 1833, the Rev. Mr. Worcester was offered a full pardon by Governor Gilmer (*The Democrat* (Huntsville, Ala.). January 31, 1833, p. 3, col. 4) if he would agree to leave the Indian country; Worcester however refused to compromise his principles and rejected the offer, but he was subsequently released on the governor's pardon.

25   "In surveying the territory, I saw many fields and huts abandoned, and was informed that they principally belonged to half-breeds and refugees, who had fled to

time propitious to renew the enrollment of Indians for removal. President Jackson promptly notified Hugh Montgomery, the Cherokee agent,[26] to give notice and to enter for enrollment the names of all persons who wished to remove to the West under the provisions of the treaty of 1828. On September 1, the president appointed Benjamin F. Currey of Tennessee superintendent for the removal of the Cherokee within the limits of Georgia. With assistants, the most of whom were named by the governor of Georgia, Currey began his work, but he met tremendous opposition. There were many Indians who wished to flee from the oppression and misery that beset them, but were restrained by the threats and persuasions of the great majority of the tribe who proposed to stand on their rights.[27]

Intrigue was met by intrigue. Currey secretly employed intelligent mixed-breeds for a liberal compensation to circulate among the Indians and advance arguments calculated to break down their resistance.[28] The state law denying an Indian the right to testify in his own behalf in a court of Georgia was employed by unscrupulous white men of the state to rob the Indians of their live stock and other property and they had no forum in which their rights could be asserted or enforced. Plied with liquor, the Indians were charged with debts for which their property was taken with or without process of law. Under these conditions, the spirit of the Indians was broken and several thousand of them would undoubtedly have enrolled for removal by autumn but for the stern opposition of their leaders; threats and even personal violence were visited upon those who were so bold as to enroll for removal. Hope was held out to them that the Congress to meet the following winter would give them the relief that President Jackson refused. Some of them who were "*inclined to go to the west are indebted to the rich and powerful chiefs, many of whom are opposed to the emigration policy, and would throw any obstacle in the way, short of open hostilities, to thwart the views of the Government on the subject, whilst those disposed to go, but not having the means to satisfy the demands*

Alabama and Tennessee to escape the jurisdiction of Georgia. . . The guard has produced a good effect in awing the chiefs to an involuntary submission to our laws" (Report of Ira E. Dupree to Governor Gilmer, June 3, 1831, *Document*, II, 488).

26 August 13, 1831 (*ibid.*, II, 320).
27 *Ibid.*, 328, 593, 619, 621, 693, 707.
28 *Ibid.*, 328, 593, 638.

of their creditors, intimidated by terrors of the law, would, in most cases, perhaps, abandon all idea of emigration, and become vassals again to the more powerful chiefs" was the report of Currey based upon rumors he had heard after two months of futile effort to secure emigrants for the West.[29] Some of the earlier emigrants tired of life in the West returned to their homes in Georgia and brought unfavorable reports of the country west of the Mississippi river; among these was Bushyhead. These reports added to the difficulty of securing recruits for emigration.[30]

29 Ibid., 612.
30 Ibid., 183.

CHAPTER NINETEEN / *Cherokee Indians Defend their*
Tribal Existence

ANOTHER council by the Cherokee people was held in October to consider their wrongs and plan for relief. Georgia soldiers were on hand to see that they did not violate the state law by enacting any legislation or pretend to exercise any of their governmental powers. The council discussed their dire situation and appointed a delegation consisting of John Ross, John Martin,[1] John Ridge, and William Shorey Coodey to Washington to present their grievances. This delegation on December 29, 1831 submitted a memorial to the secretary of war[2] in which they called attention to the taking of their gold mines by Georgia; the state authorities had taken their people from their homes at the point of the bayonet, and carried them away in chains without legal process; the state had surveyed their lands and proposed to divide them by lottery among the citizens of Georgia; a licensed trader and postmaster who had taken the oath of allegiance to the state was permitted to reside among the Indians and dispense whisky to them in violation of federal laws; intruders were suffered to come upon their lands from all sides and ravage their property and abuse the people; the government permitted citizens of Georgia to go into possession of lands vacated by Indians who had left for the West, when such lands were the common property of the Cherokee Nation; all in violation of laws enacted for their protection. "Such a mode of extinguishing the title of the Cherokees to their lands is certainly one never

1 Judge John Martin had been treasurer of the Cherokee Nation before the removal west. He was a useful and prominent citizen of the Nation; he died of brain fever near Fort Gibson, October 17, 1840, at the age of fifty-five years, eleven months and twenty-seven days. He was buried at Fort Gibson and the inscription on the monument over his stone-walled grave recites that he was the chief justice of the first supreme court of the Cherokee Nation.

2 *Document*, II, 731.

contemplated by any one until the present Chief Magistrate came into office and is at war with all the professions of the government, and the principles of its action heretofore" wrote the delegates Coodey and Martin to the secretary of war.[3] Georgia had enacted a law to prevent any Cherokee from conveying his property to any other person, white or Indian, except to the governor of the state or the general government.[4]

After the departure of the delegation, Currey wrote to Herring, the commissioner of Indian affairs, that if they failed on their visit to Washington to realize the promises held out to the Indians, their influence with them which was absolute, would be lost; and besides making the suggestion to Herring, he promised to do all in his power with the Indians to destroy the influence of their delegates.[5] They were not only handicapped by the hostilities of the officials with whom they desired to council, but they were embarrassed by the conflicting interests arising in the tribe in the West.

At a council of the western Cherokee held at Tolluntuskee at the mouth of the Illinois river in November 1831, Chief John Jolly appointed a delegation to go to Washington. The members of the delegation were Alexander Saunders, Black Coat, Capt. Rain Crow, Capt. John Rogers, and Andrew M. Vann with Edward Hicks as secretary and Capt. James Rogers as interpreter. They bore to President Jackson instructions authorizing them to solicit from the government a performance of the promises made to them in the treaty of 1828. In view of the recent removal to the West of several hundred Cherokee who came under the terms of that treaty, they asked to have the annuity of the western Cherokee increased accordingly, and for the same reason requested that the country allotted to them be increased.[6]

The instructions particularly directed them to solicit the fulfilment of the promise to cancel certain reserves to individual Osage in their treaty of 1825, and included in the lands given the Cherokee in 1828. Some of these reserves had been purchased by Sam Houston who prepared the instructions given by Chief Jolly to the delegation,[7]

3 *Ibid.*, III, 22.
4 *Ibid.*, 415.
5 *Ibid.*, II, 649.
6 *Ibid.*, 677, ff, 693; III, 275; the Cherokee complained that their country in the West was too small and too poor to sustain any more emigrants (*ibid.*, II, 690).
7 *Ibid.*, III, 2, 7.

and it was charged that Houston expected to profit largely by his influence with the Indians and by demanding a large price for his reserves.

Two of the delegates, Capt. John Rogers and Andrew M. Vann, were directed to pass through the old Cherokee Nation and engage some of the eastern Cherokee to accompany them to Washington. There they were joined by John Walker, Jr.,[8] and James Starr, who, without credentials accompanied them. Though they had no authority to represent any one but themselves they were well received by the officials[9] because they were willing to advance the cause of removal and make rash statements about the temper of the Cherokee people on the subject, and the domineering attitude of the Cherokee chiefs who opposed the wishes of the government.[10] They and their actions were repudiated by a large part of the tribe.[11]

The western Cherokee had a grievance of long standing in the failure of the government to make the payment promised them for their live stock killed and stolen by the white people of Arkansas before and during their removal from that Territory.[12] The money was due them under the terms of the treaty of 1828, but it was like many other promises made to the Indians to induce them to remove, and then forgotten. It was April 11, 1832, before they could get from Secretary of War Cass a reply[13] to their memorial which had been on file for more than four months while Jolly and his delegation waited in Washington for an answer. Cass then assured them that the government was ready to redeem its four-year-old promises by the erection of a sawmill and grist-mill, provision for a school fund, purchase of a printing press and payment for losses sustained to their property in Arkansas; but declined to do anything about extinguishing the Osage reserves.[14]

8 Walker had offered to sell to the government his influence with his tribe (*ibid.*, II, 601).

9 Cass wrote them a long deferential letter which they could exhibit at home as proof of their influence in Washington (*ibid.*, II, 810).

10 Their expenses were paid by the government (*ibid.*, 964).

11 *Ibid.*, IV, 119.

12 *Ibid.*, III, 4.

13 *Ibid.*, II, 808.

14 In the treaty of cession made by the Osage Indians in 1825 (Kappler, *op. cit.*, II, 154) a section of land was reserved to each of eight Osage half-breeds, wards and most of them children of Col. A. P. Chouteau; these reserves were located on the east

Martin, Ridge, and Coodey, the eastern delegates, remained in Washington all winter and did not leave for home until May 15, 1832. Though they repeatedly presented to the secretary of war the grievances of their people growing out of the intrusion of the whites on their lands, they were invited to solace themselves by a perusal of the president's special message and his dictum that their problem was one of remedy and not one of right. Their course was controlled to some extent by John Ross who wrote them letters of instructions calculated to stiffen their resolution. The secretary sought to have them carry home with them propositions to submit to their people, but even this, with the warning of the martinet Ross in their ears, they were afraid to do. The president[15] therefore on May 11, 1832, commissioned E. W. Chester to carry his proposals for removal to the Cherokee people in council, and ask for definite acceptance or rejection.[16]

In the meantime Currey and his assistants had been laboring against great odds to collect a party of emigrants for removal to the West. Currey had secured the assistance of Edward Adair of the western Cherokee to travel among his brothers in the East and present to them the advantage of the new home in the West.[17] In paying the Indians an annuity of fifty cents during the summer of 1831, Curry was using the opportunity to enroll them for removal; the chiefs and captains by threat of whipping compelled the Indians to refuse the annuity.[18] By the middle of December Curry had succeeded in enrolling only seventy-one families of whom twenty-one were Indians headed by white men, totalling 366 individuals. Currey's assistants were nearly all selected by Governor Gilmer of Georgia, which greatly embarrassed the movement because the Indians regarded the people of Georgia as their enemies and where persuasion was needed their words were wasted.[19] Some of them gave up and returned their commissions.

---

bank of Grand river between Fort Gibson and the present Salina, Oklahoma. When this territory was given to the Cherokee Indians by the treaty of 1828, they insisted that these reserves be extinguished (Grant Foreman, *Pioneer Days in the Early Southwest*, 258).

15 *Document*, II, 824.
16 *Ibid.*, III, 432.
17 *Ibid.*, II, 707.
18 *Ibid.*, 522.
19 *Ibid.*, III, 201.

As the season advanced and the suffering of the poor Indians increased, numbers of them sought relief in Currey's enrollment, and he was encouraged to believe that he would have a thousand ready to remove in the spring. A few preferred to leave independently and find their own way to the West by flatboats. But even these were not allowed to depart in peace. *"Unjust claims of long standing having been placed in the hands of Cherokee sheriffs, and the property of emigrants seized on the highroad, to extort money from, or annoy, them in their passage thither, and to the town of Calhoun, opposite the place of embarcation. They have been decoyed by the irrisistible influence of ardent spirits, and there induced to create debts without the prospect of advantage to themselves or families."*[20] "Delays of the most unlooked for character have also been occasioned by serving bail warrants and attaching Indian property to satisfy debts, in some instances of forty years standing."[21] Thus did Currey picture the oppression practiced by the Cherokee on their own people to discourage their removal.

In December Currey had received sixteen flatboats or arks belonging to the United States which he proceeded to repair for the use of his emigrants from Georgia, some of whom soon after began arriving at Calhoun, Tennessee. By March 10 there were 180 of them quartered in rude huts on the banks of the Hiwassee river erected for their protection against the weather, while awaiting the time to embark for the West.[22] Currey was ready by April 1832 to depart with the little band collected by him: "The Cherokees" he said "dread the length of time necessarily consumed in passing on board of flat-bottomed boats to the mouth of White river, as they are not accustomed to long voyages, would be liable to contract desease."[23] Instead of the thousand emigrants promised him, he had but 380 persons, 108 blacks, forty whites, and the remainder mixed, with a few full-bloods. Twenty-one were from Tennessee and the remainder from Georgia.[24]

They left the Cherokee agency at Calhoun on April 10 in nine flatboats, and passing down the Tennessee river through the rapids

20 Currey to Herring, January 25, 1832 (*ibid.*, III, 152).
21 *Ibid.*, III, 257.
22 *Ibid.*, I, 759; III, 270.
23 *Ibid.*, II, 648.
24 *Ibid.*, III, 430.

at Muscle Shoals arrived a week later at Waterloo.[25] They were transferred to the steamboat *Thomas Yeatman* which departed about the twentieth and passed out of the mouth of the Tennessee river three days later. They proceeded down the Ohio and Mississippi and up the Arkansas river, reaching Little Rock on the thirtieth;[26] part of them were disembarked at the Cherokee Agency just above Fort Smith, on the left bank of the Arkansas river,[27] and the remainder were taken farther up to the mouth of the Illinois. When the Indians were put ashore they learned to their dismay that there was no food awaiting them or money to purchase any. They were destitute and Currey made temporary arrangements with the Cherokee agent Vashon to furnish some rations to the Indians, but not to their slaves nor to the whites intermarried among them.[28]

About 170 emigrants had preceded them, going on their own re- sources in flatboats or arks which their men steered and worked[29] as far as the mouth of the White river. Twenty of them were carried up the Arkansas river in March on the steamboat *Elk* while others waited on White river for transportation.[30] At the request of the members of this party, the secretary of war in December, 1831, gave permission to the Rev. D. O'Bryant, a Baptist missionary and his family to accompany them to the West at the expense of the govern- ment.[31]

25 *Ibid.*, I, 760; III, 287.

26 *Arkansas Gazette*, May 2, 1832, p. 3, col. 1.

27 *Document*, III, 377. The first Cherokee Agency was located here ". . .a few miles west of the Territory and on the bank of the Arkansas river, and the cost of the dwelling, office, kitchen and stable all built of brick, in a plain substantial workmanlike manner and enclosing the agency, is estimated at five thousand dollars" (George Vashon, Cherokee Agent West, to Secretary of War, December 2, 1830, OIA). Before the government provided a building, "Captain Vashon kept his agency at the house of Mr. Looney Price" (Arbuckle to Brown, February 3, 1836, AGO, ORD, "Ft. Gibson Letter Book" No. 110, p. 157). After the steamboat *Thomas Yeatman* discharged her Indian passengers she made two trips carrying freight up from Fort Smith to Fort Gibson before she ran aground on a sandbar twenty-five miles above the former post; there she was left while her captain Mr. Irwin, and Mr. Currey descended the river in a keel boat (*Arkansas Gazette*, May 30, 1832, p. 3, col. 2).

28 *Document*, III, 378.

29 *Ibid.*, 257.

30 *Arkansas Gazette*, March 14, 1832, p. 3, col. 2.

31 *Document*, II, 381, 688; III, 152.

Thus by dint of great efforts there were 626 Cherokee collected during the autumn and winter of 1831, and removed in the spring, representing the whole of the year's work.[32] Understanding that another movement would occur in the autumn, enrollment was again undertaken by Currey who was engaged through the summer in preparing the minds of the Indians for it. He began with a prospect for a considerable enrollment; a number of the more prosperous Indians had disposed of their crops and stock, preparing to leave for the West,[33] when in September Currey received notice again to suspend his work. In the summer the news[34] of the decision of the supreme court in favor of the missionaries in the case of Worcester against Georgia, threw the Cherokee people into a tumult of rejoicing.

". . .It was trumpeted forth among the Indians, by the chiefs, head-men, and missionaries, that the decision mentioned had forever settled the controversy about their lands; that their laws and country would be unconditionally restored to them again, and the Georgians expelled from their territory. Following this, councils were called in all the towns of the nation, rejoicings, night dances, etc., were had in all parts upon the occasion, and the Indians urged and pressed not to enrol. For a time these deluded people believed in the realty of the reports and assurances, and were rejoicing, yelling and whooping in every direction. Indeed,

32   Ibid., I, 627. According to a tabulation in the office of Indian affairs of January 25, 1839, a total of 907 migrated in 1831 and 1832.

33   Document, I, 620. The subject of removing the Cherokee tribe to the mouth of the Columbia river was receiving some consideration (ibid., III, 434). Chester reported to the secretary of war in 1832: ". . .In my last I mentioned that there had been suggestions made by some of the Cherokees, about removal to the Pacific. I am inclined to think that such a plan, if possible, would be more agreeable to many of them, than a removal to the Arkansas.

"It has long been a question with me, what is eventually to be done with the country west of the Rock Mountains. It is too remote ever to be formed into a State, or States of the Union; unless rail roads, and the power of steam, are hereafter to make neighbors of antipodes. Between the Rock Mountains and the States there is a large extent of country, which must for ages be unsettled by civilized man. There is little doubt that settlements will soon be made at the mouth of the Columbia, and probably on other parts of the coast. Will not the government find it necessary, either to break them up, or establish a Government of some kind over them, to avoid the danger of many mischiefs" (ibid., 398). Some of the Cherokee thought the Creeks and Choctaw could be induced to unite with them in a removal to the Pacific Ocean (ibid., 392).

34   June 24, 1832, (ibid., III, 381).

such was their audacity, that they sent private emissaries into our camp at the Highwassee river, before the emigrants embarked for Arkansas, and persuaded them not to go; that if they would remain they would be protected; which produced some disaffection among them, and having no guard, gave us great trouble to preserve order among them, and to prevent their running off; some made the attempt to run off, but were promptly pursued and brought back. Finally, the agitation and disorder among them increased to such a degree, that on the night previous to their embarkation, we had to plant a strong chain of sentinels around their camp, composed of white men who had volunteered their services to prevent the disaffected from making their escape."[35]

The Cherokee council met again on July 23, 1832 at Red Clay, Tennessee,[36] where it would have elected a chief but for the penalty threatened by the State of Georgia for its exercising the functions of the government, so it passed a resolution continuing their chief in office; the government's proposition to enter into a treaty of removal, presented by Elisha W. Chester was unanimously rejected[37] in a resolution reciting that the Indians would consider such proposition only when offered through the regularly appointed Cherokee agent. Saying that when the government would afford them the protection guaranteed by their treaties and the decisions of the supreme court, so that they would not be compelled to act under coercion, they would treat; they would then be able to negotiate on equal terms with the more powerful government, but now they were asked to treat with their backs to the wall. This council was conducted in an atmosphere of great bitterness. Chester said there were some members in favor of a treaty but they were in a small minority and feared to urge their views.

The council then adjourned but another was called for the autumn, which convened October 8. Again Chester was on hand to urge the propositions submitted by the president, threatening the Cherokee that if for the second time they rejected this offer they would have to apply for terms to the State of Georgia. The subject was discussed for several weeks and the agent reported that the majority of the most enlightened half-breeds and white men having Indian families approved

35   Davis to Cass, ibid.
36   Ibid., I, 656.
37   Ibid., III, 421, 425.

the treaty of removal, but the full-bloods were opposed to it, having always followed the advice of Ross and others who did their thinking for them. The failure of the government to provide for and keep its agreements with emigrants on their arrival in the West and the resulting suffering had caused much discontent and complaint, news of which was circulated among the eastern Cherokee and this handicapped the efforts of the government to create a sentiment for removal. The government's propositions were rejected by the council. John Ridge offered a resolution to send a delegation to Washington with power to treat with the government on the subject of removal, but it was defeated. Instead, a resolution was adopted to send a delegation composed of Richard Taylor, John F. Baldridge, and Joseph Vann, accompanied by John Ross as chief and counselor[38] to attend to the business of the nation before the government.

In the autumn of 1831 there were comparatively few white people in the Cherokee Nation, ". . .and they were generally refugees from justice, or had come into the country to get a living by stealing and robbery. At this time [September 1832] there is at least five hundred families, half of whom are honest where they have white people to deal with. But in their dealings with Indians, who are not allowed to be a party to a suit, nor entitled to the benefits of an oath in courts of justice, they mostly take all advantages allowed by the law. Consequently, although the Indian finds a market at his own door for his stock, he cannot sell for cash, and to sell on a credit is equal to giving it away."[39] Thus does Benjamin F. Currey, enrolling agent, illustrate the operation of the infamous law enacted by Georgia, to prevent an Indian from maintaining his rights against a white man.[40]

The autumn election was now at hand and the Indians were urged to stand fast for a short time longer as Henry Clay was sure to defeat Jackson for re-election in which event Clay would see that the treaties and decisions of the supreme court were enforced and their rights protected against the encroachments of Georgia. There was a strong sentiment in favor of agreeing to a treaty of removal but the influence of Ross, Ridge, Martin, and others was too powerful to be overcome.

38 Ibid., 521.
39 Currey to Hook, September 29, 1832, Document, I, 627.
40 Ibid., II, 235.

It had been hoped that this delegation would be able to submit their grievances to President Clay where they were certain of relief; but to their sorrow Jackson was re-elected. When the result of the election was known government agents secretly engaged in efforts to call another meeting of the Cherokee favorable to removal, to destroy the influence and standing of the delegation.[41]

The delegates arrived in Washington January 8, 1833, and on the 28th submitted to the secretary of war their memorial asserting that the Cherokee Nation would never consent to remove to the West and praying the government to enforce the rights secured to them by treaty; in the face of the illegal action of Georgia in annulling their laws, and dividing their lands by lottery, the government had withdrawn its protection promised in the treaties.[42] For answer[43] the delegation was told that the president was solicitous for their welfare which could never be realized but by surrender to the policy of removal, and referred them again to the president's message for his answer on the subject.

Ross dominated the delegation at Washington and maintained his position in argument with the president; the latter offered him $2,-500,000 for all their country except that in North Carolina, and finally he was induced to raise the offer to $3,000,000 if they would all remove. But Ross told him the gold mines in Georgia were alone worth more than that. Ross inquired of the president how, if he could not protect them in their rights in Georgia, he could protect them against similar evils in the West.

On the return of the delegation May 14, 1833, the council met to hear their report,[44] which was made by Ross. His nephew, William Shorey Coodey presented a protest against the course that had been pursued by the leaders, which in the debate was urged by Coodey, Ridge, Boudinot, and many others but was opposed by Ross, Lowery and their adherents; finally, as a compromise, it was agreed that discussion of the subject go over to the October council, when all the people of the Nation would be invited to be present and express their views.

41 Ibid., III, 540, 569.
42 Ibid., IV, 63.
43 Ibid., III, 588. The delegation on February 14 submitted an argument in answer to the reply of the secretary of war (ibid., IV, 97).
44 Ibid., 411.

However, before the council adjourned on May 20, it adopted a resolution complaining of the evasive and unsatisfactory replies of the secretary of war to their memorial and proposing that the subject be referred to Congress where they hoped to receive more favorable consideration than the president would give them.[45]

Bitterness and dissension between the Ross faction and the treaty advocates continued. Currey, who was present at the council reported to the commissioner of Indian affairs: "*These resolutions, a copy of which had been promised to me, were not spread upon the journal. John Ridge, who had read a letter addressed to him and others from the department a few days before, and depicted, in an eloquent and impressive manner, the forlorn situation of the country, demanded that these resolutions should be made a matter of record, which was consented to; but his attention being turned for a moment or two towards his father, who was by this time addressing the crowd in an adjoining grove, Judge Taylor snatched the resolutions from the clerk's table, and joining John Ross, they rode off in great haste, leaving no track or trace of the resolutions further than they rested on the memory of the auditors.*

"*. . .Old Major Ridge is the great orator in the nation; he dismissed the meeting, after giving a concise and well arranged history of their present condition compared with what it had been; the probability of their being called on in a few months, for the last time, to say whether they will submit always to the evils and difficulties every day increasing around them, or look for a new home, promising them freedom and national prosperity; advising them to bury party animosity, and in case they should conclude to seek a new home, to go in the character of true friends and brothers. . .Past experience has shown that Ross and his party hold no pledge sacred.*"[46]

The condition of the whole tribe was getting more and more desperate. In the summer of 1833, with the oppression of the intruders, venders of whisky, and other troubles from Georgia, on the one hand, and the vain hopes held out to them by Ross and other influential leaders on the other, they were thoroughly demoralized. Scant provision for the future was made and few crops put in; the Indian agent reported in June that the full-bloods were in a state of wretchedness

45 Ibid., 408.
46 Ibid., 413.

-{ 248 }-

bordering on starvation, and of ten persons who had gone into the woods to dig roots for food, six died from eating a poisonous weed.[47]

At the council held at Red Clay in October 1833, another delegation was appointed to go to Washington during the succeeding session of congress. It was composed of John Ross, Richard Taylor, Daniel McCoy, Hair Conrad, and John Timson.[48] They were commissioned to represent the Cherokee Nation "on all subjects touching the rights and interests of the same, with a view to a final termination of existing difficulty." Because the delegation did not favor the removal of the tribe Governor Lumpkin wrote the secretary of war[49], that they "are wholly undeserving the courtesy and marked attention of the official authorities at Washington."

Neither was the subject of removal of the tribe viewed with complacency by the western Cherokee, who objected to receiving the emigrants except upon terms; they took the position that all the land set apart by the treaty of 1828 belonged to them and they did not intend to divide it with their eastern brothers.[50] A proposed treaty was therefore entered into between them and Cherokee Agent George Vashon February 10, 1834, at the Cherokee Agency on the Arkansas river near the mouth of the Illinois river. It was signed for the western Cherokee by the chiefs John Jolly, Black Coat, and Walter Webber. It provided for increasing the annuities and enlarging the holdings of the western Cherokee as a condition precedent to the participation in them by their brothers from the East. In view of the large number of children in the tribe whose parents had died, provision was made also for an orphan home. The treaty was submitted to the Stokes commissioners at Fort Gibson who refused to submit it to the secretary of war.

47 Ibid., 445.
48 Ibid., IV, 630.
49 November 18, 1833, ibid., 718.
50 Captain Vashon estimated the number of Arkansas Cherokee in 1833 at 3,000 and the emigrants at 1,000. "When the hunters return and those who yet remain on the waters of Red and White Rivers move within the Cherokee limits, an accurate census may be obtained, but it is hoped the above estimate will answer for the present" (Vashon to Herring, December 31, 1833, OIA, "Cherokee West").

"The Cherokees claim in the States east of the Mississippi, 7,200,000 acres of land. There was estimated to be about 2,700 families in 1828. 2,666 acres of land on an average, belong to each Cherokee family. Since 1828, about 200 families have enrolled and ceded to the Government all their right and interest in the nation east. . . Under the Cherokee laws, as they now stand and have stood for many years past, each family has a right to clear and cultivate as much land as he pleases, so he does not go nearer than one quarter mile to his neighbor" (Currey to Herring, May 1, 1833, *Document*, IV, 195). "Under the treaty of 1817 about 500 families enrolled and relinquished their interest in this country" including the 200 since 1828, said Currey in July, 1833 (*ibid.*, 490).

An official census taken in December, 1835, gave the number of Cherokee in Georgia, North Carolina, Alabama, and Tennessee as 16,542, exclusive of 1,592 negro slaves and 201 whites intermarried with Cherokee. They were distributed as follows: Georgia, 8,946, with 776 slaves; North Carolina, 3,644, with thirty-seven slaves; Tennessee, 2,528, with 480 slaves; Alabama, 1,424, with 299 slaves (*U. S. Senate Document No.* 120, Twenty-fifth Congress, second session, 535).

CHAPTER TWENTY / A Tragic Migration

OPPRESSION was employed mercilessly to break the spirit of the Cherokee who refused to leave their homes; and with the help of state laws enacted for the purpose, the homes of the wealthier members of the tribe were taken from them. Joseph Vann was a prosperous Cherokee whose plantation contained about eight hundred acres in cultivation, a residence of brick that had cost him ten thousand dollars, besides other extensive improvements. On the pretense that he had violated a law of Georgia by employing a white man to oversee his farm while he was absent from home, his property was seized in December, 1833, as forfeit to the state. The larcenous methods employed easily accounted for rival claims to the property, by white men. One, named Spencer Riley, took possession of the upper part of the house, armed for battle; when the state's agent William N. Bishop entered the lower part, March 2, 1835, a fight ensued and many shots were exchanged within the house, while Vann and his family were cowering in a room to which they had fled for safety. Riley could not be dislodged from his position upstairs, even after being wounded, so Bishop's party set fire to the house. Riley surrendered and the fire was extinguished. Vann and his family were driven out in the cold weather and compelled to wade through the snow to seek shelter across the Tennessee line, in an open log cabin, upon a dirt floor.[1]

1 Memorial and Protest of the Cherokee Nation to Congress, June 21, 1836. The man Bishop, commander of the Georgia guard, became notorious for his disregard of the law and his outrages on both white and red. In this instance he was trying to secure the valuable Vann home for his brother (George M. Battey, Jr., *A History of Rome and Floyd County*, 85). He was required to resign his post as commander of the guard and was then, in January, 1836, elected clerk of the superior court of Murray county by a vote of 158 votes to twelve for his opponent (*ibid.*).

In the spring of 1834 the fine estate of John Ross was seized by authority of the State of Georgia under another form of larceny, a lottery authorized by the state to deprive the Cherokee of their lands,[2] the title to this property having been vested in a successful drawer of lots. The newcomer took possession of his valuable ferry at the head of Coosa river and of all his extensive farm and houses, leaving only one room on the ground floor of their home for the occupancy of Mrs. Ross who was in feeble health.[3] These experiences were repeated until nearly all of the members of the tribe who had valuable property were driven from their homes. And still their spirit was not broken; but they were being worn down by the constant battle from which they could see no escape.

Benjamin F. Currey, superintendent of removal, and his assistants, were using all their resources to secure recruits to their companies of emigrants in 1834 at a time they must inevitably suffer much from disease. "This is the third season that the cholera has scattered desolation & dismay over the Western waters and during its malignant influence no bodies of people have been able to move in any considerable numbers for any length of time in contact, upon the rivers with impunity," wrote Lieutenant Harris.[4] But the government did not relax its efforts to drive the Indians through that disease infested area.

The agents had enrolled a considerable number for emigration, and a time had been fixed for wagons to come to their neighborhoods, to carry their children and baggage to the rendezvous. Before the arrival of the wagons however, the opponents of removal had called meetings where inducements, intimidations and warnings of disease along the route were employed to discourage their departure. The result was that nearly 800 of those who had enrolled, declined to leave. *"There were some families to assemble on the river from the Creek Path Valley and without my presence there was but little hope they would be able to get off. My acquaintance with the emigrants and their desire that I should accompany them until they were past the dangers of the Shoals & for the purpose of allaying their fears from Cholera which was represented to*

2 *Document* III, 418.
3 *Cherokee Phoenix,* June 5, 1834, p. 3, col. 4. Mrs. Ross died on the journey west.
4 Harris to Gibson, June 5, 1834, OIA, "Cherokee Emigration."

FROM THE GREAT SOUTH BY EDWARD KING

The home of John Ross near Ross's Landing, now Chattanooga, Tennessee

GRANT FOREMAN

Site of encampment of Lieutenant Harris's party of Cherokee Indians at mouth of Cadron Creek, Arkansas, where they suffered with cholera

be raging on the river, I went as far as the confluence of Tennessee & Ohio rivers," wrote Currey of some Indians who were emigrating at their own expense.[5]

Heavy rains and other causes delayed the arrival of the emigrants at the Cherokee Agency on the Hiwassee river; from February 1 they began straggling in to the gathering place where log shelters had been provided for them. These consisted of a "*cantonment of four blocks containing in all twenty-eight pens of rough open log work some 16 feet square each, & covered with good weather proof roofs of a suitable pitch. . . The site of the camp has been judiciously selected about three quarters of a mile from the Agency & about a half a mile below the town at one of the best landing places on the river; and by its distance & the intervening hills, securing the quiet of the peaceful settlers from the loud & boisterous riot which revels here throughout the assembling season.*

"*We already feel a serious annoyance in the trading boats, or 'floating doggeries' which now infest the river, & which coming from the upper Tennessee, the Holston & the Clinch with their loads of cakes, & pies, & fruit, and cider & apple jack and whiskey, Shark it here for the annuity arrearages of the poor Indians, or the hard earned or illicit gains of the worthless white men; & become the nurseries & receptacles of idleness, drunkeness & vice. It is from these that a torrent of tumultuous revellers is pouring itself incessantly into the town. . . introducing. . . shameful & bloody quarrels & drunken orgies into the camp. And is it not surprising that nothing apparently is done to remove the source of so much mischief, and. . . purge these waters of lawless venders who daily and every hour in the day & night are openly demonstrating them-selves to be public nuisances?*" So wrote Lieut. Joseph W. Harris of New Hampshire, a West Point graduate of the class of 1825 who had been assigned to conduct this party of emigrants to their western home.[6]

Flatboats that were to carry the Indians for some distance down the river, were tied up to the opposite shore a few hundred yards above the camp. Waiting for dilatory arrivals two weeks after the time set for departure, on March 13, 1834, the boats dropped down to the landing and the next afternoon when the *John Cox* and the *Sliger* had

5 Currey to Gibson, April 20, 1834, *ibid.*
6 Journal of Lieut. J. W. Harris, *ibid.*; the journal of this conscientious officer when transcribed from the manuscript extends to more than one hundred typewritten pages.

taken on board seventy-two emigrants they cast off. This party was in charge of Harris's assistant, a white man named John Miller who was married to a Cherokee woman; he was under orders to collect the stragglers and those living along the banks of the Hiwassee and Tennessee rivers who were ready to depart and would be awaiting the boats; and then to wait at Muscle Shoals for the remainder of the party.

Harris delayed the departure of the main body of emigrants until the arrival of a company of seventy mountain Indians known as the Valley Towns, who brought their belongings in three heavy six-horse wagons. "Immorality & misrule have continued to be the order of the day— dancing, drunkeness, gambling & fighting the pastime of the night; and their floating causes still continue triumphantly moored to the opposite bank of the river." Measles broke out among the emigrants and from the "fact that few of them have ever been visited with this disease and are consequently open to it now, and to the immense number of children in the fleet & to reports of cholera below," Harris engaged Doctor Edington of Calhoun to accompany the emigrants as far as Tuscumbia where he would be relieved by another.

After ten days rations had been issued, the next day at eleven o'clock the *Blue Buck* with 125 emigrants on board cast off. An hour later "*after some trouble in which persuasion, threats & force were alternately resorted to, the remainder of the party were embarked & the* Rainbow, *the* Squeezer *and the* Moll Thompson *unmoored & dropped into the current.*"

"*The banks of the river were thronged with people brought thither by almost as many motives; who in the language of the Country 'saw us off' & cheered us upon our journey. The parting scene was more moving than I was prepared for; when this hour of leave-taking arrived I saw many a manly cheek suffused with tears. Parents were turning with sick hearts from children who were about to seek other homes in a far off and stranger land; and brothers and sisters with heaving bosoms & brimful eyes were wringing each others hands for the last time. And often I observed some young man whom the spirit of roving or adventure had tempted to forsake all that was dear to him here, to seek alone an uncertain future in other climes; or some young wife who was tearing herself from father and mother, 'kith & kin,' to follow the fortunes of her husband whithersoever they should lead, turn again & again to the embrace of those they loved and were leaving, in seeming forgetfulness that they had already rec'd their adieus. . . We slipped gently down the river with the current, occasionally impeded in our course by a brisk head wind, now working an oar to give us head way, & now calling our strength and skill into requisition to 'dodge a snag or clear a sawyer.' "*

At midnight the party overtook the *Blue Buck* moored snugly to the bank with all on board asleep. Her skipper was ordered to cast off and an hour later the boats passed out of the Hiwassee river into the Tennessee. At eight o'clock, twenty-five miles below, Harris overtook Miller's contingent at Brown's Ferry and by noon had joined the remainder of the fleet. Before night the boats successfully negotiated the shoals and rapids in the Tennessee river known as the "Suck," the "Boiling Pot," the "Frying Pan," and the "Skillet." After safely passing through the Muscle Shoals, they arrived at Waterloo, Alabama, on the nineteenth, having made 267 miles in six days of water travel. The voyage had been uneventful thus far, though considerable trouble had been caused by the introduction of whisky among the Indians whenever stops were made near white settlements, and numerous cases of measles had developed in the party.

They were delayed a little at Waterloo, a "hamlet of doggeries & of brothels, got up to entertain the low and sensual tastes of the boat-men who navigate the river;" but on the twenty-fourth, the party with recent additions picked up at Creek Path, now numbering 457, was transferred to the steamboat *Thomas Yeatman*. The descent of the Tennessee, Ohio and Mississippi rivers with three keel-boats loaded with Indians in tow, was marked by frequent stops to make repairs to the machinery or paddle-wheels of a dilapidated old steamboat; to wash out the boats as a precaution against disease; to secure a coffin and bury a child. Stops were frequent at woodyards to "wood" the boat.

Overtaking a party of sixty-seven Cherokee emigrants who had become discouraged and bewildered and who begged to be taken in charge by Harris, their boat was "lashed abreast of the keel—filled in the night and went down. The people on board had barely time to save themselves. They lost most of their property." The steamboat *Harry Hill* came alongside and delivered to them seventy-five barrels of flour, forty-five of pickled pork, and two of salt.

Soon after the party entered the Mississippi river, Anna, the sister of Daniel Reynolds, drowned. "*She had been to one of the cooking fires upon the deck of the larboard keel and was returning below when her foot slipped & she fell over the Stern of the boat. . . The night is dark & the immense headway the boat had on at the time of the accident, left the poor wretch far behind before assistance could be properly attempted—one wild shriek rose in the distance,—& the waters closed over her forever; the yawl was ordered in & the boats resumed their voyage. I had cautioned the people against these accidents, and positively ordered that the fires should be extinguished at dark & and that after that time they should confine themselves below decks, or in their respective cabins.*"

Arriving at Montgomery's Point at the mouth of White river they found a fleet of eight or nine flatboats containing about 200 more Cherokee emigrants of those who had received the commutation allowance and were transporting themselves. They had been on the way twenty days, had suffered much from disease and several deaths had occurred among them. The undertaking had taxed their resources to such an extent that they repented not having committed themselves to a government conductor; ". . .several of them pleaded so hard to be recd. on board & their brothers & sisters who were with me were so anxious to have them" that Harris took a few aboard and arranged to transport the remainder up the Arkansas river on another steamboat.

As they ascended the Arkansas river their progress was delayed by frequent stops at woodyards. Numerous snags and shoals compelled them to travel only in the daytime and tie up to the bank at night. Sickness from measles was increasing and they occasionally stopped to bury a dead person. They arrived at Little Rock April 6 and after putting ashore ninety barrels of flour and pork to lighten the craft, proceeded the next day. Due to the difficulty of passing the shoals, stopping twice to bury children of Daniel McDonald and Henson, and repairing damages to the paddle-wheels of the boat, they made only forty-three miles in the first two days. Towing the two keel-boats over the shoals and through the swift crossings had become so difficult that Harris induced 102 of his party to go ashore at the mouth of Cadron creek and proceed overland. He paid them two dollars each for their subsistence and with this sum they expected to purchase an ox team to carry their provisions and cooking utensils. It was planned to carry the remainder of the emigrants on the steamboat and one keel-boat. They got under way on the morning of the eleventh and had proceeded only about an hour when they came to a bar across the river where there were but twenty-six inches of water, and the boat drew three and one-half feet. Further ascent being impossible they descended to the mouth of Cadron creek from which the land party had not departed.

The men were ordered ashore to prepare for their families shelters to which they were the next day to remove from the boats all of their women and children and an increasing number of sick; also to land all their personal effects, and wash and air their clothing and bedding. They were to make the best of their camp until an accession of water would enable them to renew their river journey, or teams could be found to take them overland. Many miles from their destination, these unhappy emigrants found themselves in a desperate situation, but their intelligent conductor did everything possible to relieve their distress. That night about three miles away he found Dr. Jesse C. Roberts and in the dark they groped their "way to the boats & visited the various sick."

Harris returned to Little Rock and scoured the country searching for wagons and teams with little success as the few owners needed them to begin their spring planting. A number of the emigrants named Nellums, Woodhall, Townsend, Daniel and Alex McDonald had purchased a wagon and oxen and with their families numbering seventeen in all, started by land. No wagons had been procured by Harris but the emigrants were cheered somewhat by the improvement in their health, when on the fifteenth an alarming change took place with the introduction of a malignant type of cholera. Two sisters, the wives of Black Fox and Charley McDaniel, and Robert Shelton's wife and several others died within twenty-four hours and were buried on the same day. The next day three died "before breakfast and eleven in all before the sun went down." The Indians were panic-stricken and "scattering through the woods, building their camp fires as remote from each other as their several fears direct," until they were extended over an area of two or three miles, thus adding to the difficulty of ministering to them.

"*My blood chills even as I write, at the remembrance of the scenes I have gone through today. In the cluster of cedars upon the bluff which looks down upon the Creek & river, and near a few tall chimneys—*

the wreck of a once comfortable tenement, the destroyer had been most busily at work. Three large families of the poor class are there encamped, & I have passed much of the day with them, & have devoted the larger portion of my cares to their sufferers—but in vain were my efforts: the hand of death was upon them. At one time I saw stretched around me and within a few feet of each other, eight of these afflicted creatures dead or dying. Yet no loud lamentations went up from the bereaved ones here. They were of the true Indian blood; they looked upon the departed ones with a manly sorrow & silently digged graves for their dead and as quietly they laid them out in their narrow beds. . . There is a dignity in their grief which is sublime; and which, poor and destitute, ignorant and unbefriended as they were, made me respect them.

"The grief of the whites of my party is now loud and more distressing, yet less touching than the untold sorrow of the poor Indian. The heart-broken wife or mother whose feelings had not from the cradle been nerved by the philosophy of the woods, could not, when a beloved child or husband was snatched within an hour from rosy health & from her bosom, brood over her anguish in silence. She must tell her misery to the world. The whites and the half breeds too are far more timid & far more selfish I find, in scenes of danger & of affliction than the full blooded Indian. They are ever alive to a thousand superstitious fears, and hugging closely each to his individual comfort, they churlishly & doggedly refuse all aid or relief to their suffering neighbors." The dead on the sixteenth were "Alex M'Toy, D. Ross child, Bolingers ditto, Richardsons wife, T. Wilsons child, Wm. England, Brewers' child, one of Wm. Vanns and three Black Foxes children; all of whom with the exception of Alex M'Toy have been decently buried, & his coffin will be in readiness in a few minutes."

Seven more died on the seventeenth and the same number the next day. Nearly all those afflicted with cholera were either suffering, or just recovering, from measles. The unusual confinement on the boats and privations to which they were not accustomed debilitated a large number of adults, who particularly were revolted by the daily diet of salt pork which they were not in the habit of eating. Articles of diet such as coffee and sugar they were accustomed to use in their homes were denied them unless they had the money with which to buy them. The government allowance provided nothing but salt pork for the ill and convalescent and whatever could be made from flour or corn.

Five died on the nineteenth. "*People employed in burying their dead, nursing the sick, washing, & burning the underbrush of the woods & creating a smoke. . . Thus far all my dead have had as decent burial as the circumstances would admit; in some cases when pressed we have been obliged to put two or even three bodies in one coffin, but such instances have occured rarely.*"

Doctor Roberts, the faithful country doctor who had come from Alabama to this country a few years before with his little family, attended his patients constantly day and night. His treatment was limited principally to doses of from one-half to a grain of opium, and from fifteen to forty grains of calomel. Under his ministration the death-rate dropped to one a day on the twentieth and twenty-first. That evening with the battle apparently won, the doctor was stricken and died the next day. "*I have devoted the day to my poor friend. He has none to help him! His poor weakly wife can scarcely crawl about; the only servant is better out of the way, or has her hands full to keep this houseful of children from their dying father. The two or three miserable white people who are scattered within so many miles of his cabin, though sent for, will not come. They are panic struck.*"

Doctor Roberts had attended faithfully and intelligently the sick and dying Indians and "*after a little acquaintance so pleased was I with his attentive care and industry in his calling, that at the request of his patients I engaged his services for the remainder of the trip. I had scarcely returned from making my final arrangements for securing land transportation when the excellent man was taken down and within 24 hours after his attack fell a victim to the pestilence he was so industriously striving to stay. He has left a wife and young family in embarrassed circumstances.*"[7]

From about fifteen miles away came Doctor Mennifee to see Doctor Roberts and gave Harris some instructions about administering to the ill but he was obliged to leave and look after his own patients. Doctor Fulton of Little Rock came a few days later, and thus relieved, Harris resumed his search for oxen and wagons to remove his emigrants. But Fulton succumbed to the hardships of his duties and was obliged to leave Harris alone with his sick.

7 Harris to Gibson, May 9, 1834, *ibid.*, "Cherokee Emigration."

In order to travel about looking for oxen and wagons, he had purchased a horse, but the day before Robert's death it was stolen from near the camp by white horse-thieves who took also a few ponies of the Indians that were tethered near; animals that were brought to aid in their land removal by their tribesmen who had preceded them to the West and had learned of the desperate situation in which the emigrants were placed.

On the twenty-third Harris *"Early in the morning dispatched a messenger to a carpenter 5 miles off to come & make a coffin for Dr. R. also to other neighbors 3 or 4 m from here to come and assist at the burial. Went the rounds on foot for I can get no horse—and for one sick and debilitated as I am it was no small undertaking. I am not much of a physician & feel that I am but a poor prop for these unfortunates to rest upon—but I have done and will do my best."* The next day he had *"been able to obtain a horse for a portion of the day, & have consequently had it in my power to make two or even three visits to some of my patients & watch the operation of my medicines. And it is gratifying to find upon my last visit that several of those who in the morning I was afraid I should lose before night, are now doing well."* Harris too, administered calomel: *"In urgent cases I do not stop for weight but administer it by the half tea spoonful."*

The twenty-fourth, the *"steamer Cavalier passed with sundry of the Cherokee emigrants we left at Montgomery's point, several of whom are very sick. My commissary Templin W. Ross being quite broken down himself & receiving discouraging news of his family, [on the Cavalier] begged permission to leave me and to give them the assistance & protection they so much needed. I could not refuse the poor man's request, for his is a case of trying affliction; although I can but poorly spare him just now; for there is none here but myself to supply his place."*

The next day there were several deaths and more became ill. Six teams of six-oxen and one five-horse team that had been engaged, arrived at camp. Word was received that other teamsters who had started had returned home when they learned of the death of Doctor Roberts and the extreme illness of Doctor Fulton. Two of the recently arrived teamsters loaded their wagons and crossed Cadron creek. On the twenty-sixth, Harris was attacked and after taking forty grains of calomel and half a grain of opium took a hot foot bath and *"laid myself down in a quiet corner out of the current of air & drawing my blanket over me composed myself & was soon in a fine perspiration. The medicine too operated favorably. By this time the people began to drop in and finding that the news was getting abroad that I was sick & knowing that I had not a moment to lose if I wished to keep together the few wagons I had—as I had even found it a hard matter yesterday to suppress the idle fears of their drivers & prevent their returning to their homes—I slipped on my clothes, & mounting Mr. F. Horse, rode through the camp—& although for a while I could scarcely keep my saddle, I soon satisfied all that I was not only not sick myself, but was still capable of doctoring others. In the course of the excitement of the day, I forgot my sickness, & am only convinced of it now by a feeling of great debility."*

This day the remainder of the wagons loaded with food and sick, started across Cadron creek. At sundown four more ox-teams arrived and were loaded the next morning, when the movement with fourteen wagons and teams began. The oxen were poor animals weak from the custom of feeding them nothing through the winter but the cane which they foraged for themselves. Because of the large number of ill and infirm it was necessary to carry all the provisions possible; as the great flood of the year before had left very little food in the country, which, when it could be procured at all, was surrendered grudgingly in small quantities and at a very high price. For these reasons, Harris required the Indians to leave behind all their effects but blankets, light bedding and cooking utensils, indispensable to the comfort of the sick and for their subsistence upon the road, and these things they were obliged to carry on their backs.

All the people who could stand traveled on foot, many of them barefoot, men, women, and children. Salvaging only what they could carry, they abandoned the many cherished possessions they had brought from their old homes with which to begin life anew in the wilderness: their bedding, household utensils, looms, ovens, pot-hooks, spinning-wheels, farming implements, plows, hoes, and harness.[8] Three children in this

8 Harris told the Indians soon after their arrival in camp to place their personal belongings on board the steamboat *Yeatman* to be taken down to Little Rock and stored until they could be carried up the river to their new home. But under the stress of their great affliction these instructions were not carried out and at the last minute this property was stored in a building at their camp. Later a few of the Indians came back to recover their effects, only to find that they had been stolen and carried away (*Cherokee Phoenix*, May 31, 1834, p. 2, col. 3; statement of Ruth Mator, *Cherokee Register of Claims for proprty lost on removal*, Vol. 1).

party died of the measles and were buried the first day of the march, three the next, one the next, and one on the thirtieth, when the party reached the Illinois Bayou near the site of old Dwight Mission.

One of Bryant Ward's children died May 1 and another the next day. Bob Shelton's child died and was buried on the third. Harris traveled ahead each day to locate for his party food and forage, some of which he had engaged in advance, only to find frequently that his contractors had failed him. He was compelled to make long and arduous rides scouring the country for supplies, and only after repeated refusals was he able, at rare intervals, to secure small quantities of pork and corn. The health of the party was improving and the Indians were more cheerful, but much distress was caused by blistered and bleeding feet from the long, weary march over rough and often rocky roads.

On May 8 the party crossed Lees creek and at noon entered the new Cherokee country; two days later they camped at Sallisaw Creek near the new Dwight Mission. Here the Indians made their plans to separate, part to move up to the Illinois and Grand rivers, a few to settle on the Sallisaw creek, and the larger part to proceed north to Beattie's Prairie. On the twelfth one contingent began loading its wagons with rations for three days and under the escort of Miller started west for Illinois and Grand rivers. Four other wagons were discharged and the remainder the next day started with the main body for Beattie's Prairie. In the morning Harris "overtook the main party who had started at 9 A. M. A number of the people had already abandoned the wagons for various sites which had pleased them along the road. They are jaded down too & must have rest, & to find themselves once more settled." After advising with their conductor all of this contingent of exhausted, sick, and emaciated emigrants (except one family that wished to join friends farther away), stopped in the vicinity of Dwight Mission to make their homes. The remainder traveling west over the military road dropped off from time to time at places that pleased them, the last stopping at the Illinois river, except Miller's immediate connections who settled near the Bayou Menard a few miles southeast of Fort Gibson.

At the time Harris left his people at Dwight Mission there had been eighty-one deaths, of which 50 were from cholera, among them since leaving the Tennessee river. Of the whole number of deaths forty-five were of children under ten years of age who "died chiefly of the measles, dysenteries, worms, &c, the result of exposure, confinement, want of proper cleanliness, the river water and the neglect of parents." The season following was one of great mortality among the troops at the military posts and other white people; and of the members of Harris's party who reached their new home nearly one half died before the end of the year.[9]

In commenting on the menace to the health and lives of the Indians involved in their removal Harris wrote: *"Many of them had been reared from the cradle in easy circumstances & had enjoyed through life its comforts & some of its luxuries, and there were those too of more frugal, but still sufficient means, and those again who from childhood had been pressed by the gripping hand of poverty.*

"That such a heterogeneous mass accustomed to live apart in thinly scattered settlements, suddenly crowded together in camps & afterwards in boats, some totally deprived of what habit had taught them to look upon as the necessaries of life, & others who had rarely known a season of plenty, deprived of exercise, breathing a confined & poisonous atmosphere and maintaining, as they ever will under like circumstances, a total dis-regard for personal cleanliness, should in a term of sixty days even under the most favorable circumstances, generate a pestilence within itself would not be surprising."[10]

Harris arrived at Fort Gibson May 14 and after making his reports to the western agent of the Cherokee, sick and exhausted, he descended the river to Little Rock where he completed his business with the commissary stationed there. On June 5, the river still being too low for navigation, he started on horseback to St. Louis. There was some-thing heroic in the devoted, intelligent, and indefatigable attention of this officer to his Indian charges. He continued in the service of Indian removal until his death which occurred May 18, 1837, at his home in Portsmouth, New Hampshire.

9   Arbuckle to Jones, December 31, 1834, AGO, OFD.
10   Harris to Gibson, May 9, 1834, OIA, "Cherokee Emigration."

CHAPTER TWENTY-ONE / *The Schermerhorn "Treaty."*
Last Stand of the Cherokee

JOHN ROGERS, John Drew, James Rogers, and Moses Smith of Arkansas went east and joined a delegation of eastern Cherokee going to Washington, composed of Andrew Ross, John West, James Starr, and T. F. Pack. The western delegates carried a petition addressed by them and some of the Creek chiefs to the secretary of war asking for the establishment of a line of military posts to protect the immigrants from the wild Indians. They proposed to organize a party of a thousand men to visit all the western Indians from whom acts of hostility might be apprehended, to conciliate whom they wished to be furnished money with which to purchase presents for them.[1]

In Washington on June 19, 1834, John H. Eaton as commissioner on behalf of the United States negotiated with the eastern delegation, a treaty by which they purported to cede to the United States all the Cherokee land in Georgia, North Carolina, Tennessee, and Alabama, and the Indians agreed to remove to the West. The small consideration included allowances for rifles, blankets, and brass kettles, $10,000 a year for ten years for schools, $25,000 for the erection of school houses, plows, axes, hoes, looms and wheels. Provision was made also for purchasing for the Cherokee 800,000 acres more land adjoining their holdings on the north, excepting that owned by the Seneca, Shawnee and Quapaw; but it was provided that these tribes might become members of the Cherokee Nation if they wished and merge their lands

---

1 John Rogers, Roley McIntosh, and others to Cass, May 14, 1834, OIA, "Creek and Cherokee Delegations." This was one of the numerous efforts that eventuated in the famous Dragoon expedition from Fort Gibson to the western Indians in the summer of 1834; for an account see Grant Foreman, *Pioneer Days in the Early Southwest*, (Cleveland, 1926).

with those of the Cherokee. A supplement provided that the Cherokee might negotiate with the Osage for part of their holdings west as
far as "McCoy's habitable line." The treaty also suspended the law
which prevented them taking into their country for their own use such
liquors as they desired. It provided compensation for the seizure
two years before by Captain Vashon and Major Armstrong of a quantity of liquor imported by some of the Cherokee chiefs, an act which
had produced much ill feeling on their part. This treaty was never
ratified.

For his participation in this business Andrew Ross's life was
threatened in August on his return to the Cherokee Nation. Later
in the month a meeting was called by John Ross at Red Clay, Tennessee, not far from the present Chattanooga. John Walker, who had
been very active in promoting the views of the government in favor
of removal was present, and on his departure was waylaid along the
road, shot, and killed. This killing caused great excitement.[2]

Two rival delegations from the eastern Cherokee arrived in Washington in February, 1835; that of the National Party, headed by
John Ross[3] came prepared to fight to the end for home and national

2 Walker, a man of superior education and influential connections, was married
to a niece of Cherokee Agent Return Jonathan Meigs; his murder was the out-
growth of a personal and not a political difficulty (James S. Mooney, *Myths of the
Cherokee*, Nineteenth Annual Report, Bureau of American Ethnology, Part I).

3 John Ross chief of the Cherokee; born in Rossville, Georgia, October 3, 1790;
died in Washington, D. C., August 1, 1866. He was the son of an emigrant from
Scotland by a Cherokee wife who was herself three-quarters white. His boyhood
name of Tsan-usdi, 'Little John,' was exchanged when he reached man's estate
for that of Guwisguwi, or Cooweescoowee, by which was known a large white
bird of uncommon occurrence, perhaps the egret or the swan. He went to school in
Kingston, Tennessee. In 1809 he was sent on a mission to the Cherokee in Arkansas
by Col. Return J. Meigs, the Indian agent, and thenceforward until the close of his
life he remained in the public service of his nation. At the Battle of the Horseshoe,
and in other operations of the Cherokee contingent against the Creeks in 1813-14, he
was adjutant of the Cherokee regiment under General Jackson. He was chosen a
member of the national committee of the Cherokee Council in 1817, and drafted the
reply to the United States commissioners who were sent to negotiate the exchange
of the Cherokee lands for others west of the Mississippi river. In the contest against
the removal his talents found play and recognition. As president of the national committee from 1819 until 1826 he was instrumental in the introduction of school and
mechanical training, and led in the development of the civilized autonomous government embodied in the republican constitution adopted in 1827. He was associate

existence. The other, headed by Maj. John Ridge, a prominent sub-chief, despairing of successful resistance, was prepared to negotiate for removal.[4] Rev. J. F. Schermerhorn, who was appointed commissioner for the purpose, negotiated a treaty with the Ridge party to be confirmed later by the Cherokee people in general council. It provided that the tribe was to cede its whole eastern territory and remove to the West in consideration of the sum of $3,250,000; the Ross party insisted on having $20,000,000 for its land and the price in the Ridge treaty was advanced to $4,500,000. The treaty was signed March 14, 1835, with the understanding that it was to be ratified by the tribe in full council before it became effective. Armed with the address from President Jackson, Schermerhorn spent the summer and autumn in fruitless attempts to secure the ratification of the treaty. Failing in these efforts he asked permission to offer bribes to the leading members of the tribe, but Lewis Cass, secretary of war sternly denied his request.

In October the Cherokee tribe was called to meet in full council at Red Clay, Tennessee, to consider the treaty. John Howard Payne who had just arrived at the home of John Ross nearby, describes the preparation for the meeting: Mr. Ross "received me with cordiality. He said he regretted that he had only a log cabin of but one room to invite me to." The winter before, while Ross was in Washington his beautiful home in Georgia on the Coosa river was drawn in the Georgia lottery and the evicted family retired across the line into Tennessee.

"With internal dissentions attempted to be fomented by the agents of Government, and with incessant external attacks from Georgia, and not only undefended by their legitimate protector, the United States, but threatened by the Chief Magistrate of those States, the Cherokee nation now stands alone, moneyless, helpless, and almost hopeless; yet without

---

chief with William Hicks in that year, and president of the Cherokee constitutional convention. From 1828 to the removal to Indian Territory in 1839 he was principal chief of the Cherokee Nation, and headed the various national delegations that visited Washington to defend the right of the Cherokee to their national territory. After arrival in the Indian Territory he was chosen chief of the united Cherokee Nation and held that office until his death, although during the dissensions caused by the Civil War, the Federal authorities deposed him (*Handbook of American Indians*, II, 396).

4 James S. Mooney, *op. cit.*, 126.

Copy of a portrait by C. B. King of the Rev. Jesse Bushyhead, Cherokee minister; courtesy of his granddaughter Mrs. J. W. McSpadden

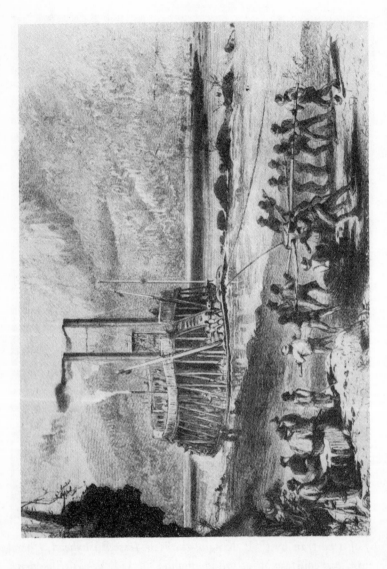

Warping a steamboat through the "Suck" on the Tennessee River during the time of the Cherokee Removal

a dream of yielding. With these clouds around them, in their little corner of Tennessee, to which they have been driven from Georgia for shelter, their national council holds its regular annual convention tomorrow. I cannot imagine a spectacle of more moral grandeur than the assembly of such a people, under such circumstances. .

"This morning offered the first foretaste of what the next week is to present. The woods echoed with the trampling of many feet: a long and orderly procession emerged from among the trees, the gorgeous autumnal tints of whose departing foliage seemed in sad harmony with the noble spirit now beaming in this departing race. Most of the train was on foot. There were a few aged men, and some few women, on horseback. The train halted at the humble gate of the principal chief: he stood ready to receive them.

"Everything was noiseless. The party, entering, loosened the blankets which were loosely rolled and flung over their backs and hung them, with their tin cups and other paraphernalia attached, upon the fence. The chief approached them. They formed diagonally in two lines, and each, in silence, drew near to give his hand. Their dress was neat and picturesque: all wore turbans, except four or five with hats; many of them, tunics, with sashes; many long robes, and nearly all some drapery: so that they had the oriental air of the old scripture pictures of patriarchal processions.

"The salutations over, the old men remained near the chief, and the rest withdrew to various parts of the enclosure; some sitting Turk fashion against the trees, others upon logs, and others upon the fences, but with the eyes of all fixed upon their chief. They had walked sixty miles since yesterday, and has encamped last night in the woods. They sought their way to the council ground. It was explained to them.

"At one moment I observed a sensation among them, and all arose and circled around their chief. Presently an old man spoke above the rest; each one went for his pack, and all resumed their way. There was something in the scene which would have subdued a sterner spirit than mine. . . Parties varying from thirty to fifty have been passing the main road, which is somewhat distant from the residence of Mr. Ross all day. All seem to contemplate the approaching meeting as one of vital import. I myself, though a stranger, partake of the general excitement."

The council rejected the Schermerhorn treaty, even Ridge and Elias Boudinot joining the majority against it. Notice was then served on the Cherokee to appear at New Echota in December to negotiate another treaty; they were informed by circulars that those who failed to appear would be counted in favor of any treaty made. The council had authorized the regular delegation headed by John Ross to go to Washington and negotiate a treaty. To prevent his departure Ross was arrested at his home in Tennessee by twenty-five members of the Georgia guard, all his private papers and the proceedings of the council being taken at the same time, and he was conveyed across the line to Spring Place in Georgia, where he was held for twelve days without a charge against him, and at last released without apology or explanation.[5] The national paper, *The Cherokee Phoenix*, had been suppressed and its office plant seized by the same guard accompanied by Stand Waitie a few days before. "Thus in their greatest need the Cherokee were deprived of the help and counsel of their teachers, their national press and their chief."[6]

5   *Ibid.*, 122; *Niles' Weekly Register*, XLIX, 239, 307, 308, 343. John Howard Payne who was a guest in the home of Chief Ross was arrested also. He was traveling through the south collecting material for a book he planned writing, describing the interesting features of the country. When he approached the Cherokee Nation he decided to meet Ross and endeavor to secure copies of manuscripts belonging to the latter, giving accounts of the early history of his tribe. He was engaged in making these copies in the home of Ross when the Georgia guard in command of Sergeant Young burst in the door and took possession of all of his papers as well as those of Ross. The prisoners were forced to mount their horses and travel twenty-five miles through a heavy rain to their place of imprisonment. Upon examining Payne's papers Bishop was enraged because in his notes the writer had said that the Georgia guard looked more like "banditti" than soldiers; but it was Payne's interest in and notice of the Cherokee primarily that brought upon him the brutality of the Georgia officials. Efforts were made to incite the people roundabout to violence against him by ascribing sinister motives to his activities, particularly by circulating the report that he was an abolitionist from the North, but as there was nothing to support it the effort failed. After thirteen days of confinement Payne was released and ordered out of the country. He then wrote a long and interesting recital of the train of infamous outrages visited upon him that was published in the *Knoxville (Tenn.) Register*, December 2, 1835; *Georgia Constitutionalist (Augusta)*, December 24, 1835; reprinted in *A History of Rome and Floyd County* [Georgia], by George N. Batty, Jr. The last contains Payne's description quoted in the text, of the Cherokee gathering near Ross's home, which is to be found also in *U. S. Senate Document No. 120, p. 573*, Twenty-fifth Congress, second session. The people of Tennessee generally were incensed at the outrage and at least one Georgia newspaper, the *Georgia Journal* of Milledgeville, deplored the lawless proceeding.

6   James S. Mooney, *op. cit.*, 123. As the Cherokee Nation was forbidden to hold councils at their ancient capital, New Echota, the National Council at Red

Although for two months threats and inducements had been held out to secure a full attendance at the December conference at New Echota, there were present when the proceedings opened, according to Schermerhorn's own report, only from three hundred to five hundred men, women and children out of a population of over seventeen thousand. Notwithstanding the small attendance and the absence of the principal officers of the Nation, a committee was appointed to arrange the details of an instrument called a treaty, which was finally drawn up and signed December 29, 1835.[7] And despite the fact that the national delegates presented to the Senate protests representing nearly sixteen thousand Cherokee, the treaty was ratified by the Senate by a majority of one vote. Councils were held in opposition all over the Cherokee Nation, and resolutions denouncing the methods used and declaring the treaty absolutely null and void were drawn up and submitted to General Wool, in command of the troops in the Cherokee country, by whom they were forwarded to Washington. The president rebuked the General for transmitting "*a paper so disrespectful to the Executive, the Senate and the American people; declared his settled determination that the treaty should be carried out without modification and with all consistent dispatch, and directed that after a copy of the letter had been delivered to Ross, no further communication, by mouth or writing, should be held with him concerning the treaty.*[8] *It was further directed that no council should be permitted to assemble to discuss the treaty. Ross had already been informed that the President had ceased to recognize any existing government among the eastern Cherokee, and that any further effort by him to prevent the consummation of the treaty would be suppressed.*"[9]

Clay directed that their printing press be removed to the latter place. Before they could remove it, the Georgia guard at the direction of Currey and Schermerhorn seized and carried it away in the summer of 1835.

7   Thomas L. McKenney, *Memoirs, with Sketches of Travels*, 264.

8   *American State Papers*, "Military Affairs," VII, 564.

9   James S. Mooney, *op. cit.*, 123. Gov. Wilson Lumpkin of Georgia wrote President Jackson on September 24, 1836, a long letter denouncing Ross and his supporters: "The statements of Ross and others that the late treaty was made contrary to the will of a majority of the Cherokee people is entitled to no respect or consideration whatever. Nineteen-twentieths of the Cherokees are too ignorant and depraved to entitle their opinions to any weight or consideration in such matters"

Before the ratification of the treaty Maj. W. M. Davis had been appointed to enroll the Cherokee for removal and to appraise their improvements. He soon learned the true condition of affairs, and addressed the secretary of war a strong letter upon the subject from which the following extract is made:

"I conceive that my duty to the President, to yourself, and to my country reluctantly compels me to make a statement of facts in relation to a meeting of a small number of Cherokees at New Echota last December, who were met by Mr. Schermerhorn and articles of a general treaty entered into between them for the whole Cherokee Nation. . . Sir, that paper. . . called a treaty, is no treaty at all, because not sanctioned by the great body of the Cherokee and made without their participation or assent. I solemnly declare to you that upon its reference to the Cherokee people it would be instantly rejected by nine-tenths of them, and I believe by nineteen-twentieths of them. There were not present at the conclusion of the treaty more than one hundred Cherokee voters, and not more than three hundred, including women and children, although the weather was everything that could be desired. The Indians had long been notified of the meeting, and blankets were promised to all who would come and vote for the treaty. The most cunning and artful means were resorted to to conceal the paucity of numbers present at the treaty. No enumeration of them was made by Schermerhorn. The business of making the treaty was transacted with a committee appointed by the Indians present, so as not to expose their numbers. The power of attorney under which the committee acted was signed only by the president and secretary of the meeting, so as not to disclose their weakness. . . Mr. Schermerhorn's apparent design was to conceal the real number present and to impose on the public and the government upon this point. The delegation taken to Washington by Mr. Schermerhorn had no more authority to make a treaty than any other dozen Cherokee accidentally picked up for the purpose."[10]

Late in 1836, John Ross, at the head of an exploring party, visited the Western Cherokee with whom he spent several weeks in an effort to arouse them against the Schermerhorn treaty.[11] He returned to

---

(U. S. Senate Document, No. 120, op. cit., p. 676; Wilson Lumpkin, The Removal of the Cherokee Indians from Georgia, II, 45).

10 James S. Mooney, op. cit., 126.

11 Army and Navy Chronicle, IV, 32.

Georgia in January, accompanied by a delegation of the western Indians headed by John Looney.[12]

About this time there was another diversion not calculated to re-assure the Indians in favor of emigration. The constitution under consideration as the basis for admission of the new State of Arkansas proposed in section eight that the western boundary of the state should extend to the former boundary[13] as fixed by the Act of Congress of May 26, 1824, "when the Indian title is extinguished." The Cherokee Indians were much exercised about it as they saw in the proposal a renewal of their controversies with the whites over their lands. Protests were signed by James Rogers and John Smith western delegates and Major Ridge, Andrew Ross, Stand Waitie, and other delegates from the East then in Washington.[14]

General Wool, who had been placed in command of the troops concentrated in the Cherokee country to prevent opposition to the enforcement of the treaty, reported on February 18, 1837, that he called them together and made them an address, but "*it is, however, vain to talk to a people almost universally opposed to the treaty and who maintain that they never made such a treaty. So determined are they in their opposition that not one of all those who were present and voted at the council held but a day or two since, however poor or destitute, would receive either rations or clothing from the United States lest they might compromise themselves in regard to the treaty. These same people as well as those in the mountains of North Carolina, during the summer past, preferred living upon the roots and sap of trees rather than receive provisions from the United States, and thousands, as I have been informed, had no other food for weeks. Many have said they will die before they will leave the country.*"

The work of disarming and overawing the Cherokee was disagreeable to General Wool whose sympathies were with the Indians, who were practically unanimous in repudiating the treaty. In one letter he

12   Ibid., 93.

13   This line was forty miles west of the present western boundary of Arkansas and embraced a large section of what is now Oklahoma. For an account of this boundary see Grant Foreman, *Pioneer Days in the Early Southwest,* and *Indians and Pioneers.*

14   *U. S. Senate Files,* Twenty-fourth Congress, first session, "Petitions and Memorials" E to J 1835-36. Sixty Cherokee who emigrated on their own resources arrived at Fort Gibson late in December, 1836 (Van Horne to Harris, January 31, 1837, OIA, "Cherokee Emigration," V 13.)

says: "The whole scene since I have been in this country has been nothing but a heartrending one, and such a one as I would be glad to get rid of as soon as circumstances will permit. Because I am firm and decided, do not believe I would be unjust. If I could, and I could not do them a greater kindness, I would remove every Indian tomorrow beyond the reach of the white men, who, like vultures, are watching, ready to pounce upon their prey and strip them of everything they have or expect from the government of the United States. Yes, sir, nineteen-twentieths, if not ninety-nine out of every hundred, will go penniless to the West."

Major Ridge, the principal signer of the treaty wrote the president: "We come now to address you on the subject of our griefs and afflictions from the acts of the white people. They have got our lands and now they are preparing to fleece us of the money accruing from the treaty. We found our plantations taken either in whole or in part by the Georgians—suits instituted against us for back rents for our own farms. These suits are commenced in the inferior courts, with the evident design that, when we are ready to remove, to arrest our people, and on these vile claims to induce us to compromise for our own release, to travel with our families. Thus our funds will be filched from our people, and we shall be compelled to leave our country as beggars and in want.

"Even the Georgia laws, which deny us our oaths, are thrown aside, and notwithstanding the cries of our people, and protestation of our innocence and peace, the lowest classes of the white people are flogging the Cherokees with cowhides, hickories, and clubs. We are not safe in our houses—our people are assailed by day and night by the rabble. Even justices of the peace and constables are concerned in this business. This barbarous treatment is not confined to men, but the women are stripped also and whipped without law or mercy. . . Send regular troops to protect us from these lawless assaults, and to protect our people as they depart for the West. If it is not done, we shall carry off nothing but the scars of the lash on our backs, and our oppressors will get all the money. We talk plainly, as chiefs having property and life in danger, and we appeal to you for protection."[15]

General Dunlap, in command of the Tennessee troops called out to prevent the alleged contemplated Cherokee uprising, having learned for himself the true situation, declared that he would never dishonor

15   James S. Mooney, op. cit., 126.

the Tennessee arms by aiding to carry into execution at the point of the bayonet a treaty by a lean minority against the will and authority of the Cherokee people.

A confidential agent sent to report upon the situation wrote in September, 1837, that opposition to the treaty was unanimous and irreconcilable, the Cherokee declaring that it could not bind them because they did not make it, that it was the work of a few unauthorized individuals and that the Nation was not a party to it. They had retained the forms of their government, although no election had been held since 1830, having continued the officers then in charge until their government could again be re-established regularly. Under this arrangement John Ross was principal chief, with influence unbounded and unquestioned. "The whole Nation of eighteen thousand persons is with him, the few—about three hundred—who made the treaty having left the country, with the exception of a small number of prominent individuals—as Ridge, Boudinot, and others—who remained to assist in carrying it into execution."[16]

By January, 1837, several hundred Indians had gathered at New Echota "who wished to remove themselves by land, many of whom had for some time been ready and only waited for the arrival of the proper officers to make a final settlement of their affairs" and deliver funds promised them. In a few weeks it was reported of them that "A large company of the most wealthy and intelligent of the Cherokee people have availed themselves of that provision of the treaty which authorizes them to emigrate themselves and families; they set out a few weeks ago for Arkansas by land. We estimate the number in this company at six hundred." Large sums of money had been placed where it would be most effective: "The policy of making prudent advances to the wealthy and intelligent, has gone far to remove opposition to the treaty among the most influential."[17]

The first party to be emigrated by the government under the terms of the treaty was in charge of Dr. John S. Young, who had three assistants, one physician, Dr. C. Lillybridge, and three interpreters. There were 466 Cherokee Indians in the party, one half of whom

16 *Ibid.*, 128.

17 Wilson Lumpkin and John Kennedy, commissioners, to Harris, March 23, 1837, OIA, "Cherokee File L" 157; *U. S. Senate Document No. 120, op. cit.*, p. 816.

were children and five Creek Indians.[18] Doctor Lillybridge was not only a zealous official but he took pains to set down accounts of the emigrants from day to day and his journal[19] covering the entire journey presents an interesting picture of the strange adventure of these simple people.

Doctor Lillybridge arrived at Ross's Landing[20] on March 1, and two days later the Indians were embarked in a fleet of eleven flatboats traveling in three sections. There was considerable intoxication and disorder among them for a time. In the open boats the emigrants were exposed to cold winds and after making five miles they landed to camp for the night. The next morning at six-thirty they resumed their journey; the doctor visited the boats and treated a number of Indians for colds and extracted a tooth for "daughter of Tese-teska and another for Mr. Arch Downing. Mrs. Waitie and James Wolf slightly indisposed from exposure—prescribed for each."

The boats reached Gunter's Landing on the sixth and were tied up to the island to prevent the Indians from going ashore and getting drunk. But in spite of precautions some of them succeeded in reaching the town, and considerable disorder was caused by drunken Indians. "*Alexander Brown an Indian six feet seven inches in height and tolerable well proportioned seized a canoe and for fear he should be interrupted before he got out of reach of the shore, paddled with all his strength; when the main current struck the canoe, he lost his balance and fell; in endeavoring to recover, the canoe dipped so much water that she immediately sank; Brown however managed to turn her and get upon her bottom, in which condition he floated down stream 200 yards to a point of land.*"

The steamer *Knoxville* was waiting for them here, and when the eleven flatboats were made fast to her, the flotilla set off at nine o'clock on the seventh. An hour later the doctor was called to "*visit an Emigrant on board the Steam Boat; the patient was found wreathing in agony, from a paroxysm of Whiskey Colic. Patient talked Coherently and said he was not drunk—that he had drank only 2 half pints of*"

18   Dr. Phil Minis to Harris, April 8, 1837, OIA, "Cherokee Emigration," M 59; Van Horne to Harris, April 7, 1837, ibid., V 13.

19   *Ibid.*, "Cherokee Emigration."

20   Ross's Landing was near the site of the present city of Chattanooga, Tennessee.

*whiskey and a few other times with his friends. Bled him 2 lbs and gave
him Gum Opii, gr. iv.*

On their arrival at Decatur the Indians were placed on board open
cars and compelled to sit in the cold from three o'clock until dark
awaiting the engine that did not arrive. The bewildered Indians who
had never before seen a railroad train were left to find a place to sleep;
"The train of Carrs from the West were momentarily expected, and
the Indians were afraid to lie down for fear of being run over. No
lights were furnished them, and they were grouping in the dark, in a
pitiful manner;" but their humane physician succeeded in having a
warehouse opened for them in which they made their beds on the
floor for the night. In the morning the emigrants were again placed
on the cars that delivered them in Tuscumbia by night.[21] Here they
camped awaiting the arrival of the boats that were to take them down
the river. While in camp it rained hard and long, the weather was cold
and windy, and the Indians were wet, cold, and miserable.

About ten o'clock on the thirteenth the steamboat *Newark* and two
keel-boats arrived and *"moored to the landing near which the Indians
encamped; immediately the whole posse of them were in motion bringing
their effects to the boats. The day was spent in getting things arranged on
board. At night the emigrants laid themselves down as they could, cheerful in the expectation of being under way in the morning."* But the next
day "some misunderstanding took place among the officers in relation
to *Rank &c.* in consequence of which the boats were detained till a late
hour in the afternoon" and the Indians were much dissatisfied with the
delay.

However, they departed at four o'clock on the fourteenth and
reached Paducah at ten the next night. The keel-boats were "very
damp and while the weather remains as cold as it is now, the emigrants

21 "Early on Wednesday morning the Indians under the direction of Gen. Smith
and Doct. John S. Young, the conducting agent of the government, commenced
debarking and by seven o'clock a handsome train of cars were snugly loaded with
about half of them and their effects." The train and cars were novel to the Indians
"who could be seen examining with their peculiar inquisitive silence and gravity,
this great enigma to them, while others apparently uninterested and thoughtless,
amused themselves with an old fiddle or sat motionless, gazing at those around"
(*Morgan Observer (Decatur, Alabama)* quoted in *Arkansas Gazette,* May 9, 1837,
p. 2, col. 3). For an interesting account of the inauguration of the Tuscumbia railroad
on July 4, 1835, see George A. McCall *Letters from the Frontier,* 276.

suffer much for want of a fire. Extracted tooth for Polly Taylor; Sally Raincrow taken with violent cramp in the stomach to which she is subject. She begged for whiskey; gave her Tinct. Myrrh compt., which relieved her in a short time." They entered the Mississippi: "*High winds from the South, with appearance of rain; during the night the boats ran foul of a snag which caused considerable alarm among the Indians; one wheel was considerably damaged and the top of the keels burst in. No new cases of sickness further than common colds and Diarrhea. The wind renders it very difficult for the Indians to cook as their fires are on the top of the Boats.*"

Doctor Lillybridge made daily rounds of all the boats looking after the ill, some of whom made his ministrations difficult by their unwillingness to take his medicine and follow his instructions. After they had been under way a few days the amount of sickness increased. The principal complaints were colds, influenza, sore throat, coughs, pleurisy, measles, diarrhea, bowel complaint, fevers, toothache, wounds from accidents and fighting, and gonorrhea among the young men.

The flotilla reached Memphis on the seventeenth. "Henry Clay a Creek has been suffering from a cough every since he joined the detachment," the doctor observes. The next morning the emigrants waited two hours at Montgomery's Point while they secured a pilot for the Arkansas river; during their stay whisky was introduced among the Indians. "*Henry Clay better than last night, got him a comfortable situation near the chimney of the Steamboat and a breakfast of Coffee & Sea Bread, which appeared to afford him much satisfaction considering his case, consumption. Daughter of Young Squirrel sick with headache and fever; gave cathartic. Arthur, son of Archilla Smith sick with influenza; gave ℞ Vin. Antim ℥ij. Applied Blister to the chest of Henry Clay. Stand has been in quite a feeble state of health since I first saw him at New Echota . . . his cough very troublesome . . . James Williams taken very suddenly with inflamation of the Spleen. Bled him and applied Blister. Prescription of ℞ Pulv. Doveri gr. viij. Sub Mur. Hydrg gr. v M.*"

Because of the danger of navigating the Arkansas river at night the boats were tied up at the bank until morning; on the twentieth the doctor reported "*Sally Raincrow has been slightly indisposed for some days. She is a doctress and a Conjueress herself. She refuses the aid of the Doctor, except when her case becomes alarming. She has acquired the* art of *Cupping with the Horn of a Yearling, which exhausts the air by sucking. She has a servant also whom she has taught the practice. Sally has great faith in Cupping & within the last three days has had the operation performed on almost every part of her body. The poor negress is kept almost constantly tugging away with her fat lips. The practice being so free from objection I have humored her caprice. An unusual number of complaints from coughs and colds through the day. Peggy Black Fox sick with influenza. Stand suffers much from his cough which is getting aggravated by change of weather. Found Henry Clay about 4 o'clock P. M. laboring under much inflamation of the chest & difficulty of respiration. Ordered him to the Steam Boat, where he could be near the fire. Got Sally Rain Crow's woman to cup him; directed her to cup him as many times as she could place the Horn on his breast."*

The emigrants arrived at Little Rock the evening of the twenty-first and were landed on the bank of the river opposite the village. In camp that night Big Coon was taken "with Pleurisy, is very corpulent and robust, bled him to syncope & gave him R. Muc. Gum Arab Zij vin Ant. Sulph. Morph. gr.ss. M. dose tablespoonful." The steamer *Revenue* took the keel-boats in tow here and started up the river the evening of the twenty-second; but that night ran aground several times. The doctor bled Big Coon twenty ounces and Water Dog ten ounces "to syncope," and they were reported the next morning much improved from cupping.

On the twenty-fifth the *"wife of Saml McCamman left on shore at Wood Yard. Her husband jumped ashore for her, the Captain of the Steam Boat made them walk. about 3 miles and then charged 2 dollars for sending his boat ashore for them. Steam Boat ran aground about 8 o'clock P. M.; in the attempt to get her off, her guard passed over the guard to one of the Keel Boats and stove in the top of the Latter, causing great alarm among the emigrants."* They arrived at Van Buren the night of the twenty-seventh and Fort Smith at noon the next day. Much whisky was introduced among the Indians and many were drunk.

The boats left Fort Smith at two o'clock but soon after Major Ridge requested to be put ashore as he had been advised by a friend at the Post that he should proceed on the road from Van Buren to reach the lands on which he wished to settle. "About 2 miles above Fort Smith the Boats landed to set Major Ridge and his friends on shore. Immediately the larger proportion of the Detachment were in motion, and in spite of the advice of the Agents and those who were acquainted with the country they landed their effects & considered themselves at home." The next day the boats continued to Fort Coffee where the remainder of the emigrants were landed. The empty boats then ascended the river to Fort Gibson.[22]

22   Journal of Dr. C. Lillybridge, March 29, 1837, OIA; *Arkansas Gazette*, April 18 and May 16, 1837, p. 2; Young to Harris, March 29, 1837, OIA, *ibid.*; *Army and Navy Chronicle*, IV, 301, 361; *New York Observer*, May 27, 1837, p. 3, col. 4. "The *Revenue* has gone up to Webbers waiting a rise in the river so she can continue to Fort Gibson. She cannot pass Webbers Falls. The steamboat *Tecumseh* which grounded last fall a few miles below Fort Coffee is still aground on a sand bar and is now six or eight feet above the water" (*Arkansas Gazette*, April 18, 1837, p. 2, col. 2).

Major Ridge's family and others of this party settled on Honey creek in the northeast corner of the Cherokee Nation near the Missouri line. Stand Waitie, who was a member of this party, was bereft of his wife, Betsy, who died in childbirth about May 1, 1836, at his home near the present Rome, Georgia; the child died also. However, another Mrs. Waitie accompanied Doctor Lillybridge's party.

G EN. JOHN ELLIS WOOL, who represented the federal government in the execution of the treaty, observed the oppression exerted on the Indians by the whites who were encouraged by local authority to intrude on the Indians and take possession of their improvements. When the courts were appealed to, the Indians were defeated by deliberate delay, the hostility of jurymen who were in sympathy with the intruders, and the denial of the right of an Indian to testify against a white man. They then appealed to General Wool, who under his instructions was required by section sixteen of the treaty, to protect the Indians against the intruders. Many such complaints were made to him, and after investigation intruders were dispossessed in favor of the Indian owners. This situation was particularly notorious in the Cherokee country in Alabama, where the majority of the white population came "for the purpose of robbing and plundering the Indians, and have exercised every species of oppression towards them."[1]

In this section of the State General Wool endeavored to protect the Indians in their homes and by the suppression of the sale of whisky, and thereby incurred the hostility of state authorities. On July 3, 1837, the governor and legislature of Alabama charged General Wool with having "usurped the powers of the civil tribunals, disturbed the peace of the community, and trampled upon the rights of the citizens;" demanded of the secretary of war that military officers be restrained from further infractions of their laws and outrages on their citizens, and asked that General Wool's conduct be investigated and condemned. The president referred the charges to a military court of inquiry at Knoxville in September, before which the governor of Alabama was

---

1 *American State Papers*, "Military Affairs," VII, 534.

invited to submit proof to support his charges, but neither the governor nor legislature offered any proof and the court vindicated General Wool of any wrong-doing.[2]

The second emigrating party numbering 365, with B. B. Cannon as conductor, was routed overland through Kentucky, Illinois and Missouri.[3] After spending two days in loading their wagons, they set out from the Cherokee Agency October 14, 1837, crossed the Hiwassee river at Calhoun and camped five miles beyond. The next day was spent in mustering the party and in the evening of the next day they reached the Tennessee river after a march of fourteen miles. On the seventeenth they were ready to commence crossing the river at daylight but were prevented by the fog, so that the crossing was not completed until four o'clock; they then advanced seven miles before they camped at eight o'clock.

The crossing of the Cumberland Mountains required four days and severely taxed the endurance of the emigrants who camped at Sequachee river. On the twenty-second they "passed through McMinnville, encamped and issued corn and fodder, corn meal and Bacon, sugar and coffee to the Waggoners and Interpreters, no water for 12 miles ahead, procured a quantity of corn meal and bacon." On the twenty-fifth "buried Andrew's child" and passed through Murfreesborough;" the next day they passed through three turnpike gates; on the next, two more, and they crossed the Cumberland river on the toll-bridge at Nashville. Their progress had been uneventful thus far; they had averaged from twelve to sixteen miles a day and there were issued corn,

---

2   *Ibid.*, 541. "On Dec. 8th Gov. Schley made an important communication to the Georgia legislature, enclosing recent dispatches sent by express from Gen. Wool touching the alarming state of things produced among the Cherokees, by the shameful practice pursued by the whites of selling to them intoxicating liquors, particularly whiskey. This abuse is carried on to a great extent in New Echota and its vicinity, and among the despatches is a remonstrance from the principal chiefs petitioning the legislature to prevent the practice. Any person by the small fee to the clerk, may obtain a license. Gov. Schley urges the passage of a law totally prohibiting such licenses. Gen. Wool implores the Governor to use his exertions to procure such a law; otherwise he fears the worst of consequences at the approaching assemblage of 1,800 Indians at New Echota, to meet the commissioners. The chiefs say their people are by the frequent potations of whiskey becoming degraded to brutes."

3   Cannon kept a journal: OIA, "Cherokee Emigration" C553, "Special File 249." See also Reynolds to Harris, December 31, 1837, file R 196.

*Above—Current River, Missouri, on the route of the Cherokee emigrants;
Below—Advance agents secured camping grounds when possible
near water mills where the Indians could have their corn
ground. A view of one in Tennessee*

C. JAS. E. THOMPSON COMPANY, KNOXVILLE, TENN.

The former home of the Cherokee Indians in East Tennessee

bacon, and flour to the Indians every second or third day and corn and fodder for their horses daily.

After crossing the river at Nashville, they "rested for the purpose of washing clothes, repairing wagons and shoeing horses. Reese, Starr, and others of the emigrants visited Genl. Jackson who was at Nashville; issued corn and fodder, corn meal and bacon." The next day they resumed their march and on October 31 reached Graves, Kentucky. November 1 they "buried Duck's child, passed through Hopkinsville, Ken." On the third they reached Princeton, and two days later Salem, both in Kentucky. Three days later they arrived at Berry's Ferry on the Ohio river opposite Golconda but the high winds on the river prevented their crossing into Illinois until the next day.

On the eighth "Mr. Reese and myself remained behind and buried a child of Seabolt's. . . James Starr & wife left this morning with two carry-alls to take care of and bring on three of their children who were too sick to travel, with instructions to overtake the party as soon as possible without endangering the lives of their children." They were detained on the tenth while they built a bridge across Cypress creek and the next day passed through Jonesboro, Illinois, and encamped at Clear creek in the Mississippi river bottom.

On November 12 the emigrants began crossing the Mississippi river, but the next day high winds arrested their progress and it was not until the fourteenth that they were all across. During this time another of Duck's children died and "Starr came up, the health of his children but little better. Richard Timberlake and George Ross overtook us and enrolled and attached themselves to Starr's family."

They marched a few days more, stopping one day to rest and wash and on the sixteenth "*left Reese, Starr and families on account of sickness in their families, also James Taylor (Reese's son-in-law) and family, Taylor himself being very sick, with instructions to overtake the Party. Passed through Jackson, Mo., halted & encamped at Widow Roberts on the road via Farmington. . . A considerable number drunk last night obtained liquor at Farmington yesterday; had to get out of bed about midnight to quell the disorder; a refusal by several to march this morning.*" However they continued and passed through Caledonia and the next day passed "through the lead mines or Courtois diggings, halted at Scott's" where they remained another day to repair wagons, shoe horses and wash, and where Starr, Reese, and Taylor caught up with them.

By the time the emigrants had crossed the Mississippi river, much sickness had developed among them from the unwholesome stagnant water in Illinois and their intemperate consumption of grapes along the route which brought on violent attacks of dysentery; nearly all the drivers were ill, some were left on the road, and substitutes hired. Finally when sixty of the emigrants became too ill to travel the physician with the party, G. S. Townsend, on the twenty-fifth called a halt. The party went into camp and the conductor obtained permission for as many as could enter, to occupy a school house near a spring two miles farther along. The doctor treated them here for about ten days during which four persons died, two children of Corn Tassel and Oolanheta, George Killion and a wagoner, a black boy.

After the illness had abated somewhat they got under way again December 4, though there was not room in the wagons for all the ill. On the fifth they camped at the Meramec river, and passed Massey's iron works the next day; on the seventh "Reese's team ran away; broke his waggon and Starr's carry-all; left him and family to get his waggon mended, and to overtake us if possible." The next day they buried Nancy Bigbear's grandchild; it rained all day and at night several Indians were drunk. On the ninth "Mayfield's waggon broke down at about a mile—left him to get it mended and overtake; halted at Waynesville, Mo." They camped at the Gasconade river on the tenth, next at Summer's, then Mr. Parke's, Eddington's on the thirteenth, and reached the James fork of White river December 14.

"December 15th, 1837—James Starr's wife had a child last night. . . Waggoners having horses shod until late at night, encamped & issued fodder & beef." They passed through Springfield, Missouri on the sixteenth and "buried Elleges wife and Chas. Timberlake's son (Smoker)." It was now snowing, much colder, and sickness was increasing. "Buried Dreadful Waters this evening." They remained in camp at Dye's several days to attend the ill and wait for medicines to be brought from Springfield; on the twenty-first they reached "Lockes on Flat Creek." The next day "Buried Goddard's Grand child." On the twenty-third "Buried Rainfrogs daughter (Lucy Redstick's child)," and halted at Reddix. Three days later they camped "at James

Coulters on Cane Hill, Ark.," and the next day "Buried Alsey Timberlake, Daughter of Chas. Timberlake. Marched at 8 oc. A.M. halted at Mr. Beans in the Cherokee Nation west."

Having crossed the line the exhausted party refused to advance farther and went into camp to minister to their sick. "Buried another child of Chas Timberlake's, and one which was born (untimely) yesterday of which no other account than this is taken. Jesse Half Breed's wife had a child last night." Two days later on December 30 Cannon remustered his party and turned them over to Lieutenant Van Horne. Fifteen deaths had occurred on the march, eleven of children, eight of them under two years of age.

In spite of threats of arrest and punishment, Ross still continued active effort in behalf of his people. In the spring of 1838, two months before the time fixed for the removal, he presented to Congress[4] another protest and memorial, dated February 22 and signed by 15,665 Cherokee, which, like the others, was tabled by the Senate. That the so-called treaty was nothing more than a transparent fraud upon the Indians had become notorious. The Indians implored the administration not to take their statement of the facts, but to make an investigation and ascertain the truth of their contention. The president and secretary of war were adamant; they answered merely that the treaty had been ratified by the Senate and that it was therefore beyond their powers to question it. And when reminded that under similar circumstances President Adams had refused to proceed under the fraudulent treaty with the Creeks negotiated in 1825 by government officials, and promptly had set it aside as a nullity, they were unmoved. In the crisis of affairs the president was willing to avail himself of the expedient presented by the Schermerhorn paper, shabby and venal as it was, to get the Indians out of Georgia for the benefit of white and red.

Martin van Buren had now succeeded Jackson as president and was disposed to allow the Cherokee a longer time to prepare for emigration, but was met by the declaration from Governor Gilmer of Georgia that any delay would be a violation of the rights of that state and in opposition to the rights of the owners of the soil, and that if trouble came

4 *New York Observer*, March 24, 1838, p. 1, col. 5.

from any protection afforded by the government troops to the Cherokee, a direct collision must ensue between the authorities of the state
and federal government.[5]

May 23, 1838, had been fixed as the time after which those who
refused to leave voluntarily would be removed by force. But such
was their love for their native land and their dread of removal, because
of the accounts they had heard of deaths on the journey and in the
new home provided for them, that few would consent to leave. Large
keel boats had been constructed and were waiting at the bank near the
Cherokee Agency to carry the emigrants down the Tennessee river as
far as "The Suck." These boats were 130 feet in length, with a house
one hundred feet long, twenty wide, two stories high, "banistered"
around the top. They were made with partitions on each floor, making
four rooms fifty by twenty feet furnished with windows. They were
provided with stoves inside and five hearths on top of each boat for
cooking.

Gen. Nathaniel Smith of Athens, Tennessee, had been appointed
superintendent of removal to succeed B. F. Currey who died December 16, 1836. Smith planned to start another party and about 300
gathered near the Agency; but the number dwindled to 250 and in spite
of warnings and threats, by March 25, 1838, only these few Indians
could be induced voluntarily to leave for Waterloo; there they were
embarked aboard the *Smelter* and a keel-boat in tow, leaving on April 5
in charge of Lieut. Edward Deas.[6]

The boats reached Paducah the second day and were anchored out in
the river to prevent white people from introducing whisky among
the Indians. When they resumed their journey in the evening the waves
from the Ohio river washed in the keel boat and the terrified Indians,
thinking it was sinking, rushed aboard the steamboat. As they could
not be induced to return to the keel-boat it was discarded and the
emigrants were all carried on the *Smelter*.

After a short stop at Memphis to secure supplies and "stopping once
to wood" they reached Montgomery's Point on the afternoon of the
ninth. Securing a pilot for the Arkansas river they passed through the
cut-off, proceeded up the river, and reached Little Rock on the morning

5 James Mooney, *op. cit.*, 120.
6 Smith to Harris, April 15, 1838, OIA, "Cherokee Emigration" S 926; *ibid.*,
Journal of Edward Deas, File D 209-217; "Special File" 249.

of the eleventh. The river had fallen so low that it was impossible for the *Smelter* to ascend higher and Lieutenant Deas secured passage for his people aboard the *Little Rock*, a steamboat of lighter draft that was "on the point of setting out for the upper Posts. . . The captain agreed to take the present Party as far up as possible for $5 each for the whole distance and proportionately for a less." The *Smelter* then proceeded up the river five miles and the passengers were landed for the night. The next day Captain Pennywit brought up his boat, the *Little Rock*, and the Indians were loaded on her and a keel boat in tow. He was towing another keel boat loaded with freight which sprung a leak and the captain found it necessary to run ashore to prevent it from sinking. This boat was then abandoned and after some delay the steamboat and one tow proceeded, arriving at the Lewiston Bar on the afternoon of the fourteenth. A week was consumed in the most laborious efforts to cross a succession of bars, during which the Indians were obliged several times to land and walk, and finally, it appearing that the boats would be unable to reach the Cherokee country on the existing stage of water, they were all landed at McLean's about forty-five miles below Fort Smith. Here Deas secured sixteen wagons drawn by oxen and one by four horses. After loading in the wagons the personal effects of the Indians the party started on the twenty-fourth; two days later two small children died. The party reached Fort Smith on the twenty-eighth and ferried the Arkansas river to the Cherokee country.

After traveling twenty-five miles farther they arrived at McCoy's on Sallisaw creek where they wanted to settle. The only source of annoyance upon the journey said Deas, "*has resulted from the people obtaining liquor, the use of which with Indians as far as I have observed results in rioting, fighting, or disorder of some kind. The infamous traffic of whiskey with Indians, is carried on to a greater extent at Fort Smith, than at any place I have seen. . . As far as I have observed there is never any difficulty in managing Indians when sober, provided they are properly treated; but when under the effects of liquor (in the use of which they have no moderation) they are unmanageable.*"[7]

7   Deas Journal; Lieutenant Deas so impressed the Indians by his humane consideration and intelligent attention to their welfare and comfort that they presented him with a sword as a token of their gratitude (*Army and Navy Chronicle*, VIII, 317).

CHAPTER TWENTY-THREE / *A Captive Nation*

IN SPITE of the pressure upon the Indians, only about 2,000 of the eastern Cherokee had removed by May 23, 1838, the expiration of the time fixed for their departure.[1] The remaining nearly 15,000 could not believe that they would soon be driven out of the country; not from a fatuous reliance on the ultimate rectitude of the government—they had no such illusion. But their fixed habits, devoted attachment to their homes, and their unfamiliarity with any other life and country prevented their comprehension of what was soon to happen to them.

Their enforced removal was entrusted to Gen. Winfield Scott who was ordered to take command of the troops already in the Cherokee country, together with reënforcements of infantry, cavalry, and artillery, with authority to call upon the governors of the adjoining states for as many as 4,000 militia and volunteers. The total so employed was 7,000. The Indians had already been disarmed by General Wool.

General Scott established headquarters at New Echota, the capital of the Cherokee Nation, whence, on May 10, he issued a proclamation to the Cherokee people, warning them that the emigration must begin at once and in haste and that before another moon had passed every Cherokee man, woman, and child must be in motion towards the West as commanded by the president, whose orders he, General Scott had come to enforce. The proclamation concludes: "*My troops already occupy many positions. . . and thousands and thousands are approaching from every quarter to render assistance and escape alike hopeless. . . Will you, then by resistance compel us to resort to arms. . . or will you by flight seek to hide yourself in mountains and forests and thus oblige us to hunt you down?*"—reminding them that

1 By May only 500 of the Treaty Party remained in the East (*Army and Navy Chronicle*, VII, 316).

pursuit might result in conflict and bloodshed, ending in a general war.[2] Even after this Ross endeavored, on behalf of his people, to secure some slight modification of the terms of the treaty, but without avail.

"The history of this Cherokee removal of 1838, as gleaned by the author from the lips of actors in the tragedy, may well exceed in weight of grief and pathos any other passage in American history. Even the much-sung exile of the Acadians falls far behind it in its sum of death and misery. Under Scott's orders the troops were disposed at various points throughout the Cherokee country, where stockade forts were erected for gathering in and holding the Indians preparatory to removal. From these, squads of troops were sent to search out with rifle and bayonet every small cabin hidden away in the coves or by the sides of mountain streams, to seize and bring in as prisoners all the occupants, however or wherever they might be found. Families at dinner were startled by the sudden gleam of bayonets in the doorway and rose up to be driven with blows and oaths along the weary miles of trail that led to the stockade. Men were seized in their fields or going along the road, women were taken from their wheels and children from their play. In many cases, on turning for one last look as they crossed the ridge, they saw their homes in flames, fired by the lawless rabble that followed on the heels of the soldiers to loot and pillage. So keen were these outlaws on the scent that in some instances they were driving off the cattle and other stock of the Indians almost before the soldiers had fairly started the owners in the other direction. Systematic hunts were made by the same men for Indians graves, to rob them of the silver pendants and other valuables deposited with the dead. A Georgia volunteer, afterward a colonel in the Confederate service, said: 'I fought through the civil war and have seen men shot to pieces and slaughtered by thousands, but the Cherokee removal was the cruelest work I ever knew'."[3]

"To prevent escape the soldiers had been ordered to approach and surround each house, as far as possible, so as to come upon the occupants without warning. One old patriarch when thus surprised, calmly called his children and grandchildren around him, and kneeling down, bid them pray with him in their own language, while the astonished soldiers looked on in silence. Then rising he led the way into exile. A woman, on finding the house surrounded, went to the door and called up the chickens to be

2 General Scott took their arms away from the Cherokee. In May 1843 there were still thirty-six boxes of their guns stored at Fort Gibson.

3 James Mooney, op. cit., 130.

fed for the last time, after which, taking her infant on her back and her two other children by the hand, she followed her husband with the soldiers."[4]

"*Camp Hetzel, near Cleveland, June 16. The Cherokees are nearly all prisoners. They had been dragged from their houses, and encamped at the forts and military places, all over the nation. In Georgia especially, multitudes were allowed no time to take any thing with them, except the clothes they had on. Well-furnished houses were left a prey to plunderers, who, like hungry wolves, follow in the train of the captors. These wretches rifle the houses, and strip the helpless, unoffending owners of all they have on earth.*[5] *Females, who have been habituated to comforts and comparative affluence, are driven on foot before the bayonets of brutal men. Their feelings are mortified by vulgar and profane vociferations. It is a painful sight. The property of many has been taken, and sold before their eyes for almost nothing—the sellers and buyers, in many cases having combined to cheat the poor Indians. These things are done at the instant of arrest and consternation; the soldiers standing by, with their arms in hand, impatient to go with their work, could give little time to transact business. The poor captive, in a state of distressing agitation, his weeping wife almost frantic with terror, surrounded by a group of crying, terrified children, without a friend to speak a consoling word, is in a poor condition to make a good disposition of his property, and is in most cases stripped*

---

4 James Mooney, *op. cit.*, 131.

5 The Indians were "taken from their houses leaving their fields of corn, their cattle, horses and most of their moveable property for any person who pleased to take it into possession" (*New York Observer*, July 14, 1838, p. 2, col. 6). General Scott wrote to Nat Smith, superintendent of emigration: "The distress caused the emigrants by the want of their bedding, cooking utensils, clothes and ponies, I much regret as also the loss of their property consequent upon the hurry of capture and removal;" but he said the Indians themselves were to blame for having faith in the ability of John Ross to save them (Scott to Smith, June 8, 1838, OIA, "Cherokee Emigration"). From a large number of "Claims for Spoliation" afterwards filed by the Indians, now among the "Ross Papers" the following are selected as representative of the whole: Fields and crops, horses, saddles, harness, rifle guns, chickens, hogs, cows and calves, ducks, geese, hoes, money, grist mills, feather beds, blankets, quilts, pots, ovens, kettles, dishes, cups and saucers, knives and forks, pails, "one set blue edged plates" one "set blue (colored) plates" belonging to Elizabeth Cooper, "paled gardens, sowed and planted," bacon, potatoes, beans, salt, cabins, looms, shuttles, weavers reeds, spinning wheels, thread reel, bedstead, cherrywood table, chairs, cupboard, wooden spoons, ploughs, chains, baskets, a "first rate fiddle" saw, shovel, and carpenter tools.

of the whole, at one blow. Many of the Cherokees, who, a few days ago, were in comfortable circumstances, are now victims of abject poverty. Some, who have been allowed to return home, under passport, to inquire after their property, have found their cattle, horses, swine, farming tools, and house furniture all gone. And this is not a description of extreme cases. It is altogether a faint representation of the work which has been perpetrated on the unoffending, unarmed and unresisting Cherokees.

"Our brother Bushyhead and his family, Rev. Stephen Foreman, native missionary of the American Board, the speaker of the national council, and several men of character and respectability, with their families, are here prisoners. It is due to justice to say, that, at this station (and I learn that the same is true of some others) the officer in command treats his prisoners with great respect and indulgence. But fault lies somewhere. They are prisoners, without a crime to justify the fact.

"These savages, prisoners of Christians, are now all hands busy, some cutting and some carrying posts, and plates and rafters—some digging holes for posts, and some preparing seats for a temporary place for preaching tomorrow. . . The principal Cherokees have sent a petition to Gen. Scott, begging that they may not be sent off to the west till the sickly season is over. The agent is shipping them off by multitudes from Ross's Landing. Nine hundred in one detachment, and seven hundred in another were driven into boats, and it will be a miracle of mercy if one-fourth escape the exposure of that sickly climate. They were exceedingly depressed, and almost in despair.

"July 10. The work of war in time of peace, is commenced in the Georgia part of the Cherokee nation, and is carried on in the most unfeeling and brutal manner. . . The work of capturing being completed, and about 3,000 sent off, the General has agreed to suspend the further transportation of the captives till the first of September. This arrangement, though but a small favor, diffused universal joy through the camps of prisoners. . . Brethren Wickliffe and O-ga-na-ya, and a great number of members of the church at Valley Towns, fell into Fort Butler, seven miles from the mission. They never relaxed their evangelical labors, but preached constantly in the fort. They held church meetings, received ten members, and one Sabbath, June 17, by permission of the officer in command, went down to the river and baptized them (five males and five females). They were guarded to the river and back. Some whites present *affirm it to have been the most solemn and impressive religious service they ever witnessed."* [6]

William Shorey Coodey was present at one of the concentration camps as the Indians prepared to march to the rendezvous where they were to organize for their departure; he wrote his friend John Howard Payne what he saw there: ". . . *At noon all was in readiness for moving, the teams were stretched out in a line along the road through a heavy forest, groups of persons formed about each wagon, others shaking the hand of some sick friend or relative who would be left behind. The temporary camp covered with boards and some of bark that for three summer months had been their only shelter and home, were crackling and falling under a blazing flame; the day was bright and beautiful, but a gloomy thoughtfulness was depicted in the lineaments of every face. In all the bustle of preparation there was a silence and stillness of the voice that betrayed the sadness of the heart. At length the word was given to move on. I glanced along the line and the form of Going Snake, an aged and respected chief whose head eighty summers had whitened, mounted on his favorite pony passed before me and led the way in silence, followed by a number of younger men on horseback. At this very moment a low sound of distant thunder fell upon my ear—in almost an exact western direction a dark spiral cloud was rising above the horizon and sent forth a murmur I almost thought a voice of devine indignation for the wrong of my poor and unhappy countrymen, driven by brutal power from all they loved and cherished in the land of their fathers to gratify the cravings of avarice. The sun was unclouded—no rain fell—the thunder rolled away and seemed hushed in the distance. The scene around and before me, and in the elements above was peculiarly impressive and singular."* [7]

When nearly seventeen thousand Cherokee thus had been gathered into the various stockades, the work of enforced removal West began. [8]

6 Letter from the Rev. Evan Jones, in *Baptist Missionary Magazine*, XVIII, 236.

7 Coodey to Payne, August 13, 1840, Newberry Library, *Ayer Collection*, "Payne Manuscrips," VI.

8 In the anti-treaty body of Cherokee were incorporated 376 Creeks who "had long been domesticated with the Cherokees, and with whom many of their warriors fought by our side at the battle of the Horse Shoe" (Gen. Winfield Scott to Governor Gilmer, October 15, 1838 in *Army and Navy Chronicle*, November 15, 1838, p. 316). After their removal, the Cherokee Council by formal enactment November 13, 1843, admitted to full membership in the tribe all Creeks who emigrated with them in

Old Mill at Shells Ford on Collins River near McMinnville, Tennessee, site of encampment of Cherokee emigrants. Local tradition tells of the Rev. Jesse Bushyhead preaching to his people at this place

FROM HISTORIC SUMNER COUNTY BY GUY CISCO

Emigrants descending the Tennessee River

Early in June companies aggregating about five thousand persons, were brought down by the troops;[9] part were taken to the old Agency, on Hiwassee river, at the present Calhoun, Tennessee, and Ross's Landing, (now Chattanooga) and Gunter's Landing, (now Guntersville, Alabama) lower down the Tennessee river, to be embarked upon boats.

Twenty-eight hundred of them were divided into three detachments, each accompanied by a military officer, a corps of assistants and two physicians. The first with about 800 in the party departed June 6; the next with 875 started on the fifteenth.[10]

The first party forcibly placed on the boats was in charge of Lieut. Edward Deas and was made up of Cherokee Indians from Georgia who had been concentrated at Ross's Landing. They were escorted by soldier guards aboard a little flotilla consisting of one steamboat of 100 tons, and six flatboats, one of which was constructed with a double-decked cabin. In the excitement and bitterness accompanying the enforced embarking of the Indians and their crowded condition aboard the boats, the conductors thought it best not to attempt to muster and count them until later.[11]

The boats were lashed together, three on each side of the steamboat and left from Ross's Landing about noon on June 6. They made four or five miles an hour until their arrival at a series of dangerous rapids called "*the Suck, Boiling-Pot, the Skillet, and the Frying pan. . . The Suck is first and most difficult and dangerous of the rapids. The river here becomes very narrow and swift and the banks on either side are rocky and steep, it being the point at which the stream passes thro' a gorge in the mountains. The S. Boat with one Flat on each side passed through, the most of the people on board, but after getting thro' the most rapid water,*

---

different detachments, some of whom had been admitted to the tribe before removal (*Laws of the Cherokee Nation*, 1868 edition, p. 109).

9 "On Tuesday morning last, about 1,000 Cherokees, men, women, and children, under an escort of two companies of infantry passed through this place on their way from the Sixes to the Agency" (*Cassville Pioneer*, copied in *Jacksonville* (*Alabama*) *Republican*, June 14, 1838, p. 3, col. 3).

10 *Army and Navy Chronicle*, VII, 45; *Louisville Public Advertiser*, August 24, 1838, p. 2, cols. 2 and 3, account from the *Hamilton Gazette*, printed at Ross's Landing in Tennessee.

11 *Deas's Journal*, OIA, "Cherokee Emigration" File D 225, Special File 249.

it was found impossible to keep her in the channel, and in consequence was thrown upon the north Bank with some violence but luckily none of the people were injured although one of the Flats was a good deal smashed. The other 4 boats came thro' two by two and the party was encamped before dark as it was too late in the day to reach the rapids in daylight."

The boats succeeded without incident in ·passing through the remainder of the rapids and into smooth water by noon the next day. They ran all that day and night; passed Gunter's Landing at nine o'clock, stopped once "to wood" and at night landed six miles above Decatur "and such of the people as choose have gone ashore to sleep and cook." Starting early on the morning of the ninth they reached Decatur at six o'clock to take the train to Tuscumbia but were compelled to remain until the next day. Then "the Indians and their baggage were transferred from the boats to the Rail Road cars. About 32 cars were necessary to transport the Party, and no more could be employed for want of power in the [two] Locomotive Engines."

As the Indians were much crowded on the train the twenty-three soldiers were discharged. The first detachment reached Tuscumbia at three o'clock and boarded the steamboat *Smelter* which "immediately set off for Waterloo at the foot of the rapids without awaiting for the 2nd train of Cars with the remainder of the Party." When the second party reached Tuscumbia they went into camp awhile awaiting transportation by water. As the guard had been discharged, whisky was introduced among them, much drunkeness resulting, and over one hundred of the emigrants escaped. The remainder were carried by water aboard a keel boat and a small steamer about thirty miles to Waterloo.

Here the party was united and set out on the eleventh aboard the steamboat *Smelter* and two large double decked keel boats; the next afternoon they reached Paducah, Kentucky, where Lieutenant Deas left one of the keel boats which he found superfluous. He succeeded in mustering the Indians after a fashion and found that he had 489. The nights were clear and calm and the boats ran both day and night, stopping only at intervals "to wood." They passed Memphis in the evening of the thirteenth and arrived at Montgomery's Point at the mouth of White River the next afternoon. Securing a pilot here they passed through the cut-off and entered Arkansas river, and, after ascending seventy miles, tied up at the bank while the emigrants went on shore to relax and encamp for the night. There were too many snags and sand-bars in the Arkansas river to permit their running at night; this program was repeated each evening and they did not reach Little Rock until the seventeenth.

Here Deas dropped the other keel boat to enable the steamboat to make better speed and reached Fort Smith and Fort Coffee on the nineteenth. The boat was tied up at the north bank of the river near the mouth of Sallisaw creek. When the emigrants went ashore to spend the night they found many of their friends who came to greet them and urge the emigrants to stop there and not continue up to Fort Gibson. After counselling together they decided to follow this advice; they took their baggage off the boat and concluded to cast their fortunes in this district with their friends who had preceded them to the West.

After their arrival at Fort Coffee Deas "*Issued a sufficient quantity of Cotton Domestic to the Indians for Tents to protect them from the weather. I have done so in consideration of their destitute condition, as they were for the most part separated from their homes in Georgia without having the means or time to prepare for camping*[12] *and it was also the opinion of the Physician of the Party that the health of these people would suffer if not provided with some protection from the weather.*" There had been no deaths in the party since their departure from Ross's Landing.

12 The emigrants had come with bitter feelings towards the authorities engendered by ". . .the precipitate manner in which they were started from the Old Nation, many of them being obliged to leave almost every particle of moveable property unsold, and as they supposed, forever lost to them" (Stuart to Adjutant General, June 29, 1838, OIA, "Cherokee Emigration").

O N JUNE 13 the second party of 875 captive Cherokee Indians departed from Chattanooga in charge of Lieut. R. H. K. Whiteley, with five assistant conductors, two physicians, three interpreters, and a hospital attendant. After the preceding day had been spent in organizing the party and reuniting separated families as far as possible, they were placed on six flatboats and dropped down the Tennessee river to Brown's Ferry where more prisoners joined them. For two days they remained there while clothing was purchased and offered to the Indians who refused to receive it "neither would they be mustered, as all attempts to obtain their names were without success."[1]

When they left there the flotilla was increased to eight flatboats; tied together in pairs these safely negotiated the dangerous rapids and arrived at Kelly's Ferry in the evening. On the morning of the eighteenth with four flatboats moored on each side, the steamboat *George Guess* continued the descent of the river. This day the Indians decided to take the clothing of which they stood in need. "*One death (a child) and one birth, were detained three hours wooding—Encamped on the bank of Tennessee River at 6 P. M. The hours of stopping and starting were so arranged as to give the Indians sufficient time to cook in the evenings and mornings the provision for the day.*"

On the twentieth they arrived at Decatur and the next morning departed on two trains, arriving at the boatlanding below Tuscumbia in the evening. One old woman died at Decatur and a man was killed by the cars when he attempted to rescue his hat. Before reaching Decatur twenty-five Indians had escaped from the party. The emigrants were required to remain at Tuscumbia several days before boats could

1 *Journal of R. H. K. Whiteley*, OIA, "Cherokee Emigration" File W 662.

be secured to carry them over Colbert Shoals, and during their stay two children died. They passed the shoals on the twenty-eighth and encamped opposite Waterloo, Alabama, while awaiting the arrival of the steamboat *Smelter*. During the stay here, three children died, there was one birth, and 118 Indians escaped.

The emigrants departed from Waterloo the last day of the month on the steamboat *Smelter* and one keel boat in tow. The next day another child died before the party arrived at Paducah. Stops were made to take on wood, to escape a wind storm, and to obtain supplies at Memphis and on the Fourth of July the boats entered the Arkansas river by way of the White river cut-off. Two children died this day and one child the next. On arrival at Little Rock the emigrants were transferred to the steamboat *Tecumseh* of lighter draft in order to navigate higher up the river.

They left on the twelfth but were unable to ascend higher than Lewisburg where the boat grounded on Benson's Bar. Here after scouring the country, twenty-three wagons were secured to haul the sick people, principally children, and they departed on the twentieth leaving eighty ill in camp. The next day more wagons were secured and the remainder of the party took up the march.

The weather was extremely hot, a drought had prevailed for months, water was scarce, suffocating clouds of dust stirred up the by oxen and wagons, and the rough and rocky roads, made the condition of the sick occupants of the wagons miserable indeed. Three, four, and five deaths occurred each day. To avoid the heat the marches were started before sunrise and ended at noon. Before the end of the month there were between two and three hundred ill.

On August first they were in camp at Lee's creek. "Did not move this day, the party requiring rest and being more than one half sick; notwithstanding every effort was used, it was impossible to prevent their eating quantities of green peaches and corn[2]—consequently the flux raged among them and carried off some days as high as six and seven." Four days later these miserable beings entered the Cherokee Nation and went into camp near the head of Lee's creek. Here they

2 At home the Indians ate peaches and corn with no bad results; but the hardships of the enforced marches, want of their customary diet, bad water, and many other causes contributed to the terrible mortality among them.

were delivered to Captain Stephenson, 602 of the original party, seventy having died in exactly three weeks.

"*Among the recent immigrants,*" wrote Mr. Washburn at Dwight, on July 31, "*there has been much sickness, and in some neighborhoods the mortality has been great. . . just returned from a neighborhood about ten miles from the mission where there have been fourteen deths within three weeks. . . want of medical aid. . . Since last October about 2,000 immigrants have come. Twenty-five hundred more are on their way. . . much sickness and mortality among them. One company of these originally a thousand, but. . . diminishing by some hundreds is expected to arrive today. . . expected that nearly all. . . will settle within ten miles of this station.*"[3]

A picture of Indian desolation in Georgia was sketched by the exulting Gen. Charles Floyd, militia officer in charge of operations against the Cherokee in that state, in his report to Governor Gilmer: "*Head Quarters, Middle Military District, New Echota, 18th June, 1838. Sir: I have the pleasure to inform your excellency that I am now fully convinced there is not an Indian within the limits of my command, except a few in my possession, who will be sent to Ross' Landing to-morrow. My scouting parties have scoured the whole country without seeing an Indian, or late Indian signs. If there are any stragglers in Georgia, they must be in Union and Gilmer counties, and near the Tennessee and North Carolina line; but none can escape the vigilance of our troops. Georgia is ultimately in possession of her rights in the Cherokee country. . .*"[4]

General Scott gave orders June 17, for the discharge of volunteer troops engaged in capturing the Indians.[5] The same day the third contingent of 1,070 captive Cherokee left Ross's Landing in wagons and on foot for Waterloo where they were to be embarked on boats.[6] These people were in a destitute condition, with very little clothing, but they refused to accept any from the emigration agent. Four children and one adult died before their arrival at Waterloo. After their departure they

3 *Missionary Herald*, XXXIV, 445.

4 *Army and Navy Chronicle*, VII, 57; Scott to Poinsett, June 15, 1838, OIA, "Cherokee Emigration."

5 Scott, order No. 46, June 17, 1838, OIA, "Cherokee Emigration."

6 *Army and Navy Chronicle*, VII, 45; *Louisville Public Advertiser*, August 24, 1838, p. 2, cols. 2 and 3.

learned that General Scott had suspended the removal until autumn, and they demanded to be allowed to remain with the other members of their nation.

Three days after their departure from Ross's Landing a number of their brothers addressed to Gen. Nat Smith, superintendent of Cherokee emigration, a touching petition to halt the movement of the party and either return them to their former encampment or establish them in a new one where they could share in the respite until a more healthful season and join in the movement in the autumn under the permission of General Scott. "*Spare their lives*," they said; "*expose them not to the killing effects of that strange climate, under the disadvantages of the present inauspicious season, without a house or shelter to cover them from above, or any kind of furniture to raise them from the bare ground, on which they may spread their blankets and lay their languid limbs, when fallen prostrate under the influence of disease. . . To this may be added the voice of our white neighbors. The cries of humanity have reached the citizens of the adjoining counties, and they have stepped forth to advocate the cause of mercy. The truth is, a general and powerful sympathy for our condition has seized the attention and affected the hearts of the white citizens generally in McMinn, Monroe and Blount counties. . . Not longer ago than yesterday the citizens of Athens, your immediate neighbors, sent a strong and affecting petition to Genl. Scott on our behalf signed by upwards of sixty of the principal citizens and physicians. . . We have today heard that the citizens of Monroe and those of Blount counties are preparing similar petitions.*"[7] This appeal was not heeded.

One hundred of the party escaped along the way and when the remainder were joined on the twenty-fifth at Bellefonte, Alabama, by Smith they "*made application to me to be suffered to return to the agency and remain until fall. . . . As they would have traveled over 120 miles, there health improving and they well provided with transportation and subsistence, I determined they should go on and so informed them. Shortly after which about 300 of them threw a part of there baggage out of the waggons, took it and broke for the woods and many of the balance refused to put there baggage into the waggons, or go any further and shewed much ill nature. Many of them told the agents who were with*

7 *John Ross Manuscripts*, in possession of his great-grandson, W. W. Ross of Park Hill, Oklahoma.

them that the white men were all Lyars and bad men; and one of them come to me and made the same observation and added further that he would go back home the next morning and shoot for Jno. Ross; that he had plenty of money and he would fight for him.

"I immediately requested the Captain of the Town Company to call out his men and aid me in starting them which he very promptly did, and we succeeded in getting off all that was left about 10 o'clock. A part of those who broke off in the morning was found and made to return. I put the party in charge of Capt. Drane of the Army and called on the citizens for 30 volunteers to accompany him to Waterloo. They turned out immediately and I had the Capt. to muster them into sirvice for 30 days unless sooner discharged.

"As verry many of this party were about naked, barefoot and suffering with fatigue although they had not traveled over 9 miles pr. day, I ditermined to purchase some Clothing, Domestic for tents & shoes, &c., &c., and issue to them which was done on the 26 ult. They rested on that day in the evening of which I called as many of the aged and Infirm and their Families as would go by water to Waterloo and took them to the river, put them on bord of the boat engaged in the upper contract and landed them next morning at Dicatur, where I learned Leut. Whiteley's party were yet at Tuscumbia. I followed on and overtook him and party at Waterloo all dooing verry well, and getting on bored of the boats to leave which they did at 10 o.c on 30 uto. We have been detained by head winds for 1 1-2 days or we should have reached this [Memphis] on the morning of 2d inst."[8]

Nat Smith accompanied this party as far as Little Rock "with 722 Cherokee out of over 1,000 who left Ross' Landing; they continued to desert some almost every night until we put them on board of the Boats" at Waterloo. On the thirtieth of June, 76 deserted before their arrival at Waterloo. "These people will have over 300 miles to travel to reach their old homes, many of them women and children and of course must suffer extremely for want of something to eat &c. Of the 3,000 which

8 Smith to Harris, July 3, 1838, OIA, "Cherokee Emigration" S 1041. "The Athens (Tenn.) Journal of July 4 says: 'Several detachments of Cherokees have passed through this place within the last two or three weeks, on their way from North Carolina to the Agency, and on last Friday 1,200 passed, conducted by two companies of artillery, under the command of Capt. Washington' "(New York Observer, July 28, 1838, p. 2, col. 4).

I wrote you from the Agency had left in the three parties, not over 2,000 will reach their new home, and all this for want of a few armed men as a guard which I have politely asked the Military for but could not get them agreably to my wish."[9]

The *Smelter* arrived at a point about sixty-five miles below Little Rock on July 20 but because of the low stage of the river could ascend no higher. The steamboat *Tecumseh* went down to bring up the Indians and Smith returned to Waterloo on the twelfth; there he found Captain Drane still detained with his land party of Indians, "supposed to consist of 800 or 900—he not having been able to muster them from their refusal to give their names and numbers of their families; the same case happened with Lieut. Whiteley's party, he had to count them out of the boats."[10]

An observer of this emigration between Memphis and Little Rock reported in September: "Eighteen hundred Cherokees have passed here by land within the last month, and they were suffering very much with measles and fever. We have had the longest drought I ever experienced in my life, and the corn crops will be light." And he predicted the tide of white and Indian emigrants would make provisions scarce and expensive.[11]

This removal, in the hottest part of the year, was attended with so much sickness and mortality that, by resolution of the Cherokee national council, Lewis Ross and other leading men submitted to General Scott a proposition that the Cherokee be allowed to conduct their own removal in the autumn, after the sickly season had ended. On June 19 the humane general agreed[12] to the proposition on condition that they would all start by September 1, and heard himself condemned

9 Smith to Harris, July 12, 1838, OIA, *ibid.; Arkansas Gazette*, July 11, 1838, p. 2, col. 1.

10 Smith to Harris, *ibid.; Arkansas Gazette*, July 25, 1838.

11 *Louisville Public Advertiser*, September 22, 1838, p. 2, col. 1.

12 Scott to Lowery and others, June 19, 1838, OIA, "Cherokee Emigration" S 1059. General Scott's agreement with Ross aroused a storm of protest and charges from a host of office-holders and owners of steamboats and wagons and other contract seekers, who saw their anticipated profits vanish (*Nashville Whig* October 29, 1838, p. 2, cols. 1 and 2).

by the impatient whites for this evidence of compassion for the unfortunate Indians. In the meantime, however, General Scott kept the
Indians under military guard in their concentration camps.[13]

However, a drought unprecedented for many years prevailed
throughout the summer and autumn, rendering it impossible to move
and subsist such large bodies of people and the cattle that accompanied
them for food, and removal was again postponed until the next month.
Officers were appointed by the Cherokee council to take charge of the
emigration, the Indians being organized into detachments averaging
one thousand each, with two leaders in charge of each detachment,
and a sufficient number of wagons and horses for the purpose. To
maintain order on the march they established in each party a sort of
police organization that punished infractions of their regulations.[14]

13 *Army and Navy Chronicle*, July 19, 1838, VII, 45. There were 2,500 at
Ross's Landing and 3,000 at the Cherokee Agency encampment covering nearly
ten square miles; 1,250 in two camps between these points; 1,500 being escorted to
these camps; two or three thousand more were prisoners at interior forts waiting to
be marched to the river camps; 3,000 had been removed and General Scott estimated
that there were fewer than 200 yet to be captured (Scott to Poinsett, June 22, 1838,
OIA, "Cherokee Emigration" S 1059). The whole number collected in North Carolina
was something more than 3,000 (Eustis to Worth, June 24, 1838, *ibid.*).

14 *Army and Navy Chronicle*, VII, 280. An effort was made to comply with the
agreement to begin the emigration by September 1; two days before that date about
2,500 emigrants in two parties had traveled twenty miles on the road when they
were obliged to stop and go into camp at Blythe's ferry. The long continued drought
had dried up all the creeks and branches in the Cumberland Mountains making it
impossible to find water for parties of more than a dozen or two men (*Knoxville
Register*, September 12, 1838, p. 3, col. 3). The delay was a serious matter for the
emigrants driven from their homes in warm weather with no clothing suitable for
winter months (*Nashville Whig*, October 5, 1838, p. 2, col. 4). However, at Nashville
the contractors engaged by Ross furnished many of the emigrants needed clothing.
Stephen Foreman's party passed through Nashville November 11; they were well
provided with teams, horses, ponies, and mules and some had private carriages; most
of them were well clothed; many were furnished with good cloaks, bearskin or
blanket overcoats, thick boots, shoes and stockings (*Nashville Union*, November 13,
1838, p. 2, col. 1). The emigrants headed by the preachers Evan Jones and Jesse
Bushyhead had an agreement with the authorities that they would be allowed to
rest on Sundays and conduct religious services. Bushyhead's party was camped four
miles from Nashville but the owner of the camp site would not permit them to remain
over Sunday and much to their regret they were obliged to march through Nashville
on that day (*Knoxville Register*, November 21, 1836, p. 2, col. 6). The last detachment
consisting of about 1,800 Indians reached the encampment on Mill Creek about four

Thus organized, numbering about 13,000 including negro slaves, they started after the drought was broken in October.

A party of Cherokee belonging to the treaty faction of the tribe who refused to emigrate under the leadership of John Ross, left the vicinity of the Cherokee Agency under the direction of Lieutenant Deas on October 11. Deas reported from Winchester, Tennessee on the twenty-seventh "*up to this time our progress has been necessarily slow, in consequence of the obstructions in the road over which we have passed. . . The Party under my charge numbers between 650 and 700 persons, and is composed for the most part of highly respectable and intelligent families, and there are but very few who have not made considerable advancement in civilization.*" Making ten or twelve miles a day and passing through Fayetteville, they reached Pulaski in November without incident except that a number of oxen belonging to the Indians died from eating poisonous weeds.[15]

On the twenty-fourth Deas finished crossing his Indians over the Mississippi river at Memphis and the next day they resumed their journey. As his party was made up of individuals who favored the plans of the government in the execution of the treaty, and they included some of the most highly civilized members of the tribe they were favored by a great increase in the allowances for transportation, subsistence and contingencies over those made for the other emigrants. A large quantity of their baggage was shipped up the Arkansas river by boat. This party reached Little Rock about the middle of December,[16] and arrived in their new home on January 7, 1839.

Those who emigrated under the management of their own officers assembled at Rattlesnake Springs, about two miles south of Hiwassee river near the present Charleston, Tennessee, where a final council was held in which it was determined to continue their old constitution and laws in their new home.[17]

---

miles from Nashville the end of November and as winter was so near at hand it was predicted that some of the detachments would be obliged to go into camp on the Ohio river until spring (*Nashville Union*, November 30, 1838, p. 2, col. 2).

15 Deas to Harris, November 3, 1838, "Cherokee Emigration," D 257.

16 *Arkansas Gazette*, December 19, 1838, p. 2, col. 1.

17 *Missionary Herald*, XXXIV, 445. Their agreement provided for subsisting them at a cost of sixteen cents per diem for each person and forty cents each for the

Crossing to the north side of the Hiwassee river at a ferry above Gunstocker creek, they proceeded down along the river; the sick, the aged, and children, with the blankets, cooking pots and other belongings in wagons; the rest on foot or on horses. There were 645 wagons and about 5,000 horses, besides a large number of oxen. "*It was like the march of an army, regiment after regiment, the wagons in the center, the officers along the line and the horsemen on the flanks and at the rear. Tennessee river was crossed at Tucker's (?) ferry, a short distance above Jolly's Island, at the mouth of Highwassee. Thence the route lay south of Pikesville, through McMinnville and on to Nashville, where the Cumberland was crossed.*"

The contingent of 1,103 Cherokee in charge of John Benge was the first to begin their journey, starting on October 1, 1838. Elijah Hicks's party of 748 started three days later and on the sixteenth reached Nashville near where they camped for several days; there they were reported as suffering sorely for the want of clothing, and it was thought that "scores of them must inevitably fall the victims of desease and death before reaching the far place of their destination. Indeed, when they passed through Nashville, 40 or 50 were on the sick list, and four or five were afterward buried near the city."[18]

---

500 horses it was expected would accompany each, 1,000 persons, two thousand pounds of soap for each 1,000 emigrants was included (*John Ross Manuscripts, ibid.*).

18 *New York Observer*, November 10, 1838, p. 3, col. 4. Mrs Rebecca Neugin, a half-blood Cherokee now living near Hulbert, Oklahoma, was three years old when she departed with her parents on the removal; from information given by her mother she told the author: "When the soldiers came to our house my father wanted to fight, but my mother told him that the soldiers would kill him if he did and we surrendered without a fight. They drove us out of our house to join other prisoners in a stockade. After they took us away my mother begged them to let her go back and get some bedding. So they let her go back and she brought what bedding and a few cooking utensils she could carry and had to leave behind all of our other household possessions. My father had a wagon pulled by two spans of oxen to haul us in. Eight of my brothers and sisters and two or three widow women and children rode with us. My brother Dick who was a good deal older than I was walked along with a long whip which he popped over the backs of the oxen and drove them all the way. My father and mother walked all the way also. The people got so tired of eating salt pork on the journey that my father would walk through the woods as we traveled, hunting for turkeys and deer which he brought into camp to feed us. Camp was usually made at some place where water was to be had and when we stopped and prepared to cook our food other emigrants who had been driven from their homes without opportunity

On the twenty-fourth Hicks, the first to reach there, reported from Port Royal near the Kentucky line "the people are very loth to go on, and unusually slow in preparing for starting each morning. I am not surprised at this because they are moving not from choice to an unknown region not desired by them. I am disposed to make full allowance for their unhappy movement." The venerable chief "White Path has been in the last stages of sickness for many days and has to be hauled & is helpless who cannot last but a few days. Nocowee has given himself up to the bane of death [whisky] and I have altogether lost his services. Our police has to drive him along the road sometimes fettered." A few days later near Hopkinsville, Kentucky, White Path succumbed to sickness, infirmity, and the hardships of the forced journey, and died at the age of seventy-five. He was interred near the Nashville road and a monument of wood painted to resemble marble was erected to his memory. A tall pole with a flag of white linen flying at the top was erected at his grave to note the spot for his countrymen who were following.[19] This party reached their destination on January 4, 1839, the first to arrive in their western home.

Nine contingents left at intervals through October and four during the next month. John Ross remained behind to supervise the preparations and he was the recipient of numerous reports of progress and requests for advice. Wilson Lumpkin of Georgia and John Kennedy of Tennessee were appointed commissioners to supervise and carry into effect the provisions of the treaty preparatory to the removal of the Indians. Their duties required them to examine and pass on the claims of the Indians for loss and damage to their property in connection with the removal as well as claims of the whites against them. The Indians who departed more or less voluntarily had the benefit of greater indulgence and leisure on the part of the commissioners than fell to the lot of the more than 13,000 who would not consent to leave until

---

to secure cooking utensils came to our camp to use our pots and kettles. There was much sickness among the emigrants and a great many little children died of whooping cough." Agents were sent in advance to select and engage camp sites at intervals of about fifteen miles; water, fuel, and grazing for their animals were essential, and the neighborhood of a water mill for grinding their corn was also an important factor in selecting a camping place.

19 Draper Collection, 26 cc 15; Hopkinsville (Kentucky) Gazette, quoted in Jacksonville (Alabama) Republican, November 22, 1838, p. 2, col. 4.

the last moment; as it was manifestly impossible to give them more than perfunctory attention before their departure, the commissioners proceeded to hear and determine them after the Indians had gone.

As these Indians now on the way were driven from their home without either their property or compensation for its loss their bitterness of spirit was greatly aggravated. At McMinnville, Tennessee, Rev. Jesse Bushyhead's party held a council and sent a message to Ross saying they had been compelled to leave without satisfaction of their claims and they feared fraudulent demands would be made to defeat them; and they urged that no further consideration of them be had while the Indians were denied the opportunity of being present or represented.

The party in charge of Rev. Evan Jones, a Baptist missionary, traveled sixteen miles on October 16 but the people were so fatigued with the effort, that they remained in camp at McMinnville several days to rest. They "paid forty dollars at the Walderns Ridge toll gate and the man agreed to let the other detachments pass at half price viz., 37 1-2 [cents] for four wheeled carriages and 6 1-2 for a horse. On the Cumberland mountains they fleeced us, 73 cents a wagon and 12 1-2 cents a horse without the least abatement or thanks." Rev. Jesse Bushyhead's detachment was delayed by their oxen eating poison ivy and they were passed by Jones. Bushyhead "has had a distressing time with the discontents."

Bushyhead reported from his party on October 31: "We have a large number of sick and very many extremely aged and infirm persons in our detachment that must of necessity be conveyed in waggons. Our detachment now consists of about 978 or 79 Cherokees and there are forty-nine waggons" and they would be unable to haul the corn needed for the horses. They often found it necessary to double the teams in ascending the mountain roads.

The route carried all the emigrants through Nashville where the contractors furnished them with supplies. In November it rained excessively and the roads, cut up by thousands of horses, cattle, and people and hundreds of wagons and carts, became an appalling morass through which locomotion was accomplished with great difficulty and distress. The infirm and sick suffered in the wagons and carts that pitched and jolted behind the struggling oxen and horses; and they were obliged to await until stops were made at night for the attention

C. JAS. E. THOMPSON COMPANY, KNOXVILLE, TENN.

Type of primitive turbine grist mill operated in the Cherokee country of East Tennessee and North Carolina

of their physicians, who, tired after a day of travel, spent most of the night making brief calls upon the large number of patients. After the Indians left those who had driven them from their homes, they found the white people sympathetic with them in their distress, and as the third detachment of about 1,200 camped near Hopkinsville, Kentucky, on November 13, the citizens made generous donations for their comfort.[20]

The last party conducted by George Hicks did not start until November 4. Hicks sorrowfully reported that day to Chief Ross: "*We are now about to take our final leave and kind farewell to our native land, the country that the great spirit gave our Fathers; we are on the eve of leaving that country that gave us birth. . . it is with sorrow that we are forced by the authority of the white man to quit the scenes of our childhood. . . we bid a final farewell to it and all we hold dear. From the little trial we have made in a start to move, we know that it is a laborious undertaking, but with firm resolution we think we will be able to accomplish it, if the white citizens will permit us. But since we have been on our march many of us have been stopped and our horses taken from our Teams for the payment of unjust & past Demands; Yet the Government says we must go, and its citizens say you must pay me, and if the debtor has not the means, the property of his next friend is levied on and yet the Government has not given us our spoliation [compensation] as promised; our property has been stolen and robbed from us by white men and no means given us to pay our debts. [The Government officers will not protect us, our property is] robbed of us in open Day light and in open view of hundreds, and why are they so bold; they know that we are in a defenseless situation. . .*"

A sympathetic traveler who met them on the road describes the appearance of these unhappy people:

"*. . .On Tuesday evening we fell in with a detachment of the poor Cherokee Indians . . .about eleven hundred Indians—sixty waggons— six hundred horses, and perhaps forty pairs of oxen. We found them in the forest camped for the night by the road side . . .under a severe fall of rain accompanied by heavy wind. With their canvas for a shield from the inclemency of the weather, and the cold wet ground for a resting place, after the fatigue of the day, they spent the night . . .many of the aged Indians were suffering extremely from the fatigue of the journey, and*

20 *Hopkinsville Gazette,* quoted in *Army and Navy Chronicle,* VII, 363.

the ill health consequent upon it . . . several were then quite ill, and one aged man we were informed was then in the last struggles of death.

". . . About ten officers and overseers in each detachment whose business it was to provide supplies for the journey, and attend to the general wants of the company. . . We met several detachments in the southern part of Kentucky on the 4th, 5th and 6th of December. . . . The last detachment which we passed on the 7th embraced rising two thousand Indians with horses and mules in proportion. The forward part of the train we found just pitching their tents for the night, and notwithstanding some thirty or forty waggons were already stationed, we found the road literally filled with the procession for about three miles in length. The sick and feeble were carried in waggons—about as comfortable for traveling as a New England ox cart with a covering over it—a great many ride on horseback and multitudes go on foot—even aged females, apparently nearly ready to drop into the grave, were traveling with heavy burdens attached to the back—on the sometimes frozen ground, and sometimes muddy streets, with no covering for the feet except what nature had given them. We were some hours making our way through the crowd, which brought us in close contact with the wagons and multitude, so much that we felt fortunate to find ourselves freed from the crowd without leaving any part of our carriage. We learned from the inhabitants on the road where the Indians passed, that they buried fourteen or fifteen at every stopping place, and they make a journey of ten miles per day only on an average. One fact which to my own mind seemed a lesson indeed to the American nation is, that they will not travel on the Sabbath. . . when the Sabbath came, they must stop, and not merely stop—they must worship the Great Spirit too, for they had divine service on the Sabbath—a camp-meeting in truth. One aged Indian who was commander of the friendly Creeks and Seminoles in a very important engagement in the company with General Jackson, was accosted on arriving in a little village in Kentucky by an aged man residing there, and who was one of Jackson's men in the engagement referred to, and asking him if he (the Indian) recollected him? The aged Chieftain looked him in the face and recognized him, and with a down-cast look and heavy sigh, referring to the engagement, he said 'Ah! my life and the lives of my people were then at stake for you and your country. I then thought Jackson my best friend. But ah! Jackson no serve me right. Your country no do me justice now!'

"*The Indians as a whole carry in their countenances every thing but the appearance of happiness. Some carry a downcast dejected look bordering upon the appearance of despair; others a wild frantic appearance as if about to burst the chains of nature and pounce like a tiger upon their enemies. . . Most of them seemed intelligent and refined. Mr. Bushyhead, son of an aged man of the same name, is a very intelligent and interesting Baptist clergyman. Several missionaries were accompanying them to their destination. Some of the Cherokees are wealthy and travel in style. One lady passed on in her hack in company with her husband, apparently with as much refinement and equipage as any of the mothers of New England; and she was a mother too and her youngest child about three years old was sick in her arms, and all she could do was to make it comfortable as circumstances would permit. . . she could only carry her dying child in her arms a few miles farther, and then she must stop in a stranger-land and consign her much loved babe to the cold ground, and that too without pomp or ceremony, and pass on with the multitude. . .*

"*. . .When I past the last detachment of those suffering exiles and thought that my native countrymen had thus expelled them from their native soil and their much loved homes, and that too in this inclement season of the year in all their suffering, I turned from the sight with feelings which language cannot express and 'wept like childhood then.' I felt that I would not encounter the secret silent prayer of one of these sufferers armed with the energy that faith and hope would give it (if there be a God who avenges the wrongs of the injured) for all the lands of Georgia! . . .When I read in the President's Message[21] that he was happy to inform the Senate that the Cherokees were peaceably and without reluctance removed—and remember that it was on the third day of December when not one of the detachments had reached their destination; and that a large majority had not made even half their journey when he made that declaration, I thought I wished the President could have been there that very day in Kentucky with myself, and have seen the comfort and the willingness with which the Cherokees were making their journey. But I forbear, full well I know that many prayers have gone up to the King of Heaven from Maine in behalf of the poor Cherokees.*"[22]

21   James D. Richardson, *Messages of the Presidents*, III, 497.
22   "A Native of Maine, traveling in the Western Country" in *New York Observer*, January 26, 1839, p. 4. The last detachment, numbering about 1,800 passed through Nashville December 2 and the *Nashville Banner* predicted that they would

The Ohio river was crossed at a ferry near the mouth of the Cumberland, and the army passed on through southern Illinois until it reached the Mississippi river opposite Cape Girardeau, Missouri. The drought having delayed the start so long, it was winter when the emigrants reached that great river. "*In talking with old men and women at Tahlequah, the author found that the lapse of over half a century had not sufficed to wipe out the memory of the miseries of that halt beside the frozen river, with hundreds of sick and dying penned up in wagons or stretched upon the ground, with only a blanket overhead to keep out the January blast. The crossing was made at last in two divisions, at Cape Girardeau and at Green's ferry, a short distance below, whence the march was on through Missouri to Indian Territory, the later detachments making a northerly circuit by Springfield, because those who had gone before had killed off all the game along the direct route.*"[23]

Nineteen hundred of these Indians passed through Jackson, Missouri, early in December. "Some of them have considerable wealth, and make a very respectable appearance; but most of them are poor and exceedingly dissipated."[24] Another detachment passed near Batesville, Arkansas, December 15. Of this party John Benge was conductor, George Lowery assistant, Dr. W. P. Rawles of Gallatin, Tennessee, surgeon and physician, and William Shorey Coodey, contractor. Many of them came through the town to get their carriages repaired, have their horses shod and for other reasons. "They left Gunter's Landing on Tennessee River 35 miles above Huntsville, Alabama, October 10, since which time, owing to their exposure to the inclemency of the weather, and many of them being destitute of shoes and other necessary articles of clothing, about 50 of them have died."[25] Twelve hundred

---

suffer intensely from the cold before they reached their new home (*New York Observer*, December 15, 1838, p. 3, col. 5).

23 James Mooney, *op. cit.*, 133. As the Indians organized and managed the movement of this great body of people and the government had nothing to do with it, there were no journals of their experiences kept so far as the author has been able to ascertain; information and descriptions of this terrible undertaking are therefore meager. James Mooney's account written from the lips of survivors of that sad migration is the most complete of any extant.

24 *Jackson Advertiser*, in *Arkansas Gazette*, December 26, 1838, p. 2, col. 1.

25 Account from *Batesville (Arkansas) News*, in *Arkansas Gazette*, December 20, 1838.

Cherokee emigrants passed through Smithville, Lawrence County, Arkansas on December 12, "*many of whom appeared very respectable. The whole company appear to be well clothed, and comfortably fixed for travelling. I am informed that they are very peaceable, and commit no depredations upon any property in the country through which they pass. They have upwards of one hundred wagons employed in transporting them; their horses are the finest I have ever seen in such a collection. The company consumes about one hundred and fifty bushels of corn per day. It is stated that they have the measles and whooping cough among them and there is an average of four deaths per day.*"[26]

Evan Jones, with his party at Little Prairie, Missouri, wrote, December 30: "*. . .We have now been on our road to Arkansas seventy-five days, and have traveled five hundred and twenty-nine miles. We are still nearly three hundred miles short of our destination. . . It has been exceedingly cold. . . those thinly clad very uncomfortable. . . we have, since the cold set in so severely, sent on a company every morning, to make fires along the road, at short intervals. This. . . a great alleviation to the sufferings of the people. At the Mississippi river, we were stopped from crossing, by the ice running so that boats could not pass, for several days. Here Br. Bushyhead's detachment came up with us, and before our detachment was all over, Rev. Stephen Foreman's detachment came up, and encamped along side us. I am sorry to say that both their detachments have not been able to cross. I am afraid that with all the care that can be exercised with the various detachments, there will be an immense amount of suffering, and loss of life attending the removal. Great numbers of the old, the young, and the infirm will inevitably be sacrificed. And the fact that the removal is effected by coercion, makes it the more galling to the feelings of the survivors.*"[27]

Rev. Jesse Bushyhead wrote from Park Hill, March 19, that his party which departed October 5, was detained by the ice in the Mississippi river for a month, and that there were eighty-two deaths among them while on the road; they reached their destination on February 23 and he expected all the other parties would be in within a week or two.[28] Several hundred of the emigrants in Jones's and Bushyhead's

---

26 *Ibid.*, January 2, 1839, p. 2, col. 2.

27 *Baptist Missionary Magazine*, XIX, 89.

28 *Ibid.*, 178. Just after they crossed the Mississippi river, there was born to Reverend and Mrs. Bushyhead on January 3, 1839, a daughter who, in commemoration

parties were members of their church, the Baptist; "thus enabling them to continue, amidst all the toils and sufferings of the journey, their accustomed religious services."[29]

At last their destination was reached. It was now March, 1839, the journey having occupied nearly six months of the hardest part of the year. Some of those whom sickness had prevented from emigrating by land with the main body of emigrants, were in a party of 228 Cherokee aboard the steamboat *Victoria*, which arrived at Little Rock about February 1, 1839. Among them were Chief John Ross and his family who had more cause to mourn than many at their enforced removal which was in part responsible for the death of Mrs. Ross as the boat landed at Little Rock; she was buried in the little cemetery at this village.[30]

On the march there were many deaths, a few desertions and accessions and occasional exchanges from one party to another where some by sickness were obliged to drop out on the way and join those coming after; so that an accurate statement of the number removed and of those who perished on the way became impossible. But the following particulars concerning the movements of the emigrants are available:

Elijah Hick's party increased by accessions to 858, and traveling with forty-three wagons and 430 horses, arrived in their new home January 4, 1839, the first party to reach their destination, reduced then to 744; of the missing, thirty-four were accounted for by death, but they were offset by five births on the way. The next company to arrive three days later was that which started in charge of Hair Conrad, numbering 858, and ended the journey 654 in number commanded by Lieutenant Deas. Three days after these John Benge arrived in his

---

of the state in which she was born, was named Eliza Missouri; she was married to David Rowe Vann in 1858, and after his death became the wife of Bluford West Alberty in 1873. Aunt Eliza Alberty, as she was affectionately called, reared a large number of orphan children, and sent others through the Cherokee and other academic and professional schools; she exercised a tremendous influence for good on the lives of many Cherokee citizens, some of whom have risen to important stations.

29 *Ibid.*, 127.

30 *Little Rock Advocate*, February 4, 1839; *Army and Navy Chronicle*, VIII, 156. Mrs. Ross was known as Quatie Martin Ross; the monument at her grave is marked "Elizabeth Ross, wife of John Ross." John Ross was married to Mary B. Stapler of Wilmington, Delaware, at Hartwell's Washington hotel, Philadelphia, September 2, 1844.

new home in charge of a party of 1,103 remaining of a total of 1,200 who began the journey. Daniel Colton arrived January 16 with 651 emigrants.

A company of 1,033 Cherokee from the Valley Towns of East Tennessee in charge of the Rev. Evan Jones arrived February 2; these were all that remained of the original party numbering 1,250, headed by Situakee, who traveled with sixty-two wagons and 560 horses. There were seventy-one deaths and five births among them. The people of this party were strongly religious and maintained their church organization and services on the road with the inspiration of their Baptist conductor. Next behind them was the party headed by Rev. Jesse Bushyhead, a Cherokee Baptist minister who interpreted for Mr. Jones. His people numbered at the beginning 950, but he lost thirty-eight by death and after accounting for six births, he delivered 898 in their new home February 23.

Rev. Stephen Foreman, also a Cherokee preacher, who had been educated at Union and Princeton theological seminaries brought the next party of emigrants made up largely of Cherokee Indians of religious attachments who arrived February 27; they began their journey in charge of Capt. Old Field 983 in number, but there were fifty-seven deaths and nineteen births on the road and after accounting for a few desertions and accessions they numbered 921 on their arrival in the West. The party of Choowalooka began their journey numbering 1,150 but on arrival at their new home in the West March first there were but 970 of them. Mose Daniel's party originally numbering 1,035 suffered forty-eight deaths on the march, but there were six births, and Captain Stevenson, the certifying agent, receipted for only 924 in their new home March 2. James Brown's contingent of 859 was reduced to 717 when it reached their destination March 5, by thirty-four deaths and other causes. George Hicks reported to Captain Stevenson, March 14, 1,039 of his original enrollment of 1,118.

John Drew delivered a small party of 219 emigrants in their new home on March 18 of 231 who started with him. Richard Taylor began his journey in charge of 1,029 emigrants and after fifty-five deaths and fifteen births in the party he brought 944 survivors to their new home March 24. Peter Hilderbrand's caravan of 1,776 emigrants extended for several miles along the highway. Eighty-eight wagons contained the young children, the sick, aged and decrepit, and the personal effects of the emigrants. There were 881 horses in the equipment of the party, some of which were employed with the oxen in pulling the wagons; the remainder were used as riding horses for women and girls many of whom bore infants on their backs. Men, boys, and able bodied women and girls walked along in company with the wagons and horses containing members of their families and their property. Only 1,312 of this party were delivered to the agent in the West March 25, the difference, 464, being accountable probably to diversion of some of them to another party and not altogether to deaths.[31]

31 These figures were turned in by the conductors of the parties; there was much disagreement on the subject. John Ross claimed a total of 13,149 removed under his supervision. Captain Stevenson, who receipted for the Indians on their arrival, reported 11,504; and Captain Page, the disbursing officer, said there were 11,702 (C. E. Royce, op. cit., 292). All told, about 4,000 died during the course of capture and detention in temporary stockades, and the removal itself. See also Emmet Starr, History of the Cherokee Indians, 103.

BOOK FIVE / *Seminole Removal*

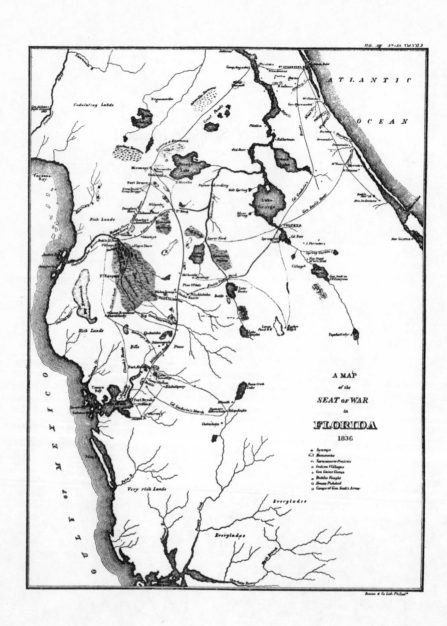

Pl. 24 N° 138 Vol VII 3

A MAP
of the
SEAT OF WAR
in
FLORIDA
1836

CHAPTER TWENTY-FIVE / *The Seminole Indians*

I N THE dishonorable record of our dealings with the Indians there is perhaps no blacker chapter than that relating to the Seminole people. These are a Muskhogean tribe, originally made up of emigrants from the Lower Towns on the Chattahoochee river who moved down into Florida after 1700; at first classed with the Lower Creeks, about 1775 they began to be known as Seminole, meaning "separatist" or "runaway". They consisted chiefly of descendants of Muskogee (Creeks) and Hitchiti, with a considerable number of refugees from the Upper Creeks together with Yamasee and other conquered tribes, Yuchi, and a large negro element from runaway slaves.[1]

Long before the Revolution, slaves of the Indians and of the whites of South Carolina fled to Florida and became Spanish subjects. They were later joined by other escaped slaves and by Creek Indians who were also slave owners; and generations of their descendants cultivated the soil and raised herds in entire freedom in this Spanish country. These negroes and the Indians were amalgamated with the Seminole tribe. The Seminole Indians were themselves slave owners who held their vassals in a form of benevolent bondage, exacting only their fealty and a small amount of corn, stock or peltries.

When the Creek Indians made their first treaty with the United States on August 7, 1790,[2] in order to placate the people of Georgia, the government induced the Indians to promise the return to the whites of all negroes living among the Seminole. The latter declared that the Creeks had no control over them and repudiated their undertaking. This claim of the whites and the promise of the Creeks and their assumption of authority over the Seminole, were destined to

1   Frederick W. Hodge (ed.) *Handbook of American Indians*, II, 500.
2   Kappler, *op. cit.*, II, 19.

influence profoundly the history of these people, who for many years had lived in a state of peace broken only at intervals by slaving raids of Georgians.

In July 1816 Col. D. L. Clinch was ordered with his command into Florida, then a Spanish province. There he joined a company of 200 Creek Indians of Coweta Town, under the command of William McIntosh, a half-breed whose interests and activities were closely identified with those of the whites of Georgia. He said his mission there was to capture negroes "and restore them to their owners." A number of them, to avoid capture, had taken refuge in Fort Apalachicola, an old fortification on the bank of Apalachicola river. It contained a large quantity of arms and ammunition and was manned by negroes and Indians. This fort was in Spanish territory about sixty miles from the boundary line of the United States. The settlements of the inhabitants in the vicinity of the fort were ravaged by the United States troops and Creek Indians who destroyed their fields of corn and melons and drove into the fort such of the people as they could not capture. The invaders then mounted cannon on two boats and on shore and bombarded the fort. At the time there were over 300 people in the fort of whom one hundred were men and the remainder women and children, thirty-one of the men being Seminole.

On the twenty-sixth a heated cannon ball entered the magazine and blew up the fort. "*The explosion was awful and the scene horrible beyond description.*[3] *You cannot conceive, nor I describe the horrors of the scene. In an instant hundreds of lifeless bodies were stretched upon the plain, buried in sand and rubbish, or suspended from the tops of the surrounding pines. Here lay an innocent babe, there a helpless mother; on the one side a sturdy warrior, on the other a bleeding squaw. Piles of bodies, large heaps of sand, broken guns, accoutrements, etc, covered the site of the fort. The brave soldier was disarmed of his resentment and checked his victorious career, to drop a tear on the distressing scene.*"[4]

3 *Army and Navy Chronicle*, II, 115. During the six years of warfare in Florida, army officers wrote frequent unofficial accounts of Indians, operations, scenes, and conditions that came within their observation. These letters and many official reports which are part of the archives of the war department, were copied in the *Army and Navy Chronicle*, which thereby became the outstanding contemporary source of authentic information touching this interesting subject. The many references herein to the *Chronicle* are to such letters and reports.

4 *Ibid.*, 116.

Two hundred and seventy unfortunates were killed by the explosion and sixty escaped with injuries. These wounded were cared for, taken as captives to Georgia and delivered to men who claimed to be descendants of others who had owned the ancestors of the captives.

The Seminole Indians and blacks resisted the raiders and made bloody reprisals along the Georgia line, in which white people were killed and their houses burned. The next year they massacred a company of forty white men and a number of women and children who were ascending the Apalachicola river. A small army of white soldiers aided by the Creeks and headed by Gen. Andrew Jackson invaded the Seminole country, punished the Indians and negroes, burned many of their towns and captured a few slaves. This was a phase of the first Seminole War which was officially ended in May, 1818. The Indians had not long been at peace when the United States purchased Florida from Spain by the treaty of 1819; and its ratification two years later brought the Seminole Indians within the jurisdiction of the United States where the slavery problem could be handled more easily.

The people of Georgia were insistent that steps be taken to secure the Florida slaves claimed by them or compensation for their loss, and commissioners were appointed by the president to negotiate with the Creeks.[5] In their letter of instructions the commissioners were informed that the treaty was to be for the benefit of Georgia and her wishes should control them. The commissioners informed the Indians that they were responsible for the actions of the Seminole Indians who were former members of that tribe; and demanded that the Creeks not only deliver to the whites all negroes who had fled to Florida, but that they pay for those who had been carried away by the British, and those killed by the Americans in the massacre at Fort Blount.[6]

Under these demands the "Treaty of Indian Springs" was negotiated January 8, 1821,[7] by which the Creek Nation ceded to the United States for the benefit of Georgia, five million acres of land for a consideration of $200,000 to be paid in instalments, and another sum not to exceed $250,000 was to be paid to citizens of Georgia to satisfy claims for slaves who in years past had escaped to Florida for which the Creeks had undertaken in their treaty of 1790 to become responsible.

5 *American State Papers*, "Indian Affairs," II, 416.
6 Ibid., 253.
7 Kappler, *op. cit.*

Proof was later made before a commissioner showing that ninety-two slaves had left their masters in Georgia between 1775 and 1802 and their value was fixed at $109,900 which was appropriated by Congress and paid to the claimants.

The Seminole had suffered much and were now a body of "dejected wretched beings. . . their defeats of 1818 having completely broken them up and dispersed them in small squads. . . They are humbled to the dust," wrote a citizen of Florida in 1821. Capt. John Bell was sent the next year to make an examination of their condition; he wrote that the original Seminole settlers in Florida composed only a third of the whole Indian population in that territory. *"The other two-thirds are from the Upper Creeks and other bands of the Creek Nation. Many of these left their country as followers of McQueen and Francis[8] their prophets. . . This nation was before the destruction of their settlements in 1812, numerous, proud, and wealthy, possessing great numbers of cattle, horses, and slaves; they are now weak and poor, yet their native spirit is not so much broken as to humble them to the dust. They appear sensible of their reduced situation; that they are too weak to make resistance in war."[9]*

As the white population increased in the adjoining states, the number of negroes escaping to Florida increased and there were more raids into the country by white people after slaves and other property. The Indians and negroes retired farther into the interior to escape these incursions. Commissioners were then sent to Florida to negotiate the first treaty with the Seminole tribe of Indians since they came under the sovereignty of the United States. On Moultrie creek September 6, 1823 seventy Seminole Indians met the commissioners. The Indians were told that they must remove from the fertile lands and cultivated fields on the Suwanee and Apalachicola rivers to the interior country below Tampa Bay. Eneah Emathla objected to moving south because the soil was poor and not capable of supporting them. "We rely on your justice and humanity; we hope that you will not send us south to a country whether neither the hickorynut, the acorn, nor the persimmon grows; we depend much upon these productions

8 Francis the Prophet, or Hillis Hadjo; for an account of this interesting Indian who was the father of Millie Francis, see F. W. Hodge, *op. cit.*, I, 549, and Grant Foreman, *A Traveler in Indian Territory.*

9 *American State Papers*, "Indian Affairs," II, 416.

of the forest for food; in the south they are not to be found."[10] The chiefs reported a population in their tribe of 4,883, living in thirty-seven towns.

To remove the principal opposition to the terms proposed, six of the most influential chiefs were bribed by reservations of extensive tracts of land where they were living, north of Tampa Bay. These chiefs were Eneah Emathla, John Blunt, Tuski Hadjo, Mulatto King, Emathlochee, and Econchattemicco. After many troubled[11] conferences, thirty-one of the Indians present signed the treaty[12] on September 18. The principal feature was that by which the Indians agreed to prevent runaway slaves from entering their country and to assist in returning those living among them, to their agent. For $6,000 worth of cattle and hogs and an annuity of $5,000 promised them, they gave up all their best lands desired by the whites—all but the six favored chiefs—and agreed to retire to the poor swamp land in the interior.

The land reserved to the Indians was not seen by representatives of the government until two years after the treaty was signed. The Seminole agent William P. Duval then went to examine it and he reported that it was so poor that no settlement could ever be made on it as there was no part of it "worth cultivation. The best of the Indian lands are worth but little; nineteen-twentieths of their whole country within the present boundary, is by far the poorest and the most miserable region I ever beheld." In one place where fire had run over it "the burnt and blackened pines, without a leaf, added to the dreary poverty of the land, presents the most miserable and gloomy prospect I ever beheld."[13]

Under these conditions the Indians could not sustain themselves on the land to which they were limited, and many of them remained in their old homes in sections which the whites began to settle, creating a situation calculated to produce difficulties between them. Slaves continued to escape from Georgia and seek refuge among the Seminole. With the permission of the secretary of war, white men claiming to

10 Ibid., 439.
11 American State Papers, "Indian Affairs," II, 429; Document, III, 597.
12 Kappler, op. cit., II, 141.
13 American State Papers, "Indian Affairs," II, 664.

have lost slaves went among the Indians and seized the negroes belonging to the latter as well as those born in freedom as Spanish subjects. These raids caused excitement and bitterness on the part of the Seminole and negroes; the latter had too long lived a life of indolence and ease to yield without a fight; and the Indians were incensed that their own slaves or the freemen among whom they were intermarried should be taken from them. The rapacity of the whites continued to the point where hostilities again became imminent. Indians had been flogged and killed, their slaves taken, their stock killed and houses burned until they were driven to desperation and in turn had committed unbridled excesses and cruel murders upon the whites. The Indians were then approached on the subject of removing to the west of the Mississippi river with their slaves where they could avoid further outrages by their white neighbors. The Indians, and especially the free negroes among them, were suspicious of the movement as they feared it was promoted with a view of enabling the Creeks to enslave them.

After the passage of the Indian removal act of 1830, Col. James Gadsden was sent in 1832 to attempt a treaty with the Indians providing for their removal. When he arrived in their country they were scattered over the peninsula in search of game to relieve their starving condition, as a devastating drought in 1831 had destroyed their meager crops. Most of them had been for three months subsisting on roots and the cabbage of the palmetto tree.[14]

The destitution of the Indians facilitated the negotiations by Gadsden who offered them food if they would remove to the West. They stubbornly refused to agree however, until the government would provide for sending an exploring party of Seminole[15] to the country in which it was proposed to locate them[16] and they could determine from the report of the explorers whether the lands and conditions offered them were suitable. A large majority of the Indians were naked and protested against leaving a warm country for the cold of the West. To meet this objection Gadsden provided in the treaty for a blanket and a shirt for each of them on their arrival in their new home. The

14 Gadsden to Cass, June 2, 1832, OIA, "Seminoles"; *Document*, II, 752, 772; ibid., III, 263, 281, 368.

15 *Document*, III, 321, 538.

16 The agent was authorized to employ a physician to vaccinate the Indians against smallpox (Duvall to Cass, April 25, 1832, OIA).

government was determined that the Seminole should unite with the Creeks in the West, and they were told that their annuity would thereafter be paid to the Creeks and only by this union would they receive the small sum unconditionally promised them in the former treaty. Under this pressure a treaty[17] was negotiated at Payne's Landing May 9, 1832.

The deputation of explorers provided by the treaty, in charge of their agent[18] reached Little Rock aboard the steamboat *Little Rock* November 3, 1832; here they were furnished horses and left for Fort Gibson where they arrived a few weeks later.[19] They had no authority to make an agreement with any one, yet they were inveigled into entering into a compact, purporting to bind the tribe, with[20] the commission composed of Stokes, Ellsworth, and Schermerhorn at Fort Gibson March 28, 1833; in this the delegation were made to say that they were satisfied with that part of the Creek Nation between the Canadian river and the North Fork provided in the recent Creek treaty for the location of the Seminole, and with the favorable disposition of the Creeks to unite with them as one people. The Seminole treaty of Payne's Landing had recited that should "they," obviously meaning the Seminole Indians, be satisfied after examination to be made by their delegation, they would agree to remove; but in the treaty at Fort Gibson, this preamble was made to read, "should this delegation be satisfied," in order to commit them to something on paper that they had never even considered. The government then insisted that the treaty of Payne's Landing had become effective and demanded that the Indians prepare to remove to the West within the three years provided by the treaty. The effort to take advantage of the Indians by this duplicity brought on the second Seminole war.[21]

17 Kappler, *op. cit.*, II, 249.

18 *Document*, IV, 58.

19 *Arkansas Gazette*, November 7, 1832, p. 3, col. 1.

20 Kappler, *op. cit.*, II, 290; *Document*, IV, 540.

21 Major Ethan Allen Hitchcock when engaged in the Seminole War, noted in his diary: "The treaty of Payne's Landing in 1832 by which it was attempted to remove the Indians, was a fraud upon them and they have in fact never agreed to emigrate. I say therefore that the Indians are in the right to defend themselves in the country to the best of their ability."

The exploring delegation included John Blunt,[22] Charley Emathla, Holahte Emathla, and Jumper, who was also known as the "Sense-keeper" of the tribe; they were accompanied by their interpreter Abraham. While they were waiting at Fort Gibson for the arrival of the commissioners, they were taken on a buffalo hunt by the Creeks, and had an opportunity to learn of the marauding Indians of the prairies, who were to be their neighbors when they removed; so when the delegation returned to report to the tribe, they said they were pleased with the land, but they were violently opposed to being located near the bad Indians, the Wichita, Kiowa, and Comanche who were constantly engaged in stealing horses.[23] Jumper was indignant that the government proposed to locate them with rogues, as it implied that they, too, were dishonest.

There was much complaint of their conductor John Phagan, who maneuvered them into making the treaty at Fort Gibson; on their return to Florida[24] Phagan was removed from his office as Seminole agent for defaulting with funds belonging to the Indians. The Indians denied that the action of the delegation at Fort Gibson was binding on them and vainly requested their agent to call a council where the tribe could consider the report of the delegation. He refused and told them that as they had sold their lands nothing remained but for them to prepare for removal. The Indians realized that they had been tricked and being almost unanimously opposed to removal, made no effort to comply during the three years provided in the treaty of 1832 and the time of removal was extended three months longer.

There was an exception in the case of John Blunt the head of the Apalachicola band. He had been paid $3,000 when the treaty was signed and was to have $10,000 more when he removed his band. He agreed to emigrate at once but as the season advanced much sickness prevailed among the Seminole, and their departure was delayed. In time however, Blunt, Osiah Hadjo who was also called Davey or Davey

22 John Blunt was chief of one of the Apalachicola bands favored by the treaty of 1823 by exempting him from the number who were required to remove and allowing him to remain on a fertile tract of land where his home was located. He was an intelligent Indian who had served as guide for Andrew Jackson during the first Seminole war.

23 Thomas L. McKenney, Memoirs, 278; Document, IV, 154.

24 Document, IV, 190, 195.

Elliott, and Yellow Hair and their people were ready; each family loaded their effects into canoes and paddled down the Apalachicola river to the bay where they were placed aboard a vessel bound for New Orleans. It was known that a man named William Beattie who lived at Columbus, Georgia, was following the Seminole emigrants, seeking an opportunity to rob them; hoping to circumvent him their agent Wiley Thompson had directed the master of the vessel to land them fifty-six miles from New Orleans, but regardless of instructions the Indians had been brought close to the city. Thompson then took the chiefs to a bank and paid them $8,000 promised by the treaty[25] and urged them to depart at once; the agent then left for Florida.

Unfortunately while the Indians in their camp below the city were making preparations to leave, after the agent had departed, Beattie on April 8, 1834, filed a suit to enforce a fraudulent claim against them, secured an attachment for their persons and had them thrown into jail. Being ignorant of their rights, and threatened with confinement until the case could be tried months later, in order to obtain their release they paid Beattie $2,000 in money and delivered to him two slaves worth a thousand more. The Indians then ascended the Mississippi river "in their boats as far as Plaquemin, about one hundred miles from this place, thence down that Stream across the lakes into Bayou Teche, and up that Bayou to Opelousas whence they traveled by land to their place of destination" on Trinity river in Texas where lived an old chief, the uncle of Blunt, named Red Moccasin, who emigrated there many years before.

John Blunt and Davey Elliott had 276 followers of whom 35 died between the date of the treaty and the migration and fourteen died at Apalachicola bay. John Yellowhair was accompanied by twenty-one. Some deserted and only 152 in all actually emigrated. Blunt himself died soon after his arrival in Texas.[26]

25 Ibid., 648.
26 American State Papers, "Military Affairs," VI, 485.

FEAR of being compelled to unite with the Creeks and thus be subject to their government and control and entailing the surrender of a large number of their slaves to the Creeks caused the remainder of the Indians to oppose going west. When the government took from the Creeks in their treaty of 1821 $250,000 to compensate the people of Georgia for slaves claimed by them to have fled to Florida, some of the Creeks in turn determined to be compensated by the Seminole Indians and had been attempting since to take from the latter slaves whom admittedly they could not identify as the escaped property of either Georgians or the Creeks. Another influence against removal was that of the negroes themselves whose wishes and advice measurably controlled the action of the Seminole Indians.[1]

Among the white traders who infested the Seminole country was one Carlton Welborne who lived in Columbus, Georgia. With his confederates he planned to steal the twenty slaves belonging to the Seminole chief Econchattemicco, as well as that many more free negroes who lived with him on his reservation on Apalachicola river. Finding that the chief and his retainers were armed and prepared to defend themselves, Welborne and his associates succeeded in creating an alarm among the white people in the vicinity with the false report that the Indians were planning to attack them. Econchattemicco was a peaceful, guileless old man and a friend of the government; he and his people were easily persuaded to give up their arms as a means of convincing their neighbors that they meditated no hostilities. Welborne's crew then on March 1, 1836, came armed and easily captured the negroes on the old chief's plantation, and carried them off to

1 *American State Papers*, "Military Affairs," VII, 454.

Georgia. The United States court for the West Florida district indicted Welborne and eight other men on the charge of robbery and larceny, but the culprits made their escape and Econchattemico's subsequent petition for relief availed him nothing.[2]

These slaves had descended to Econchattemicco by an interesting rule of descent. An unsuccessful assault had been made on his title and possession through the machinations of the ubiquitous scamp Ben Hawkins, the Arkansas Creek Indian who was associated with Sam Houston in some of his ventures. In this instance Hawkins was operating with slave traffickers of Columbus, Georgia and Econchattemicco successfully invoked the jurisdiction of the United States court at Pensacola to defend his title. The court found that prior to the termination of the War of 1812, the universal law of inheritance among the Creeks and Seminole was that brothers first inherited in preference to children and all others, and then the sons of sisters; *"from the belief entertained by the Indians that a brother or a sister's son would be more likely to have the same blood with the deceased flowing in their veins than even the children of the wife of the deceased, although those children might be reputed to be the children of the deceased. . . . After the close of the late war, McIntosh, the Indian chief, procured the Indian law of inheritance to be altered, and under the new law children inherited in preference to brothers or nephews. Immediately on the alteration of the law, the alteration was made known to the lower Indians, and was agreed to in council."*[3]

The negroes in the Seminole Nation dreaded the *"idea of being transferred from their present state of ease and comparative liberty to bondage and hard labor under overseers on sugar and cotton plantations. They have always had a great influence over the Indians. They live in villages separate, and, in some cases, remote from their owners, and enjoy equal liberty with their owners, with the single exception that the slave supplies his owner annually, from the product of his little field, with corn, in proportion to the amount of the crop; and in no instance, that has come to my knowledge, exceeding ten bushels; the residue is considered the property of the slave. Many of these slaves have stocks of horses, cows,*

2   Ibid., VI, 461 ff. Blunt had been robbed by white men who came to his home in the spring of 1833 (*Document*, IV, 404).

3   Ibid., 536; *American State Papers*, "Military Affairs," VI, 468.

and hogs, with which the Indian owner never assumes the right to inter-
meddle.

"I am thus particular on this point that you may understand the true
cause of the abhorrence of these negroes of even the idea of any change.
And the indulgence so extended by the owner to the slave will enable you
to credit the assertion, that an Indian would almost as soon sell his
child as his slave, except when under the influence of intoxicating liquor."[4]

The date had been fixed for the Seminole to assemble at Tampa Bay
preparatory to board the transports for New Orleans on their way to
their new homes. It was January 8, 1836. Gen. Duncan L. Clinch had
been provided 200 soldiers with which it was supposed he could
handle the removal and he had notified the Indians that if they did not
come voluntarily, he would take them by force.[5] Lieut. Joseph W.
Harris was sent in October, 1835, to New York to engage vessels.
While there he advertised for bids to furnish 1,400 hunting shirts for
the men and 13,000 yards of "plaided woolseys" for the petticoats and
wrappers for the women.

Charley Emathla, one of the chiefs who signed the treaty at Fort
Gibson, Holahte Emathla, and other chiefs met their agent Wiley
Thompson in council in May, 1835, and agreed to remove to the West.
As the time approached, those opposed to removal became more bitter
and on November 26 as a warning to all against yielding to the government, Charley Emathla was killed by or through the agency of Osceola
(or Powell).[6]

Wiley Thompson, the Seminole agent, warned the Indians that if
they were not ready to embark at the time appointed, the troops would
be sent for them. Osceola blamed Thompson for the seizure of his
young wife who was carried off into slavery; he had a further grievance
from Thompson's having placed him in irons on a recent occasion. On
December 28 as Thompson and Lieut. Constantine Smyth were walking
just outside of the fortifications at the agency at Fort King, a band of
forty or fifty Mickasuki Indians under the leadership of Osceola fired
on and killed them both. They also attacked the sutler Erastus Rogers
in his home and killed him and his two clerks.[7]

4   Thompson to Cass, April 27, 1833, *ibid.*, 533.
5   *Ibid.*, 60.
6   Wiley Thompson report, November 30, 1835, OIA, "Seminole Emigration."
7   Harris to Gibson, December 30, 1835, *ibid.* "The Indians scalped their victims
and beat in their skulls" (*Army and Navy Chronicle*, II, 43).

On the same day six or seven miles north of Withlacoochee river near the Great Wahoo swamp a large party of Indians and negroes ambushed a company of troops who were proceeding under Maj. Francis L. Dade from Fort Brooke to Fort King to aid in the enforced removal of the Indians. Of that company of eight officers and 102 noncommissioned officers and privates, all were killed but three. No other troops ventured in the vicinity until the twenty-second of the following February, when the battle ground was visited by a detach- ment of men under Capt. Ethan Allen Hitchcock who buried the dead and wrote a graphic description of the scene.[8]

This bold challenge inaugurated the second Seminole war. Osceola wrote a letter of defiance to General Clinch in January, saying that if the general would only give him a few days for preparation he would be prepared to carry on a war for five years. "The letter is written in a style very concise, and quite characteristic of its daring and intrepid author. '. . .You have guns, and so have we—you have powder and lead, and so have we—you have men, and so have we—your men will fight, and so will ours, till the last drop of the Seminole's blood has moistened the dust of his hunting ground'."[9] Three days after the massacre of Dade's command, an engagement took place on the With- lacoochee river about forty miles from Fort King, in which thirty or forty Indians were killed by white troops.

To escape the fate of Charley Emathla, his followers of the "friendly towns" fled to the Tallahassee country and had scarcely settled down when they were forced to flee to Tampa Bay for protection; there were about 500 of them headed by the chiefs Holahte Emathla, Fukeluste Hadjo (or Black Dirt), and Econchattemicco. They all desired to emi- grate to Texas and join John Blunt's band, and they waited at the bay for protection and for the transports that would take them away from the hostiles of their tribe.[10] A number of their warriors joined the troops under General Clinch, to put down the uprising among the hostile elements; in their absence their families, destitute, hungry, and cold, some of them naked from their precipitate departure from their

8 Ibid., 55, 168; George A. McCall, *Letters from the Frontier*, 299; *American State Papers*, "Military Affairs," VI, 565.

9 *Army and Navy Chronicle*, II, 99.

10 *American State Papers*, "Military Affairs," VI, 61, 476.

homes, remained at Tampa Bay, panic stricken from fear of reprisals at the hands of the hostiles.[11]

Charley Emathla was one of the party that went to explore the proposed new home of the Seminole in the West. "He was a firm advocate of emigration; he spoke a little English and this faculty with his amiable, sociable countenance and manners, made him an object of interest to all the garrison. He was about 50 years of age, and about 5 feet 11 inches high—his frame was large and muscular. In council he discovered more foresight and common sense than any other of the Chiefs. He has left two or three very interesting daughters to mourn his loss; and now whilst I fancy them in their neat dresses and orderly deportment following their becoming father into garrison, and then think that that kind and beloved father is no more, I feel inclined with them to drop a tear to his memory.

"Oceola is an upstart in the nation; but one who has obtained his present high elevation by his energy and his talents. He was at one time in the employ of the garrison at Fort King, to inflict the penalties of the Indian law upon all those of his nation, who were found outside of their boundary. For a while it is said, he proved both vigilant and efficient; but then he became more and more relaxed in his castigations; was full of solicitations for immunity to the aggressors; and finally went over to the Micasoukies, as one of their sub-chiefs. Though he never took an open part in the National Councils, he was always believed to have considerable influence; he has an unbounded ambition, and I suspect, is second only to Jumper in determination and in vigorous intellect. He is a half-breed— is about 6 feet high, of a spare frame, and has a 'lean and hungry look.' At first sight you would suppose him feeble; but on a closer view, you will find him of a structure well knit and sinewy; his face is all vivacity, and marked as it is with the worn lineaments of incessant thought and ever active passions, it is strikingly expressive. In his salutations, he is full of smiles, exceedingly courteous, and hearty in the shake of the hand. I recollect once to have seen him on the piazza of the officers quarters, whilst Micanope, the ostensible chief of the nation, was closeted with General Clinch, in his office which opened upon the stoop. Micanope is a fat, lubberly Guloseton kind of a man, and is ever a stupid fool, when not replenished by his 'sense bearer,' (as he calls him) Abraham, who

11 Ibid. There were thirteen transports in the bay by February and Harris dismissed eight of them (Army and Navy Chronicle, IV, 347).

was on the present occasion absent. Oceola well knew this, and therefore, it was, that he betrayed the anxiety he did, to be near Micanope, to give him the proper que for a non-commitment. He would stand at the door apparently in the attention of an eaves-dropper; then he would be peeping into this and then into that window; ever assuming that peculiar air of curiosity, discernible only in the Indian. Becoming more and more impatient of his exclusion from the conference, he suddenly stalked across the stoop, jerked out his knife, and flourished it around his head with the most savage vehemence. Never have I seen a more striking figure than he presented at that time. Of a fine rigid frame— his costume as appropriate as it was striking, gave grace as well as dignity to his attitudes. On his head was a turban, garnished with two long drooping feathers— his hair of glossy blackness, fell in thick profusion around a face of the most beautiful variety of expression when unruffled; but now exhibiting a mixture of hate and unconquerable resolution. Couple these characteristics with his sturdy stride, his significant shake of his head, and his uplifted hand, clenching and flourishing with savage ferocity his knife, and you may form some conception of him as he then appeared to me.

"Oceola is not the chief of the Seminole, as some suppose. He is, as I have said before, a subordinate Chief among the Micasoukies. The nominal Chief of the nation is Micanope; though Jumper, who is exceedingly intelligent, and I suspect the most influential Chief in the nation, has always taken the lead in Council. Oceola, however, I should think the more active Chief as well as the better General; Jumper being now rather old. Oceola, I should say, is about 35 years old, and Jumper about 55. Oceola seems to have headed all the large parties in the late engagements. At the battle of the Withlacouchie, he is said to have been very conspicuous. He is reported to have used all his eloquence to encourage his men—ever and anon he was heard to cry out to them, not to flinch before the pale faces—that the river was between them and the enemy; and that there were but a handful of regulars. . .

"Oceola is a wonderfully shrewd man, as his politic conduct towards General Thompson will show. Thompson it would seem, proved a dupe in his beneficence to Oceola. I have been told that he had such a regard for the Chief, that when he went to Savannah to visit his family—he purchased a beautiful rifle for him; and there is but little doubt, if Thompson gave it to him, that that was the rifle Oceola used, when he added his bullet to the fifteen which passed through his benefactor. Are such men to be amused with attempts to excite their beneficence?"[12]

Regular troops and volunteers from surrounding states were ordered into Florida to put down the uprising. Gen. Edmund P. Gaines took command of 1,100 men including 700 volunteers at New Orleans and sailed with them in three steamboats on February 4, reaching Tampa Bay five days later. Accompanied by seventy-seven friendly Indians he marched through the country to Fort King and when he got there, finding there were no provisions for men or horses he hastily turned back and attempted to regain Tampa Bay. When about to cross the Withlacoochee river on February 27 his command was attacked by several hundred Indians under Osceola, Jumper and other leaders. Gaines's command were forced to fortify themselves and the Indians who increased to over a thousand, kept them in this situation for ten days, during which time their provisions gave out and they were obliged to kill some of their horses for food. A number of men were killed here including Lieut. James F. Izard. Finally the Indians proposed a truce and a conference was held with Captain Hitchcock, participated in by Jumper, Osceola, Mikanopy (Hulputta Hadjo, Crazy Alligator) Abraham, and Caesar, negro advisers.

The hostiles said they were tired of fighting and it was proposed that if they would withdraw below the Withlacoochee river and cease hostilities, the troops would pursue them no further. A formal treaty was to be considered later. They had agreed on these terms when General Clinch appeared with reinforcements and not understanding the conference, fired upon the Indians who fled thinking they had been betrayed.[13]

It was believed that the war was now over and many of the volunteers were returned to their homes in Alabama, Georgia, South Carolina, and Louisiana. Others with the regulars were retained in garrisons where much sickness developed with the coming of warm weather, until more than half were disabled, and many died. Some of the Creek Indian soldiers were discharged so they could remove to the West. The truce was observed for a while, but before long the burning of homes of the whites and killing the Indians were resumed. Marauding

12 Correspondence in *Newbern, North Carolina, Spectator*, February 26, 1836, copied in *Army and Navy Chronicle*, II, 197.
13 *Ibid.*, II, 201, 214, 226; III, 81.

parties of Indians scattered in small bodies, suddenly appearing out of the swamps and forests, attacking a home or exposed detachment of troops and as suddenly disappearing; and the soldiers were unable to follow or find them in their retreats. The families of the Indians had been removed far into the inaccessible swamps and it was impossible to engage any considerable number of warriors in action except in the "Battle of Micanopy" on June 9, in which about 200 attacked the post of that name.[14]

The outstanding results of the campaign were the failure to make any effective impression on the Indians; the charges and recriminations touching the situation; the castigation administered by Gen. Winfield Scott to General Gaines for his futile march to Fort King and an arraignment of General Jesup for a similar adventure to Fort Mitchell in the Creek "war" in Alabama; and his equally scathing characterization of the conduct of the white people of Florida as evidence of cowardice that increased the difficulty of protecting them.[15]

14 Ibid., II, 411.
15 Ibid., 378.

Lieut. Joseph W. Harris, at Fort Brooke, Tampa Bay, on April 11 and 12, embarked on transports 407 of Holahte Emathla's friendly Indians including Fukeluste Hadjo (or Black Dirt) his confidential chief, and his family, and arrived with them at New Orleans on the twenty-third.[1] The Indians were there placed aboard a steamboat and a keel boat in tow and arrived at Little Rock May 5, numbering then only 382, twenty-five having died on the way. The mortality "*resulted from the perversity of the Indians in adhering to their own peculiar treatment of the sick; which being confined to frequent deluging the patient with cold water, & to a constant kneading of the body, terminated—inasmuch as the diseases consisted of coughs, slight disentaries, &c—almost invariably in death. And this could not be obviated, although after having exhausted advice, entreaty and expostulation, we resorted to watching, threats and force.*"[2]

Harris was too ill to accompany the party farther and after resting near Little Rock two days, the Indians in charge of Lieut. George G. Meade[3] were reëmbarked on the steamboat *Compromise* and a keel boat in tow on May 7 and started up the river.[4] Two days later the rapid decline in the stage of the river compelled the conductor to put the Indians ashore at McLean's Bottom a few miles below Fort Smith, where wagons were procured to take them overland. Lieut. Jefferson Van Horne was sent to relieve Lieutenant Meade and conduct the Indians to their destination. He reached their encampment on the thirteenth, he relates in his journal,[5] and found that seventy-eight of the party were ill.

1 Harris to Gibson, April 25, 1836, OIA, "Seminole."
2 Ibid., May 11, 1836.
3 Who afterward became Major general Meade of Civil War fame.
4 *Army and Navy Chronicle*, II, 348.
5 Van Horne's *Journal*, June 5, 1836, OIA, "Seminole Emigration," File 67.

"In this state of things, guided by the Doctor's opinion that the party were unable to travel, Lieut. Meade who had charge, was delaying. As the Teams, Agents, &c., were waiting at a heavy expense, and as it was the Doctor's opinion that the Measles would run through the whole party, and the sickness was likely to continue on the increase for some time rather than to diminish, the more especially as it was understood they would not submit to the Doctor's prescriptions; and their proximity to the river enabled them to bathe the sick constantly in cold water, which was sending them rapidly to the grave; as their camps were very filthy, and the people in the neighborhood were complaining of their destroying their timber, and as it appeared to me they would be as likely to improve in health by traveling slowly, as by laying in a pollutted camp, I thought it best to urge an immediate departure. Besides the Indians, there were two Waggon Loads of Indian Goods to transport. Lieut. Meade had directed the employment of Twelve Waggons, eleven only were procured. I issued Four days rations of corn, and started the party four miles in the evening. On account of the great number of sick, and the great quantity of surplus Corn and Meat, these Indians had accumulated, their stubbornness and obstinacy, and unwillingness to move, I was obliged to leave four Waggon loads behind, and return for them, taking up two loads in the evening and two the next morning.

"May 15th. It rained heavily. After getting up the sick, we started about Eleven O'Clock, though with great difficulty on account of the great number of sick and dying among whom was the son of the Principal Chief, very low. We placed the sick in the Waggons ourselves, and in spite of every effort were obliged to leave a load behind. We made six miles. It rained all day. Roads bad; two of the party died.

"May 16th. It continued raining heavily. The Indians begged for the sake of the sick, of whom there are from one hundred and thirty to one hundred and fifty, many very low, that I would not move today. We had every difficulty to contend with, in the way of rains, bad roads, sickness, unwillingness to move, and the degree to which those people seem to have been humored, petted, and pampered. Teams loaded with corn and flour, great quantities of which they wasted or left on the way. They desired not to travel until the sick were recovered. We were every day using efforts to get additional Teams, but thus far without success.

"May 17th. It continued raining. At length we obtained an additional Waggon, and brought up the sick from Camp. People indisposed to moving.

Great numbers very sick. They begged not to be moved in the rain. A principal Man very low, they begged me to let them stay till he died and was buried. He died and was buried.

"May 18th. Started at Nine O'Clock. Made ten miles to the commencement of a prairie, where we were obliged to encamp at three O'Clock, as we could find no encamping place for Ten miles farther. Issued beef.

"May 19th. It rained powerfully. An Indian Doctor (Hotulgee Yohola), a principal man, dying. All the Chiefs were very urgent to remain until he should die and be buried. All joined in the request and evinced such unwillingness to go, that I thought nothing but force would start them; I wished to leave that as a last resort.

"May 20th. Started at Nine O'Clock, made 10 miles to the Vache Grasse.[6] Continued raining. Part of the road very bad. Many of the Teams mired down constantly, and we were compelled to haul the Waggons through deep mire for long distances with ten yoke of oxen to each. We continued at this with five teams in rear, until late at night, trying in vain to get them out of the swamp. They remained two miles in rear until morning of

"May 21st. When we hauled them out by main force. It rained every day powerfully, the Streams very full, roads miry. We passed on to Camp; and as our Oxen and drivers were worn out and exhausted, we stopped at Barlins', five Miles, at four O'Clock at a good encamping place convenient to good water and wood. Issued Beef.

"May 22d. Started at Nine O'Clock. Made ten miles to Poteau River. Road boggy in places—Poteau not fordable, obliged to travel without a road two and a half miles through the woods and ferry over it. I rode forward and made an advantageous agreement for crossing our party at the ferry at a reduced rate. An Axel tree gave way one mile short of the Poteau, Waggon detained; it joined our party at the Agency. Occupied until dark crossing Waggons over Poteau; broke the boat and unable to cross four teams until morning. The party encamped early in the afternoon. After dark a Choctaw introduced a Gallon of Whiskey into Camp, which I took from him. He had escorted two Seminoles to a Store at Fort Smith; each of the three had bought a Gallon of Whiskey. In the morning I found the same Choctaw with two Bottles of Whiskey in our Camp. I took them from him and poured the Whiskey

6   Vache Grasse, a creek about fifteen miles southeast of Fort Smith.

on the ground. This was the only occasion on which Whiskey found its way among the party while under my charge.

"May 23. Making Axel tree and repairing the Boat detained us. Started about ten O'Clock, reached the Choctaw Agency, nine miles, about three O'Clock, except three Waggons (including the one which had broken its Axel tree) which arrived at dark. I intended going three miles further, but the Superintendent said he had been delaying his journey to Red River two or three days, to have an interview with the Seminoles, and recommended me to encamp at his Agency for the purpose. Issued Corn in the evening.

"May 24th. It rained heavily last night. Three died in the morning, Black Dirt's wife and daughter and Tustenuggee Harjo's principal warrior; others very low. Having heard they were to have a talk, they dressed themselves in the morning, and nothing could induce them to omit it. They urged on the Superintendent the great number of sick, the Dead and unburied, others near their end; that their effects were soaked with rain; the sick suffering from exposure to it. The Superintendent thought the circumstances rendered it necessary to lay by for the day and asked if I did not think so also. I told him it was not for me to dissent from his opinion, but that this had been the language and the posture of affairs each day since I took charge; that each day, I had equal, nay superior difficulties to combat with, and that at no time on our journey had the morning opened with so fine a prospect of a good day's journey; and conjured him to give his influence in urging them forward so soon as he was done talking with them.

"I then retired until his talk was closed; when finding that they were pitching their Camps with the fixt purpose of remaining at least for the day, I very reluctantly yielded. It rained very powerfully during the after part of the day and the night. Some one ready to breed trouble had put Black Dirt up to require of me Coffins and burial for his Wife and daughter; this had been done for them on the water; myself and Mr. Chase were obliged to expose ourselves to a soaking rain to effect this.

"May 25th. Wet Morning. Found it difficult as usual to start them. We made about five miles through the rain, which fell in a constant torrent. The earth covered with water, thus becomes so soft that our Waggons mired at every step. We were obliged to drag them in succession with Ten or Twelve Yoke of Oxen which we did until we got them all together at a small Creek at dusk. Every soul soaked with rain; some of the Teamsters shivering with Ague, the poor Indians suffering intensely. Some of our Waggons broke down, the Oxen were exhausted by floundering in the mud. The whole country one Quagmire.

"May 26th. Found it impossible to proceed. To attempt it is to exhaust ourselves and endanger the safety of the Indians, drivers and Oxen. Before us within a few miles are several impassible streams. Behind us the Poteau has cut off our supply of Beef; the contractor having toiled several days in fruitless efforts to cross our Beef Cattle. He drowned three today in the attempt. We are today making repairs to the Waggons. The Indians drying their effects. Myself and Mr. Chase broken down and exhausted by toil and exposure of preceding day and night, being soaked with rain.

"May 27th. Numbers very low and dying, several died. They again besought me to remain. I was obliged to return to the Agency and purchase Beeves at an exorbitant price as our own could not be crossed over the Poteau, & Indians were in want of Beef. Found Indians obstinately bent on remaining and that only force could remove them. Issued Beef in the evening.

"May 28th. After much difficulty in getting our Sick in the Waggons, being obliged to carry and lift them in ourselves, we started about Ten O'Clock. In crossing the Cache one Waggon upset. Roads boggy in places. Banks of stream very steep and difficult of ascent. Made fifteen miles to a good camping ground near the Sans Bois, which we had hoped by this time to find fordable, having had no rain for the last day or two. Found it out of its banks, rapid, and entirely impassable. During the night it fell about Seven feet. Contractor not come up with the Beef Cattle. On account of the Continual heavy rains and exposure, the sickness and mortality has increased ever since we started. From one, two, to three deaths per diem, we now have four. The effluvia and pestilential atmosphere in the Waggons, where some twenty sick or dying lay in their own filth, and even the tainted air of their camps is almost insupportable, and affects more or less those exposed to it. 15 m. "May 29th. Obliged to wait the subsiding of the waters.

"30th. Sans Bois still deep and rapid, so much so that the Indians with their usual perverseness were unwilling to cross, and we were obliged to take a Team one Mile, and let them see it cross over and return in safety before they would venture.

"According to the Contract made before my taking charge, the Teamsters were to subsist themselves and their Oxen. In consequence the Oxen turned loose to graze, were frequently astray in the morning. Such was the case this morning. As we were starting, a woman died, and her relations desired to wait and bury her. These things delayed us and we were late in starting. The roads were deep in places, so that we had frequently to double our teams, and the crossing of the Great and Little Sans Bois so bad, that notwithstanding all my cautions to the drivers to be careful, two of the Waggons overturned; one at each of these streams. We encamped on the Bank of the Little Sans Bois, about half an hour before sun set, having made five miles. Issued Beef.

"May 31st. I was obliged to hire a driver in place of one whose oxen were strayed off, and who had gone in pursuit of them. I had frequent and importunate applications from the Chiefs to buy Horses for them; Holahte Emathla and Tustenuc Harjo, Prncipal Chiefs were very urgent this morning. My private means would not admit of this; and I was ignorant of their public resources. Holahte Emathla was hauled in a Waggon today. Started about Ten O'Clock. One of the Teamsters sick. We had much difficulty to get his team along. Teamsters and all attached to the party seem more or less affected by the prevailing sickness.

"In the post oak woods the roads very deep, so that we had to double teams, and were often obliged to raise the Waggon Wheels from the mire with levers and other means, to get along. A Waggon overturned at the steep and difficult crossing of a Creek. While I was exerting myself to extricate the sick the Indians by concert quickly threw out the Sick and baggage from the other Waggons, before they could cross the Creek. We were thus obliged to stop short of our intended goal. We made eight miles. I rode on two miles to get information of the route. 8 m.

"June 1st. The Doctor who had given Holahte Emathla repeated portions of Calomel, pronounced him very sick. He said he expected to die in a few hours, and begged that I would detain the party until he was buried, or at least until morning. I told him that if he could not go with the party, that he had better remain with his family at a Choctaw house near by, and let the party proceed. All were unwilling to leave their chief, and represented the piteous condition of the sick. We remained and issued Corn and Beef.

"June 2nd. Holahte still low; and the whole renewed their request to wait another day for Holahte to die, pledging themselves to take him with them in the morning if he lived. I found that force only could move them as on yesterday; and they were so well provided with arms and ammunition and seem so intractable and stubborn, that such a resort might have been hazardous. They have all along thrown every difficulty in the way; and on my urging them, they said I might abandon them. This I did not wish to do, except in the very last resort. Their suffering condition and the number of Sick and dying was such that I deemed it best to yield to this delay rather than desert them. Since we left the Choctaw Agency they seem wilful and to consider themselves beyond the reach of restraint.

"June 3rd. Started at ten O'Clock; made Eleven Miles. Had several bad Creeks with Steep Banks to cross. Had some difficulty in finding the correct route. In some places roads almost impassable; obliged to Bridge and cut tree out of the way, and to select the best ground for our route, road miry in many places. In the evening we came to a deep and boggy Creek whose course we had to search for some miles to find a practicable crossing place. We were finally obliged to unload and haul the Waggons over empty; this detained us until morning.

"Holahte Emathla principal Chief died during the night. He was buried in the morning by his people on a handsome eminence overlooking the stream, one and a half miles from the Canadian. His body and his effects were encased in a strongly built wooden pile, built to the height of Five feet above the surface of the Earth. The neighboring ground was carefully cleared of grass and leaves, and a fire left burning near his head. He declared from his first attack that he could not survive. He was of pleasing manners, and good person, cool, crafty, and politic; he was wanting in decision, and could not be depended upon.

"June 4th. Started about nine o'Clock. The frequent recurrence of deep Creeks and ravines with abrupt banks obliged us to pursue a circuitous route. For the last few days we are obliged to hunt out open woods or make our own roads, as the Waggons cannot follow the little Horse trail which we follow with the assistance of a guide that I found it necessary this morning to employ, as we once missed our way. The tongue of a Waggon broke today which detained it until early next morning. We had two high, steep and very rocky hills to ascend today. Flies bad on the prairie. Some of the Waggons stuck fast repeatedly which detained them until near dark. Made Ten Miles.

"June 5th. Started at Eight O'Clock. We had much difficulty in ascending a very steep and Rocky Mountain. I rode on to the Canadian about Ten Miles and endeavored to find a ford. My guide could not find the way around a deep Creek putting in between us and the fording place. We could not understand the Indians living here[7] until our interpreter came up with the Waggons, when a Creek Indian told me he could show me the way over. As I was very anxious to get the party over on to their own Lands as soon as possible after so much delay; I mounted my horse and the Waggons followed us. The route soon became very bad, impassible; and while we were endeavoring to find a better one, the Indians apprehensive of danger in crossing this boggy river, and persevering to the last in their disposition to retard our progress and prolong the journey, were clamorous to have me encamp for the night, and commenced unloading and encamping.

"Finding on examination that it was entirely impossible to cross our Waggons, I caused them to be drawn up close on the bank where was a Spring of excellent water and a handsome encamping place. I immediately obtained two Canoes with which the party commenced crossing the river. I discharged the Teams, issued Beef and the Articles guaranteed by the Treaty. The party continues very sick. Three or four die daily. They continue in spite of all that can be said to them to bathe those in cold water who have the measles; and to press unmercifully the stomachs of all the sick whatever the disease be. I was desired by them to name the successor to Holahte as principal Chief. I told them that Eneah Thlocco, son of Holahte, had been very sick ever since I had joined, and I could not therefore judge so well of his fitness or indeed of the fitness of others, as they themselves from my short acquaintance with them, and urged them to make the selection themselves agreably to their usages. Eneah Thlocco was appointed principal Chief. Fukeluste Harjo or Black Dirt is the most able and influential Chief. 10 miles.

"Although we were told at McLain's Bottom that the distance to the Seminole Lands was but one hundred miles; we thus found the whole distance travelled by land 127 Miles through a Country unfrequented except by Hunters."

Of this party of 407, which on their arrival at Little Rock had been reduced by death to 382, twelve more died during the next week, and when Van Horne took charge of them May 14, there were but 370 left.

7 The unhappy emigrants have arrived in the Shawnee settlement on the south side of the Canadian river in the present Hughes county, Oklahoma.

Fifty more died during the terrible march of the next twenty-two days and Van Horne located on their new domain 320 of the original party of 407, an appalling loss by death of eighty-seven in less than two months.

This little band of Seminole Indians had suffered fearfully for their friendschip to the United States according to the sympathetic Lieutenant Harris: "*They have lost every thing. . . The wealth of the Seminole Indian consists in ponies, hogs, poultry, perhaps some peltries in hand, and in the fall and winter seasons a scanty store of maize, rice and roots. With the number of these—particularly of cattle & hogs, who roam at large over the range & through the hammocks for subsistence—he seems rarely to be acquainted. 'Many' or 'few' are terms sufficiently definite to his thinking to indicate the extent of his riches or poverty. . . The loss to which the claimants attached the greatest importance was that of their ponies.*

"*By reference [to his letters and journal] . . .you will read the history of this unfortunate band, reduced by disease and accident from some four hundred & fifty, to scarce more than three hundred strong—of their losses, their privations, their dangers, trials, troubles. Objects of the suspicion and hatred for more than a year past, of their fellow countrymen, most of them have led a wandering & anxious life, many of them driven from their homes. Their cabins burned; their property destroyed or driven away; their aged & their infirm made martyrs to their faith by the exposure, fatigue & privation of the wretched condition to which they were reduced—themselves alternately assailed by the persecutions, temptations, promises & threats of our enemies—& finally, persued & persecuted, their numbers fearfully thinned & many of the most loved & venerated laid cold by a cruel disease on their long & tedious journey to a distant and unknown land.*

" '*Holati-Emarthla!' a name that will never be breathed by those who knew him but with respect & love—a name which, had his destiny lain in a more favorable path, might have shown amongst those of the greatest & the best of the age in which he lived— their venerated chief, their father, guardian, friend; he who had been their prop & stay through the trials & afflictions of the past, & who was the anchor of all their future hopes— he too has been taken from them. The bones of the aged warrior repose in peace upon the banks of the Arkansas, [Canadian?] &, in the language* of an eye witness—'his disconsolate & broken hearted people' mourn over his loss at length in their too dearly found homes.

"Our country owes to his memory a debt of gratitude—liberally should it be paid to his bereft family & to his afflicted people. Instances of such integrity as his are rare indeed. His was the directing & controuling spirit that guided this little band along its mazy path—his the hand that bound them with the friendly tie & which watchfully held each link together; and his the heart at which the deadliest shafts were levelled. His virtues would have honored the patriot & the sage, & long & reverently should his name be cherished. . . How great must have been the fortitude which enabled these people to resist the many temptations which assailed them to abandon our cause—a cause at one time apparently to them so hopeless; and which exposed them to such imminent dangers & inconveniences both present and prospectively until they or their countrymen in arms should be annihilated."[8]

8   Harris to Cass, July 25, 1836, OIA, "Florida Emigration."

CHAPTER TWENTY-EIGHT / *Hunting the Seminole*
out of the Swamps

A MORE aggressive campaign was inaugurated by General Jesup during the following autumn and winter. Several thousand troops scoured deep in the Indian country, burning towns and destroying the stores of coontie root of which the Indians made bread;[1] killing hundreds of the cattle on which they subsisted; and capturing other hundreds of cattle and their ponies, the latter in many cases loaded with packs containing the sole possessions of these people, men, women, and children, now living like hunted animals, prepared to flee at a moment's notice; occasionally encountering small parties of the elusive enemy, a few score of whom were killed or taken prisoners. In these engagements the Indians and their allies fought with such bravery and coolness as to challenge the admiration and evoke tributes from the white soldiers and their officers.

At one little encampment *"the Indians took the alarm and plunged into a thick growth of palmettos and small trees immediately beyond their camp. The more advanced men of the party fired upon the Indians as they fled, and, it is thought, wounded one warrior; at the camp were found three pots of coontie and cabbage (palmetto cabbage) boiling on the fire; wooden spoons lying by, in a small wooden bowl, indicating preparations for a meal. A rifle, a bow and arrows, two shot pouches*

---

1 *Army and Navy Chronicle*, V, 41. "They take the [coontie] root which is something like a turnip in appearance, tho' longer and larger; they scrape off the exterior, pound it, completely mashing it; put it into a bag and drain off the liquid; the liquor settling leaves a substance at the bottom which is the proper flour, the water being poured off. The flour is washed two or three times, settling each time, the water being poured off. The powder finally is then used as flour" (Diary of Ethan Allen Hitchcock).

and powder horns, a tomahawk, two axes, scalping-knives, blankets, skins, besides several ornamental trinkets of silver and beads—etc., etc., were picked up in the camp, besides a large supply of coontie which was lying in a heap near the fire. Thus it is. The poor devils are driven into the swamps and must die next summer if not before, from the effects of being constantly in the damp, low, and foggy ground. And yet they will not go. . . There is a charm, a magic. . . in the land of one's birth.[2]

An army officer recorded in his journal in January, 1837: "A scout of mounted men and Indians, under Lt. Colonel Cauldfield, was sent out in search of the enemy, and at about 1 P. M. joined the main body, having killed the chiefs Cooper and We-a-Charley, the son of the former, and an Indian Doctor. They took sixteen prisoners, consisting of the families of the slain, and some negroes who were with them.

"My heart bled for two of the recent widows, when I saw them prisoners; they were on horseback, each with a little child on her back, and another at her breast; and when I remembered that the sun rose upon them with peace in their cabins, and in company of the husbands of their youth; but ere the noon had arrived, they were bereft and desolate, and their children fatherless. The grief and distress of these two female inhabitants of the forest were apparent to the slightest observation, and few could look upon them without pity and commiseration. . . Cooper was brother-in-law to Mikanopy and the immediate commander of the negroes, and conspicuous for his cruelties and courage. I saw his bleeding scalp in the hands of his conqueror, a Creek warrior—it was nearly oval in shape, about two and a half inches long by one and a half broad, and the hair formed two braids."[3]

Three days later they captured 300 head of cattle: "We also took 300 Indian ponies, some of which were loaded with dried beef, and the koun-tee root, which the Seminoles use for bread in place of corn which they used to raise in times of peace; this is sometimes called the cherry-briar root. . . The hostile chief Cloud, has long commanded the war party in the neighborhood of the Wah-hoo and the Withlacoochee, and has been aided by Osceola and the Mikasuki and other scattering desperadoes from all directions, who have attached themselves to the desperate fortunes of these men; both of these Indians have declared their determination to die

2   *Army and Navy Chronicle*, VIII, 220.
3   Ibid., 94.

on the soil that has for centuries furnished places of sepulture for the bones of their fathers; and where every hill and valley bears upon its breast the recollections of childhood and the attachments of early life; where their first-born has been nourished, and where the wives of their youth have followed them through all the windings of the dark forest."[4]

They had captured a negro named Ben, a slave of Mikanopy, who told the officers that Jumper and Abraham were in the neighborhood and would come in if they were sure of their lives. Accordingly on January 31, Ben was sent to Jumper with offers of a liberal treaty. Three days later Abraham came in with pacific messages from Jumper and Alligator whom he brought in on February 3. Their families were suffering, they were tired of fighting, and agreed to bring their chiefs to Camp Dade and make a treaty of peace.[5]

Accordingly, largely through the negotiations of the negro, Abraham, on March 6, 1837 at Camp Dade, a treaty was concluded between Jesup and the Seminole chiefs Jumper and Holahtochee (or Davy) claiming to represent Mikanopy [or Hulputta Hadjo]. By the terms of this treaty the Indians agreed to cease their hostilities, come to Tampa Bay by April 10, and board the transports for the West. The chief Mikanopy was to be surrendered as a hostage for the performance of their promises. However, to induce them to accept these terms, General Jesup was obliged to agree to the one condition that the Indians had insisted on from the beginning; and that was that their allies, the free negroes, should also be secure in their persons and

---

4 *Ibid.*, 154.

5 "Abraham who is sometimes dignified with the title of 'Prophet,' . . .is the prime minister and privy counsellor of Micanopy; and has through his master, who is somewhat imbecile, ruled all the councils and actions of the Indians in this region. Abraham is a non-committal man, with a countenance which none can read, a person erect and active and in stature over six feet. He was a principal agent in bringing about the peace, having been a commander of the negroes during the war, and an enemy by no means to be despised." When sent for by General Jesup "Abraham made his appearance bearing a white flag on a small stick which he had cut in the woods, and walked up to the tent of Gen. Jesup with perfect dignity and composure.

"He stuck the staff of his flag in the ground, made a salute or bow with his hand, without bending his body, and then waited for the advance of the General with the most complete self-possession. He has since stated that he expected to be hung, but concluded to die, if he must, like a man, but that he would make one more effort to save his people" (*ibid.*, IV, 378).

property; and "that their negroes, their *bona fide* property shall accompany them to the West."⁶

Though this treaty was made with only a faction of the tribe, the war was again believed to be over. Mikanopy came to Camp Dade March 18 and agreed to the treaty and said he was ready to go west. About 250 hostiles also assembled near the post prepared to emigrate. Osceola was not among them however, having *"folded his arms and walked away. If only half that has been said of this indomitable warrior be true, he is a most remarkable man. The war is believed to have originated, and been carried on, mainly by his influence with the savage brethren, and yet he is now discarded from their councils because he would not embrue his hands in the blood of his captives."*⁷

Jumper, Abraham, Alligator, and Mikanopy all came in. *"Alligator is a most sensible, shrewd, active, and jocose man, worth all the Indians I have seen. Jumper is in a decline from a pulmonary affection. He is a sensible man; but from the state of his health, and consequent low spirits, much disposed for peace. Abraham is a cunning negro, of good consideration with the Seminoles, and who can do more than any other. Micanopy is not the fat old fool we thought him, but certainly possessing good sense, and actually exercising regal powers. He was respectable in appearance with the council, his remarks evincing judgment, and his deportment suitable and comporting with his nominal rank."*⁸

Gradually through April chiefs and subchiefs were bringing detachments of their people in to Tampa Bay; among them was Cooacoochee (or Wild Cat) the "son of Philip the principal chief on the St. John's river. His influence is greater than that of his father. Gen. Jesup states that he is the most talented man he has seen among the Seminoles, and will no doubt be the principal chief of the nation."⁹ The Indians were bringing in their cattle and horses to be purchased by the quartermaster's department of the army. By the early part of May Osceola and Philip with several hundred of their warriors on the way to

6 *Ibid.*, 215, 220.

7 From *Pensacola Gazette* in *Army and Navy Chronicle*, IV, 220, 236.

8 *Ibid.*, 234. After their removal Mikanopy served his people well in helping them solve the problems of readjustment to their new environment, and died near Fort Gibson near the end of December, 1848 (*Cherokee Advocate*, January 1, 1849).

9 *Army and Navy Chronicle*, IV, 265; *American State Papers*, "Military Affairs," VII, 848.

Tampa Bay stopped near Fort Mellon to dispose of their cattle. It was observed here that the hardships of the war had been felt most by the women who seemed in a most depressed condition.[10] "They are the most destitute looking beings we have yet seen. Most of them are almost naked. They are a fine hearty looking set of fellows, and none look the worse for wear, except in dress. It would be difficult to starve them out; they came in with loads of coonty root, all prepared for making bread."[11]

The Indians were congregating in two large camps in the vicinity of Tampa Bay where they waited in a tentative spirit to test the good faith of the whites of whom they were suspicious. *"Parties visit the post to satisfy themselves of the sincerity of our troops; and being satisfied, go out to report to others. They draw rations, and procure articles of clothing. They say that their women and children are naked, and that they cannot bring them in till they have clothing for them, and that they are busy making up the materials they obtain in articles of dress."*[12] The Indians were as suspicious of the motives and intentions of the whites as the latter were of them; everything depended on winning the confidence of the Indians until all should come in and board the transports. Capt. John Page who was to have charge of the removal remained in one of their camps to gain their confidence.

They were long engaged in hunting and collecting their cattle in order to bring them in for sale before their departure; so that their arrival was delayed and they begged that the time for taking the boats be extended to autumn; this was refused by General Jesup but the long delay permitted the operation of sinister influences. White people honestly seeking the recovery of runaway negroes and other whites hoping to seize those to whom they had no claim, began clamoring for permission to enter the Seminole camps and settlements in quest of slaves. This was opposed to General Jesup's orders and would violate the express terms of the treaty under which the Indians came to Tampa Bay. Under the pressure of strong influence however, Jesup modified his orders so that whites were permitted to go among the Indians. They naturally took alarm and many of the negroes hastily disappeared; they in turn were followed by bodies of Indians and

10   *Army and Navy Chronicle*, IV, 282, 301, 313, ff, 329.
11   *Ibid.*, 330.
12   *Ibid.*, 348.

General Jesup regretfully reported that his hopes of ending the war, and the peaceful removal of the Indians had given way to misgivings. Jesup then ordered the Indians present to be enrolled so that they could depart by June 15 but they objected, saying they could not be ready before autumn. Becoming suspicious the general sent a detachment to their camp and learned that they had all left, including Mikanopy and Jumper. However, an epidemic of measles in the camp from which twenty had died was one reason for their leaving. But they were charged with having outwitted General Jesup by obtaining government rations for several weeks and securing immunity from attacks by the troops while they raised crops and prepared for futher resistance. It was discovered that Mikanopy and Jumper had been kidnapped and carried off by Osceola and other hostiles.[13]

The troops could not operate against the Indians during the sickly summer season, and General Jesup employed the time preparing for an autumn campaign. The services of the Creeks had not been a great success though near June 1, Paddy Carr and his band brought in 150 head of cattle and mules for sale, which they had captured from the Seminole. "*Paddy Carr is a dark Indian, about forty years of age, five feet eight or nine inches, handsomely proportioned, and muscular in his person, very intelligent in conversation, and has no doubt received a good education. He speaks our language with fluency, is correct in his deportment, and rather polished in his manners; the latter acquirements have obtained for him admittance into some of our most respectable families—he is fond of the society of the ladies, and looses no opportunity to visit them—in fact for an Indian, he is rara avis.*"[14] He belonged to the regiment of mercenary Creeks in the service of the United States. The Creek and white troops had captured and brought in 125 negro slaves, thirty-five of whom were returned to their owners and the remaining ninety, General Jesup sent to Fort Pike near New Orleans,

13   Ibid., 393. However, about eighty of them were placed aboard a vessel and carried to New Orleans where they were confined in the jail while awaiting transportation up the Mississippi and Arkansas rivers (*New Orleans Courier,* June 19, 1837, p. 3, col. 2).

14   *Army and Navy Chronicle,* IV, 379. Paddy Carr [Patrick Carey] married a daughter of Col. John Crowell, Creek agent; he named his twin daughters Ari and Adne. His portrait is included in the McKenney and Hall collection of Indian portraits. He did not emigrate with his tribe, but continued to live in Alabama.

pending further orders for their disposition. The Creek warriors suc-cumbed to the unhealthful surroundings;[15] they were discharged from time to time and sent to their people, the last of them sailing from Tampa Bay September 11 for Pass Christian to join their families.[16]

Efforts were now made to secure the services of Indians of other tribes to come to Florida and hunt the Seminole from their hiding places; orders were given by the secretary of war in July to recruit 400 Shawnee, 200 Delawares, 100 Kickapoo, 100 Sauk and Foxes, and 200 Choctaw, for that purpose. Shawnee and Delaware volunteers arrived at Tampa Bay in November, 1837; and by January, 900 Indian allies were assisting the white army in Florida.[17]

Through the summer a few stragglers came in and placed themselves in the custody of the troops. In preparation for an aggressive fall cam-paign, the secretary of war made a call for volunteers and General Jesup issued an order fixing the shares of officers and privates in the loot—slaves, cattle, and ponies, expected to be taken from the Seminole Indians.[18]

15 Ibid., V, 10; American State Papers, "Military Affairs," VII, 865. The Creek regiment included 450 warriors enlisted under Jim Boy. The command of the regiment was entrusted to Capt. John F. Lane, promoted to lieutenant colonel for the purpose, a graduate from the United States Military Academy, aged twenty-six years. Septem-ber 20, 1836, they boarded steamboats twelve miles below Fort Mitchell for Tampa Bay. After several skirmishes and the killing and capture of 500 head of cattle, the com-mand, numbering 690 Creeks and ninety white soldiers, arrived at Fort Drane October 19. Colonel Lane was ill of fever and hardship and complaining of a pain in his head, and when no one was watching he ran a sword through his right eye into his brain. His friends claimed his death was accidental. The Creek warriors, with Florida and other white troops, on November 21 took part in a difficult engagement in the Wahoo Swamp. For several hours in the early part of the action the Creek soldiers were sent in front to bear the brunt of the fight and their tribesman Maj. David Moniac was the only officer killed besides a number of privates of both races (Army and Navy Chronicle, IV, 8). Lieut. T. B. Wheelock, said to have been temporarily demented by the hardships of the service committed suicide by shooting himself with his rifle earlier in the year. Col. Julius F. Heilman and Capt. Lemuel Gates, besides many privates, died also at Fort Drane (Army and Navy Chronicle, III, 217, 281, 326).

16 Ibid., V, 236.

17 Ibid., 253; American State Papers, "Military Affairs," VII, 522 ff, 888. Gov. R. K. Call of Florida was at the head of the troops opposing the Seminole until December 8, 1836, when the command by order of the president was transferred to Gen. T. S. Jesup.

18 Army and Navy Chronicle, V, 171.

In September Jesup directed Lieut. Frederick Searle to go to Pass Christian and muster out the Creek warriors; then he was to go to New Orleans and procure funds with which to pay the Creeks for their services as slave catchers. "The chiefs and warriors who were actually in the field, and present at and aiding in the capture of the negroes are alone to receive any part of the sum allowed." Twenty dollars was to be paid the Creeks for each of the thirty-five slaves captured who was the property of a white person. The other negroes who were not known to belong to the whites but who nevertheless had been captured and confined at Fort Pike were to be sold by the Creeks to the United States as slaves for $8,000. Searle was commissioned to make the division of the reward intended for the Creeks. "The amount allowed for the Seminole Negroes will be apportioned as follows, viz: to the first battalion, five thousand seven hundred dollars, to the second battalion, two thousand dollars, and to the spy battalion three hundred dollars."[19] However, the Creeks refused to dispose of the negroes to the government, and they were saved to furnish material for discord, contention, and bloodshed in the western home of the Indians.

General Jesup not only assisted in launching the United States government in the slave business, but he impressed the smartest of his negro prisoners in his service. "*The Seminole negro prisoners are now all the property of the public. I have promised Abraham the freedom of his family if he be faithful to us, and I shall certainly hang him if he will not be faithful. . . The Creek Indians were entitled to all the Indian property they captured. I compromised with them by purchasing the negroes from them on account of the Government for which I agreed to pay them eight thousand dollars. . . I was also compelled to pay the Indians a reward of twenty dollars each for the negroes captured by them, the property of citizens.*"[20]

In September, though no depredations by the Indians had been reported, troops began scouring the country and on the ninth a detachment of 170 men led by a hired Seminole, surrounded a little camp containing the old chief Philip, his family, three warriors and women and children to the number of thirty-five whom the battalion brought in to St. Augustine. The disappointment of Jesup and every one else

19 Jesup to Searle, September 9, 1837, OIA, "Seminole Emigration," File J 153.
20 Jesup to Harris, September 25, 1837, *ibid.*

concerned over the situation was deep and poignant and this little exploit revived them so wonderfully that much jubilation was indulged in.[21]

Reports were received from Mikanopy, Jumper, and Alligator that they were willing to abide by their agreement to remove west, and General Jesup sent them word that they must be at Fort Brooke on Tampa Bay ready to sail by October 1. They thought the time too short and agreed to consult and communicate with him later. However, the impacable Mikasuki through their indomitable chief Abiaca (or Sam Jones) insisted that they were still at war and would on no account agree to leave the country.[22]

Nearly three weeks after the capture of Philip, his son Cooacoochee (or Wild Cat) came to St. Augustine under a flag of truce to consult his father about the future policy of his people.[23] Wild Cat expected to be permitted to return to his people but instead he was imprisoned with his father. However he was the next month released to carry messages to the Indians who were thereby induced to send in a number of negroes. Wild Cat returned according to promise and was again locked up in the fort.[24]

That which gave the greatest joy to the army officers was the capture of Osceola, resulting from Wild Cat's visit. Expecting to be recalled from his command for his failure to conquer the Indians, public criticism and chagrin rested heavily on General Jesup and he resorted to measures that he found it difficult to justify. The treaty made by him in March had been observed by the Indians as a treaty of peace. But there were points concerning their slaves and terms upon which removal was to proceed that were not understood by them. In response to messages carried by Wild Cat, Osecola and a party of his warriors

21 *Army and Navy Chronicle*, V, 200, 203.

22 Sam Jones was "represented as being a well set, neatly formed and perfectly finished small man, with locks white as the driven snow—aged and venerable, yet active as a hind, and intrepid as a lion, struggling for the home of his childhood and the grave of his forefathers. He was born in the Creek country" (*ibid.*, 382).

23 *Ibid.*, 236; "He was mounted on a spirited horse and attired in his native costume; he rode into town with a great deal of savage grace and majesty. His head dress was a plume of white crane feathers and a silver band. He is now confined in the fort with his father" (*ibid.*, 270).

24 *Ibid.*, 285.

about October 20, came to a point seven or eight miles from St. Augustine whence they sent word to General Jesup that they desired a conference. The general did not meet them, but instead sent General Hernandez who was directed first to charge Osceola with responsibility for failure to return stolen slaves according to the promise of an obscure chief with which Osceola had nothing to do, and then if his replies should not be satisfactory, as it was known in advance they would not be, to make that an excuse to seize him and his followers. After formal salutations a conference was begun and while it was in progress under the direct orders of General Jesup a considerable force quietly surrounded the Indians and at a signal closed in and made them prisoners.[25]

General Jesup had been the object of bitter criticism from many quarters for his failure to conquer the Indians or to achieve even a slight advantage over them and he felt that his violation of the trust implied by Osceola's seeking a conference with him would be condoned by the country. But when it was known how he had taken the intrepid chief, condemnation was almost as bitter in its denunciation of the means employed as it had been of his former failure. Jesup then undertook to placate his critics by detailing facts about the affair as mitigating the violation of his obligation to a trusting foe. In some quarters his explanation was accepted and he was acquitted of wrong doing for the reason, as one lame apologist said: "*However revolting the violation of a flag of truce may at first appear, yet when we reflect that the General was dealing with savages, who had once forfeited their plighted faith, and deceived him—that the interview was sought by them, and probably with the worst of motives—it is believed that he will not only be justified by public opinion, on the expediency of the measure, but will be commended for it.*"[26]

On November 9 General Hernandez returned to St. Augustine with fifty-three Indians and sixteen negroes captured by him; twenty of them were warriors including the eldest and youngest sons of King Philip. A general order was issued, heralding the success of the troops to "all the posts on the east of St. John's."[27]

25 *Ibid.*, 377.
26 *Ibid.*
27 *Ibid.*, 328, 329.

CHAPTER TWENTY-NINE / The Capture of Osceola

THOUGH the Cherokee Indians were deeply immersed in their own difficulties with the government, they were so moved by the greater sufferings of the Seminole that their chief then in Washington consented to attempt a mediation between them and the United States. The undertaking had been proposed by John H. Sherbourne, a special agent of the United States; whereupon the Cherokee chief, John Ross, named a delegation of Cherokee to go to Florida. Before entering upon their mission, however, Ross discussed the subject with the secretary of war, who gave it his hearty approval. Ross then on October 18, 1837, indicted a talk to the chiefs of the Seminole tribe, and this was conveyed by the Cherokee delegation consisting of Hair Conrad, Jesse Bushyhead, Thomas Woodward, Richard Fields, and the interpreter, Major Polecat.[1]

The Cherokee delegation proceeded from their Nation to Augusta, Georgia, where they met Sherbourne and with him on November 6 arrived at Charleston whence they sailed.[2] On their arrival in Florida they went to see General Jesup at his headquarters at Picolata, and the next day proceeded to St. Augustine, where November 10, the delegation accompanied by the commander of the fort visited the Seminole prisoners confined there.

1 "This was done at the instance of the Secretary of War" (*Army and Navy Chronicle*, V, 314).

2 *Ross Manuscripts*, belonging to W. W. Ross, of Park Hill Oklahoma. Said the *Charleston Courier*: "We have obtained a copy of the talk to be delivered to the Seminoles, and insert it below. It contains sentiments highly honorable to the influential Cherokee who penned it" (*Army and Navy Chronicle*, V, 331); here the "talk" is given in full).

"*Soon after, the whole procession, with the Cherokees in full costumes, arrived, and were formally introduced, by all shaking hands, etc. Benches were then brought in the great square of the Fort, and the Seminole Chiefs took their seats; the Cherokees sat facing them with Colonel Sherbourne on their right, and next to him sat Captain Brown, the General's aid, and all the other officers standing by, surrounded by about one hundred warriors, all dressed in full costume.*"[3]

One of the Cherokee delegation through a black interpreter delivered the talk sent by Ross and a reply was made by Coahadjo; at the end of these talks the peace pipe was smoked and the Seminole asked the visitors to go into the forests and see the warriors and try to induce them to come in and make ready to remove to the West, though Wild Cat warned them that it would be a dangerous mission. Osceola spoke briefly and said he was tired of fighting but he was too ill to say more.[4]

The Cherokee delegation remained here until the twenty-eighth; messages had been sent by the prisoners in the fort to the chiefs advising them to come in, and Mikanopy sent word that he thought he could induce many of his people to surrender, but he desired a conference with the Cherokee delegation. General Jesup gave his consent. Arrangements were then made and with Coahadjo as a guide the Cherokee delegation left Fort Mellon November 28, and penetrated the deep swamps and hammocks of Florida a distance of sixty miles; at Chickasaw creek they met the Seminole and Mikasuki chiefs and warriors in council, and delivered to them the talk prepared by Chief Ross; after reading and explaining it through the interpreter, the chiefs and warriors agreed to receive it in friendship as coming through their red

3 *Ibid.*, 364, 395. General Jesup addressed a letter to the Cherokee delegation saying that "The interview which has just terminated has been highly satisfactory to me and I appreciate fully the benevolent and humane motives which have impelled your chief to order, and you to undertake, the perilous enterprize in which you propose to engage" (Jesup to Fields, Conrad, Bushyhead, and Woodward, November 13, 1837, 1837, OIA, "Florida" File R. 1). Such missions were dangerous because the chiefs and warriors had decreed the penalty of death for Indians consenting to emigrate and for white or Indian emissaries seeking to confer with them on the subject. "From signs made in the sand, supposed to be made by Alligator, and which the Interpreter Abraham had seen, the latter gives it as his opinion that the Indians intend to war to the death" (*Mercantile Advertiser* (Mobile) January 8, 1838, quoted in *Nashville Union*, January 13, 1838, p. 3, col. 1).

4 *U. S. House Document*, No. 327, Twenty-fifth Congress, second session.

brethren the Cherokee with the utmost sincerity and good feelings, from their elder brother the secretary of war, who represented their father the president of the United States.

After smoking of the pipe of peace and other Indian ceremonies were concluded, Mikanopy the principal chief with Cloud, eleven other chiefs and fifteen or twenty warriors, agreed to accompany the Chero- kee delegation to General Jesup's headquarters to negotiate with him; they accordingly went under a flag of truce into the headquarters of the United States army at Fort Mellon where they arrived December 3.

A conference was held in which Mikanopy said he desired peace, and was ready to surrender and bring his people in for removal, but they were widely scattered by the warfare that had been waged against them and the necessary search for food, and he would need time to collect them. To this request General Jesup answered that he had been deceived many times by them and did not propose to be deceived again. He accordingly had his visitors imprisoned in the fort of St. Augustine and held as hostages for the surrender of their families to whom messages from the prisoners were sent with directions to come in.[5] Because the Indians had outwitted him General Jesup was not averse to violating the most elemental rules of civilized warfare. He wrote the secretary of war when he gave his consent for the Cherokee delegation to visit Mikanopy: "If the council have no other effect, it will cause the Indians, who are now much dispersed, to reassemble, when they can be more readily attacked."[6]

The Cherokee delegation were so mortified at appearing to share in the treachery by which the Seminole were trapped, that they begged for an opportunity to clear themselves with the captives; after several refusals one of them was permitted to go to St. Augustine and in the confines of the prison protested to the unhappy Seminole any guilty responsibility for their situation. Chief John Ross was so incensed and humiliated that he and his tribesmen should have been com- promised by the treachery of the whites, that he addressed an indignant

5 *American State Papers*, "Military Affairs" VII, 890; *New York Observer*, December 16, 1837, p. 3, col. 4; *ibid.*, December 23, 1837, p. 2, col. 4; *ibid.*, January 27, 1838, p. 4, col. 3.

6 Jesup to Poinsett, November 28, 1837, *American State Papers*, "Military Affairs," VII, 890.

*View of Florida Swamps in which the Seminole Indians
secreted themselves*

protest to the secretary of war in which he said: "*Under this extraordinary state of affairs it has become my imperious though painful duty, for the defense of my own reputation as well as that of the deputation who acted under my instructions for carrying out the humane objects of this mediation; also in justice to the suffering chiefs and warriors, whose confidence in the purity of our motives as well as the sincerity of the Government, by the assurance held out to them under your authority, in my talk, had thus placed themselves under the flag of truce before the American army. I do hereby most solemnly protest against this unprecedented violation of that sacred rule which has ever been recognized by every nation, civilized and uncivilized, of treating with all due respect those who had ever presented themselves under a flag of truce before their enemy, for the purpose of proposing the termination of a warfare.*"[7] In this and in subsequent letters, Ross who was in Washington, repeatedly pleaded with the secretary of war to release the Seminole captives.

General Jesup characterized the Cherokee mission as a failure, but said that the Cherokee delegation ". . . *acted with the most untiring zeal and earnestness in endeavoring to convince the misguided chiefs of the Seminoles and Mickasukies, as well as their own people, of the advantages of peace and the necessity of fulfilling their treaty engagements . . . they have acted throughout in perfect good faith and with sincere desire to serve you and our country, and to benefit the Indians by enlightening them in regard to their true interests.*"[8]

Wild Cat had made his escape from the fort at St. Augustine[9] and fled to his people whom he inflamed with news of his imprisonment after acting as envoy for General Jesup. The latter hurried his troops out in pursuit of the Indians. Col. Zachary Taylor at the head of about 800 regular troops, 180 Missouri volunteers, and seventy Delaware

7 *U. S. House Document*, No. 285, Twenty-fifth Congress, second session; this document contains an extended account of this affair; see also Joshua R. Giddings, *The Exiles of Florida* (Columbus, 1858), 166 ff. The report of the Cherokee delegation to chief John Ross, dated February 17, 1838, with footnotes by Grant Foreman, appears in *Chronicles of Oklahoma*, IX, 423.

8 *American State Papers*, "Military Affairs," VII, 891.

9 Visitors to St. Augustine are shown the room about twenty feet square in which the Indians were confined, and marvel at their exploit as they gaze at the small hole—the only one in the room—about eighteen feet from the floor, through which Wild Cat and his companion made their remarkable escape (J. R. Giddings, *op. cit.*, 167).

Indians proceeded from Tampa Bay to scour the country along the Kissimmee river. Jumper and his family and other Seminole and negroes to the number of about 250 surrendered to him.[10] In addition he secured 600 head of cattle and one hundred horses which seriously impoverished a considerable number of Indian owners. During this campaign Taylor captured in all 484 Indians and negroes.[11]

On Christmas day Colonel Taylor's command engaged near Lake Okechobee a body of Seminole warriors who were well concealed in a dense hammock surrounded by a swamp which separated them *"from the enemy, three quarters of a mile in breath, being totally impassable for horse, and nearly so for foot, covered with a thick growth of saw-grass five feet high, and about knee-deep in mud and water, which extended to the left as far as the eye could reach, and to the right to a part of the swamp and hammock we had just crossed, through which ran a deep creek."*[12]

The soldiers were obliged to proceed on foot through this swamp to a disastrous engagement with the Indians who had skilfully planned the setting for it. The loss of the attacking force was twenty-six killed and 112 wounded, a large portion of whom were officers. The bodies of ten Indians were found and it was learned that four others had been killed.[13] A month later another engagement occurred at a crossing on

10 Jumper and his party numbering sixty-four surrendered on December 19, arrived at Tampa Bay January 19, and immediately were placed aboard a vessel bound for Camp Pike near New Orleans (*Army and Navy Chronicle*, VI, 81).

11 *Ibid.*, VI, 51. Many Creek refugees who had fled from the terrors of Alabama had taken refuge among the Apalachicola Indians. By January 4, 1838, 136 of them had been collected. "They are nearly naked and have been starving ever since they left the Creek Nation. They have consumed what little provisions was in the neighborhood Towns, and all hands are now without provisions" (Smith to Harris, January 4, 1838, OIA, "Florida Emigration" File S 741).

12 This saw-grass on other occasions had cut the legs of the Delaware warriors so badly that they were forced to drop out. Taylor was brevetted brigadier general for his services in this engagement.

13 *New York Observer*, January 20, 1838, p. 3, col. 4; *Army and Navy Chronicle*, VI, 42, 43, 59, 69, 73, 76, 81, 154; *American State Papers*, "Military Affairs," VII, 985. It was in his official report (*ibid.*, 81) of this engagement that Colonel Taylor made reference to the Missouri Volunteers in terms that brought upon his head the censure of the people of that state, and provoked a long drawn out controversy in and out of Congress.

St. John's river between a force under General Jesup and a body of Indians in which seven soldiers were killed and twenty-nine wounded.

The Indian prisoners at St. Augustine were removed in the custody of Capt. Pitcairn Morrison and forty soldiers, placed aboard the steamer *Poinsett*, carried to Charleston and confined within Fort Moultrie on Sullivan's Island where an escape such as that of Wild Cat's could not be repeated. The party of prisoners included Mikanopy, Coahadjo, King Philip, Osceola, Little Cloud, 116 warriors and eighty-two women and children.[14] After being confined here about a month, these captives together with others to the number of 220, on February 22 were placed aboard the brig *Homer* in charge of Lieut. J. G. Reynolds and an escort of twenty-nine soldiers and on March 12 all but five who died on the voyage, were landed near New Orleans and confined in the barracks at Fort Pike.[15]

There was one of that company of Indians who was not able to leave Fort Moultrie with the others; that was the young chief Osceola who had been ill since before his capture. When the special agent Sherbourne was preparing the mission of the Cherokee Indians to the Seminole, he arranged with the artist George Catlin to visit the chiefs. Catlin arrived at Fort Moultrie January 17 prepared to begin at once painting the portraits of Osceola, Coahadjo, Little Cloud, and King Phlip and said that when his work was done he would *"hasten back with all speed to show the citizens of New York how these brave fellows look. . . Osceola is a fine and gentlemanly looking man with a pleasant smile that would become the face of the most refined or delicate female, yet I can imagine when roused and kindled into action, it would glow with a hero's fire and a lion's rage. His portrait has never yet been painted."*[16]

"Osceola seems to be in great distress of mind, and it is my opinion as well as that of the surgeon of the Post, that he will not live long in his present condition; he is losing his substance very fast, and when I left

14. *American State Papers*, "Military Affairs" VII, 891; *Charleston Courier*, in *Army and Navy Chronicle*, VI, 42. Cloud was commissioned a major in the Confederate army and was killed in the Civil War.

15. *Ibid.*, VI, 202; *Arkansas Gazette*, March 28, 1838, p. 2, col. 1; Reynolds to Harris, March 13, 1838, OIA, "Florida Emigration" File R 220.

16. *Missouri Saturday News*, February 10, 1838, p. 3, col. 3.

there he was upon the floor, without being able to stand or to speak. This however, was the result of a very severe attack of the Quinzy."[17]

The last day of his sitting for Mr. Catlin, Osceola was too ill to con-tinue. ". . .Mr. C. last saw him lying before a fire, both his wives being in affectionate attendance upon him. It was the artist's intention to paint the likeness of these two women, but the sickness of their chief prevented, all their time being required in taking care of him. . . His bold spirit took its flight on the evening of January 30. The papers say that his disease was an affection of the throat, but grief and mortification doubtless had their share in bringing him to his end. He died at Fort Moultrie, where he was confined. Every attention was paid him that skill and compassion could suggest, by the officers having charge of the prisoners."[18] Catlin reached New York January 30 with his portraits of five chiefs and five other Indians."[19]

By the latter part of February, 1838, General Jesup had brought his army to a point east of Lake Okechobee and erected a little post called Fort Jupiter. From here he sent out detachments to scour the swamps for Indians, but their service was not only well nigh fruitless, but was performed with great hardship and suffering.[20]

17 Catlin to Harris, January 31, 1838, OIA, "Florida Emigration," File C 535.
18 From *Commercial Advertiser*, quoted in *New York Observer* February 10, 1838, p. 3, col. 1; Capt. P. Morrison in command of the Indian guard sent to Maj. H. J. Hook Osceola's effects as follows: four black and two white ostrich feathers, large silk shawl used for head dress, a splendid belt made of ornamented beads, an Indian belt ornamented with beads, a blue guard made of beads, three silver gorgets, and a hair brush with a glass mirror on the back (*Army and Navy Chronicle*, VI, 234).
19 Catlin to Harris, January 31, 1838, OIA, "Florida Emigration," File C 535.
20 *Army and Navy Chronicle*, VI, 216. An army officer at Fort Jupiter wrote: "137 negroes were sent off to Tampa Bay day before yesterday—an accession to our Indian camp; Tuskegee gave a ball and invited the officers—they kept up whooping and yelling all night. . . When we left here about the 7th or 8th of last month to pursue the Indians on their trail south, one of the soldiers was taken sick two miles from this place, and ordered back. On the return of the army, he had not reached here, nor had he been heard of. He had two days' provisions in his haversack when he was ordered back. On the evening of the nineteenth day from the time that he left the army, he was brought in by an Indian, who found him about twelve miles north, asleep at the root of a tree. The savage waked him up much to his alarm, and as he was nearly exhausted from fatigue and exposure, the Indian took his musket, accou-trements, and knapsack and brought them safe to camp. The soldier had reserved a biscuit and a half, and a small piece of meat, which the savage although nearly starved himself, did not molest. The soldier appears to have kept a diary on the first days of

At times the soldiers could not even carry their cartridge-boxes. They were compelled to deposit them, with their muskets, in light boats, which they pushed before them through the mud for many miles.[21] "*You have no conception of the manner of our living in the field*" wrote an army officer; "*we scarcely have transportation enough to carry the pork, bread, and coffee, which alone comprises our bill of fare and the blanket which shields us from the storm. Yet amidst all this, our troops, often barefooted, and their pantaloons cut off as high as the knee with the saw palmetto, press forward in defense of their country and in checking the depredations of the savage upon the inhabitants of this region whose presses teem with abuse upon the army now serving in the Territory. The officers are alienated from home, kindred, and friends, and com-pelled to remain in this inglorious war, defending a domain which can never be densely populated, and protecting some of its inhabitants who would suffer much in comparison with the savages.*"[22]

The officers were disheartened, discouraged and sick of the service and longed to get out of the country. On February fifth Gen. Abram Eustis urged Jesup to end the war by a truce with the Indians by which they would be left in the southern part of Florida. The next day Col. David E. Twiggs and a committee representing all of the superior officers of his command came to the general and joined in the prayer of Eustis. The officers were united in the opinion that they could never conquer the Indians in the swamps and Jesup agreed with them. He thereupon called into requisition the strategy he had employed in the capture of Osceola, Mikanopy, and others. By a Seminole negro he sent word to the Indians to come in for a conference. Soon "*General Eustis reported to me that several Indians were waiting for me with a flag of truce in advance of a cypress swamp in front of the army. I met them: a young chief Hallec Hadjo conducted the conference on their part. He spoke of the wretched condition of the Indians, and of their ardent desire for peace; but declared that the greater part of them*

---

his peregrination, on the blank leaf of his Bible, the style of which was somewhat like that of Jeremiah's Lamentations (*ibid.*, 217).

21 *Ibid.*, VII, 53. Another expedient was to suspend their burden from a pole carried on the shoulders of two soldiers.

22 *Ibid.*, 105. At times officers could not be distinguished from their men for they had all grown long beards and were equally dirty and black from the smoke of their camp fires in which they sought refuge from the mosquitoes (*Hitchcock Diary*).

wished to remain in the country; that they would thankfully receive from us any part of it, however small, that we might think proper to assign for their residence." The next day Jesup conferred with their principal chief Tuskegee and it was agreed that the Indians would assemble within ten days near Fort Jupiter and wait there while the general communicated with the president to learn whether they might remain in Florida.[23]

General Jesup then took the next step in what was to result in peace or a treacherous conquest of some of these harried people. The 8,000 troops employed in Florida through the winter campaign had achieved a pitiful measure of success against the Indians. Jesup and his whole army were under fire of criticism and he was ready to admit defeat. He wrote the Secretary advising the abandonment of the war. "*In regard to the Seminoles, we have committed the error of attempting to remove them when their lands were not required for agricultural purposes; when they were not in the way of the white inhabitants; and when the greater portion of their country was an unexplored wilderness, of the interior of which we were as ignorant as of the interior of China. . .*

"*As a soldier, it is my duty, I am aware, not to comment upon the policy of the Government, but to carry it out in accordance with my instructions. I have endeavored faithfully to do so; but the prospect of terminating the war in any reasonable time is anything but flattering. My decided opinion is, that unless immediate emigration be abandoned, the war will continue for years to come, and at constantly accumulating expense.*"

He proposed that the Indians in Florida be permitted to remain, provided they were confined to the country from the Kissimmee river and Lake Okechobee southward to the end of Florida; and that the Indians who were confined at Charleston and New Orleans be taken to the new country west of Arkansas.[24] The secretary of war found the suggestions of Jesup's letter very interesting but said that he was powerless to suspend the operations of the policy of the government; however, he gave Jesup some latitude in making a temporary truce with the Indians, but directed him to drive out or destroy the hostiles who had depredated on the settlers.[25]

23 Army and Navy Chronicle, VII, 52.
24 Jesup to Poinsett, February 11, 1838, ibid., VI, 177.
25 Ibid., 178.

Exasperated by the facility with which the Indians eluded him, chagrined by his failures and the criticism poured on his head from all quarters, Jesup improvised ways to cope with his agile enemies fighting desperately for their homes and families. If the Indians had outmaneuvered him he must find a way to trick them. In the warfare he was waging against the Indians and negroes he construed all the rules of war against them strictly and for infractions he imposed penalties conceived by himself.

So-called treaties between Jesup and certain chiefs of the tribe through the medium of the negro Abraham and others, which had never been dignified by ratification by the Senate were used by Jesup to impose certain obligations, pains, and punishments on all the Indians whether they were parties to them or not. The whites had violated the security guaranteed to the Indians in the possession of their slaves after they had come in for removal, and Jesup would give them no assurance that if they removed they would not be placed under subjection to the Creeks who would take their slaves from them. The Indians returned to their swamps and whenever expediency could be served, Jesup declared that they were violators of paroles and had thereby forfeited all rights that attached to a flag of truce and all other rights that it was convenient to disregard.

Jesup had the Indians at Fort Jupiter in his power and giving as an excuse a rumor that their slaves would join their masters if hostilities broke out again, he told them that their slaves "must be separated from them and sent out of the country. On the 27th of February, I sent off a party of Indians and negroes to Tampa Bay on their way to the west." This however was not unusual as he had on other occasions separated the negroes from the Indians when captures or surrenders had occurred, and he had sent the negroes to Tampa Bay and to New Orleans to be looked over by slave traders before sending them farther west.

Jesup received the reply of the secretary of war on March 17 and two days later he called a council of the Indians. Having received an intimation that all was not well the Indians refused to attend the council and made preparations to leave and retain their liberty. Jesup was too quick for them however and ordering out his troops captured all those in camp and those who had left. "Five hundred and thirteen Indians were secured on the 21st and two succeeding days, which, with a hundred and sixty-five negroes that at different times were taken and sent to Tampa Bay, made an aggregate taken at Jupiter of six hundred and seventy-eight."[26]

Jesup then on March 24, 1838, sent Abraham and Holahtochee to General Taylor with word of his success and messengers carried to Alligator and his band on the west side of Lake Okechobee news of their disaster with the result that that chief and his band of 360 Indians and negroes of whom one hundred were warriors, gave up the fight and surrendered to General Taylor.[27] They were then marched to Tampa Bay and encamped under the surveillance of the troops. Here they were kept for more than two months convenient for slave traders to come and look over the negroes. But on June 4, the anniversary of the escape of Mikanopy, Jumper, and their people, Alligator's company attempted a similar escape. A dance had been held all day and at night it was attended by the officers. After they had returned to their quarters "the Indian drum was yet beating in the 'white feather' when the alarm was given in camp that the *Indians were going off!* The troops turned out and prevented all but 30 from escaping. The whole party except Alligator was the next morning put on board vessels and sent to New Orleans."[28]

Maj. J. C. Clark at New Orleans reported April 6, 1839 that "yesterday eleven Seminole Indians arrived here from Charleston; three chiefs in irons." And because he had no instructions, the facetious officer added "I don't know whether to shoot or hang them." Six straggling Creeks from St. Andrews, Florida arrived on July 4. A schooner from St. Augustine brought him forty-eight more captive Seminole Indians. They were put ashore at New Orleans and Clark

26 *Ibid.*, VII, 53.
27 *Ibid.*, VI, 332; Freeman to Harris, March 24, 1833, OIA, "Florida Emigration," File 61.
28 *Army and Navy Chronicle*, VII, 44. *American State Papers*, "Military Affairs," VII, contains many pages of official accounts relating to the campaign in Florida and the hostilities in Alabama. "White Feather" was the name of one of the dances of the Seminole and Creeks. One hundred sixteen Seminole captives arrived at their western home in charge of William Neilson June 19, 1838, and sixty-six more August 5 in charge of Lieut. J. W. Reynolds. These included thirty-four negroes that had been held in jail in New Orleans pending efforts by white people to take possession of them. Two hundred seventy-two Seminole and negro captives arrived January 10, 1839 and 204 more April 13.

reported that he would "keep them in barracks and wait for instructions." On August 26 fifty-four Seminole prisoners, men, women, and children captured in Florida were confined at Charleston in a destitute condition.

General Jesup was recalled from the command of the Florida army and he made a long and interesting report of the campaigns in which he had engaged.[29] He summarized as follows: *"The number of Indians and negroes altogether, who surrendered or were taken by the army, from the 4th of September, 1837, until I left Florida, amounted to 1,978, twenty-three of whom escaped, leaving 1,955 actually secured; I estimated the killed at thirty-five, though I am confident from the admission of the chiefs, that with those who died of their wounds, the number of killed was much greater. Of this number killed and taken, the warriors, or those capable of bearing arms, exceeded six hundred.*

"From the time I commenced operations, in December, 1836, to the 4th of September, 1837, the number of Indians and negroes killed and taken by the different detachments of the army, were equal to about four hundred, over a hundred of whom were warriors or men capable of bearing arms.

"The villages of the Indians have all been destroyed; and their cattle, horses, and other stock, with nearly all their other property, taken or destroyed. The swamps and hammocks have been every where penetrated, and the whole country traversed from the Georgia line to the southern extremity of Florida; and the small bands who remain dispersed over that extensive region, have nothing of value left but their rifles."

29 Jesup to secretary of war, July 6, 1838 (ibid., 49).

CHAPTER THIRTY / Seminole Captives Deported

JUMPER and his people were confined in the barracks at Fort Pike near New Orleans with other captives awaiting transports to take them to their western home; more than one hundred of them were ill and on April 18 occurred the death of the distinguished chief Jumper who for a long time had been dying of consumption. He "was buried in the afternoon. In his coffin were placed his tobacco, his pipe, his rifle, and other equipment according to his people's custom. The military and a number of citizens attended his funeral, which was conducted with all the honors of war."[1]

By May 1, 1838 there, were a thousand Indians and negroes at the New Barracks near New Orleans awaiting transportation up the Mississippi and Arkansas rivers and more were coming from Tampa Bay. Half of those present in the barracks were ill and the number was increasing daily; the Indians were discontented and unhappy from long confinement and eager to be on their way; suitable boats for their transportation had been difficult to obtain.[2] On May 14 Lieutenant Reynolds reached New Orleans from Tampa Bay with

1 From a New Orleans paper quoted in *Arkansas Gazette*, May 9, 1838; *Army and Navy Chronicle*, VI, 297. Jumper claimed to be descended from two Yamasee Indians, the sole survivors of a band of that tribe driven by the Creeks on an island in the Everglades, where all perished but these two. Alligator also claimed to be descended from the Yamasee.

2 Clark to Harris, May 1, 1838, OIA, "Florida Emigration," File C 652. Eight Spaniards and 129 Indians from "Bunce's Rancho" were brought from Tampa Bay to New Orleans on April 5 and four days later another party of three Indians and eighty-five negroes came. A week later they were joined by two parties of captives from Indian river aggregating 350. Early in May the schooners *Caspian* and *Randolph* arrived at New Orleans with twenty-six Indians, seventy-nine negroes and two Spaniards; on the thirtieth they were joined by forty-two more negroes from Tampa Bay.

another party of Indians and negroes that brought the total awaiting transportation up the river to 1,160.[3]

In charge of Lieutenant Reynolds, the chiefs Mikanopy, King Philip, Little Cloud, and Coahadjo, and the other captives at New Orleans, were embarked on two steamboats, 453 aboard the *Renown*, which departed May 19, and 674 on the *South Alabama* which sailed three days later. Nearly one third were negroes who had been reared among the Indians.[4] Seven Spaniards of the party who objected to going farther were left upon their promise not to return to Florida until the close of the war. Reynolds on the *South Alabama* reached Vicksburg the twenty-sixth and reported that since he had taken command of the party there had been forty-seven deaths and five births.

The *Renown* reached Little Rock May 26 and passed up the river the same night, but because of low water could not ascend more than one hundred miles farther.[5] "*Among those who have gone up are about 150 Spanish Indians or Spaniards who have intermarried with the Seminoles. Take the whole party as a body, it is the most dirty, naked, and squalid one that we have seen. Armed sentries and U. S. soldiers were stationed in different parts of the boat, and not one Indian was permitted to step ashore during the few hours the boat laid at our landing.*"[6] The *Gazette* did not explain that the appearance of these unhappy wretches was in a large measure due to the fact that they had been hunted out of the fastnesses of their native country like wild animals and had been herded aboard the boats with no opportunity to secure and bring with them their meager personal belongings.

Ninety negroes represented the loot taken by the Creek mercenaries who served in Florida. They had been carried to Fort Pike to wait further disposition. During their stay here of more than a year fraudulent claims to them were made by slave traders of Georgia and Florida. Finally James C. Watson, a slave trader of Georgia, purchased the slaves from the Creek owners for between fourteen and fifteen thousand dollars. Watson then commissioned his brother-in-law, Nathaniel F.

3 Reynolds to Harris May 15, 1838, OIA, "Florida Emigration," File R 246.

4 *New York Observer*, June 30, 1838, p. 3, col. 5; Reynolds to Harris, May 21 and 26, OIA, "Florida Emigration."

5 Reynolds to Harris, June 2, 1838, OIA, "Florida Emigration," R 275.

6 *Arkansas Gazette*, May 30, 1838, p. 2, col. 1.

Collins, to go to New Orleans and secure the negroes. Gen. E. P. Gaines then in New Orleans undertook by recourse to the courts to prevent the carrying of the negroes into bondage, but he received little encouragement from the court. The Seminole Indians were owners of most of these negroes and bitterly protested against departing from New Orleans without them; and their delay at New Orleans and resultant deaths during their confinement in the barracks were attributable in a measure to the efforts to deprive them of their negroes encouraged by the government.

After much controversy Lieutenant Reynolds succeeded in embarking most of the negroes with the Seminole with whom they had been reared and proceeded up the Mississippi river. Collins who was absent at the time of their departure pursued and overtook them at Vicksburg. Here he exhibited to Reynolds an order from the commissioner of Indian affairs directing him to deliver the negroes to Collins. The Indians objected strenuously and Mikanopy protested that the effort to take their negroes from them was a violation of the express agreement made by General Jesup.

As Reynolds had not a sufficient force to compel the surrender of the negroes, on their arrival at Little Rock, on June 3 he requested the governor of Arkansas to use the power of his office to effect the transfer. After due consideration of the matter the governor declined to comply with Reynold's request.[7]

The river continued falling so fast that Reynold's boats were unable to ascend higher than seven miles below Little Rock, and his Indians

7 OIA, "Florida Emigration," File R 275. When Reynolds reached Fort Gibson he asked General Arbuckle to enforce the delivery of the negroes and the General also declined (ibid.). Reynolds descended to New Orleans and brought up the remainder of the Seminoles' ninety negroes except those who had died. Watson subsequently filed a claim with Congress for reimbursement of the sum paid by him for the negroes; the matter dragged in Congress for many years, and resulted in some illuminating debates during which the public learned something of the amazing activities of the administration in trafficking in slaves and endeavoring to send these free negroes into bondage. It also became clear that the war in Florida was conducted largely as a slave catching enterprise for the benefit of the citizens of Georgia and Florida. One of the members of the House of Representatives who engaged in the debates was J. R. Giddings of Pennsylvania, who was so astonished by the developments that he wrote a book (*The Exiles of Florida*, Columbus, Ohio, 1858) in which he details much of what he learned in these hearings and exhibits many official documents bearing on the subject.

were transferred to the *Liverpool* and *the Itaska*, steamboats of lighter draft, each with two keel boats in tow. They proceeded up the Arkansas river without accident and reached Fort Gibson June 12. Since leaving New Orleans fifty-four deaths had occurred in the party, including that of old King Philip, who succumbed to the hardships of the journey and died on June 7 about fifty miles before the party reached Fort Gibson. "A coffin was made and on the morning of the 8th both Steamers were stopped, and the guard of each amalgamated, and proceeded the Corps to the grave, followed by nearly the whole party—he was buried with the honors of war" including a salute of one hundred guns over his grave on the banks of Arkansas river.[8] With the arrival of this party at Fort Gibson, Capt. R. Stephenson receipted for 1,069 Seminole out of a total of 1,160 on Reynolds' muster roll.[9]

Another party of 117 Seminole and two negro emigrants from Charleston arrived at New Orleans May 28 and three days later were embarked on the steamer *Ozark* for the journey up the river; a short distance below Pine Bluff, Arkansas, the boat ran on a concealed snag which tore a hole in the bottom of the vessel;[10] she was immediately run on a sand-bar where she sank to the guards. The Indians cheerfully joined in the rescue of the cargo which they carried ashore, and but for their help would have been lost. The passengers were transferred to the steamboat *Mt. Pleasant* and brought up to Little Rock; there the Indians were placed on the steamboat *Fox* and departed June 12, 1838 for Fort Gibson.[11]

Captain Morrison arrived at New Orleans June 14, 1838 with 305 Seminole and 30 Seminole negroes—men, women, and children—whom he brought from Tampa Bay. They were embarked aboard the steamboat *Livingston*[12] and passed Little Rock June 23.[13] On the way Morrison picked up some additions so that he delivered 349 emigrants

8 Reynolds to Harris, June 18, 1838, OIA, "Florida Emigration"; *Army and Navy Chronicle*, VII, 45.

9 Reynolds to Harris, *ibid.*; 200 of this party of emigrants were negroes (Arbuckle to Poinsett August 27, 1838, OIA, "Florida Emigration," A 452.

10 Clark to Harris, May 31, 1838, OIA, "Florida Emigration," C 652.

11 *Arkansas Gazette*, June 13, 1838, p. 2, col. 1; *Army and Navy Chronicle*, VII, 46.

12 Morrison to Harris, June 14, 1838, OIA, "Florida Emigration," M 396.

13 *Arkansas Gazette*, June 27, 1838, p. 2, col. 3.

to Captain Stephenson at Fort Gibson on the twenty-eighth after an unusually quick passage.[14]

Lieut. John G. Reynolds embarked at New Oeleans July 11, on the steamboat *Itaska* in charge of sixty-six Seminole Indians including the chief Alligator and his family. They arrived at Little Rock in eight days but were delayed there by the low stage of the river. "Take them as a body, they are as likely a party of Indian emigrants as we have ever seen."[15] At Clarksville they picked up a number of Seminole negroes who had ascended with a party of Cherokee Indians but had been forced by the low water at Louisburg to disembark and attempt passage by land. They resumed their river journey the twenty-second and reached a point two miles below Fort Coffee before low water compelled them on the twenty-ninth to abandon further progress by boat. After securing wagons and teams to transport the sick, baggage, and provisions, they set out two days later and reached Fort Gibson August 5. Proceeding three and one half miles to the ferry Reynolds encamped the party and turned them over to Captain Stephenson.[16]

The steamboat *Rodney* was engaged to transport the whole of the Apalachicola tribe numbering 300, and 34 Creeks who had taken refuge on Dog Island. These Indians refused to embark until they were paid the pittance promised them for their land and this was done as soon as they boarded the boat at Pensacola. "General" Welborne, in charge of the Alabama militia, refused to surrender a number of Creek children and he and others were afterwards charged with holding them in slavery.

Gen. Zachary Taylor advised against the risk of taking so many Indians to sea on one steamboat and Daniel Boyd the conductor of the emigrants chartered two schooners, the *Vesper* and the *Octavia* to carry part of the emigrants as far as New Orleans. They sailed from Pensacola October 29 and arrived at New Orleans four days later. There the passengers on the schooners were transferred to the *Rodney* and passage up the Mississippi river began. By the eleventh they were

14 Morrison to Harris, June 14, 1838, OIA, "Florida Emigration;" Stephenson to Harris, August 8, 1838, OIA, "Western Superintendency;" *Arkansas Gazette*, June 27, 1838, p. 2, col. 3.

15 *Arkansas Gazette*, June 25, 1838, p. 2, col. 3; *Army and Navy Chronicle*, VII, 105.

16 Reynolds to Harris, August 18, 1838, OIA, "Florida Emigration."

The Mississippi River at New Orleans where the Creeks and Seminole began their river journey

opposite Princeton, Mississippi. The emigrants, said Boyd, had *"suffered very much from sickness. Six have died since we left Chattahoochee
and more than twenty are now on the sick list. The weather has been unusually cold for the season, which has no doubt increased the number of
invalids. The water in the Mississippi river is very low; we lay two days
upon a sand bar about twenty-five miles above Vicksburg."*[17]

Boyd with his emigrants arrived at Montgomery's Point at the
mouth of White river on the thirteenth, where he was obliged to wait
for an increase in the stage of the Arkansas river, which brought him
to Little Rock on November 22. As there was not sufficient water for
the *Rodney* to ascend higher, the emigrants were transferred to the
North St. Louis a steamboat of lighter draft; they took their departure
soon after and had gone about fifty miles when further progress was
prevented by a bar in the shallow river. The Indians were then put
ashore; their conductor hired teams to haul their sick and provisions
and started with his people for Fort Gibson.[18]

The treaty made by the Seminole delegation at Fort Gibson March
28, 1833[19] stipulated that a tract of land separate and apart from the
Creeks would be provided for Seminole occupancy; the tract designated
lay between the Canadian river and the North fork of that stream and
extended west to the forks of the Little river. Later the Creeks wished
to change this arrangement and require the Seminole to occupy part of
their land and be incorporated with them. A large number of Creeks
who had emigrated ahead of the Seminole had settled on the lands
designated for the latter. When the Seminole arrived at Fort Gibson
on June 12 a council was called by General Arbuckle which was
participated in by some of the Creek warriors headed by Roley McIntosh and by the Seminole. The meeting was cordial until the subject
of location was mentioned. Mikanopy and the other Seminole chiefs
positively refused to consent to any change from the arrangements
made for them in their treaty, and as that land was already well occupied by the Creeks the Seminole remained in camp around Fort
Gibson.[20]

17   Boyd to Harris, November 11, 1838, *ibid.*
18   *Ibid.*, December 3, 1838.
19   Kappler, *op. cit.*, 290.
20   Reynolds to Harris, June 18, 1838, OIA, "Florida Emigration," 275.

The Seminole heard with much alarm that it was planned to locate them in the Creek Nation as they feared the latter Indians intended to overwhelm them and take their negro slaves and allies; "they look upon us as runaways, and would treat us just as they would so many dogs."[21] As subsequent parties arrived they all settled around Fort Gibson until there were 2,000 of them stubbornly refusing to remove to the Creek country.

In the summer of 1838 Holahtochee, Coahadjo, and several other chiefs and warriors who had removed to the West were induced to return to Florida to exert such influence as they had with the Indians remaining there to emigrate. By September they had helped to collect at Tampa Bay about one hundred Tallahassee Indians who came in to negotiate with General Taylor.[22] In two months this number had increased to 200.[23]

Through the winter captives were slowly being assembled at Tampa Bay, and February 25, 1839, "*General Taylor shipped 196 Indians, consisting of warriors, women, children and negroes westward.*[24] *The women were very reluctant to go and upbraided the men with cowardice, in refusing to die upon their native soil. The vessel departed amid their lamentations and taunts, and reproaches upon the conduct of their warriors. Among the negroes is Abraham, well known as an interpreter and a wily and treacherous rascal.*"[25] In charge of Capt. Pitcairn Morrison the party ascended the Mississippi river in the steamboat *Buckeye* and passed Natchez March 28.[26] Later a boiler of the steamboat exploded and killed a number of the emigrants. The party arrived at Little Rock April 2, but because of low water the boat was compelled to remain here for some time. An observer said they appeared well fed and cheerful.[27]

21 Holahtochee and others to Jesup, September, 23 1838, OIA, "Florida Emigration," A 458.

22 Ibid., Abercrombie to Poinsett, September 29, 1838; Army and Navy Chronicle, VII, 219.

23 Ibid., 315.

24 Ibid., X, 50.

25 Ibid., VIII, 205.

26 Natchez Free Trader, March 29, 1839.

27 Arkansas Gazette, April 3, 1839, p. 2, col. 3; Army and Navy Chronicle, VII, 268.

ARLY in April, 1839, Gen. Alexander Macomb arrived in Florida and superseded General Taylor in command of the army. He had been sent from Washington with the belief that his high rank would make an impression on the Indians that would lead to important negotiations for peace.[1] He released Taylor's prisoners and sent them back to their people in the swamps, with offers of peace. Subsequently Halek (or Aharlock, Aha-lek) Tustenuggee, a Mikasuki chief, and other warriors came to Fort King for a conference. "*They were received by Gen. Macomb with much form and ceremony, and with every mark of friendship and kindness. All of them were much embarrassed by the appearance of so many officers and soldiers in uniform, and it was not until they were told that they pertained to the rank of the Great Chief that was sent to talk to them, that they were at all satisfied. The appearance of these Indians was indeed interesting; some of them had had no intercourse with the whites for at least three years. The chief Har-lock-tustenugge was a man about thirty years of age, well dressed, tall, commanding person, manly—prepossessing countenance, and an expressive and fluent speaker. The others were quite young, and remarkable for their hideous and repulsive faces, and their fine, well proportioned—athletic persons, which were well displayed, they having no other garb than a rough buck-skin shirt. The General explained to them clearly and briefly the object of his visit among them, and if they were willing to comply with his demands the white and red man could once more be at peace.*"

The Indians departed the next day and eight days later returned with a body of one hundred, headed by Chitto Tustenuggee sent as his deputy by Sam Jones, principal chief of the Mikasuki who had become

[1] *Army and Navy Chronicle*, IX, 253, 280.

too old and decrepit to travel. The deputy chief was "*about forty years of age—remarkably pleasant and affable when spoken to, but at other times very dignified and reserved. By his conversation and conduct in and out of council, he showed himself to be a man of much intelligence and observation. The Indians paid him great respect, and seemed gratified in having so able a counsellor.*

"*The last council was held on the 22d inst.; both chiefs were present, together with forty-five Seminole and Mickasukie warriors. Gen. Macomb, upon this occasion, as upon all others, gave to it a degree of excitement and interest by adhering to imposing forms and ceremonies. Indeed, this is indispensable in all negotiations with Indians; for among the most degenerated these customs are retained from generation to generation, and attach to all that is said a degree of solemnity which they believe is gratefully received by the Great Spirit.*

"*A large council chamber was erected, and the General and his staff, with all the officers at the post, in uniform, were escorted to the council by the band of the 7th infantry and a company of dragoons on foot. White flags were hoisted at different points; a fire was built in the centre of the chamber, around which the Indians were seated in profound silence; pipes and tobacco were given to them; and, amid a cloud of smoke, the Indians passed round, shaking hands with all present.*"

The terms of peace were explained to them—that they were to retire to the country near Lake Okechobee with guarantee of protection from the whites if they would remain in the country designated. After being in session about four hours the Indians agreed to the terms proposed and the council broke up. "*Every act and expression on the part of the Indians evinced the utmost sincerity and friendship. They attributed the war to the proper cause—the aggression of the whites, and were willing to retire to any part of Florida to avoid those unfortunate collisions which have existed for so many years. The men were destitute of clothing other than a buckskin shirt; and the women and children were almost in a state of nudity. Those who had covering were wrapped up in old forage bags, picked up in the vicinity of abandoned posts; they were truly objects of commiseration.*"[2]

General Macomb's announcement on May 18 of peace with the Indians was received with much satisfaction by the country generally,

2 Ibid., VIII, 363, 379 ff.

as it promised an end to the enormous expenditure of lives and money entailed in the prosecution of the war for which no adequate advantage or credit was perceptible; but the treaty was denounced by the people of Florida[3] who demanded nothing short of absolute removal or annihilation of the Indians. Keeping and feeding large numbers of troops in Florida had brought a measure of prosperity to some of the inhabitants of that Territory who were unwilling to see it discontinued. The treaty was expected to withdraw scattered bands of Indians from their hiding places contiguous to white settlements and roads, and concentrate them in one section remote from the whites.

Agreeable to the promise made them in this treaty by General Macomb, Col. William S. Harney proceeded to a point about eight miles above the mouth of the Coloosahatchie (or Synabel) river in a steamboat with a trader and a stock of goods to establish a trading post within the region reserved for the Indians. Before the establishment had been completed, before daylight on the morning of July 23, 1839, the company of thirty-two men were attacked by what were called Spanish Seminole[4] who killed eighteen of the party. The result was that General Macomb and his treaty came in for much criticism; but some of the leaders among the Indians hastened to report to the posts and disclaim any participation in the bloody affair.[5] A week later when forty-five Indians visited Fort Mellon to receive rations, the officer in command made them all prisoners and took them on a steamboat to Fort Moultrie.[6]

Futile scouting expeditions were continued through the summer and in the autumn the yellow fever appeared in the country to make the labor of the troops more difficult and hazardous. Every body was ill at Tampa Bay and in St. Augustine not a physician was able to minister to the ill.[7]

During the year of his administration, 1839, Taylor undertook to traverse the country with roads and erect forts at strategic points; and by the end of the year seventy forts had been established. Some of these were merely stockades, but they bore testimony to the amazing

3 Ibid., IX, 253.
4 A faction of the tribe living in the south end of Florida.
5 Army and Navy Chronicle, IX, 121, 173, 138, 280.
6 Ibid., 105.
7 Ibid., 364.

tenacity and resourcefulness of the Indians who made the efforts of the army almost futile.[8] Through the whole summer the troops had discovered only a small part of the well concealed fields of the Indians and had destroyed 1,500 acres of their corn and pumpkins "and some hundred or two sheds were burnt (for they can hardly be called houses) but so far from being induced to come in and surrender themselves to our arms, few, very few Indians were seen and still less killed or captured."[9]

Every stream, and lake, and swamp abounded with good fish, game was plentiful, the coontie root for making their bread grew abundantly, and it was impossible to threaten the food supply of the Indians. The army had made such slight impression on them that the officers were in despair. The soldiers in their pale blue and white uniforms were conspicious at a distance, while the Indians often concealed themselves by standing stock-still in view of the enemy, their dark skin and soiled garments if any, giving them the appearance of a stump.[10]

The campaign of 1839 failed so signally that the governor and council of Florida sent to Cuba and purchased thirty-three bloodhounds that had been employed in the pursuit of negro slaves. When information of this new branch of the service against the Indians became known, indignant protests from over the country poured into Washington. The subject engaged the attention of Congress and the secretary of war sought to placate criticism by ordering that in the pursuit the dogs should not be allowed to attack the Indians. While General Taylor favored the use of the dogs, it was demonstrated that they were of little value.[11]

In preparation for the campaign of 1840 Capt. John Page prevailed on two of the principal Seminole chiefs, Holahtochee and Nocoseohola, twelve other Indian immigrants, and two interpreters to accompany him from Fort Gibson to Florida for the purpose of exerting their influence on the resident Indians to remove to the West. The parting from their families and friends on October 1, 1840, was an affecting scene. Holahtochee and other chiefs made parting addresses, and the old chief Alligator "formerly one of the most uncompromising, as well

8   Ibid., 89.
9   Ibid., XI, 220.
10   Ibid.
11   Ibid., X, 114, 115, 117, 124, 135, 173, 187, 221, 239.

as brave and successful among the emigrated Seminole warriors, then took the stand in behalf of the people (with whom he remains) and in an animated strain, conjured the members of the deputation to neglect no effort with their suffering brethren" to induce them to join the immigrants in the West. The party descended the Mississippi river and traveled from New Orleans aboard the ship *Harbinger*, arriving at Tampa Bay one month and two days after their departure from Fort Gibson. On this ship came also Maj. W. G. Belknap and four companies of the Third Infantry from Fort Smith.[12]

In October an expedition under Maj. Greenleaf Dearborn was ordered out. "*About forty miles distant an old women was met having sixteen sticks in her hand. She asked for sixteen days when some Indians would come in for a 'talk' . . .The sixteen days expired yesterday and the squaw returned saying that two chiefs and ten warriors were eight miles distant waiting to see the General. This morning the General [Armistead] took a troop of Dragoons and went out to hear what they had to say. . . 9 P. M. the General has returned after a 40 mile ride. He says he met Tiger Tail & Halec Tustenuggi & the warriors & that they say— here comes the old story 'he say him tired of the war—him want to fight no more.' The Gen'l says they seem to be really in earnest; they say their corn has been destroyed & their women are broke down with labor in preparing countiroot, that they are in a starving condition & can fight no longer—that the country is theirs & that we have no right to it; but that if we will not let them have a part of it, they must go. That they hope we will let them stay, but they will do as we say. . . The Genl. told them that he could give them no answer, but would write for instructions to Washington. In the meantime they have promised to come into Fort King with their families and to induce all of the others to come in. . . Whether this is to be a farce like all the other talks remains to be seen.*"[13]

Escorted by Capt. B. L. E. Bonneville[14] and his dragoons, General Armistead on November 7 joined the Arkansas delegation and a large

---

12 *Ibid.*, 329. Four more companies of this regiment marched from Fort Towson to Little Rock where they arrived on November 6; here they were embarked on the steamboat *Corvette* and two keel boats in tow for New Orleans (ibid., 362).

13 Maj. E. A. Hitchcock to Samuel Hitchcock, October 22, 1840, *Hitchcock Manuscripts.*

14 For accounts of Bonneville see Washington Irving, *Adventures of Captain Bonneville;* Grant Foreman, *Pioneer Days in the Early Southwest.*

number of troops near Fort King. Some of the Indians who came in to the camp loaded with venison reported the approach of Halek Tustenuggee and his band at Tampa Bay. They shook hands with the visiting delegation, "some of them coldly, others with smiles of recognition. The principal men from Arkansas then (all being seated) commenced talking & continued talking a long time."[15]

Gen. Walker K. Armistead with Col. William J. Worth and several other officers, escorted by a company of dragoons, went out to the camp of Halek Tustenuggee for an interview on the subject of emigration. Colonel Worth thought there *"were 50 or 70 Indians about the place of meeting which he describes as one of the most dense hammocks he has ever seen. Their rifles were laid upon logs, loaded and ready for use. Suspicion is the order of the day. They cheated Genl. Jesup who took revenge by seizing a party under a flag of truce & they are afraid of being taken now. . . . The Indians thus far seen are well dressed. Some few are dressed entirely in deer skins, but some have cloth leggings and nearly all have calico shirts. We see but few blankets. There is so far as seen a full proportion of ornaments—beads and feathers."*[16]

Tiger Tail sent word that he would be present for a talk with General Armistead, but suddenly on the night of the fourteenth the 200 Indians in the neighborhood suddenly disappeared and General Armistead "was entirely subdued and broken spirited. His confidence in his success had been boundless and his letters to Washington have doubtless been in that temper."[17] He was so exasperated that he gave

15 Manuscript Diary of Col. Ethan Allen Hitchcock, the property of Mrs. W. A. Croffut, Washington, D. C. Colonel Hitchcock served many years among the Indians and recorded in a series of diaries his impressions and experiences among these people: for an account of him see Grant Foreman, *A Traveler in Indian Territory, the Journal of Ethan Allen Hitchcock, late Major General in the United States Army;* W. A. Croffut, *Fifty Years in Camp and Field.*

16 Hitchcock Diary.

17 *Ibid.* The following illuminating account is taken from a long letter written at Tampa Bay, Florida, October 22, 1840 by Major Ethan Allen Hitchcock to his brother Samuel Hitchcock of St. Louis, now in the possession of Mrs. W. A. Croffut of Washington, D. C.

"In 1836 . . .I thought . . .when I heard of the massacre of Maj. Dade and his command . . .that the Indians had made a treaty to emigrate in good faith and had violated their engagements, signalizing their violation of faith with the most wholesale and barbarous murders. In that opinion, as you know I entered Florida as a volunteer, being on furlough at the time. I no sooner reached Fort King and had access to

orders for his troops to pursue the Indians and in the event that any of
them thereafter should present themselves with a flag of truce, they

---

officers who had been witnesses of the proceedings of the Govt. than I entirely changed
my mind and I ascertained the history of the matter to be substantially this: That
some 20 years ago a treaty was made at Fort Moultrey by which the Govt. undertook
to secure the Seminoles in the peaceable possession of this country for the period of
20 years. This is important, for if the Indians had no right to the country before the
treaty (which has been alleged) they had an undoubted right after it.

"When negotiations were opened with them in 1832 to induce their emigration,
the Indians at once answered 'let the 20 years pass and we will talk with you.' This
was the language to the Govt. Commissioner for several days in succession, when
the articles in the treaty proposed for their acceptance were altered by introducing
one article giving the interpreter $100 and another by which the Indians were to send
a delegation of 6 Indians to examine the new country west of the Arkansas.

"Now the interpreter was a runaway slave from Pensacola on whom the $100
in prospect operated as a *bribe* and it was so spoken of by the Comr. in an interview
with Gen. Jackson in the presence of Capt. Thruston, who stated the fact to me.
Col. Gadsden, Commr. remarked to President Jackson, that he 'never could have
done anything with the Indians if he had not bribed the interpreter with $100'."

"The Indians have always held one language in regard to their understanding of
the treaty. They have from first to last uniformly declared that the deputation to
examine the new country had no power to confirm the treaty, but were to return and
report the result of their observations when they, the tribe, were to assent or dissent.
The deputation however were induced while at Fort Gibson (as I have heard, even
under menaces that they should not otherwise return to their friends) to sign a paper
signifying that they were satisfied with the country designed for them in the Treaty.
This paper was regarded by President Jackson as completing the treaty and the Senate
ignorantly ratifying it, it became to appearance the law of the land in '33 I believe.
2 or 3 years were lost however before any decided step was taken by the Govt. to
enforce the treaty, during which time the President was fully advised of the state
of the facts and of the disposition of the Indians, in the face of which he ordered the
treaty to be carried into effect.

"The immediate consequence was the murder by the Indians, of the principal
Chief who was favorable to emigration, which was followed by the murder of the
Indian Agent, whose arrogance and insolence had been conspicuous in Council with
the Indians, extending to the usurpation of authority by which he confined Oscola
(sic) in chains and went through the form of degrading sundry Chiefs from their
dignity in the tribe; a thing unheard of before and impossible in execution from the
nature of the case. The war was then fairly entered upon and we are now after five
years exertion and some 20 millions expenditure no nearer its termination than when
we commenced; while Florida, from its present condition opens a field for runaway
negroes and desperate white men where they are rather growing stronger than weaker
every day, and there is reasonable ground to doubt whether fewer than 20,000 men
could quiet the country short of five years to come and it might require ten years.

were at once to be made prisoners. The troops however, were unable to overtake or discover any of them for some time.[18]

The hunt continued and on March 21, 220 captive Tallahassee Indians were embarked from Tampa Bay for New Orleans; there on April 4 the party, reduced by death to 205 Indians and six negroes, boarded the steamboat *President* in charge of Maj. William G. Belknap for the ascent of the Mississippi river. On the nineteenth they were landed on the Arkansas opposite the mouth of the Grand river. Wagons were provided and the emigrants were taken from here to join their chief Mikanopy on the Deep Fork. Another party of 200 in charge of L. E. Capers, disbursing agent, left Tampa Bay on May 7 and reached New Orleans six days later. The emigrating agent was instructed to have them vaccinated and then permit them to see the city before sending them on; but he learned that there were lurking in the city "a sett of loafers from Georgia looking for negroes they pretended to claim, when in fact they have no more legal claim than I have." For safety the agent kept the Indians in confinement and on the sixteenth embarked them on the steamer *John Jay* in charge of Capt H. McKavett who landed them June 13 at the Choctaw Agency whence they marched overland to their new home.[19]

Alligator, Hotulke Emathla, and Waxie Emathla in charge of Capt. S. B. Thornton were employed to return to Florida and use their influence to secure more emigrants.[20] They descended the Arkansas river from Fort Gibson and on September 20, 1841, with six companies of the Fourth Infantry in command of Col. John Garland, they departed from Fort Smith for Florida. Each of the Indian emissaries was permitted to take with him one other and an interpreter.[21]

"I give you this little sketch in order that you may estimate the feelings with which I now enter this country. Five years ago I came as a volunteer, willingly making every effort in my power to be of service in punishing as I thought, the Indians. I now come, with the persuasion that the Indians have been wronged and I enter upon one of the most hopeless tasks that was ever given to man to perform."

18 *Army and Navy Chronicle*, X, 361, 377, 395, 426.

19 *Arkansas Gazette*, April 14, 1841; Capers to Crawford, April 4, 1841, OIA, "Seminole Emigration;" Arbuckle to Jones, April 20, 1841, AGO, OFD, 146 A 41.

20 Taylor to Jones, September 24, 1841, *ibid.*, 283 T 41.

21 Taylor to Worth, September 22, 1841, AGO ORD, *Fort Smith Letter Book* A (8).

In May Halek Tustenuggee sent to the post at Tampa Bay 115 sticks to indicate that his band numbering that many people would come in and surrender. A number of Indians bearing a passport signed by Colonel Worth and accompanied by a negro interpreter named Joe came into Fort Pierce and reported that Wild Cat had sent them to say that he was ready to surrender "if it was all right." Maj. Thomas Childs said it was all right and sent Lieut. William Tecumseh Sherman *"with eight or ten mounted men to accompany Joe and one Indian to bring in the chief. Six or seven miles away they found Coacoochee (Wild Cat), a handsome young Indian of twenty-five years, and a dozen other warriors, and invited them to go to the fort. They had some little difficulty in persuading them to do so, but finally Coacoochee dressed himself in all his finery and went to the Fort. There he said he was tired of the war and wanted to go with his people to the Indian Territory, but he wanted rations for a month, which time it would take to get his people together for the journey. This was agreed to and then the great chief got gloriously drunk. A few days later he went away, but frequently sent back messengers for more whiskey and provisions. At the end of the month he was but little nearer ready to travel than before. A council was accordingly called at which Coacoochee became drunk again. Then Sherman and some of his men put the whole party in irons and they were promptly shipped off to the Indian Territory."*[22]

In all several hundred Indians were captured and concentrated at Tampa Bay through the summer of 1841; two hundred were started west of whom three died on the way and 197 were delivered at Fort Gibson November 12; under the influence of Mikanopy they agreed to remove from the vicinity of the post to the Deep Fork river and had crossed the Arkansas when they were overtaken by a blizzard. These wretched half-clad Indians who were unused to cold weather, huddled around camp fires on the bank of the Arkansas river where is now the Muskogee water works, and for some time refused to budge farther.[23] The steamer *Little Rock* passed Little Rock early in November with 207 Seminole Indians, sixty of whom were warriors, besides women and children. They included Wild Cat and Hospitake, and were in charge of Capt. Washington Seawell and Lieut. Forbes Britton; detained by

22 W. Fletcher Johnson, *Life of Wm. Tecumseh Sherman*, 43.
23 Clark to Armstrong, December 1, 1841, OIA, "Seminole File" A 1135.

the low stage of the river they did not reach Fort Gibson until near two months later.[24]

More Indians were captured during the next winter and in the spring were transported to New Orleans in the brig *Laurance Cope-land*. Three hundred of these left New Orleans aboard the steamer *President* in charge of Capt. T. L. Alexander but on May first their progress was interrupted sixty miles below Little Rock by the low stage of the Arkansas river. With an accession of water later in the month they reached Webbers Falls June first; as the boat was unable to proceed farther, the Indians were put ashore and ordered to march to their new home on Deep Fork river and join the earlier arrivals. This they refused to do, and insisted on crossing the Arkansas river and proceeding to Fort Gibson to join the Seminole living there with Alligator; and it became necessary to order out five companies of troops from Fort Gibson to the mouth of the Illinois river to force the Indians across the Arkansas on the way to the Deep Fork.[25] Another party of one hundred under Lieut. E. R. S. Canby that left New Orleans aboard the steamboat *Swan* July 22 was forced by low water to abandon the boat six miles below Little Rock and march overland by Fort Smith and the Choctaw Agency to the Creek council ground where they were delivered to the agent on September 6, 1842.

General Taylor, then stationed at Fort Smith, estimated that by March 21, 1842, 2,833 Seminole Indians had been removed and located: 1,097 of Alligator's and Holahtochee's bands from nine to fifteen miles north, and seventy of Wild Cat's band three miles south of Fort Gibson. Mikanopy's town numbering 827 people ten to forty miles southwest, and Concharte Micco's band of 479 twenty miles south of the Fort. Black Dirt's band of 360 survivors were located on the Little river ninety miles southwest of the post.[26] Some of the Seminole located on Cherokee land, planted crops there with the consent of the owners, and General Taylor gave them permission to remain until their crops were gathered.[27]

24 *Arkansas Gazette*, November 10, copied in *National Intelligencer* December 2, 1841; Clark to Armstrong, February 6, 1842, OIA, *ibid*.

25 Alexander to Crawford, May 18, and Alexander to Seminole agent, June 1, 1842, OIA, "Seminole Emigration" A 1238, 1269, 1273.

26 George W. Clark to William Armstrong, March 21, 1842, OIA, "Seminole Emigrant File."

27 Taylor to adjutant general, May 15, 1842, AGO, OFD, 158 T 42.

Fort Gibson boat landing. This ledge of rock determined the location of the post at this place

General Worth "succeeded by an act of perfidy in seizing some Indians he had himself invited within his guards, and they were sent out of Florida, whereupon the *end of the war* was proclaimed, and through the influence of Gen. Scott, Worth was brevetted a Brigadier General."[28] But it was soon discovered that the war was not over. One of the chiefs of the Mikasuki who it was supposed had surrendered, escaped with some of his companions, and on November 28, 1842, Col. Ethan Allen Hitchcock "received an order to re-open the War which has been *closed* so often heretofore. I am to operate along the Apalachicola river."[29]

Hitchcock declined the offer of two companies of civilian volunteers he was authorized to accept and with two companies of his regiment, the Third, on December 12, 1842, on the steamboat *William Gaston*, began the descent of the Apalachicola river in quest of Pascofa and his band of "Ocklocknee" Indians, the hostiles who yet stood in the way of peace in Florida. These were Creek Indians who fled from the terrors of Alabama in 1836 and took refuge in Florida.[30] They had made their escape from the party of Creeks that emigrated from the Apalachicola in 1838, and since had been a scourge to the settlements on that river, killing the inhabitants and burning their buildings. For four years futile efforts had been made to capture them or bring them in by negotiation.[31]

By the exercise of patience and perseverance Hitchcock succeeded through his messengers in bringing to his camp some members of Pascofa's party with assurances that the chief himself would visit the colonel in three days. There was some rivalry among the officers and detachments operating in Florida, and this news which presaged a real ending of the war, was followed by demonstrations of joy by officers and soldiers comparable to the jubilation produced by an armistice between much greater forces. Pascofa appeared on the seventeenth and had a long talk with Colonel Hitchcock whose honorable and sympathetic treatment of the Indians had won their trust and respect. Pascofa expressed his joy that peace was to be established between them and explained the ceremony he desired observed in celebrating

28 Hitchcock's Diary, *ibid.*
29 *Ibid.*
30 *Ibid.*
31 *New Orleans Weekly Picayune*, February 13, 1843.

that peace: "*As he is the last chief to give up, he said he would do something in especial. Of course I humored him & told him to do what he pleased. About 3 P. M., his warriors appeared. I had furnished him a horse in the morning & the runner Nocose, had another. These were on the lead, each horse carrying double, the remaining warriors being in Indian file on foot with feathers in their scalp locks all singing a war song. When within some one or two hundred yards they discharged their rifles and continuing past my guard entered the center of the Camp where I received them with my officers. Of course I gave them a talk after shaking hands all around. . ."* After the chief made his talk "*. . .the liquor was brought by Lt. Henry who handed me a tin cup filled with the most abominable stuff. I took the cup & without blessing it led off, to their good health & handed it to the chief who pronounced 'iste linus tcha' & passed it on, all his warriors drinking 'iste linus tcha.'*

"*The chief wanted a blanket—begged & plead for one—even an old horse blanket if I could give him no other. He wanted it he said, for his wife—he was ashamed to have her seen as she was almost naked. . . his warriors are wretchedly dressed, mostly in skins, i. e. leggings, but with very dirty and tattered shirts; one or two had pieces of blankets about them. They were not all armed and they told my interpreter that they generally hunted with the bow and arrow and could kill a deer with an arrow almost as certainly as with a ball.*"[32] The chief required four days time to assemble his people and board Colonel Hitchcock's boat and as he desired one big drunk and grand frolic for his people before leaving, he sent in a doeskin which Hitchcock filled with five gallons of liquor to meet his requirements. While waiting here Colonel Hitchcock learned that Tiger Tail and his party had been taken to Cedar Keys under an escort of troops.

Hitchcock's boat descended the river to the bay and then ascended the Ocklocknee river thirty miles to receive Pascofa's party. Their canoes being in bad condition there was some delay and they did not reach the steamboat until January 9. When they boarded the boat they numbered twenty-one men, nineteen women and ten children; and there was issued to each of them a blanket, to each man a shirt and turban, and to each woman a calico dress and a head kerchief. They then descended the river with much difficulty from snags and bars, and Hitchcock received "*accounts of the seizure at Tampa bay of the party of*

32 Hitchcock's Diary, *ibid.*

Ochacker, a Creek Chief who has been tampering with the authorities since last May or June. They were seized by Order of Genl. Worth by Capt Seawell of the 7th Infy. Seawell it appears invited them to receive presents & when assembled surrounded them and took them prisoners and sent them to Sea Horse Key, one of the Cedar Keys."

As Hitchcock's boat approached "Port Leon yesterday morning about 9 o'clock, the Indians wished to give the war yell. I gave permission & it was done, but soon afterwards a revulsion of feeling seemed to overcome the whole of them; for on nearing the wharf and seeing the people the Indians appeared to be struck with the conviction that they were now, indeed, in our power. The men became silent and serious—sad—while the women were nearly all in tears. I took occasion to speak to them, telling them not to lose heart, that they were among friends who would take care of them, that I was glad to see they had feeling hearts, but to make sure they would be treated well. The chief himself even was so affected that his lips trembled and he could not say a word. . .

". . .A story exists that in the early part of the war, the children of this band were put to death by their parents to prevent being discovered by their noise and to make themselves light for hasty retreats; and it is a fact that the children among them extend up from infancy to 4 years of age—mostly to but 3 and then jump to 15 or 16. It would really seem from this that some 4 years ago they did put some of their children to death. Yesterday morning just before leaving the boat, I had an opportunity of speaking to a very matronly looking woman, the mother of two grown women & an infant, the infant being in her arms, and I took the occasion, the interpreter being by, to tell her that she would soon be happier than she had been &c., reminded her of their having lived more like wild animals than like human creatures, but that now they would begin to have houses and make gardens etc., and could bring up their children to something besides war.—The old woman dropped her head and burst into tears."[33]

And now after more than six years of cruel and futile fighting and killing, entailing the expenditure of the lives of 1,500 white soldiers and twenty millions of dollars, and untold suffering, misery, and mortality of the Indians in defense of their homeland, the Seminole war was actually terminated; and Colonel Hitchcock was credited with that bloodless achievement by his fellow officers, the press, and by

33 Ibid.

Gov. R. K. Call in a special message to the Florida legislature recommending a vote of thanks to him.[34]

The steamer *William Gaston* with Pascofa's band on board departed for New Orleans but lost her rudder in a violent storm on January 29, and little hope for the vessel was entertained by her officers. However by skillful handling she succeeded in reaching Pensacola where a temporary rudder was rigged with which she made New Orleans some days later. Here the Indians were landed at the barracks and consolidated with earlier arrivals soon to ascend the Mississippi river.[35] These Indians in charge of Lieutenant McKavett left New Orleans March 4 and on the eleventh reached Little Rock where they were detained by low water; they were landed on the south bank of the Arkansas river opposite the mouth of the Illinois on April 26.[36] From here they were taken overland to their agency.

Making a virtue of the necessity, General Worth agreed that several hundred Seminole Indians might remain for the present in Florida upon conditions to which the Indians paid little attention.[37] They continued to live immured in the fastnesses of Florida, but the government was not allowed by the white people to forget their presence. Through emissaries of their own tribe in 1849 large financial inducements were offered them to join their brothers in the West. They were promised $500 a head for each man and boy capable of bearing arms, and $100 for each woman or child. The government promised to subsist them for a year after their removal and to pay for all cattle, hogs, crops and other property abandoned or left behind; to make them presents of clothing and blankets before starting; to pay all expenses enroute, and furnish a physician for the journey; and in addition large sums were offered by army officers to individual Indians of influence in the tribe, amounting in one case to $10,000. No such inducements were ever held out to any other tribe, but they failed to influence the Seminole Indians to leave their native land. These efforts were supplemented by a military force sent to overawe them, but the four or five hundred Indians hidden

34 *Apalachicola Journal*, December 31, 1842; *National Intelligencer*, January 19, 1843.

35 *New Orleans Weekly Picayune*, February 13, 1843.

36 McKavett to Jones, March 31, May 1, 1843, AGO, OFD, 121 M 43, 145 M 43.

37 Report of Commissioner of Indian Affairs, 1849.

in Florida refused to yield. In 1851 a commission was issued to Luther Blake to go to Florida and attempt their removal. He was authorized to offer $800 to each warrior and $450 for each woman and child who would agree to emigrate; but this effort also was fruitless.[38]

An abortive attempt was made in 1856 by army officers at Fort Gibson to take a delegation of Indians to Florida for their influence on those remaining there; but the Indians convinced them that if the enterprise were directed by the military it was doomed to failure. In the winter of the next year Elias Rector, superintendent of Indian affairs for the southern superintendency, S. M. Rutherford, the western Seminole agent, and W. H. Garrett, Creek agent, took to Florida a delegation of forty Seminole and six Creeks. At the cost of a large sum of money Rector engaged the services of a number of influential Florida Seminole Indians, including the chiefs Holahta Micco and Billy Bow Legs;[39] and with their assistance and by dint of weeks of labor and searching through the Everglades secured 165 of what Rector called the hostile Indians for removal to the West. Of this number 121 were women and children and the remainder warriors. They included ten of the Mikasuki band, leaving twelve warriors and five very old men who declined to emigrate and abandon their venerable but implacable chief Sam Jones, then 108 years old, but promised they would remove after his death.[40] Rector's party sailed from Fort Myers, Florida, May 4 and proceeded by way of New Orleans, the Mississippi and Arkansas rivers; on the steamboat *Quapaw*, they arrived at Fort Smith May 28, and in a few days, after securing wagons for their transportation, in charge of Rutherford, they proceeded overland, reaching their agency June 16; after their arrival an epidemic of fever took a number of lives in the party.

At last Indian removal was an accomplished fact. The white people had come into possession of the ancestral domain of the aboriginals. Exulting town boomers, land speculators and farmers overran the land

38 *U. S. House Executive Document No. 2, p. 306*, Twenty-third Congress, first session. A deputation of Seminole Indians headed by their chief John Jumper, in charge of Maj. Horace Brooks departed from Fort Smith April 22, 1850, in the steamboat *J. B. Gordon* enroute to Florida where they were to use their influence to induce their brothers to emigrate at once (*Fort Smith Herald*, April 27, 1850, p. 2, col. 1).

39 Bow Legs (Bolek) was a brother of Alligator (*American State Papers*, "Military Affairs," VII, 848).

40 Rector to Thompson, May 9, 1858, OIA, "Seminole."

and appropriated the sites that so recently had been cherished spots—the homes, villages, fields and burying grounds of the Indians, even while the sad expatriates were toiling over cruel and forbidding highways. With bitter sorrow in their hearts, weakened by hardship and privation, decimated by disease, oppressed by penury, despondent and disheartened, they traveled on.

All but hopeless the Indians were as they approached their new home, forbidding and strange. And yet there was a wistful hope of a partial recompense—that in this remote country they would find surcease from the cruelty, sordidness, and rapacity of the frontier white man. Hope that in the country he did not covet and would not have, they would be allowed to live in peace to restore their broken health and homes, institutions and governments. With this hope after their arrival they resolutely attacked the problems of pioneering in the strange country that confronted them. The rehabilitation of these five Indian nations, their readjustment to their new surroundings, the recovery of their national spirit and enterprise, the building of their farms and homes, their governments and schools upon the raw frontier, bringing into being a higher civilization of Indians, this was an achievement unique in our history, that compares favorably with the best traditions of white frontier civilization.

FINIS

BIBLIOGRAPHY

BIBLIOGRAPHY

Removal of the Indians was committed to the commissary general of subsistence subject to the orders of the secretary of war. A large staff of army officers and civilian employes in the field maintained extensive correspondence with the commissary general's office and other branches of the war department. Endless negotiations and controversial exchanges with the Indians, frequent reports on their condition and activities and on every phase of the subject of removal, requests for information and solution of a multitude of problems, complaints and instructions passing between the agents and officers engaged in the removal and their superiors in Washington; the furnishing of rations, supplies, and equipment, and execution of other contracts, swelled this correspondence; added to this was an endless series of correspondence between superintendents and other persons of authority in the field with their subordinates, contractors, and local army officers, which in turn was forwarded to Washington; all this resulted in a vast accumulation in the war department of manuscript material bearing on the subject of Indian removal.

Other divisions of the war department including the secretary himself were also engaged in endless exchanges of letters touching this unprecedented enterprise. Administration of Indian affairs proper belonged to a division of the war department created by law for this purpose. In 1849 when the Indian office was transferred from the war department to the department of the interior, most of this correspondence was transferred to and is now deposited in the office of Indian affairs. But there is a residue of thousands of pages of such material remaining in the various branches of the war department.

Primary Sources

This book is written in the main from this large mass of unpublished correspondence, reports, and journals of events, in the office of Indian affairs and in the war department. Reference herein to the material in the office of Indian affairs is abbreviated to OIA. In the war department material the references are shortened as follows:

Adjutant general's office, old files division: AGO, OFD.

Adjutant general's office, old records division: AGO, ORD.

Adjutant general's office, old records division, war department files: AGO, ORD, WDF.

Quartermaster corps: QMC.

Other primary sources drawn upon for the contents of this book are the missionary letters recently in the custody of the American Board of Commissioners for Foreign Missions at Boston and now deposited in the Harvard-Andover Theological library; The Alabama State Department of Archives and History, and the Mississippi State Department of Archives and History; United States Senate files; manuscript division of the Library of Congress; Ayer collection, Newberry library, Chicago; Draper Manuscript collection the State Historical Society of Wisconsin; Ross Manuscript collections belonging to Mrs. E. W. Piburn, Denver, Colorado, and W. W. Ross, Park Hill, Oklahoma.

Secondary Sources

The United States Senate on December 27, 1833, adopted a resolution calling for the correspondence relating to the subject of the emigration of the Indians, between that date and November 30, 1831. In response to the resolution the commissary general of subsistence submitted a mass of material that was published by Congress in five volumes, making over four thousand two hundred pages. It appears as *U. S. Senate Document No. 512, Twenty-third Congress, first session, "Indian Removal."* As the contents of this document are frequently referred to herein, for brevity the long title is shortened in the references to *Document* followed by the volume number.

American Historical Association, Annual Reports for 1901, 1906, 1907.

American State Papers. Documents, legislative and executive, of the Congress of the United States. Class II, Indian Affairs," vols. I-II. Class V, "Military Affairs," vols. IV-V-VI-VII (Washington, 1832-60).

Nathan Bangs, D. D., *An Authentic History of Missions of the M. E. Church, 1778-1862* (New York).

George M. Battey, *History of Rome and Floyd County [Georgia]* (Atlanta, 1922).

Cherokee Nation vs State of Georgia, Peters United States Supreme Court Reports, V, 1.

J. F. H. Claiborne, *Mississippi as a Province, Territory, and State*, (Jackson, Mississippi, 1880).

M. M. Cohen, *Notices of Florida and the Campaigns with a map and portrait of Osceola* (Charleston, 1836).

Reports of the Commissioner of Indian Affairs (Washington, 1832-60).

Reports of the Commission to the Five Civilized Tribes, 1899 to 1905 (Washington, 1899-1905).

G. W. Cullum, *Biographical Register of the Officers and Graduates of the United States Military Academy* (New York, 1879).

H. B. Cushman, *A History of the Choctaw, Chickasaw, and Natchez Indians* (Greenville, Texas, 1899).

Abbé Emmanuel Domenech, *Seven Years Residence in the Great Deserts of North America* (London, 1860).

Charles Dickens, *American Notes* (Various editions).

Samuel B. Drake, *The Aboriginal Races of North America* (Boston, 1848; Philadelphia, 1860; New York, 1880).

The War in Florida: Being an Exposition of the Causes, and Accurate History of the Campaigns of Generals Clinch, Gaines and Scott, by a Late Staff Officer (Baltimore, 1836).

George W. Featherstonhaugh, *A Canoe Voyage up the Minnay Sotor* (London, 1847).

Grant Foreman, *Indians and Pioneers* (New Haven, 1930).

————, *Pioneer Days in the Early Southwest* (Cleveland, 1926).

————, *A Traveler in Indian Territory* (Cedar Rapids, 1930).

Frederick Gerstaecker, *Wild Sports in the Far West* (London, 1854).

Joshua R. Giddings, *The Exiles of Florida* (Columbus, 1858).

Francis B. Heitman, *Historical Register and Dictionary of the United States Army* (Washington, 1903).

F. W. Hodge, ed., *Handbook of American Indians* (Washington, 1912).

Washington Irving, *The Conspiracy of Neamathla*, "Geoffrey Crayon Papers" (Various editions).

Charles J. Kappler, ed., *Laws and Treaties* "Indian Affairs" (Washington, 1903).

Wilson Lumpkin, *The Removal of the Cherokee Indians from Georgia* (New York, 1907).

Printed Laws of the Cherokee Nation (Various editions).

George S. McCall, *Letters from the Frontier* (Philadelphia, 1868).

Thomas L. McKenney, *Memoirs with Sketches of Travels* (New York, 1846).

———— and James Hall, *History of the Indian Tribes of North America*, Vols. I-III (Philadelphia, 1854; same in various editions).

George W. Manypenny, *Our Indian Wards* (Cincinnati, 1880).

Mississippi, High Courts of Errors and Appeals, Reports I.

James Mooney, *Myths of the Cherokee* (Nineteenth Report, Bureau of American Ethnology, pt. 1, Washington, 1900).

Narcissa Owen, *Memoirs of* (Washington, 1907).

A Narrative of the Early Days and Remembrances of Oceola Nikkanochee, Prince of Econchatti (London, 1841).

Publications of the Mississippi Historical Society.

Publications of the Alabama Historical Society.

James Richardson, *Messages of the Presidents* (Washington, 1903).

John Ross, *Letter from John Ross, Principal Chief of the Cherokee Nation of Indians, in Answer to Inquiries from a Friend Regarding the Cherokee Affairs with the United States* (Washington, 1836).

————, *Letter from the Principal Chief of the Cherokee Nation to a Gentleman of Philadelphia* (Washington, 1838).

Charles G. Royce, *The Cherokee Nation of Indians* (Fifth Report, Bureau of American Ethnology, Washington, 1887).

————, *Indian Land Cessions in the United States* (Eighteenth Report, Bureau of American Ethnology, pt. 2, Washington, 1899).

Sketch of the Seminole War, by a Lieutenant of the Left Wing (Charleston, 1836).

George G. Smith, *Life and Times of Bishop George E. Pierce* (Nashville, 1888).

James F. Smith, *The Cherokee Land Lottery* (New York, 1838).

W. W. Smith, *Sketches of the Seminole War and Sketches of a Campaign* (Charleston, 1836).

Speeches on the Passage of the Bill for the Removal of the Indians, Delivered in the Congress of the United States, April and May, 1830 (Boston, 1830.)

Emmet Starr, *History of the Cherokee Indians* (Oklahoma City, 1921).

John R. Swanton, *Early History of the Creek Indians and their Neighbors* (Bulletin 73, Smithsonian Institution, Bureau of American Ethnology, Washington, 1922).

———, *Social Organization and Social Usages of the Creek Confederacy* (Forty-second Report, ibid., Washington, 1928).

R. G. Thwaites, ed., *Early Western Travels*, III (Cleveland, 1904-08).

United States Statutes at Large.

United States Senate, *Executive Document No. 386*, Twenty-third Congress, first session.

———, *Executive Document No. 512*, Twenty-third Congress, first session, vols. V.

———, *Document No. 120*, Twenty-fifth Congress, second session.

———, *Document No. 107*, Twenty-eighth Congress, second session.

United States House of Representatives, *Document No. 56*, Twenty-second Congress, first session.

———, *Executive Document No. 171*, Twenty-second Congress, first session.

———, *Report No. 502*, Twenty-second Congress, first session.

———, *Document No. 2*, Twenty-third Congress, first session.

.———, *Document No. 149*, Twenty-third Congress, first session.

———, *Report No. 474*, Twenty-third Congress, first session.

———, *Document No. 2*, Twenty-fourth Congress, first session.

———, *Document No. 27*, Twenty-fifth Congress, first session.

———, *Document No. 285*, Twenty-fifth Congress, second session.

———, *Document No. 327*, Twenty-fifth Congress, second session.

———, *Document No. 453*, Twenty-fifth Congress, second session.

———, *Document No. 129*, Twenty-sixth Congress, first session.

———, *Document No. 107*, Twenty-eighth Congress, second session.

———, *Document No. 2*, Thirty-second Congress, first session.

United States Supreme Court Reports, "Peters" V, VI.

Autobiography of Martin Van Buren, Annual Report of the American Historical Association for 1918 (Washington, 1920).

Cephas Washburn, *Reminiscences of the Indians* (Richmond, 1869).

Muriel H. Wright, *The Removal of the Choctaws to the Indian Territory, 1830-33*, Chronicles of Oklahoma, VI, 103 (Oklahoma City, 1928).

Worcester vs State of Georgia, Peters United States Supreme Court Reports, VI, 515.

Journals

Army and Navy Chronicle, I to IX.

Baptist Missionary Magazine, XIV, XVIII.

Chronicles of Oklahoma, V, VI.

Missionary Herald, XXIX to XXXIV.

Niles' Weekly Register, XXXVIII to XLIX.
Religious Intelligencer, XIV, XV, XVI.

Newspapers

Alexandria (Louisiana) Gazette.
Apalachicola (Florida) Journal, 1842.
Arkansas Advocate (Little Rock), 1831, 1832, 1836, 1839.
Arkansas Intelligencer (Van Buren), 1845.
The Arkansas Gazette (Little Rock), 1832, 1833, 1835, 1837, 1838, 1839.
Athens (Tennessee) Journal, 1838.
The Batesville (Arkansas) News, 1838.
Cassville Pioneer.
Charleston (South Carolina) Courier, 1837.
Cherokee Advocate (Tahlequah, Indian Territory), 1843-45.
Cherokee (New Echota, Georgia) Phoenix, 1832, 1833, 1834.
Commercial (Montgomery, Ala.) Advertiser, 1838.
Columbus (Georgia) Inquirer, 1835.
Fort Smith (Arkansas) Herald, 1849.
Hopkinsville (Kentucky) Gazette, 1838.
Huntsville (Alabama) Democrat, 1830, 1832, 1833.
Huntsville (Alabama) Southern Advocate, 1836.
Jackson (Tennessee) Advertiser, 1838.
Jackson (Tennessee) Gazette, 1830-24.
Jacksonville (Alabama) Republican, 1837, 1838.
Knoxville (Tennessee) Register, 1835.
Louisiana (Alexandria) Herald, 1825.
Louisville (Kentucky) Public Advertiser, 1838.
McMinnville (Tenn.) Gazette, 1838.
Memphis (Tennessee) Morning Enquirer, 1836.
Memphis (Tennessee) Gazette, 1837.
Milledgeville (Georgia) Recorder, 1831.
Mississippi Free Trader (Natchez), 1839.
Missouri Saturday News (St. Louis) 1838.
Mobile Daily Commercial Register and Patriot, 1830, 1831, 1835, 1837, 1838.
Morgan (Decatur, Alabama) Observer, 1837.
Alabama Journal (Montgomery), 1836.
Montgomery Commercial Advertiser (Alabama), 1836, 1837.
Nashville Banner and Nashville Whig, 1830.
Nashville (Tenn.) Whig, 1838.
Nashville (Tenn.) Union, 1838.
National Intelligencer (Washington, D. C.), 1830, 1839, 1841, 1843.
Newbern (North Carolina) Spectator, 1836.
The Louisiana (New Orleans) Courier, 1837.
New Orleans Weekly Pickayune, 1843.

New Orleans Free American, 1837.
The New Orleans Bee, 1837.
New York Observer, 1832, 1836, 1837, 1838.
Pensacola (Florida) Gazette, 1837.
St. Louis Commercial Bulletin, 1837.
Vicksburg (Mississippi) Advocate and Register, 1831-1832.

INDEX

INDEX

Benge, John: conducts Cherokee emigrants: 302.

Benson's Bar; 295.

Benton county (Ala.): 122 *footnote* 7; 163.

Bernard, Wm.: 28 *footnote* 16.

Big Bear, Nancy: 282.

Big Black river: 89.

Big Coon: 277.

Bishop, William N.: 251.

Mrs Black's: resting place for emigrants, 93, 101; 159 *footnote* 25; 207.

Black Coat (Cherokee chief); 239, 249.

Black Dirt (Fukeluste Hadjo, Seminole): 327, 332, 339, 380; wife dies, 335.

Black Warrior river, 143.

Black Fish lake (Ark.): 207.

Black Hawk: 226.

Black Fox (Cherokee): 257, 258.

Blake Luther: 130.

Bloodhounds: used in Seminole War, 374.

Blue (De L'eau Bleu, Low Blue, Loe Blue, Oak-she-me-la) river: 35; 220 *footnote* 9; 225.

Blunt, John (Seminole chief): 319; 322 *footnote* 22: his party of emigrants, 323.

Blythe's Ferry: 300 *footnote* 14.

Boggy Depot: rations issued to Chickasaw immigrants, 220.

Boggy river: 33, 36, 68, 72, 221, 225.

Boiling Pot: The, 291.

Bonneville, Capt. B. L. E.: 375.

Boudinot, Elias: 267.

Bowlegs, Billy, (Seminole chief): 385 *footnote* 35.

Boyd, Daniel: 369.

Brandon (Miss.): 89.

Brashears, Lewis (Choctaw): 203 *footnote* 35.

Bribery of Indians: 27, 28, 29, 230, 319, 322.

Bridges: built for emigrating parties, 54 *footnote* 39.

Brodnax, Maj. John H.: 107.

Broken Arrow (Creek town): 152 *footnote* 1.

Brooks, Maj. Horace; 385 *footnote* 38.

Brown, Capt. Jacob: 53, 65, 69, 78, 96.

Brown's Ferry: 284.

Brown's Hotel (Washington): 110.

Brown, Maj James (Chickasaw): 203.

Brushy Creek: 203 *footnote* 35; 221.

Buckner, Capt. Simeon: contracts to remove Chickasaw on steamboats, 213.

Burnett, David: 135.

Burney, David (Chickasaw): 226.

Burney, Simon (Chickasaw): 226.

Bushyhead, Rev. Jesse (Cherokee): 300 *footnote* 14; 304, 309, 311, 352.

Buzzards Roost: 200 *footnote* 26.

Bynum, John A.: 198.

Cache creek: 207.

Caddo (Indians): 36, 196.

Caddo river: 82, 211.

Cadron creek: 256 261.

Cahawba river: 142.

Caledonia (Mo.): 281.

Calhoun (Tenn.): 242, 291.

Call, Gov. R. K.: 348 *footnote* 17.

Campbell, John A.: 161.

Canadian river: 34, 194, 221, 321.

Canby, Lieut. E. R. S.: 380.

Cannon, B. B.: conducts Cherokee emigrants, 280, 283.

Cape Girardeau (Mo.): 71, 308.

Carmel Mission: 234.

Paddy Carr (Patrick Carey, Creek): 107, 130.

Carr Thomas: 107, 110 *footnote* 14.

Carroll county (Ga.): 229.

Carroll, William, Gov. of Tenn.: 230.

Carter, Henry B.: 204.

Cass, Lewis: 74, 108, 113, 115, 116, 119, 132, 240; 264 *footnote* 1.

Catlin, George: paints Indians at Fort Moultrie, 357.

Chambers county (Ala.): 122 *footnote* 7; whites kind to Creek Indians, 124.

Charleston (Ala.): 363.

Charleston (N.C.): 352.
Charleston (Tenn.): 302.
Chase, Capt.: 204.
Chattahoochee river: 137, 145, 150, 315.
Chattanooga (Tenn.): 265; 274 *footnote* 20; 294.
Cheemalee (Creek Indian): 152.
Cherokee (agency): 243, 252, 291; 300 *footnote* 14; 301; in West, location of, 243 *footnote* 27; 249.
Cherokee Phoenix: suppressed, 268.
Cherokee (Indians): 141 *footnote* 3; council in 1830, efforts to induce removal, 232; council in 1831, 238; at Red Clay in July, 1832, 245; council rejects removal treaty, October, 1832, 246; council at Red Clay May 1833, 247; in October, 1833, 249; in October, 1835, Schermerhorn treaty rejected, 266, 267; delegations to Washington, 241, 246, 247, 249, 264; plundered by whites, 200; losses, 200 *footnote* 5; 279, 287, 288; 300; oppressed by whites, 229, 248, 251, 252, 271; by Georgia, 238; no remedy but by removal, says president, 232; denied oath in Georgia courts, 229; country incorporated in Georgia, 229; gold mines seized, 230; missionaries imprisoned, 235; cast down by decision in Cherokee Nation vs. Georgia, 233; printing press seized, 268 *footnote* 6; send delegations to Washington, 332, 238; dissension on subject of removal, 247, 265; treaty of 1828, terms not performed by United States, 240; of 1834 not ratified, 249, 264; Schermerhorn "treaty" of 1835, 266; fraud exposed, 270; opposition to, 272; protest against, 269; west, delegation to Washington, 264; intermarried with Creeks, 188; Creeks admitted to Cherokee tribe 188, 290 *footnote* 8; John Howard Payne describes Cherokee, 266; desolation of Cherokee country, 290; western Cherokee, 249 *footnote* 50; grievances against government, 239; plundered by whites of Arkansas, 240; oppose emigration from east, 249; delegation to Washington, 264; protection against wild Indians sought, 264; intercede with Seminole to make peace, 352, 353.

Cherokee (Indians): emigration, 230; efforts made in 1831, 235, 241; in 1832, 244; renewed, 252; hindered by chiefs, 235, 242; promoted by president, 232; few go by water in 1831, 242; consider emigration to Pacific coast, 244 *footnote* 33; hope for election of Henry Clay, 247; emigrants assemble at rendezvous, 242, 253; departure, affecting scene, 254; experiences of, 255; suffer from cholera, 252, 257; destitution of emigrants, 231, 243, 248, 296, 298; party conducted by Dr. John C. Young, 273; description by Dr. C. Lillybridge, 274; second volunteer party, description of, 280; passes through Illinois, 280; starting of another party, 284; emigrants reach destination, 277, 278; medical treatment of emigrants, 276; nation made captive by army, 271, 296; confined in stockades, 289, 290, 300 *footnote* 13; removal by force begun, 286, 294; forced on boats, 291, 296; resist and escape captors, 297; plead for respite, 297; sickness and mortality of emigrants, 257, 275, 295, 296, 297, 299, 304, 307; death of Chief White Path on the road, 303; suffering on the way, 289, 308, 309; pathos of, 286, 287, 288, 289; descriptions of, 291, 302 *footnote* 18; 280; births and deaths 310; outrages committed on emigrants, 287, 288, 289; emigration suspended by drought, 299; management assumed by Cherokee officers, 300, 301, 302, 303; resumption attempted in autumn, 300 *footnote* 14; difficulties, 300; resumed in October, 301; emigrants plundered by whites,

101; first to reach destination, 41; emigrants, imposition on by whites, 54
footnote 40; emigrants of Leflore's
district, 84,87; embark at Memphis,51;
detained at Arkansas Post, 52, 53; embark at Vicksburg, 49; condition of
roads, 54 *footnote* 40; emigrants, condition of, 39, 42, 60, 61, 64, 94; emigration resumed in 1832, 71, 78, 87,
88; menaced by cholera, 70 *footnote*
30; 77, 78, 81, 89, 91, 93; subsistence
on the march 55; method of travel, 49;
efforts to remove in 1833, 99, 100;
difficulties of travel in the swamps,
61, 62 *footnote* 24; 80; emigrants
greeted by earlier arrivals, 82, 87;
equipment of emigrating parties, 56,
58, 60, 67; movement of horses, 53
footnote 35; 62 *footnote* 24; emigration
in 1833, 101; provisions on the march,
55, 56; rationing in new home, 68, 69,
82; estimates of emigrants, 95; remaining in Mississippi, 102; condition of,
74; emigration ended, 102; emigration
in 1843,103; in 1846 and 1847, 104, *footnote* 40; emigrants suffering on the
march, 53, 54; 57 *footnote* 7; 58 *footnote* 13; 60, 61, 62, 63; 64 *footnote* 29;
77, 78, 79, 80, 91, 93, 94; immigrants
in new home, 72 *footnote* 7; location
of 79, 95, 96; losses from floods, 97, 98;
destitution of, 96, 97, 99; deaths from
sickness, 98; subsist on spoiled meat,
99.
Cholera: 76; deters Chickasaw exploring
party, 199; in West, 76; 98 *footnote*
22; menace to emigration in 1834, 252;
among Choctaw emigrants, 77, 81, 83,
91; ravages Lieutenant Harris's party
of Cherokee, 257.
Chouteau, Col. A. P.: Osage reserves,
240 *footnote* 14.
Chupco John (Creek Indian): 187.
Clarendon (Ark.): 75 *footnote* 20.
Clark, Capt. J. B.: 43.
Clark, Maj. J. C.: 362.

Clay, Clement C.: governor of Alabama,
142, 146, 148, 183; explains Creek
disturbances, 149.
Clay, Henry: election as president desired
by Cherokee, 246.
Clay, Henry (Cherokee): 277.
Clean House (Chickasaw Indians): 215.
Clear creek: 82, 87.
Clear Boggy creek: 220.
Clements, Col. Benj.: 222.
Clewalas (Huhliwahli, Creek Indians):
40.
Clinch, Gen. Duncan L.: 253, 316, 326,
327, 329.
Cloud (Seminole, Indian): 343, 354; 357
footnote 14.
Coahadjo (Seminole, Indian): 353, 357,
365, 370.
Co-cha-my, Ward (Creek, Indian): as-
sists Creeks to emigrate, attempts
rescue of Creek slaves, 190 *footnote* 35.
Coffee, John: 26, 48, 193, 195, 197, 198.
Colbert, George (Chickasaw, Indian): 33,
193, 198, 200, 203, 217, 224.
Colbert, James (Chickasaw, Indian): 198,
201, 203, 224, 226.
Colbert, Levi (Chickasaw, Indian): 33,
36, 193, 196, 197, 198, 199; death of,
200 *footnotes* 26 and 28.
Colbert, Martin (Chickasaw, Indian):
200, 202.
Colbert, Pitman (Chickasaw, Indian);
33, 198, 199, 202, 203 *footnote* 35; 217.
Colbert, Robert (Chickasaw, Indian):
217.
Colbert, Samuel (Chickasaw, Indian):
226.
Colbert, Susan (Chickasaw, Indian): 226.
Colbert, Thomas (Chickasaw, Indian):
202.
Colbert's Shoals: 295.
Cole, Robert (Choctaw, Indian chief):
30 *footnote* 24.
Colquhoun, Lieut. William S.: 44, 48, 59,
60, 87; attacks Armstrong, 90; journal, 88.

Creek (Indians): emigration started, 125, 126, 142, 160, 162, 216; experiences, 143, 160, 161, 162; journals of events, 159, 166; contractors indifferent to comfort of emigrants, 166; appreciation for conductor's kindness, 176; consumption of supplies, 176; condition of emigrants, 127, 128, 162, 178, 189; compelled to abandon personal effects, 156 footnote 19; suffering of, 127 footnote 27; 159, 160, 164; 169 footnote 1; 173, 174, 177, 178; demoralized by whisky introduced by whites, 156 footnote 19; destitution of, 115, 136, 157; 158 footnote 23; 163, 164, 188, 189; equipment, 158, 166; deaths among, 160.

Creek (Indians): "war" started, 137, 140, 142, 145, 146; incited by whites, 147; causes of, 148, 149, 150; warriors arm to put down, 148; military operations against, 150; corrections of frauds stopped, 147; wholesale removal by force ordered, 147, 152; prisoners concentrated at Fort Mitchell, 152; removed to Montgomery 152, 183; embarked there, 154, 184; captives reach New Orleans, 154, 158; hardships of emigrants, 158; embarked on Mississippi river, 155; land at Rock Roe, 156; death rate among, 156; destitution of, 157; party under Captain Belton, 158; soldiers in Seminole War, 128 footnote 21; 161; 179 footnotes 6 and 7; 180, footnote 8; 348 footnote 15; families remain in Alabama, 180; soldiers rewarded for catching slaves, 249; dismissed from service, 348, 349; families driven out of Alabama, 182, 183; concentrated at Pass Christian, 185, 186; deaths among, 184; joined by warriors from Florida, 186; embarked at New Orleans, 187; large number drowned in Mississippi river by sinking of steamboat, 187; remaining in Alabama, in bondage, 190 footnote 35; some hanged,

189; emigration in 1848, 190 footnote 35; in West, 125; 128 footnote 32; complain of conditions, 138; camped at Fort Gibson, 178; difficulties with McIntosh faction feared, 157.

Craval, John: 217.

Crawford, Robert L.: 113.

Creek Path (Ala.): 255.

Crockett, R. B.: 215, 216.

Cross, S. T.: 59, 77, 78, 81, 102.

Crowell, John: 109, 110, 116.

Currey, Benj. F.: 236, 239, 241, 242, 244, 246, 248, 252, 284.

Cumberland Mountains: 300 footnote 14; 304.

Cumberland river: 280.

Curnell, Anne: 180.

Cutchathlipee creek: 87.

Dade, Camp (Fla.): 344, 345.

Dade, Maj. Francis L.: command massacred by Seminole, 327; 376 footnote 17.

Dancing Rabbit Creek, treaty of: 28, 29.

Daniel, Mose (Cherokee, Indian): 311.

Dardennelle Rock: 80.

Davis, Maj. W. M.: 270.

Dawson, Lieut. J. L.: 33.

Dearborn, Maj. Greenleaf: 375.

Deas, Lieut. Edward: 142, 143, 163, 165, 184, 189, 284, 291, 293, 301, 310; Indians present sword to, 285 footnote 7; Journal, 189 footnote 34.

Decatur (Ala.): 163, 275, 292, 294.

Deep Fork river: 378, 379, 380.

De Kalk county (Geo.): 229.

Delaware (Indians): warriors in Florida war, 348; 355 footnote 12.

Deposit Landing (Ala.): 163.

Descent, rule of in Creek and Seminole tribes: 325.

Destitution of Indians: 42, 124, 296, 372.

Disease of Indians: 185, 186; cupping, 277; treatment of, 274, 332, 333, 339.

Doaks, Josiah: 31; 213 footnote 7.

Doaksville (Ind. Ter.): 203, 217, 221, 224.

Fort Mitchell (Ala.): 114, 116, 121, 123, 136, 138, 146, 151, 152, 331.
Fort Mellon (Fla.): 346, 354.
Fort Myer (Fla.): 385.
Fort Pearce (Fla.): 379.
Fort Pike (La.): 349, 365.
Fort Smith (Ark.): 32; 43 *footnote* 34; 67, 69, 71, 73, 75, 80, 144, 221, 231, 243, 277, 285, 293, 334, 385.
Fort Towson (Ind. Ter.): 41, 42, 44, 65, 66, 68, 71, 72, 83, 84, 90, 95, 158, 199, 203, 208, 211, 216, 217, 219, 223.
Forts in Florida constructed by General Taylor: 373.
Fourche Maline river: 220.
Fournois river: 86.
Francis the Prophet (Hillis Hadjo, Creek Indian): 318 *footnote* 8.
Francis, Millie: 318 *footnote* 8.
Franklin (Tenn.): 193.
Franklin county (Ga.): 180.
Frauds on Chickasaw Indians: 201, 202, 218; on Creek Indians, 129, 145, 147; on Seminole Indians, 321 *footnote* 21; 322, 323; 377 *footnote* 17.
Frazier, Anderson (Chickasaw, Indian): 217.
Frederick (Md.): 150 *footnote* 28.
The Frying Pan: 291.
Fukeluste Hadjo (Black Dirt, Seminole Indian): 327, 332, 339, 380.
Fulton, Dr. John T: 51.

Gadsden, Col. James: 320.
Gaines Creek: 33, 220.
Gaines, George S: 27, 32; 34 *footnote* 10; compensation denied, 37 *footnote* 13; conducts Choctaw exploring party, 32, 33, 34, 45, 46, 47, 48, 90.
Gaines, Gen. E. P: 331.
Gardner, Joel (Choctaw): 60.
Garland, Samuel (Choctaw): 51.
Garrett, W. H., Creek agent: 385.
Gasconade river: 282.
Gayle, John, governor of Alabama: 122 *footnote* 7; asks for protection for

whites, 136, 137, 138.
Georgia: 19, 20; extends laws over Cherokee Nation, 229; claims Cherokee gold mines, 230, 267, 268.
Gibson, Felix G.: 167, 170.
Gibson, Gen. George: 43, 63, 91, 102; 156 *footnote* 19.
Gilman (contractor): 170.
Gilmer, Geo. R., governor of Georgia: 230, 234, 235.
Glover's Fork river: 54.
Going Snake (Cherokee): 290.
Golconda (Ill.) 281.
Government, Indian: 20, 23, 24.
Grayson, Sampson (Creek, Indian): 128, 138.
Great Wahoo Swamp: 327.
Greenwood, Captain: 198.
Gunstocker creek (Tenn.): 302.
Gunter's Landing (Ala.): Indians embark, 163, 189, 230, 274, 291, 292, 308.
Guntersville (Ala.): 291.
Guy, William R: 204, 206, 208; 209 *footnote* 8; 219 *footnote* 8; 222.
Gwinnett county (Ga.): 229, 234.

Habersham county, (Ga.): 229.
Hadjo, Yelka (Creek): 161.
Halec Hadjo (Seminole): 259.
Halek (Aharlock, Ahalek) Tustenuggee (Mikasuki): 371, 375, 376; offers to surrender, 379.
Haley, D. W: 22, 23; 39 *footnote* 21.
Hall county (Ga.): 229.
Hardage, David (Creek): tried and acquitted, 190.
Harkins, George (Choctaw): 2, 30, 31, 32; named chief, 38, 48, 59; 72 *footnote* 7; supplies rations for emigrants 96; 203 *footnote* 35.
Harney, Col. William S.: 373.
Harreld's Bluff: 98.
Harris, Daniel: 217.
Harris, Lieut. Joseph W.: 256, 260, 326; *journal* of experiences with Cherokee

emigrating party, 252, 253, 262; with Seminole party, 332; death of, 263.

Hawkins, Benjamin (Creek): 125, 135; 136 *footnote* 15; 325.

Hawkins, Sam (Creek): 136 *footnote* 15.

Helena (Ark.): 216.

Henderson, W. S.: 206 *footnote* 2.

Henry, Jim (Jim McHenry) Creek warrior: 150, 151; sketch of, 152 *footnote* 1; 153 *footnote* 4; 155 *footnote* 15; tried and acquitted, 190.

Hernandez, General: 351.

Herring, Elbert (Commissioner of Indian Affairs): 239; 249 *footnote* 50.

Hetzel, Camp: 288.

Hicks, Elijah (Cherokee): 302, 303.

Hicks, George (Cherokee): 305, 311.

Hicks, Wm. (Cherokee): 266 *footnote* 3.

Hightower: 234.

Hildebrand Peter (Cherokee, conductor): 312.

Hilibi (Creek town): 142.

Hill, William K: 197.

Hitchcock, Col. Ethan Allen: 321 *footnote* 21; 327; *views* on Seminole war, 376 *footnote* 17; 381; captures Pascofa, 381.

Hitchiti (Creek, Indians): 145, 148.

Hiwassee river; 242, 253, 291, 301, 302.

Hoffman, D. A.: 136 *footnote* 15.

Hogan, John B.: 134, 140.

Holahte Emathla (Seminole chief): 327; party starts west, 332; death of, 338; *appreciation* of, 340.

Holahtochee (Davey, Seminole): 344, 362, 370.

Holly Springs (Miss.): 225.

Holston river: 253.

Hoo-wan-nees (Choctaw Indians): 89.

Hopkinsville (Ky.): 281, 303.

Horse Prairie: 68, 72.

Hotchkiss, Archibald: 135.

Hotulke Emathla (Seminole): 378.

Houston, Sam: 136 *footnote* 15; 239, 325.

Huntsville (Ala.): 163, 308.

Hurricane creek: 84.

Hutchechubbee river, 148.

Illinois Bayou: 262.

Illinois river: 239, 262.

Indian confederacy: proposed, 194, 195.

Indian Mission conference: 152 *footnote* 1.

Indian removal bill: 21, 107.

Indian removal, completed, 385.

Indians: advancement of, 20.

Indians, wild: Chickasaw ask protection ·from, 200.

Irving, Washington: 89 *footnote* 9; 151 *footnote* 29; 226.

Irwin's stand (Ark.): 162.

Irwinton (Ala.): 114 *footnote* 24.

Ish-ta-ho-ta-pa (Chickasaw king): 200; 219 *footnote* 8; 223.

Island Bayou: 203, *footnote* 35.

Izard, Lieut. James F.: 330.

Jackson, President Andrew: 21, 22, 42, 107, 109, 136, 193, 230, 235, 281; refuses to protect Cherokee Indians against whites, 232; campaign in Florida 317.

Jackson (Mo.): 281, 308.

Jesup, Gen. Thomas S.: 148, 160, 166, 180, 344; 353 *footnote* 3; advises abandoning Seminole war, 360; bought Florida negroes for United States, 349; captures Seminole by strategy, 361; *summary* of Florida campaign, 363.

Jim Boy (Creek chief): 135, 148, 179, 184, 186, 187; 190 *footnote* 35; commands Creeks warriors in Florida, 348 *footnote* 15.

Jolly, John (Cherokee chief): 239, 249.

Jones, Rev. Evan: 300 *footnote* 14; 304, 309, 311.

Jones, Dr. J.: 160.

Jones, Robert M. (Choctaw): 48 *footnote* 11; 57, 60; 203 *footnote* 35.

Jones, Sam (Abiaca, Mikasuki chief): 351, 371; remains in Florida, 385.

Jonesboro (Ill.): 281.

Journal of events during emigration: 83, 159, 160, 166, 207.

Jumper, (Seminole chief): 322, 329, 330, 344, 345, 347, 350; and party embark for West, 355 *footnote* 10.

Jumper, John (Seminole): accompanies delegation to Florida, 385 *footnote* 38.

Juzan, Pierre (Choctaw): 51 *footnote* 21; 56.

Juzan, William: 89.

Kan-tcati (Creek, Indians): 141.

Kasihta (Creek, Indians): captives, 131, ·154; 166, 175.

Kearney, Maj. S. W.: 72.

Keenan, Dr. C. C.: 206, 208.

Kelly's Ferry: 294.

Kemp, Jackson (Chickasaw): 224, *footnote* 20.

Kennedy, John: 273 *footnote* 17; 303.

Kerr, Joseph: 63, 64.

Key, Francis Scott: investigates Creek situation, 123, 124, 125.

Kialachies (Kealedji, Creek Indians): 140, 142, 148.

Kiamichi river: 32, 41, 42; 53 *footnote* 35; 54, 59, 68, 94.

Kickapoo: warriors in Florida war, 348.

Kincaid, Joseph (Choctaw chief): 50; 203 *footnote* 35.

King, William D.: 33.

Kingsbury, Capt. G. P.: 212 *footnote* 6; 219, 225.

Kin-hi-cha (Chickasaw chief): 216.

Kiowa (Indians): 322.

Kissimmee river: 360.

La Blanc, Louis: 40 *footnote* 23.

Lake, Captain (Choctaw Indian): 89.

Lake Okechobee: 372.

Lake Providence: 61, 64.

Lake Washington: 90.

Lane, Capt. John F.: 348 *footnote* 15.

Langtree, G.: 206 *footnote* 2; 214.

L'Eau Bleu river: 35, 220.

Leflore, Greenwood (Choctaw chief): 22, 23, 27, 32, 38, 84; inaugurates emigration, 38; asked for advice by government, 44, 72, 74, 81; his district, 99, 194.

Leflore, Thomas (Choctaw chief): 203 *footnote* 35.

Leavenworth, Gen. Henry: 219.

Lees Creek: 262, 295.

Lewis, Felix: 222.

Lewisburg (Ark.): 172 *footnote* 3; 295; bar, 285.

Lillybridge, Dr. C.: *journal* of Cherokee emigration, 273, 274, 276.

Little Cloud (Seminole): 343; embarked for West, 357, 365.

Little Doctor (Creek): 161.

Little Missouri river: 79, 86, 94.

Little river: 54, 68, 86.

Little Rock (Ark.): 45, 52, 58, 75, 82, 84, 92, 93, 94, 101, 102, 127, 143, 162, 164, 171, 172, 178, 199, 209, 214, 215, 219, 231, 256, 263, 277, 284, 295, 298, 332, 365, 366, 368, 370.

Live stock of emigrants: 53, 57; 59 *footnote* 15; 81, 82, 83, 164, 214.

Logan, William O.: 136 *footnote* 15.

Looney, John (Cherokee): 271.

Love, Benjamin (Chickasaw): 193 *footnote* 2; 200, 203; removes company of emigrants, 225.

Love, Henry (Chickasaw): 33, 199, 200, 203.

Love, Sloan (Chickasaw): 224.

Lovely, Maj. William L.: 159.

Lowery, John: 232.

Lumpkin, Gov. Wilson: 249; estimate of Cherokee people, 269 *footnote* 9; 273 *footnote* 17; 303.

Lutcapoga (Creek town): 148.

Macomb, Gen. Alexander: assumed command in Florida in 1839, 371; criticised for peace policy with Seminole, 373.

Macon county (Ala.): 122 *footnote* 7; citizens deprecate frauds on Creeks, 136, 137.

Riley, Spencer: 251.
Roanoke (Ala.): 153 *footnote* 4.
Roberts, Dr. Jesse C.: 257, 259, 260.
Rock Roe (Ark.): 70, 75; sketch of, 75 *footnote* 20; 77, 79, 81, 84, 92, 93, 101, 155, 162, 164, 171, 207.
Rogers, Erastus: 326.
Rogers, Capt. James (Cherokee): 230, 239, 240, 264.
Rogers, Capt. John (Cherokee): 239, 240, 264.
Ross, Andrew (Cherokee): 264; life threatened, 265.
Ross, George (Cherokee): 281.
Ross, John (Cherokee chief): 232, 238, 241, 249, 252, 265, 269, 272, 273, 301, 303; in Washington, 247; dominates Cherokee council, 246; sketch of, 265 *footnote* 3; arrested by Georgia guard, 268; visits western Cherokee, 270; at tempts to end Seminole War, 352; resents Jesup's treatment of Seminole, 355; supervises Cherokee removal, 303.
Ross, Mrs. John: death of on removal west, 310 *footnote* 30.
Ross's Landing (Tenn.): 274 *footnote* 20; 291, 296, 298; 300 *footnote* 13.
Ross, Lewis (Cherokee): 299.
Ross, Templin W. (Cherokee): 260.
Russell county (Ala.): 122 *footnote* 7; 137, 146, 181.
Russell's stand: 88.
Rutherford, S. M.: 58, 385.
Ryan, Lieut. Stephen Van Rennssalaer: 52; conducts Choctaw emigrants, 53; 86.

Sabine river: 135, 196.
St. Augustine (Fla.): 349, 351, 352, 357, 362.
St. Francis river: 64, 206.
St. Johns (Fla.): 351.
St. Louis: 76.
Sakapatayi (Creek, Indians): 141.
Saline creek: 95.

Saline river: 54.
Sallisaw creek: 262, 285.
Salt works: 33.
Sanford, J. W. A.: 129, 133, 145, 155, 234.
Sans Bois river: 336.
Sauk and Foxes warriors: in Florida war, 348.
Saunders, Alexander (Cherokee): 239.
Schermerhorn, Rev. John F.: 239, 270, 321; negotiates Cherokee "treaty," 266; ratified, 270; 283.
Schley, Gov. William of Georgia: 280 *footnote* 2; explains Creek troubles, 149.
Scott, Gen. Winfield: 150, 286, 296, 331; compassion for Cherokee people, 299; postpones Cherokee removal, 300.
Screven, Lieut. R. B.: 162.
Sealey, Samuel (Chickasaw): 193, 208, 212.
Seawell, Capt. Washington: 379.
Secretary of War: characterizes wrongs on Creeks, 122; ignores frauds on Creeks, 130; takes notice of them, 132; gives orders to protect Creeks, 113, 116.
Seminole (Indians): 19, 317; rule of descent, 325; Spanish, 364 *footnote* 2; 365; appearance of, 346; treaty of 1823, 319; treaty of 1832, 320, 321; treaty of 1833, 321; War, 226, 317, 324; re newed in 1837, 349; responsibility for, 377 *footnote* 17; hardships of, 359; abandonment advised by army officers, 359, 360; government calls on Creeks for help, 161; warriors from other tribes recruited, 348; reinforcements from Fort Smith, 375; western Semi nole intercede for peace, 374, 375, 376, 378; Cherokee Indians inter cede for peace, 352; negotiations for peace, 344; Indians taken un der flag of truce, 351; 354; object to incorporation with Creeks, 360; peace made with Gen. Macomb, 371,

372, 373; prisoners released by Macomb, 371; condition of in 1821, 318; land claimed by whites, 318; protest treaty made at Fort Gibson, 322; amalgamation with Creeks attempted, 321, battle at Withlacoochee, 330; battle with Gen. Taylor at Lake Okechobee, 356; confer with Jesup about peace, 359, 360; resources of Seminole country, 374; inducements to remove west rejected, 384, 385; exploring party sent west, 321, 322; imposed upon by whites, 321; robbed by whites, 323; fraud committed on, 377 *footnote* 17; ravage white settlements, 317; massacre whites on Coloosahatchie river, 373; Seminole slave owners, relation to negroes, 326; freedom of negroes guaranteed by Jesup, 344; negroes restored to whites, 346, 347; negroes, loot of the Creek captors, 365; Seminole protest separation from their negroes, 370; uprising believed ended, 330; country ravaged by troops, 342, 343; failure of campaign, 374.

Seminole (Indians) emigration: ordered, 326; Seminole opposed to, 326; friendly, desire to go to Texas, 327; captured by Gen. Armistead, 377, 378; friendly, embark in 1834, 322, 323; under Lieut. Harris, 332; others plan to surrender, 326, 375; collection for emigration, 345, 348; captives escape, 347; 358 *footnote* 20; concentrated at Tampa Bay, 365, 379; embark for West, 357; 358 *footnote* 20; 361, 362, 378, 379; captives embarked by Gen. Taylor, 370; emigration of John Blunt's band in 1834, 322, 323; captives sent to New Orleans, 347, 370, 380; arrive at New Orleans, 362, 363, 367; confined at New Orleans, 364; ascending Mississippi river, 365, 367, 368; sickness among, 333, 334, 335, 336; treatment of disease, 332, 333, 339; destitution of, 318, 319, 320, 362, 363, 365, 372,

382; mortality among, 323, 339, 340; suffering and hardship, 332, 341; death of Black Dirt's wife, 335; suffer from cold in West, 379; estimate of number of, 380; settle near Fort Gibson, 380; controversy with Creeks over new home, 369; treatment of sick by Seminole, 333; Wild Cat surrenders to Lieut. William T. Sherman, 379; Pascofa's band surrenders to Major Hitchcock, 382; removal efforts in 1856, 385.

Seneca (Indians): 264.

Setelechee (Creek council ground): 138.

Shearer, Gen. Gilbert: 146.

Shawnee (Indians): 35, 264; on Choctaw land, 36, 66; warriors in Florida war, 348.

Shelton, Robert: 257, 262.

Sherbourne, John H.: 352.

Sherman, Lieut. William T.: 379.

Shorter, Eli S.: 121, *footnote* 4; 132.

Simonton, Lieut. Isaac P.: 91, 94.

Six Towns (Choctaw, Indians): 56, 89, 91; 84 *footnote* 5.

The Skillet: (291).

Slave: traders among Seminole Indians, 325, 346.

Slaves among Seminole: sought by white people, 346; escaped to Florida, 315, 318; efforts to catch in Florida, 316; claims of Georgians to, 317; stolen by whites, 324, 325; relation to Seminole owners, 326; captured in Florida by Creek warriors awarded to captors, 349.

Slaves: Creek captives made by white people, 190 *footnote* 35.

Sloan, Lieut. T. P.: 182.

Smallpox: ravages Creek Nation, 110 *footnote* 11; introduced among Chickasaw emigrants, 222 *footnote* 13, 223; devastates Chickasaw and Choctaw nations, 221, 222, 223, 224.

Smith, Archilla (Cherokee): 276.

Smith, Moses (Cherokee): 264.

Welborne, Gen. Carlton: 182, 324.

Welborne, W. J.: 206 *footnote* 2; 214, 215.

West, John (Cherokee): 264.

Wetumka (Ala.): 146.

Wetumpka (Creek town): 113, 115, 142, 162.

Wharton, Dr. W. L.: 110.

Wheelock, Lieut. T. B.: 348, *footnote* 15.

Whisky: 162, 210, 248, 285, 292; used by whites to demoralize and defraud Choctaw Indians, 39, 44, 74, 100; Creek Indians, 112, 136, 137, 138, 142; Chickasaw, 202, 212; Cherokee Indians, 248; 280 *footnote* 2; difficulties of emigration caused by whites selling to emigrating Indians, 143; 156 *footnote* 19; 185, 212, 221, 253, 254, 255, 277,280,286; sale to Indians prohibited by Memphis, 171.

Whiteley, Lieut. R. H. K.: conducts Cherokee emigrants, 294; *journal* of 294.

White Path (Cherokee chief): dies on way west, 303.

White river: 51, 64, 85, 77, 90, 91, 171, 207, 242, 256, 292, 295.

White people: intruders in Chickasaw country, 197, 199, 200, 201; in Cherokee country, 246; in Choctaw country, 31, 39, 73, 74, 100; in Creek country, 109, 112, 113, 114, 115, 117, 124; oppression of Indians: Choctaw, 73, 74, 76; Creek Indians, 117, 119, 120, 121, 122, 123; Cherokee, 248, 271; plunder Indians: Chickasaw, 201, 202, 204; Creeks, 120, 126, 161, 181; 182 *footnote* 11; Cherokee, 235, 236, 279, 287, 288, 305; Seminole, 320; emigrants, 62, 68, 69, 305; persecute Creek Indians, 114, 115; kill live stock of Cherokee, 240; slave raids in Florida, 318, 320;

not all cruel to Creeks, 124; compassion for emigrants, 63, 305, 306; of Alabama, deprecate frauds on Indians, 136; protest to Washington against frauds, 136.

Wichita (Indians): 322.

Wild Cat (Cooacoochee, Seminole): 245; taken under a flag of truce, 350; escapes from St. Augustine fort, 355; offers to surrender, 379; surrenders to Lieut. Wm. T. Sherman, 379; embarked for the West, 379.

Williams, Loring S.: 79 *footnote* 31.

Williamson, James: 206 *footnote* 2.

Winchester (Tenn.): 301.

Witchcraft: among Choctaw Indians, 66 *footnote* 38.

Withlacoochee river: 343; massacre of Dade's command, 327; battle with Seminole, 330.

Wolf, Col. James (Chickasaw): 217, 274.

Wolf, James (Cherokee): 274.

Woodward, General: 132.

Woodward, Thomas (Cherokee): 352.

Wool, Gen. Ellis: 188, 285; describes condition of Cherokee Indians, 271; sympathy for Cherokee, 279; rebuked by president, 269.

Worcester, Samuel (Choctaw): 203 *footnote* 35.

Worcester, Rev. Samuel A.: 234; imprisoned by Georgia, 235.

Worcester vs. Georgia: 244.

Worth, Gen. W. J.: announced end of Seminole War, 381; consents to Seminole remaining in Florida, 384.

Wright, Daniel W.: 73.

Yellow Hair (Seminole): 323.

Young, Dr. John S.: 273; 275 *footnote* 21.

Young Squirrel (Cherokee): 276.

Yuchi (Creek Indians): 144, 145, 156, 315; made captives, 152, 154.

Date Due